Yeats AT WORK

Yeats AT WORK

Curtis B. Bradford

SOUTHERN ILLINOIS UNIVERSITY PRESS
Carbondale and Edwardsville

Library of Congress Catalog Card Number 64–19799
Printed in the United States of America
DESIGNED BY ANDOR BRAUN

IN MEMORY OF

Professor H. O. White

1885–1963

PREFACE

YEATS has left his students two problems with which students, say of Milton, do not have to deal: (1) many of his works went through a complex textual evolution following their first publication; (2) for many of his works a complex tangle of prepublication manuscripts survives. Colonel Alspach has dealt with one part of the first problem in his invaluable *Variorum Edition* of Yeats's poems, and is dealing with another part of it in his forthcoming variorum edition of Yeats's plays. A collected edition of Yeats's prose with textual notes is badly needed, for in his prose too Yeats made many textual changes, some of them outrageous, as when he introduced Leda into "The Adoration of the Magi" when revising it for *Early Poems and Stories* (1925). In this book I address myself to the second problem by presenting and analysing successive manuscript versions of chosen poems, plays, and prose works other than plays.

I am by no means the first student of Yeats to work with his manuscripts — Hone, Jeffares, Ellmann, Stallworthy, Parkinson, and others — have consulted and used this material in various ways, but my study of it is more extensive than any that has yet appeared and the first that attempts to survey Yeats at work in all his varied genres. I have not, with a very few exceptions which will be noted, reproduced any manuscripts previously printed. Besides trying to avoid doing again what has already been done, I have avoided works whose manuscript development was so complex that a study of it would require a monograph or even a book (*On Baile's Strand* (1903), *Deirdre* (1907), *The Player Queen* (1922), *A Vision* (1937)). The manuscript material available has also necessarily governed my choice; it is simply not possible to choose in advance of an investigation of the surviving manuscripts those works one would most like to study.

i

AFTER OBSERVING that Yeats himself set his students the problem of examining his manuscripts by saving so many of them or allowing them to be saved, I wish to consider briefly the use of such studies as the present one. Many manuscript studies have appeared in recent years; those of Shelley, Mark Twain, and especially of Joyce come immediately to mind. My own feeling is that such studies have often disappointed their readers and sometimes even their writers. If we come to them with any expectation that they will once for all dispel the mystery surrounding the creative process, we are bound to be disappointed, for no manuscript can provide a record of the internal or mental aspect of creation. Everyone who has ever written knows that writing involves more than pushing words around on paper, yet by the very nature of things this is the only aspect of an act of writing, however great, that can survive. After studying a run of manuscripts, even though it be complete, the mystery of creation remains a mystery still: the Heavens have not opened and no doves have descended. Many aspects of the creative process will remain forever unknowable.

I do not wish, however, to imply that manuscript studies do not have their uses, or that, to paraphrase Falstaff, rebellion against archetypal criticism lay in my way and I found it. From Aristotle almost to the present, criticism has had of necessity to deal with literature as a mode of being, for no record of literature's becoming had survived — in English literature there are almost no extensive autograph manuscripts earlier than Pope's (and many of these had dropped out of sight at the time when the Twickenham Edition was being prepared). Now, rather suddenly and on an increasing scale, records of the external aspects of literature's becoming are available. The problem is to define the uses of this new, and to some students of literature unwelcome, dimension or in other words to say what light the record of becoming throws on the being.

One use of manuscripts has long been recognized, that of correcting or improving the received text. A good many Yeats manuscripts serve this use as I shall show, indeed most if not all the manuscripts of poems printed after his death could serve it. A knowledge of the manuscript development of a work may also help us to explicate it. Here the use is perhaps more negative than positive, since there is no single right reading of a work of any complexity. Wrong readings are, however, all too possible and frequent, and a knowledge of a work's becoming can save us from such mistakes. Yeats's "Byzantium" is an instance of this: the development of the manuscripts shows that some of the earlier readings proposed are demonstrably wrong. And, positively, the manuscripts do at least help us toward a right reading, assist us, sometimes greatly, in the work of explication. My own readings of Yeats's works whose manuscripts I have studied have always been enlarged and refined by that study, and one of my reasons for writing this book was a wish to share this experience with others.

A knowledge of the manuscript development of a given work has a further use than those already discussed; such a knowledge can and often does open new and unexpected critical insights into that work. This happens frequently with the works of Yeats which I present, as when Yeats abandons realism to achieve a necessary symbolism in the drafts of stanza 1 of "The Wild Swans at Coole," but I should like to take my principal exemplum from Joyce.

The recently published first-draft version of the Shem the Penman section of *Finnegans Wake* (David Hayman, *A First-Draft Version of Finnegans Wake*, pp. 108–12) is a very poor thing indeed. This comes as a surprise, for Shem is clearly an extension of the Stephen myth and Joyce had been working on the Stephen myth during most of his creative life. So the reader begins to ask why Joyce has so much trouble getting the episode underway. I think he gets an answer very early when Joyce writes "Cain — Ham (Shem) — Esau — Jim the Penman." Translated out of Joyce's shorthand this must mean "I, the writer James Joyce, am Cain-Ham-Esau: I want to kill my insufferably righteous brother 'in the Meddle of [my] might . . . to find out how his innards [work],' I have seen the nakedness of my father — that is of my fatherland, and I have sold my birthright for a mess of pottage though I have also been done out of it." This points to many themes of the finished episode, but it also points to the fact that Joyce is having trouble controlling his accidence, trouble creating a myth out of a man. And in fact he never did quite manage to control his accidence here and elsewhere in *Finnegans Wake*. In the Shem the Penman episode Joyce's paranoid feelings toward Ireland are apparent in spite of the pyrotechnics of his style, as are also such naked biographical facts as his eschewing his native victuals by preferring canned salmon to Liffey trout and white wine to Guinness, and his irritation over the pirated editions of *Ulysses* printed in the United States. In the great moments of Shem the Penman Joyce becomes if not everyman at least everyartist, when he works "kuskykorked . . . up tight in his inkbattle house," when he refuses his "birthwrong . . . to fall in with Plan," when he as every great writer must becomes a "Europaisianised Afferyank." But elsewhere, though it is simplistic to separate what is being said from how it is being said, only his "quashed quotatoes" and "his cantraps of fermented words" save Joyce from sounding maudlin, if indeed they do save him. Which may in part explain the quashed quotatoes and fermented words.

Perhaps I, who am not a Joyce critic but only one of his common readers, can go further from this instance and hazard some generalizations which a Joyce critic might properly hesitate to make. The exegesis of *Finnegans Wake* has made it clear that in the *Wake* Joyce sooner or later worked off every irritation he had accumulated during his literary life — and he had accumulated a great many. In one aspect it is his *Dunciad*. Now the *Dunciad*, excepting the fourth book, hardly seems to me to belong with the best of Pope, with "An Essay on Criticism," "The Rape of the Lock," and "Moral Essays: Epistle IV," partly because Pope's pain shows through in spite of the technical brilliance of the poem. *Finnegans Wake* is not the best of Joyce and for the same reason. In *Dubliners, Portrait, Ulysses* Gabriel and Gretta are not James and Nora Joyce, Cranley is not J. F. Byrne, and, especially, Stephen and Buck Mulligan are not Joyce and Gogarty. In this last instance mythical figures of great dimension stalk the streets of Dublin; the accidence in which they began has been wholly transcended. Too often in *Finnegans Wake* once we have penetrated the verbal texture we find James Joyce in all his accidence. I've had lots of fun at Finnegan's wake, but reading the first-draft version has made me aware of one reason why I do not think it as great as Joyce's other fictions.

Many of the Yeats manuscripts studied here show Yeats involved in this very problem of controlling his accidence. And when Yeats's poems occasionally fail or relatively fail — one of the most remarkable things about Yeats's work is the high level of the whole corpus, his great poems start up out of it already a mile above sea level like the peaks of the Colorado Rockies — it is usually because he does not manage to control his accidence. "The Municipal Gallery Revisited" is a case in point as Thomas Parkinson has recently demonstrated in

The Later Poetry. These are the kinds of critical insight that may grow out of a study of art's becoming.

ii

WRITING WAS ALWAYS DIFFICULT for Yeats. When he began in the 1880's he was prolix. The manuscripts of such unpublished apprentice works as have survived show little revision, but these plays, stories, and verses are loose, thin-spun, tedious. Yeats began to publish in 1886, but only a few of the works published before 1895 seem to have satisfied him; these early published works were either abandoned or carefully rewritten before they were included in the various collected editions. By 1895 Yeats had developed more effective habits of work; he now began to put both prose and verse through many drafts, to stick with poem, play, story, or essay until much hammering had worked it into shape.

Yeats's apprenticeship as a poet ended, as Thomas Parkinson has shown in *W. B. Yeats: Self-Critic*, when he revised his early verse for *Poems*, 1895. The legends and lyrics printed with *The Countess Kathleen* (1892) are clearly the work of a man who is forming a style whereas the poems collected in *The Wind Among the Reeds* (1899) display one of Yeats's styles fully formed. Yeats himself must have felt that this was so, for he continued to revise his early poems through many successive editions; the text of *The Wind Among the Reeds* remained, to the contrary, remarkably stable. During these same years Yeats completed his apprenticeship as a prose writer. For me, the stories included in *The Celtic Twilight* (1893) show an apprentice hand whereas parts of *The Secret Rose* (1897) do not. "Rosa Alchemica" is a finished work and, again, Yeats must have felt that this was so, for during the course of many reprintings he made very few changes in its text.

The road to a master's certificate as a playwright was both longer and harder: Yeats's whole practice of playwriting shows him intent on developing antirealistic dramatic modes. He achieved the first of these in his early heroic plays based on traditional Irish themes, but it took him more than twenty years to do it (he began planning *The Countess Cathleen* in 1889 and he finished the rewriting of *The Hour-Glass* in 1913; by that time all his early plays except *The King's Threshold* had reached pretty much the form in which we know them). He invented a second mode, the heroic farce, while at work on *The Green Helmet*, and in the version of that play published in 1910 we reach the moment of relative textual stability which Yeats had reached in his poetry with *The Wind Among the Reeds*. He went on to invent a third mode, the most successful of all, when he completed and produced in 1916 *At the Hawk's Well*, his first play for dancers.

Even though Yeats achieved mastery of the technical means of his art rather early in his career, he at no time found the act of writing easy. It was for him always an "unnatural labour." Yeats worked as hard at his writing in the 1920's and 30's as he had in the 1890's. Up to about 1920 his method of composing was physically tedious. He wrote always in longhand, very slowly, revising as he went along. Before his marriage he wrote usually in bound manuscript books, often cheap copy books intended for school exercises. He never at any time in his life produced a prose manuscript that could be transcribed by a secretary so Yeats's customary practice was to dictate from his manuscripts. Only two of all the prose manuscripts I have examined have been transcribed ("The Speckled Bird," and parts of "The Tragic Generation" and "The Stirring of the Bones"), and both transcriptions are extremely inaccurate. Verse manuscripts were, I believe, usually transcribed because of the difficulty of indicating line ends during dictation. When the manuscript on which he was working became nearly illegible because of over-writing and cueing in from the margins and the opposite page, Yeats would either copy it out, dictate it to a secretary, or have it transcribed. He always introduced further changes while rewriting or dictating. If Yeats had dictated or had a work transcribed, he would go to work on the manuscript or typescript his secretary had produced, carrying on in his own hand the process of revision. There was much work to be done on such a draft. Since Yeats was thrown off completely if interrupted while dictating, his secretaries had to write what they thought they heard; when transcribing they sometimes misread his writing. There are still many places where Yeats's printed texts inaccurately represent his original intention because his various secretaries misheard what he said or misread his hand, and Yeats happened to miss the mistake while correcting.

After his marriage Yeats worked out with Mrs. Yeats's help a method of composition that was less demanding physically. Now he usually wrote in looseleaf notebooks, except when he was away from his Dublin study, at Coole, for instance, or in Italy. When away from home he continued his earlier practice of writing in bound manuscript books. Looseleaf notebooks had one great advantage. Throughout his life Yeats continually rearranged the order of his material while composing, especially when he was writing prose. When he wrote in a bound manuscript book, he had to indicate by notes the order he wanted, or tear out or cut out the pages (Yeats did this even with books, including his own books) he wished to put earlier or later. Loose leaves were more easily rearranged. Often a looseleaf manuscript page will have at the top a series of page numbers indicating the various places it has occupied in a work.

When Yeats had achieved something of the order and style he wanted, he would, as he had earlier, dictate the work to a secretary or have it transcribed — he greatly preferred to work with Mrs. Yeats. He had by now developed a truly remarkable ability to improve both his prose and verse while working on these typed versions. Sometimes successive typescripts were needed, each dictated as the preceding script grew illegible: this happened with *A Vision* and *On the Boiler* (1939). But often in the 1920's and 30's Yeats finished his writing on the first typescript.

We have seen that Yeats nearly always wrote in a book either bound or looseleaf; apparently he liked the two page spread each opening provided. He usually started on the right-hand page; when this became too overwritten, he would move over to the left-hand page and continue his revision there, cueing the passage into its proper place on the right-hand page by drawing arrows. Another aspect of Yeats's practice is worth noting, since it is often a source of confusion. When Yeats wrote in a bound manuscript book, he rarely used the sheets in order. He would move from place to place in the book, or both forward and back from the page on which he had begun to write. This means that the order of drafts, particularly drafts of poems, often cannot be determined by the order in which they occur in the book. When, finally, Yeats felt reasonably satisfied with a work, he would usually initial it, or even sign it in full, "W. B. Yeats," and often add the date. When a manuscript written in a looseleaf notebook had once been dictated or transcribed, Yeats would remove the sheets and put them into a file envelope. He would sometimes note the principal contents on the flap of the envelope, and the date of filing.

Yeats's manuscripts and typescripts are extremely interesting to any student of the writing process, for it is nearly always possible to reconstruct from them at least the external aspects of how a poem, play, or essay was put together. One can also watch lines of poems and single sentences of prose emerge from the inchoate as Yeats achieves with immense labor the expression he wants. For Yeats the construction process usually meant adding on; his works accumulated slowly, as a coral reef accumulates. The "First Draft," for instance, of the *Autobiographies* is a manuscript of about 42,000 words. The material in "First Draft" parallels "The Trembling of the Veil" (1922) and parts of "Dramatis Personae" (1938); these run to nearly 100,000 words. In poem or play as well as prose work, such a result is typical. The things added were usually detail, incident. Though some early drafts are too encumbered with detail, most of them show, as Yeats often complained, that his writing at the outset of a work tended to be abstract. In a lyric the rich fabric of metaphor and symbol as well as Yeats's characteristic staging of a poem builds up slowly through many drafts. This was notably true of "Sailing to Byzantium." In his play *The Resurrection,* what was little more than a dialogue on the nature of God slowly becomes a play with dramatic tension and climax. In "The Trembling of the Veil" Yeats slowly envelops certain personal reminiscences with the rich fabric of his System.

Yeats's characteristic styles were also achieved with difficulty; this is equally true of the hushed, autumnal tone of *The Wind Among the Reeds,* the splendid baroque diction of the great poems of the 1920's, and of the crackling, slashing sentences of the late prose works. In plays the adjustment of word and phrase to the actor's speaking voice was given minute attention, and plays were seldom printed until after production. After a certain point in the composition of nearly all his works, Yeats's revisions are largely concerned with improving the style.

There were exceptions to these usual procedures: During the many years he spent working on *The Player Queen,* Yeats accumulated a great deal of material he had to discard, including many pages of verse and much hard-worked-for incident. Yeats wrote many conclusions to *A Vision* in which he projected his System into the future before he finally decided to avoid the prophet's role and print none of them. In style, too, a particularly happy phrase would sometimes occur early and persist through many drafts while the context of the phrase changed out of all recognition.

iii

A TYPICAL YEATS MANUSCRIPT seems on first examination to resemble the daw's nest Yeats described in "The Tower"; it appears to be a jumble, a mere heap of confusion. If the work was of any length, it would have been put together slowly. This means that the paper is often of various sizes, the inks of various colors. Revisions in pencil were always done with soft pencil in a very light stroke, so they are now nearly indecipherable. Yeats's hand, in spite of the fact that it was remarkably uniform, is very difficult to read. The writing, especially when intended for Yeats's eye alone, is in very rough state. The spelling is atrocious. Prose is badly overpunctuated by commas or dashes. Whenever Yeats paused momentarily in a sentence to get his bearing, or felt a poet's longing for caesura or line end, he inserted a comma or dash. Capital letters cannot surely be distinguished from small, which, taken together with a near absence of end punctuation, makes it difficult to distinguish sentences. A single stroke of the pen, nearly indistinguishable in shape, stands for both "I" and the ampersand. A little cross stands for "to," "too," and "two." "Of," "by," and "my" are nearly identical. Most suffixes are reduced to a squiggly down stroke. Many necessary words are omitted. Though all I have written above is true, I should add that when Yeats was well he could at any time in his career produce a legible manuscript when he wished for some reason to do so.

Because of these difficulties, I have edited prose manuscripts radically. I have silently corrected the spelling, expanded abbreviations, and am responsible for most of the punctuation. I have been careful to inclose all words that I have added in square brackets, but have dropped silently many uncancelled words which revision has made redundant. Yeats's many cancellations raise serious editorial problems, for they seldom indicate exactly what is to be cancelled. I have tried to produce a clean, readable text which will adequately represent Yeats's latest intention.

My editing of the manuscripts of poems is conservative, though I have not attempted to produce a diplomatic text. Jon Stallworthy did attempt this when he printed manuscripts of Yeats's poems in *Between the Lines*, and David Hayman has carried the effort even further in *A First-Draft Version of Finnegans Wake*. I have not tried to produce a diplomatic text of Yeats's manuscripts because I do not think it can be done, and because such a text makes a reader's already hard task even harder. Nothing that typography can do will actually reproduce the peculiarities and difficulties of Yeats's manuscripts; even photographic reproduction does not always do this very well because of the varieties of inks used and the frequent intermixture of ink and pencil.

In my editing I have expanded abbreviations and silently corrected obvious misspellings, but I have not added any punctuation. I have used the following devices in reproducing manuscripts of poems. An × before a line means that Yeats has cancelled it; revisions within a line are printed in cancelled type, as in this example:

> ~~Why dost thou brood~~ Linger no more where the fire burns bright

The original reading is followed immediately by the revised reading. This practice is followed even when Yeats eventually abandoned the whole line, cancellations and all. When alternate readings occur and Yeats has allowed both of them to stand, they are printed in this way, separating these readings with a slant sign:

> For hands wave to them / are waving and eyes are a gleam.

Actually Yeats's revisions were written above and below as well as at the side of the words he first wrote. When lines of poetry are printed without normal spacing between them, this indicates that Yeats has tried various versions of a single line but has cancelled none of them. Whenever a line of verse reaches the form in which it was first printed, I place before it the number assigned to it in the *Variorum Edition.* I have likewise numbered the lines of plays in verse as they reach the form in which they were first printed, following the system used by Colonel Russell Alspach in printing *The Shadowy Waters.* In transcriptions of both prose and verse whenever I have been unable to decipher a word or group of words, I have indicated my failure and the length of the undeciphered passage. I have nowhere used the word "sic," and have tried to reduce to a minimum editorial queries indicating doubt of the accuracy of my reading. I have many doubts, but in the interests of a clean page use a query only when I cannot reduce Yeats's hieroglyph to any word which fits the context.

My work on this book was done at the libraries of Harvard University (particularly Houghton and Widener), at the library of Trinity College, Dublin, at the National Library of Ireland, and at Burling Library, Grinnell College. I wish to acknowledge the unfailing kindness of the staff members of all these libraries, especially of the staff of the Houghton Library Reading Room, which is presided over by Shannon's portrait of Yeats.

My greatest debt is to Mrs. W. B. Yeats who first in 1954–55 and again in the summer of 1960 made Yeats's manuscripts available to me, and who has placed no restrictions on my quotations from them. Next this is my debt to Sheldon P. Zitner, who encouraged my enterprise from the start, who has read the whole work twice and parts of it more often, and whose advice has been invaluable. The late Professor H. O. White of Trinity College, Dublin — "HO" to his innumerable friends — to whose memory I have dedicated this book, introduced me to Mrs. Yeats and never failed to be interested in and helpful to my work. Dublin cannot be the same without him. A Ford Faculty Fellowship made possible my year in Dublin in 1954–55; a grant from the Lilly Endowment enabled me to return to Dublin in the summer of 1960.

C. B. B.

Grinnell, Iowa
June 1964

CONTENTS

Yeats AT WORK

PART ONE

Poems

AN INTRODUCTION

AMONG THE YEATS PAPERS IN DUBLIN are working or draft versions of a great many poems. The manuscripts of Yeats's earlier poems, up to the poems printed in The Green Helmet (1910), are usually late versions written into bound manuscript books. Few of the rough papers which preceded these versions seem to have survived. The situation is sometimes different with the poems Yeats wrote after 1908. From then on his rough papers were sometimes kept and filed, or he sometimes did all his work on a poem in a bound manuscript book. With many late poems it is possible to study the entire external process of composition, beginning with their prose sketches and continuing through successive drafts until Yeats corrects the final typescript. Chance more than any other factor seems to have governed what was kept and what thrown away.

From this material I have reproduced and analysed draft versions of the following poems: "The Hosting of the Sidhe" and "The Host of the Air," 1893; "The Lover asks Forgiveness because of his Many Moods," 1895; "Words," 1909; "The Wild Swans at Coole," 1916; "Nineteen Hundred and Nineteen"; section III of "The Tower," 1925; "Lullaby," 1929; "The Mother of God," 1931; section VIII of "Vacillation," 1932; "Ribh considers Christian Love insufficient," 1934; "The Gyres," 1937; "The Circus Animals' Desertion,"

1937–38. This selection illustrates the normal process Yeats went through in composing poems. I have avoided on the one hand poems which Yeats largely composed in his head and then wrote down, such as "The Wheel," or poems which gave him particular trouble, such as "Parnell's Funeral." Yeats forced himself to write "Parnell's Funeral" at a time when he had not written a poem in over a year, using as his theme a passage from a lecture, "Modern Ireland," prepared for his last American lecture tour. When Yeats forced the creative process, for whatever reason, the work of composition was too long drawn out and complicated to be easily described.

i

Yeats almost always began work on a poem by composing what he called a "sketch" or "subject" in prose. These subjects state the content of the poems and note the principal images to be developed in them. They were often brief, though sometimes they were put through successive drafts. Some subjects are as long as the poems that grew out of them, some rough poems already. The subjects of section I of "The Tower" and of "Among School Children" are both short:

What shall I do with this absurd toy which they have given me, this grotesque rattle? O heart, O nerves, you are as vigourous as ever. You still hunger for the whole world, and they have given you this toy.

Topic for poem. School children, and the thought that life will waste them, perhaps that no possible life can fulfill their own dreams or even their teacher's hope. Bring in the old thought that life prepares for what never happens.

[*Transcribed from a manuscript book begun at Oxford, April 7, 1921.*]

Both these subjects, and indeed most others, show that while Yeats was actually composing poems they seldom worked out exactly as he had planned. The rattle became a kettle tied to a dog's tail in section I of "The Tower"; "Among School Children" loses its nostalgic tone during its course and becomes one of Yeats's most powerful statements of Unity of Being. The subject of "Among School Children" fails notably even to suggest the great poem that grew out of it.

Yeats put the "Creed" which is the subject of "Under Ben Bulben" through three drafts. All three manuscripts are extremely difficult to read: the first, which is the longest, I was unable to transcribe; the second is a brief, summary version, perhaps the earliest of the three; the third draft, based directly on the first, went approximately as follows. (The title is taken from the head of the first draft.)

CREED

I

I believe as did the old sages who sat under the palm trees, the banyan trees, or among the snowbound rocks, a thousand years before Christ was born; I believe as did the monks of the Mareotic Sea; as do country men who see the old fighting men and their fine women coming out of the mountain, moving from mountain to mountain.

II

And this is what I believe: that man stands between two eternities, that of his race, that of his soul. Further I declare that man serves these sword in hand and with an amoured mind. That only so armed does man pick the right mate, and only in the midst of a conflict which strains all his mind and his body, and to the utmost, has he wisdom enough to choose his right mate. The wisdom I seek is written on a sword, mirrored on a sword, on Sato's sword, a sword wrapped in a woman's old embroidery.

III

I declare that no evil can happen to the soul except from the soul — that death is a brief parting and brief sickness. What matter though the skies drop fire — children take hands and dance.

[*Transcribed from a late looseleaf manuscript notebook. This may be seen as Yeats left it in a microfilm copy at the Houghton Library. The materials in this notebook have now been distributed.*]

The subject of "On Woman" anticipates the development of that poem very fully; that of "Lines Written in Dejection" is itself almost a poem [*transcribed from the manuscript book begun Christmas, 1912*]:

SUBJECT FOR POEM

I give God praise for woman, what is a man's friendship worth beside hers? I praise God because she is a woman, and in her our minds and our bodies find rest. I praise first for her mind where she covers our vague thoughts with the substance of her revery, for Solomon grew wise in talking to her; and then for her body and the pleasure that comes with sleep; and because in her the vague desires of the dim sky meet the violent, and the curtain shivers: O God, grant me for my gift, not in this life for I begin to grow [old], but somewhere, that I shall love some woman so that every passion, pity, cruel desire, the affection that is full of tears, the abasement as before an image in a savage tent, hatred even it may be, shall find its prey. O God, it is a pity that even you cannot [grant] this to the old, in whom only the heart is insatiable.

No longer the moon
Sends me dark leopards
Green eyed, and wavering [?] in the body
Nor longer her white hares
And that holy centaur of the hills
And the young witches with lofty dissolute faces
Now that I grow old
I have nothing but the harsh sun
I no longer climb in the white mountain valleys
Our heroic mother the moon has vanished
I am alone with the timid sun.

It is difficult to state exactly the role played by these "subjects" in the total economy of poetic composition as Yeats practiced this, difficult because the relations of subjects to finished poems differ greatly. The physical process of working out a poem through successive drafts usually began with these subjects, but it is clear that before writing the subject Yeats had carried the internal, mental aspect of composition much further with some poems than with others. The subjects of "Among School Children" and "Byzantium" illustrate extremes of preparation and lack of preparation. After writing the subject of "Among School Children" Yeats still had nearly everything to do: the poem's principal themes are not anticipated in the subject, among the correlatives used in the poem only the children and the schoolroom setting have been chosen.

In the subject of "Byzantium," on the contrary, the materials of the poem are almost all assembled, and are with one exception in the order in which they appear in the finished poem.

Describe Byzantium as it is in the system towards the end of the first Christian millennium. A walking mummy; flames at the street corners where the soul is purified. Birds of hammered gold singing in the golden trees. In the harbour [dolphins] offering their backs to the wailing dead that they may carry them to paradise.

[*Transcribed from the* MS. *of the 1930 Diary.*]

The question cannot be fully answered until all surviving "subjects of poems" by Yeats are collected and studied, including "subjects for poems" — and there are many such — which never developed into poems. Meanwhile here are some tentative conclusions based on such subjects as I have studied: (1) Yeats wrote subjects at various stages of his thinking about a poem; sometimes he had the poem rather fully formed in his mind, at other times he was only beginning to plan it. (2) A close relation of finished poem to subject does not indicate that Yeats found the actual writing of the poem easy. The subjects of "Coole Park, 1929" and "Byzantium" rather fully anticipate the poems that grew out of them. Jon Stallworthy has shown that Yeats had extreme difficulty composing "Coole Park, 1929"; in writing "Byzantium," as I have shown elsewhere,[1] *his whole attack shows complete mastery of his ideas and of his technique. (3) Such subjects as I have studied do not by themselves indicate whether Yeats is recording a major or a minor inspiration; they do not even hint at the greatness or lack of greatness of the poems that will grow out of them. Until a full study is made we shall have to be content to conclude that these subjects were for Yeats a necessary beginning. Soon after composing a subject, at times on the same day, Yeats would start work on the poem.*

ii

Once he had written his subjects, Yeats had "to find for them some natural speech, rhythm and syntax, and to set it out in some pattern, so seeming old that it may seem all men's speech" ("The Bounty of Sweden" — 1925). This involved great labor of which Yeats often complained. He had to develop a form suited to his particular subject, he had to find and invent descriptive detail and correlatives that would put flesh on its bare bones, and he had — hardest of all — to make "some natural speech." He accomplished this in stages when his poem was at all complex; in some short poems he seems to do everything at once. He always, I think, worked on the whole poem though sometimes he started in the middle or even at the end; he did not try to finish one part of it before moving on to the next. Sometimes he wrote drafts not governed by his intended form; these are always, I think, very early. Then he wrote a series of early drafts where everything he does is, after some experimenting, governed by the chosen pattern of line length and rhyme scheme. Then in intermediate drafts Yeats would assemble his whole poems; if these pleased him at all he would initial or sign them. He often made clean copies of such intermediate drafts so that his typist could transcribe them. Yeats then went to work on these transcriptions; he would improve his phrasing, make subtle metrical adjustments, and systematically punctuate his poem. Very often in these transcriptions various parts of a poem are in various stages of finish. When Yeats detected a bad spot, he would make further manuscript drafts until he had got the poem right. He carried on the process of revision in his proofs, and even after printing.

Yeats sometimes made drafts for parts of poems before he had decided on the form of the poem. Yeats probably wrote many such drafts, but very few have survived. Such as have survived are among his most interesting and tantalizing manuscripts; interesting because they record the earliest stages of Yeats at work, tantalizing because they are almost impossible to read. One draft of this sort has been printed three times, that of the first stanza of "Sailing to Byzantium." [2] I print below an early draft of what is now stanza v of "Among School Children" as another illustration of what Yeats did in the early stages of forming a poem. Yeats began work on stanza v of "Among School Children," perhaps on the whole poem, in this manuscript: [3]

<table>
<tr><td>lap</td><td>fears</td><td></td><td>lap</td></tr>
<tr><td>shape</td><td><s>tears</s></td><td></td><td>made</td></tr>
<tr><td></td><td><s>years</s></td><td></td><td>escape</td></tr>
<tr><td></td><td><s>forth</s></td><td>birth</td><td>betrayed</td></tr>
<tr><td></td><td>forth</td><td></td><td>shape</td></tr>
<tr><td></td><td></td><td></td><td>head</td></tr>
</table>

× What mother of a child shrieking the first scream
× Of a soul

Of a soul struggling to leave
× Degradation of the [word undeciphered]
× Still knowing that it is betrayed [?]
Still half remembering that it [is] betrayed

What mother with a child upon her breast
Shedding there its tears, all the despair
Of the soul betrayed into the flesh
Would think — [if] it came before her in a vision
~~The image~~ What the child would be at sixty years
A compensation for the

[*There are some other jottings on this page which I cannot transcribe.*]

Here the lines Yeats drafts are not governed by the stanza form of "Among School Children," his adaptation of ottava rima. This was Yeats's favorite eight-line stanza, and he used it for many of his most famous meditative and philosophic poems. Since almost the first thing Yeats did when starting to work on a poem was to establish his form, a practice illustrated by most of the manuscripts I reproduce, the fact that he had not chosen his form is a fairly certain indication that Yeats began "Among School Children" with what is now stanza v. *It seems hardly possible that were he past the midpoint in composing the finished poem he would draft a stanza not governed by form.*

There are other bits of evidence that Yeats began "Among School Children" with stanza v, *these external. Shortly before writing out the "topic" from which the poem developed (already quoted), Yeats made this entry in the same manuscript book:*

I think of my grandfather and grandmother, to whom I was so much, and as I look in the glass, as I look at old age coming, I wonder if they would [have] thought it worth the bother. What have I that they value? I think of my father and mother, and of my first coming to their house. What have I that they value, what would have seemed sufficient at the moment? My thoughts would have seemed superstition to the one and to the other a denial of God.

This is essentially the thought expressed in stanza v of the poem, which repeats one of Yeats's most repelling ideas, a young mother's prevision of her infant son as an old man, expressed earlier in the second stanza of the song that opens At the Hawk's Well. *Here as so often with Yeats a new poem uses material found in an already finished poem. In stanza v of "Among School Children" it is content, not form, that governs the draft lines Yeats writes, though if we combine the last two words from the list of rhyme words in the middle of the manuscript page with the list on the right they point clearly to an ottava rima rhyme scheme and include all the rhyme words in the finished stanza except "decide." Choosing his rhyme words or rhyme sounds was a standard practice with Yeats when blocking out a stanza.*

I reconstruct the order in which Yeats wrote the material on this manuscript page as follows: First he wrote the list of rhyme words in the center of the page which ends with the rhyme words of his closing couplet (birth, forth) carefully reversed from the order in which he originally wrote them down. Then I think he invented the fine couplet:

> A compensation for the pang of his birth
> Or the uncertainty of his setting forth.

Perhaps he wrote this down some place else or was trusting his memory, for here he merely dubs it in by writing "A compensation for the." In the draft lines found on this page Yeats was trying to invent matter that might introduce this couplet and fill out his stanza. Yeats then went back to the top of the page and wrote the list of rhyme words to the right. This includes enough of the controlling words of the stanza to indicate that it was now rapidly shaping up in his mind.

A draft of stanza v from a manuscript of the whole poem finished June 14, 1926, makes it almost certain that Yeats worked with the above sheet of notes before him, for as we move back and forth from notes to draft we find that in the draft Yeats further explores nearly every detail found in the notes: the child's cries, its struggle to escape the degradation of incarnation, its recollections of immortality. Yeats slowly discards details that do not work as he finds the details he needs to fill out his stanza.

5

What youthful mother, rocking on her lap
× A fretful thing that knows itself betrayed
× And struggles with vain clamour to escape
× Before its memory and apprehension fade
× Before ~~its~~ the memories of its freedom fade
× Would think — had she ~~foreknown~~ foreknowledge of that shape
× Would think her son could she foreknow that shape
× Her son with sixty winters on his head
× With maybe sixty winter ~~on~~ upon his head
× With sixty or more winters upon his head

[*The next twelve lines were written on the facing page.*]

A thing, the ~~oblivious honey has~~ generative honey had betrayed
× And that shrieks out and struggles to escape
35 And that must sleep, ~~or~~ shriek struggle to escape
× As its drugged memories gleam or fade
× As it
× As still but half drugged memories decide
× As its drugged memories may decide
× Where some brief memories or the drug decide
× ~~As flitting~~ As sudden memories or the drug decide
36 As recollection or the drug decide
37 Would think her son, ~~could she foreknow~~ did she but see that shape
38 With sixty or more winters on ~~his~~ its head

[*Returns to the principal draft.*]

39 A compensation for the pang of his birth
40 Or the uncertainty of his setting forth? [4]

Many early drafts controlled by a form Yeats had invented or was soon to invent have survived, though often they represent only parts of a poem. Apparently Yeats normally started without a fully set form. Indeed in only one manuscript known to me ("Byzantium") does Yeats set his rhyme scheme at the top of his first draft. Characteristically he feels his way into the form by experimenting with rhyme schemes and, especially, line-lengths. In the early drafts of section III of "The Tower" we will find Yeats trying lines with three or four stresses before deciding on three; in early drafts of "Lullaby" and "The Gyres" the stanza form emerges, so to speak. But the first thing Yeats did was to set his form; once he had set it he rarely changed. Rhyme words and rhyme sounds were also established very early in the process of composing and they will often stand firm while the entire context changes around them. They are abandoned only when Yeats has decided that a radical new beginning is needed to remove a bad spot from a poem.

In these early drafts Yeats slowly accumulates additional correlatives, that is the descriptive detail, objects, and images he needs to express the idea contained in his subject. With these change is constant; they come into a poem and go out of it through a long process during which Yeats will finally select those details that best serve his purpose. The multiple drafts of lines 9–32 of "Nineteen Hundred and Nineteen" illustrate this refinement. As this process is going on Yeats will slowly — sometimes with agonizing slowness — find the words he wants, find that "natural speech so seeming old that it may seem all men's speech." The early drafts of "The Wild Swans at Coole" brilliantly illustrate this slow improvement of Yeats's diction.

Most of the surviving manuscripts of Yeats's poems are intermediate drafts, drafts that is of whole poems which are very often initialed or signed, and dated. (Incidentally, these are usually the dates given by Richard Ellmann and others for the composition of particular poems; Yeats rarely recorded the dates on which he actually finished a poem. Often many months elapsed between intermediate and final drafts.) These are always working drafts in which Yeats constantly revises as he goes along. In most intermediate drafts the various parts of the poem show various states of finish. There is no pattern I can discover in the occurrence of bad spots in particular poems. The first two stanzas of "Sailing to Byzantium" had to be rewritten; stanzas 2 and 3 of part I of "Nineteen Hundred and Nineteen"; the last stanza of "The Circus Animals' Desertion." These intermediate drafts are fully illustrated in the discussion of particular poems which follows. Very often Yeats made a clean copy of such intermediate drafts so that a typist could transcribe it.

Yeats's poems were typed at this point, usually in multiple copies. Yeats preferred to have Mrs. Yeats transcribe his manuscripts, but *whether she or another made the typed versions, great care was taken not to add anything, particularly not to add any punctuation. When Yeats went to work on a typescript, he would first of all correct it, filling in blanks which the typist had left when unable to read his writing, improving spelling and capitalization. He would make careful adjustments of meter by dropping or adding syllables, usually one syllable words. Yeats manuscripts are very lightly punctuated, and he often used one copy of a typescript solely for punctuation. A typescript of "News for the Delphic Oracle" with the punctuation Yeats added inserted in brackets illustrates this practice.*

NEWS FOR THE DELPHIC ORACLE

I

There all the golden codgers lay[,]
There the silver dew[,]
And the great water sighed for love
And the wind sighed too[.]
Man-picker Niamh leant and sighed
By Oisin on the grass[;]
There sighed amid his choir of love
Tall Pythagoras.
Poltinus came and looked about[,]
The salt flakes on his breast[,]
And having stretched and yawned awhile
Lay sighing like the rest.

II

Straddling each a dolphin's back
And steadied by a fin
The Holy Innocents re-live their death[,]
Their wounds open again[.]
The ecstatic waters laugh because
Those cries are sweet and strange[,]
Through their ancestral patterns dance
And the brute dolphins plunge
Until in some cliff-sheltered bay
Where wades the choir of love
Proffering its sacred laurel crowns[,]
They pitch their burdens off.

III

Slim adolescence that a nymph has stripped[,]
Pelius on Thetis stares[,]
Her limbs are delicate as an eyelid[,]
Love has blinded him with tears[;]
But Thetis' belly listens[.]
Down the mountain walls
From where Pan's cavern is
Intolerable music falls[.]
Foul goathead, brutal arm appear,
Belly, shoulder, bum
Flash fishlike[;] nymphs and satyrs
Copulate in the foam.

This is an excellent example of rhetorical as opposed to grammatical punctuation; it suggests to us, if we remember that in his own readings Yeats always paused at line ends whether there was a mark of punctuation or not, how Yeats heard the poem and how he wanted us to hear it.[5]

If Yeats became seriously dissatisfied with some section of a poem that had already been typed, he would usually start work on the offending lines in the margins and between the lines of typing. When he had used up the available space, he would begin again in manuscript. This process is illustrated below in the drafts of "Nineteen Hundred and Nineteen" and "The Circus Animals' Desertion." These new manuscripts were in their turn typed and corrected until Yeats was satisfied with a poem. A final typescript was made from which the poem was printed. Yeats continued correction in proof, though in later years he made few changes. Even this was not the end, for Yeats continued to improve his poems after he had had them printed; he used successive editions for such improvement. Here again in his later years his practice grew more conservative. Readers of the Macmillan Wild Swans (1919), Michael Robartes (in Later Poems, 1922), The Tower (1928), The Winding Stair (1933), and A Full Moon in March (1935) generally found the final versions in these books.

iii

Yeats's revisions move in three directions, though the third is not operative in his early poetry. The first is toward correctness, toward an effort to make a poem in process, say a ballad such as "The Hosting of the Sidhe," conform more fully with Yeats's abstract ideal or norm of what a ballad should be. A second type of revision, which might be called mimesis or imitation — though given the long history of these words in literary criticism one would like to find a fresh word — involves an effort to make the imagined scene or action of a poem increasingly vivid sensuously. Both types of revision involve primarily meter and diction, both are illustrated in the revisions of "The Hosting of the Sidhe" and "The Host of the Air." A third type of revision is concerned with the management of the personae invented or being invented for a particular poem; such revisions demonstrate Yeats's effort to control the expressiveness of this personae, to properly modulate the voice speaking the poem.

The personae of most of Yeats's early poems are so vague and abstract that they have almost been refined out of existence. And herein, I think, we find one source of the limitation of Yeats's poetry up through The Wind Among the Reeds. *The vagueness and abstractness of the personae of Yeats's early poems will be discussed in the following chapter. Here it is enough to say that because Yeats often failed to define sharply the personae of his early poems his revisions of them are two dimensional only, involve what we have called correctness and mimesis. But sing song, however subtle and refined it may become, is good only in limited contexts, and realism is not the goal of a lyric poet.*

Wordsworth defined the poet as a man speaking to men, and, however much Yeats disliked Wordsworth's moralizing and didacticism, he came fully to agree with his definition of a poet. Yeats came into his own as a poet when he developed and then made operative a belief that a poem must be a personal utterance, though the phrase "personal utterance" may easily mislead us unless we define it by observing how it worked in Yeats's own poetry and the various ways in which he qualified it by later observations, as in his description of an effective poetic persona in "The First Principle" quoted below. Certainly Yeats at no time in his life regarded poetry as a mode of what is loosely called "self expression"; the very complexity of his concept of the self as involving the "mask" and the "anti-self" make us sure of this. And in the same essay from which "The First Principal" is quoted Yeats wrote "I knew . . . that I must turn from that modern literature Jonathan Swift compared to the web a spider draws out of its bowels; I hated and still hate with an ever growing hatred the literature of the point of view."

Still Yeats did believe that the voice of a poet is the voice of a man, that this must be so because poetry is memorable speech and speech comes from a man. Beginning with "Adam's Curse" most of Yeats's poems are personal utterances, and because they are Yeats is constantly involved in managing the personae he has invented to speak them. This is particularly true of poems using an I-persona. This is Yeats's favorite; sixty-two of Yeats's poems begin with the word "I" to count those instances alone. Much of Yeats's revision of his later poetry is concerned with developing and controlling the expressiveness of his personae. Such revisions are both more important and more revealing than revisions made in the interests of correctness and mimesis. Three dimensional revision will be found at work in the successive drafts of "The Wild Swans at Coole."

Yeats stated his concept of an effective persona far better than I can state it in the opening sentences of "A General Introduction for My Work" written in 1937 and recently printed for the first time in Essays and Introductions. *He called this part of his essay "The First Principle":*

A poet writes always of his personal life, in his finest work out of its tragedy, whatever it be, remorse, lost love, or mere loneliness; he never speaks directly as to someone at the breakfast table, there is always a phantasmagoria. . . . Even when the poet seems most himself, when he is Raleigh and gives potentates the lie, or Shelley 'a nerve o'er which do creep the else unfelt oppressions of this earth,' or Byron when 'the soul wears out the breast' as 'the sword outwears its sheath,' he is never the bundle of accident and incoherence that sits down to breakfast; he has been reborn as an idea, something intended, complete. A novelist might describe his accidence, his incoherence, he must not; he is more type than man, more passion than type. He is Lear, Romeo, Oedipus, Tiresias; he has stepped out of a play, and even the woman he loves is Rosalind, Cleopatra, never The Dark Lady. He is part of his own phantasmagoria and we adore him because nature has grown intelligible, and by so doing a part of our creative power.

Yeats sometimes had difficulty achieving this ideal; there is always a danger when using an I-persona that too much of his accidence will creep into a poem, and we will find that this indeed happened in early drafts of many of the poems studied below. Yeats's principal problem in revision was then to control this accidence. This was particularly difficult when the persona was Yeats himself, for Yeats had then to invent a phantasmagoric Yeats, had to refine the accidence of a particular man involved in an actual situation in the alembic of his imagination. Perhaps the greatest paradox in Yeats's development as a poet was that he became truly a public poet only after he had become a private one; eventually he came to express whatever was nearest to hand, say a statuette carved in lapis lazuli standing on the mantel in his study, in the mode of public speech for which he has so justly been praised.

Eight of the later poems studied use variations of the I-persona, though sometimes only incidentally: "Words," "The Wild Swans at Coole," "Nineteen Hundred and Nineteen," section III *of "The Tower," section* VIII *of "Vacillation," "Ribh considers Christian Love insufficient," "The Gyres," and "The Circus Animals' Desertion." In "Words," "Vacillation," "Ribh considers Christian Love insufficient," and "The Gyres" Yeats had little or no trouble managing his personae, and it is, I think, because their personae came right from the start that Yeats appears to have written these poems with relative ease. In the others Yeats had trouble managing the personae, sometimes serious trouble. When the trouble is serious Yeats will write draft after draft until he has transmuted accidence into permanence. In "Lullaby" and "The Mother of God" Yeats invents more objective personae, the mother who speaks the lullaby, and Mary. But even in these poems Yeats's belief that a poem should be in some way a personal utterance controls what Yeats writes, indeed enables him in the later poem to use material he might not otherwise have managed.*

1

POEMS FROM *The Wind Among the Reeds*

THE earliest bound manuscript book preserved among the Yeats papers in Dublin is inscribed "W. B. Yeats. August 29th. 1893." It contains draft and final versions of many of the poems Yeats published in *The Wind Among the Reeds,* along with others which he printed but never collected and some which have never been printed. There are several lists of poems, in which Yeats explores the order of poems to be included in *The Wind Among the Reeds,* and partial working drafts of *The Shadowy Waters* (1900). The latest date in the book is December 1895. This manuscript book is particularly interesting because it contains love poems addressed to both Maud Gonne and Diana Vernon: the uncollected poem "The Glove and the Cloak" (poem jj in the *Variorum Edition*) obviously refers to Maud Gonne; "The Lover asks Forgiveness because of his Many Moods" is just as obviously about Diana Vernon. Manuscripts of both poems occur in this book.

i

"The Hosting of the Sidhe"

YEATS TRIED TO RESERVE his bound manuscript books for clean copies of poems he had finished or nearly finished, but very often in the process of copying out a poem he would start revising it, sometimes going on to successive revised versions. I believe that the 1893 manuscript book was used in this way, and doubt if it records the earliest versions of any of the poems included in it. The three poems chosen for study are among the most revised poems in the book. Yeats has numbered the pages of the book; three successive versions of "The Hosting of the Sidhe" are found on pages 1–6:

1

They call from the cairn on Knocknarea
They are calling calling from Knocknarea
They call from the grave of Clooth-na-Bare
And the ~~water~~ pool that is over Clooth-na-Bare
Caolte tosses his burning hair
But Niam murmurs 'away come away'

2

'~~Why dost thou brood~~ Linger no more where the fire burns bright
6 Filling thy heart with a mortal dream
~~White~~ ~~Our~~ ~~Her~~ For hands wave to them/ are waving and eyes ~~are~~ a gleam
8 ~~To draw it away~~ Away, come away to the dim twilight'

3

White arms glimmer and red lips are apart
If any man gaze on the Danaan band
They come between him and the deed of his hand
They come between him and the hope of his heart

4

× But some afar on their way
Ah somewhere afar on their ringing way
— No hope or deed was a whit so fair —
And no hope or deed is a whit so fair
And the world has not hope or deed/ deed or hope ~~so~~ as fair
Caolte tosses his burning hair
But Niam murmurs
'Away come away'
August 29th [1893]

Yeats first dated the next draft August 29th, then cancelled 29 and wrote 30 above it.

They are calling calling from Knocknarea
They rush from the cairn of Knocknarea
To the pool

× They call and they rush from Knock etc
And the pool that is over Clooth-na-Bare
Caolte tosses his burning hair
But Niam murmurs 'away come away'

'Linger no more where the fire is bright
6 Filling thy heart with a mortal dream
For hands are waving and eyes ~~are bright~~ a-gleam
For our breasts are heaving our eyes a-gleam
8 Away come away to the dim twilight'
'Our white breasts heave and our red lips part;
Our ~~arms~~ white arms wave and our red lips part
If any man gaze on our ~~ringing~~ rushing band
11 We come between him and the deed of his hand
12 We come between him and the hope of his heart'

They are rushing by on their ringing way
And there is not a hope nor deed as fair;
Caolte tosses his burning hair
But Niam whispers 'away come away'

In the third version Yeats gets closer to the wording of the poem as it was first printed in *The National Observer* on October 7, 1893.

The host is calling from Knocknarea
And the pool that is over Clooth-na-Bare
Caolte tosses his burning hair
But Niam murmurs 'Away come away'

*

'Linger no more where the fire is bright
6 Filling thy heart with a mortal dream

For our breasts are heaving ~~our~~ and eyes agleam
8 Away come away to the dim twilight

*

~~Our~~ And arms are waving our lips apart
10 And if a ~~man~~ any gaze on our rushing band
11 We come between him and the deed of his hand
12 We come between him and the hope of his heart.

*

13 The host ~~rushes by~~ is rushing twixt night and day,
~~And~~ There is not a hope nor a ~~dream~~ deed as fair,
Caolte tosses his burning hair
But Niam murmurs
'Away come away'

Apparently Yeats had done the rough work on this poem before copying it into his manuscript book, for his stanza form and rhyme scheme have been determined, as well as his allusions to Knocknarea, Clooth-na-Bare, Caolte, and Niam. In these drafts Yeats is working for correctness and a more vivid imitation of the imagined scene, a process which he continued in printed versions of the poem until it reached final form in *The Wind Among the Reeds.* To help us see just what Yeats did with this poem by revising it, the successive versions of each line are assembled below, beginning with the earliest MS. and ending with the text found in *The Wind Among the Reeds.* (Manuscripts are designated "MS. 1," "MS. 2," "MS. 3." Printed versions are given the designations found in the *Variorum Edition.* NO stands for *The National Observer,* October 7, 1893; 7 for *The Celtic Twilight,* published December, 1893; 11 for *The Wind Among the Reeds.* I have ignored typographical changes, and changes in punctuation at the ends of lines.)

1 They call from the cairn on Knocknarea MS. 1
They are calling calling from Knocknarea MSS. 1 and 2
They rush from the cairn of Knocknarea MS. 2
They call and they rush from Knocknarea MS. 2
The host is calling from Knocknarea MS. 3
The host is riding from Knocknarea NO, 7, 11

2 They call from the grave of Clooth-na-Bare MS. I
And the pool that is over Clooth-na-Bare MSS. I, 2, and 3
And over the grave of Clooth-na-Bare NO, 7, II

3 Caolte tosses his burning hair MSS. I, 2, and 3
Caolte tossing his burning hair NO, 7, II

4 But Niam murmurs 'away come away' MSS. I, 2, and 3
And Niam calling, 'away, come away NO, 7, II

5 Linger no more where the fire burns bright MS. I
Linger no more where the fire is bright MSS. 2 and 3
And brood no more where the fire is bright NO, 7
Empty your heart of its mortal dream II

6 Filling thy heart with a mortal dream MSS. I, 2, 3; NO, 7
The winds awaken, the leaves whirl round II

7 For hands are waving and eyes agleam MSS. I and 2
For our breasts are heaving our eyes a-gleam MS. 2
For our breasts are heaving and eyes a-gleam MS. 3
For breasts are heaving and eyes a-gleam NO, 7
Our cheeks are pale, our hair is unbound II

8 Away, come away to the dim twilight MSS. I, 2, 3; NO, 7
Our breasts are heaving, our eyes are agleam II

9 White arms glimmer and red lips are apart MS. I
Our white breasts heave and our red lips part MS. 2
Our white arms wave and our red lips part MS. 2
And arms are waving our lips apart MS. 3
Arms are a-waving and lips apart NO, 7
Our arms are waving, our lips are apart II

10 If any man gaze on the Dannan band MS. I
If any man gaze on our rushing band MS. 2
And if any gaze on our rushing band MS. 3; NO, 7, II

11 They come between him and the deed of his hand MS. I
We come between him and the deed of his hand
MSS. 2 and 3; NO, 7, II

12 They come between him and the hope of his heart MS. I
We come between him and the hope of his heart
MSS. 2 and 3; NO, 7, II

13 Ah somewhere afar on their ringing way MS. 1
They are rushing by on their ringing way MS. 2
The host is rushing twixt night and day MS. 3; NO, 7, 11

14 — No hope or deed was a whit so fair — MS. 1
And no hope or deed is a whit so fair MS. 1
And the world has not hope or deed as fair MS. 1
And there is not a hope nor deed as fair MS. 2
There is not a hope nor a deed as fair MS. 3
And where is there hope or deed as fair NO, 7, 11

15 Caolte tosses his burning hair MSS. 1, 2, and 3
Caolte tossing his burning hair NO, 7, 11

16 But Niam murmurs 'Away come away' MS. 1
But Niam whispers 'Away come away' MS. 2
But Niam murmurs 'Away come away' MS. 3
And Niam calling 'Away come away' NO, 7, 11

This run of drafts is a simple but characteristic illustration of what Yeats accomplished when he revised his poems. By revision Yeats increased the degree of energy both within the single lines and among the lines that constitute a verse unit — here a four line stanza rhymed abba. I think his revisions always achieved this result; though I sometimes feel that Yeats carried some detail of a revision beyond the point where he achieved the best expression, I have never felt that revision has failed to improve a poem as a whole. As for diction and phrasing, Yeats, early and late, worked hard to achieve Swift's ideal — "Proper words in proper places." He sought at once to find the inevitable word, and to arrange these words according to a syntax based on the spoken language. The finished version of "The Hosting of the Sidhe" is both more energetic and more colloquial than the drafts. Finally, we observe that Yeats finished his poem a part at a time: lines 1–4 and 14–16 in *The National Observer,* lines 5–9 in *The Wind Among the Reeds,* lines 10–13 in manuscripts 2 and 3. Again, this is typical.

I have divided my commentary on the details of Yeats's revisions into units corresponding to the stanzas. In the manuscripts and in the two earliest printings of the poem the stanzas are separated; in the finished poem they are printed without breaks.

LINES 1–4. Here Yeats's principal revisions affect his verbs; they involve both the form of his verbs and the content. Yeats shifts from the present tense to the progressive present — the progressive present dominates the finished poem — while moving towards increased energy of statement. Yeats tries two forms of lines 1–2 in MS. 1:

> They call from the cairn on Knocknarea
> They call from the grave of Clooth-na-Bare

and

> They are calling calling from Knocknarea
> And the pool that is over Clooth-na-Bare

The repetition of "They call from" is at once too easy and too static, so Yeats introduces the progressive present "are calling," doubling the participle in line 1 and dropping it from line 2. There has been some gain in energy, but the solution is still too easy. In MS. 2 Yeats tries two solutions: "They rush from the cairn of Knocknarea/ To the pool" and "They call and they rush from Knocknarea/ To the pool." At this point Yeats perhaps realized that he was involved in a double difficulty; he has been using the pronoun "they" without an antecedent with the result that when his reader gets to the names Caolte and Niam in lines 3–4 he will assume that "they" refers to them, "call" and "rush" do not combine happily because they are necessarily unsimultaneous. In MS. 3 Yeats solves the first problem by introducing the noun "host" in place of the pronoun "they":

> The host is calling from Knocknarea
> And the pool that is over Clooth-na-Bare

Eventually this reading will supply the titles, successively "The Faery Host," "The Host," and "The Hosting of the Sidhe," and meanwhile the poem moves better when first the "host" and then two individuals from that host, Caolte and Niam, summon mortals to join the Sidhe. But "calling" is still static; the movement involved in the cancelled word "rush" has been lost, and now Yeats merely summons us to join the Sidhe on Knocknarea. Before Yeats printed the poem in *The National Observer*, he completed the procession image with which the poem now begins:

> The host is riding from Knocknarea
> And over the grave of Clooth-na-Bare.

While all this change was going on in lines 1–2, lines 3–4 remained untouched until Yeats revised his poem for *The National Observer:*

> Caolte tosses his burning hair
> But Niam murmurs 'away come away.'

Yeats finished stanza 1 when he changed his verbs to the progressive present and transferred the summons from the host to Niam:

> Caolte tossing his burning hair
> And Niam calling, 'away, come away.'

LINES 5–8. Yeats's revision of stanza 2 was radical, but far less complicated. The stanza remained fairly stable through its second printing in *The Celtic Twilight;* then Yeats rewrote it for *The Wind Among the Reeds.* In this rewriting he replaced lines 5 and 8 by new lines which he put into the middle of his stanza (as lines 6 and 7); he revised his old lines 6 and 7 and transposed them so that they now provide his "a" rhymes at the beginning and end of the stanza:

> And brood no more where the fire is bright
> Filling thy heart with a mortal dream,
> For our breasts are heaving and eyes a-gleam;
> Away, come away to the dim twilight.
>
> Empty your heart of its mortal dream.
> The winds awaken, the leaves whirl round,
> Our cheeks are pale, our hair is unbound,
> Our breasts are heaving, our eyes are agleam,

Perhaps Yeats made these changes partly because of the sheer weakness and emptiness of the lines he abandoned; line 8 in the original version was particularly weak and empty. Certainly Yeats's new lines are far more energetic than his old; the whirling leaves are particularly interesting because they adumbrate the gyre of Yeats's later poetry. Another possible explanation, and here I am on surer ground, is that the changes are involved with Yeats's decision to abandon the separation of his stanzas. It would not have been enough merely to shove together the successive stanzas, keeping a full stop at the end of every fourth line; some enjambments are needed. Yeats provided a forced enjambment, so to speak, at line 4 when he replaced a period with a colon; by the revision described above he provided a true enjambment here at line 8. He increased the force of this enjambment by his revision of line 9.

LINES 9–12. Yeats did most of his revising of these lines in manuscript. The development of line 9 is complicated by the fact that Yeats decided while working on MS. 2 to rearrange some of his descriptive detail. The "heaving breasts" of the revised ninth line he put into stanza 2, the "waving hands" of the original seventh line he brought down into stanza 3. During the transposition "white breasts heave" became "breasts are heaving." Perhaps this is an example of Yeats's timidity in handling details involving sexual attraction in *The Wind Among the Reeds,* a timidity certainly illustrated in his revision of "The Lover asks Forgiveness," discussed below. "White arms" are less suggestive than "white breasts." Yeats revised the line again in MS. 3, getting rid of the eight low words that had crept into it and changing "wave" to the progressive present "waving." The line now read "And arms are waving our lips apart," which without punctuation seems rather silly. Before printing the poem in *The National Observer* Yeats dropped the initial "and"; he also invented the awkward form "a-waving" to replace the syllable lost at the beginning of the line. Revisions like this one are frequent in Yeats's later poetry. Their result is to begin a line with a strong accent, and with an important word. When Yeats revised the line for *The Wind Among the Reeds,* he got rid of "a-waving" and cast the line in its final form. In the successive versions of this line we observe again continually increasing energy and movement. Here Yeats moved from "White arms glimmer and red lips are apart" of MS. 1 to "Our arms are waving, our lips are apart." The rest of the stanza caused less trouble, though the revisions made have the important effect of changing the point of view. In MS. 1 we are observing the host of the Sidhe from the outside:

> If any man gaze on the Danaan band
> They come between him and the deed of his hand
> They come between him and the hope of his heart.

When Yeats finishes these lines in MS. 3, we are part of the host:

> And if any gaze on our rushing band
> We come between him and the deed of his hand
> We come between him and the hope of his heart.

The change from "Danaan band" to "rushing band" shows what revision of a single word can accomplish. The exotic word "Danaan" will puzzle most readers, thereby interrupting their experience of the poem; it is also static, whereas the participle "rushing" sustains the image of the riding host.

LINES 13–16. Since stanza 4 largely echoes stanza 1 in its development — the echo of the rhyme sounds is exact — most of the changes made in four follow from the changes already made in one. When, for example, Yeats in MS. 3 changed line 1 to read "The host is calling from Knocknarea" he also changed line 13 to read "The host is rushing twixt night and day"; when in *The National Observer* he changed lines 3 and 4 to read "Caolte tossing" and "Niam calling" he made the same changes in lines 15 and 16. During the process of revision Yeats noticeably increased the similarity of stanzas 1 and 4; they are far more alike in the finished poem than in MS. 1. Only the complex revision of line 14 is not explained by Yeats's endeavor to make the echo of stanza 1 more exact. From MS. 1 on Yeats uses line 14 to pick up the thought of stanza 3 by repeating the words "hope" and "deed," uses it, that is, to express again the attraction of the invitation to join the faery host. While revising this line Yeats shifts from direct statement of the contrast between our world and faeryland ("And the world has not deed or hope as fair"), to an implied statement of the contrast ("There is not a hope nor a deed as fair"), to a question ("And where is there hope or deed as fair"); his expression of the attraction of faeryland grows increasingly subtle, increasingly tantalizing.

The total effect of Yeats's revision can be judged best when MS. 1 and the finished poem are put side by side; indeed the great effect of his typographical revision can be judged only when the two versions are brought together.

1

They are calling calling from Knocknarea
And the pool that is over Clooth-na-Bare
Caolte tosses his burning hair
But Niam murmurs 'away come away'

2

'Linger no more where the fire burns bright
Filling thy heart with a mortal dream
For hands are waving and eyes a gleam
Away, come away to the dim twilight'

3
White arms glimmer and red lips are apart
If any man gaze on the Danaan band
They come between him and the deed of his hand
They come between him and the hope of his heart

4
Ah somewhere afar on their ringing way
And the world has not deed or hope as fair
Caolte tosses his burning hair
But Niam murmurs
'Away come away'

THE HOSTING OF THE SIDHE

The host is riding from Knocknarea
And over the grave of Clooth-na-Bare;
Caoilte tossing his burning hair,
And Niamh calling *Away, come away:*
Empty your heart of its mortal dream.
The winds awaken, the leaves whirl round,
Our cheeks are pale, our hair is unbound,
Our breasts are heaving, our eyes are agleam,
Our arms are waving, our lips are apart;
And if any gaze on our rushing band,
We come between him and the deed of his hand,
We come between him and the hope of his heart.
The host is rushing 'twixt night and day,
And where is there hope or deed as fair?
Caoilte tossing his burning hair,
And Niamh calling *Away, come away.*

ii "The Host of the Air"

YEATS WROTE "The Host of the Air" while he was working on *The Land of Heart's Desire* (1894). Both poem and play exploit the theme of the mortal woman who leaves her husband to join the Sidhe. This theme attracted Yeats because it seemed to him to express his relations with Maud Gonne: in section XXIV of the manuscript "First Draft" of Yeats's *Autobiographies* he says, "I began to write *The Land of Heart's Desire* . . . and put into it my own despair. I could not tell why Maud Gonne had turned from me unless she had done so from some vague desire for some impossible life, for some unwearying excitement like that of the heroine of my play." Yeats wrote the poem in 1893; the version printed in *The Bookman* in November of that year is dated October 1. In a note included with this first printing (*Variorum Edition,* p. 143) Yeats says that he has put into verse a story told him by an old woman at Ballysadare, Sligo. Ballysadare was the home of his Middleton cousins and the seat of the Pollexfen Mills. This note suggests that when Yeats came to write the poem its simple story was fully arranged in his mind. The form he chose for it is a ballad stanza of four lines, lines two and four rhyming. The fact that Yeats is retelling a story in a simple metrical form suggests that composition may have been easy, that perhaps most of the process of composing is illustrated in the versions given below. These are found on pages 20–29 and on part of page 31 of the 1893 manuscript book. The repeated reference to reeds in the first draft of the poem suggested to Yeats the title *The Wind Among the Reeds,* for on the bottom of page 19, opposite the first draft, Yeats has written, "Name for a book of verse 'The Wind among the Reeds!' "

MacMara drove with a song
2 The wild duck and the drake
3 From the tall and tufted reeds
Of the dim Heart Lake

And he saw the ~~tall~~ reeds darken
6 At the coming of night tide
And dreamed of the long brown hair
8 Of Bridget his bride

He heard in his song and dream
10 A piper piping away
× And never was piping so mournful
11 And never was piping so sad
12 And never was piping so gay.

13 And he saw ~~that~~ young men and young girls
14 ~~Danced~~ Who danced on a level place
15 And Bridget his bride ~~danced with them~~ among them
With a sad and a merry face

And then they crowded about him
18 And many a sweet thing said
19 And a young man brought him red wine
And a merry young girl white bread.

× But Bridget took hold of his sleeve
× And led him away from the throng
× To where old men were at cards
× And he went on with his song

× But Bridget/ his bride drew him by the sleeve
× Away from the dancing band
× To where old men were at ~~play~~ cards
× Twinkling their
To old men sitting at cards
And the twinkling of ancient hands.

She had fear of bread and the wine
Of those people of the air
But he sat and played in a dream
A dream of her long bright hair

She had fear of the bread and the wine
Of the people of the air
But he sat and played in a dream
A dream of her long dim hair

29 He played with the merry old men
× Nor had the thought of home
× Till his Bridget
And he thought not of evil chance
31 Until one bore Bridget his bride
Away in his arms from the dance

And then he stood up in a rage
And scattered the cards on the ground
× But the piper, the dancer and old

But the old men and young men and girls
Faded away like a cloud

× He knew who the dancers were
× And his heart was black with dread
He knew who the dancers were
And his heart was black [with] dread
And he ran to his cabin door
Old women that keened for the dead

41 But he heard high up in the air
42 A piper piping away
43 And never was piping so sad
44 And never was piping so gay

On the opposite page Yeats drafted what was to be his ninth stanza.

33 He bore her away in his arms
That handsome young man there
And his breast and his face and his arms
Were drowned ~~by~~ in her long dark hair.

The second draft follows immediately.

1 O'Driscoll drove with a song
2 The wild duck and the drake
3 From the tall and the tufted reeds
4 Of the ~~dim~~ drear Heart Lake

And he saw where reeds grew dark
6 At the coming of night-tide
7 And dreamed of the long dim hair
Of Bridget his new wed bride.

He heard in his song and dream
10 A piper piping away
11 And never was piping so sad
12 And never was piping so gay.

13 And he saw ~~where~~ young men and young girls
14 Who danced on a level place
15 And Bridget his bride among them
16 With a sad and a gay face

And then they/ And the dancers ~~came~~ ~~crowding~~ crowded about him
18 And many a sweet thing said
19 And a young man brought him red wine
And a merry young girl white bread.

21 But Bridget drew him by the sleeve
22 Away from the merry bands
~~Where~~ Unto old men ~~were at~~ who played at the cards
24 With a twinkling of ancient hands;

For the bread and the wine brought doom
26 For these were the folk of the air;
And he played at the cards in a dream
In a dream of her long dim hair.

29 He played with the merry old men
30 And thought not of evil chance
31 Until one bore Bridget his bride
32 Away from the merry dance.

33 He bore her away in his arms —
34 The handsomest young man there,
35 And his neck and his breast and his arms
36 Were drowned in her long dim hair

O'Driscoll got up in a rage
38 And scattered the cards with a cry,
39 But the ~~old~~ ~~young~~ old men and ~~girls~~ dancers were gone
40 As a cloud faded into the sky

× He knew who the dancers were
× And his heart

40a He knew now the folk of the air
40b And his heart was blackened by dread
40c And he ran to ~~his cabin door~~ the door of his house
× And he [word undeciphered]
40d Old women were keening the dead;

41 But he heard high up in the air
42 A piper piping away
43 And never was piping so sad
44 And never was piping so gay.

Yeats wrote another version of stanza 10 at the bottom of page 31 of the manuscript book; it was first printed in *The Wind Among the Reeds.*

37 O'Driscoll scattered the cards
38 And out of ~~his~~ the dream awoke
39 Old men, and young men, and young girls
Were gone like a fading smoke.

Yeats's second draft is essentially what he printed in *The Bookman.* In revising the poem for *The Wind Among the Reeds,* Yeats replaced stanza 10 with the new version given at the end of the second draft, and omitted the stanza beginning "He knew now the folk of the air." The omitted stanza tells of Bridget's death, an event already implied in her rape by the Sidhe, so the effect of the omission is to make the poem less obvious and more suggestive.

The details of Yeats's revision are less interesting than the details of his revision of "The Hosting of the Sidhe," and the revision as a whole had a far less radical effect on the poem. Even though this is true, a few of the changes Yeats made deserve particular comment: In the second draft of line 4 "dim Heart Lake" becomes "drear Heart Lake"; the word "drear" has far more emotional force than "dim," and the change has the farther result of reserving "dim" for the description of Bridget's hair. Yeats revised line 5 twice: "And he saw the ~~tall~~ reeds darken" (MS. 1)/ "And he saw where reeds grew dark" (MS. 2)/ "And he saw how the reeds grew dark" (*Bookman*). Cutting "tall" unifies the visual impression; with it we see tall reeds in a darkening landscape, without it the darkening landscape is stressed. The revision also shifts the metrical accent from "tall" to "reeds." The revision of lines 7, 28, and 36 all involve abandoning various adjectives descriptive of hair in favor of a single adjective "dim."

7 long brown hair (MS. 1)/ long dim hair (MS. 2)
28 long bright hair/ long dim hair (MS. 1)
36 long dark hair (MS. 1)/ long dim hair (MS. 2)

Yeats made a change similar to those listed above in line 22 of "The Lover asks Forgiveness." The successive versions of that line go as follows: "dark shadowy hair" (MSS. 1 and 2)/ "~~long~~ dim shadowy hair" (MS. 3)/ "dim heavy hair" (*Wind*). In all of these revisions an adjective commonly, even tritely used to describe hair is replaced by an adjective not ordinarily used to describe hair. In the context of *The Wind Among the Reeds* I do not think this is a source of true surprise, for there the adjective "dim" seems always to hand, evocative of the Celtic twilight that pervades. In addition to contributing to this twilight effect, the changes enable Yeats to avoid certain Romantic clichés, particularly "bright hair." In revising line 9 Yeats raised a prepositional phrase to an adverbial clause: "He heard in his song and dream" (MSS. 1 and 2)/ "He heard while he sang and dreamed" (*Bookman*). Replacing nouns with verbs makes for greater energy of expression. In line 16 Yeats while revising introduced a spondaic close, a device he had used to great effect in "The Lake Isle of Innisfree." "With a sad and a merry face" (MS. 1)/ "With a sad and a gay face" (MS. 2). Finally, the changes introduced in lines 25–26 give those lines a folksy, perhaps even folk-lorish tone in keeping with the ballad meter.

She had fear of the bread and the wine
Of the people of the air
(MS. I)

For the bread and the wine brought doom
For these were the folk of the air
(MS. 2)

The bread and the wine had a doom,
For these were the host of the air;
(*Bookman*)

In spite of these evidences that Yeats took normal care in writing "The Host of the Air," in spite of the fact that the poem grew out of Yeats's unrequited love for Maud Gonne, it still seems all too facile. Yeats himself in "Ireland after Parnell" (1922) provides a commentary appropriate to it. There he recalls the comment of a fellow art student on one of George Russell's visionary paintings, "That is too easy, a great deal too easy!" Yeats's early poems in ballad meter strike me as a great deal too easy. They lack the verbal and technical ebullience of the late poems in ballad form, and above all they lack Yeats's marvelous, and marvelously controlling refrains. Poetry of this early sort could proliferate intolerably. Perhaps Yeats realized this, for beginning in 1895 (after he had met Diana Vernon) there came a change in his creative economy. He turned to those compact, carefully worked short lyrics that give *The Wind Among the Reeds* its characteristic autumnal tone. The poem to be studied next is a poem of this sort.

iii

"The Lover asks Forgiveness"

ON PAGES 107–16 OF HIS MANUSCRIPT BOOK Yeats wrote out three successive drafts of "The Lover asks Forgiveness." The first of these is already highly finished; it suggests that much work had been done on the poem elsewhere. Perhaps the surest indication that Yeats thought it finished or nearly so is the carefulness with which the first of the drafts has been pointed. Yeats gave attention to pointing very late in the process of composing a poem; if a draft is carefully punctuated then it is certainly late. Each of the drafts is dated; they are the work of successive days: August 23, 24, and 25, 1895. Their special interest is that they show what Yeats could do to a poem at such close intervals. When Yeats wrote the poem he was considering an affair with Diana Vernon, and it seems to reflect his doubts and hesitations, caused by the fact that Maud Gonne pre-empted his affections. He simply could not free himself for another woman. It also reflects his belief that some apocalypse is at hand, that somehow the world from which he suffers will shortly disappear, give place to a world presided over by the Rose.

THE TWILIGHT OF ~~PEACE~~ ~~MY PEACE~~
FORGIVENESS

1 If this importunate heart trouble your peace
With hopes lighter than air,
Or plans that in mere planning flicker and cease
Draw down your long dim hair,
And make a twilight over your lips, and say:
Torn/ O piteous candle flame
Wavering in winds, older than night or day,
That murmuring and longing came
From marble cities loud with tabors of gold,
From dove-grey faery lands,

And/ From altars, behind purple fold on fold
From bridal curtains fold on purple fold
From bridal beds fold falling on purple fold
behind many a purple fold

12 *Queens wrought with glimmering hands;*

From Usheen gazing on Neave's love-[*pale* — cancelled] *lorn face*
That saw young Neave [*ride* — cancelled] *mourning with love-pale pale*

Amid the Wandering tide,

[*From* — cancelled] *And lingering/ And lingered in a hidden desolate place*

16 *Where the last phoenix died,*

And blowing the flames above his holy head;
[*That have* — cancelled] *rolled the flames above his sacred head*

18 *And still murmur and long;*

O piteous hearts that till all hearts are dead
Waver in winds of song.

Then cover the pale blossoms of your breast
With your dark shadowy hair
And ~~bid~~ heave a sigh for ~~all~~ this heart without rest
And/ Trouble the twilight there.
August 22nd. 1895

THE TWILIGHT OF FORGIVENESS

1 If this importunate heart trouble your peace
2 With words lighter than air
3 ~~Or~~ And hopes that in mere hoping flicker and cease,
Draw down your long dim hair
~~Loosen~~ Unbraid your shadowy hair
And make a twilight over your lips, and say:

O piteous candle flame!
O heart like a thin flame
Wavering in winds, older than night or day,
That murmuring and longing came

9 *From marble cities loud with tabors of* [*gold* — cancelled] *old,*

10 [*From* — cancelled] *In dove-grey faery lands,*

From [*bridal* — cancelled] *battle curtains, fold* [*on* — cancelled] *upon purple fold,*

12 *Queens wrought with glimmering hands;*

That saw young Naeve wander with love-lorn face

Amid the wandering tide

15 *And lingered in the hidden desolate place*

16 *Where the last phoenix died*

And rolled the flames above his sacred head

18 *And still murmur and long:*

O piteous hearts that till all hearts be dead

Waver in winds of song.

Then cover the pale blossoms of your breast

With your dark shadowy hair

And heave a sigh for all hearts without rest

And trouble the twilight there.

~~W B Yeats~~ August 23rd. /95

Yeats's cancellation of his own signature is charming. When Yeats signed a poem and dated it, that meant he thought the poem finished. On the next day when Yeats went to work once more, he apparently started by cancelling his signature at the end of the previous draft.

THE TWILIGHT OF FORGIVENESS

1 If this importunate heart trouble your peace

With ~~words~~ plans lighter than air

3 And hopes that in mere hoping flicker and cease

Unbraid your shadowy hair

4 Crush the rose in your hair

And shed a twilight over your lips and say:

5 Cover your lips with rose heavy twilight, and say:

6 'O hearts of windblown flame!

7 'O winds ~~older~~ elder than changing of night and day,

'That murmuring and longing came

9 'From marble cities loud with tabors of old
10 'In dove-grey faery lands,
11 'From battle banners, fold upon purple fold
12 'Queens wrought with glimmering hands;
13 'That saw young ~~Neave~~ Niam ~~wander~~ hover with love-lorn face
14 '~~Above~~ ~~Amid~~ Above the wandering tide,
15 'And lingered in the hidden desolate place
16 'Where the last phoenix died
'And rolled the flame above his sacred head
18 'And still murmur and long.
19 'O piteous hearts changing till change be dead
20 'In the ~~nine winds of~~ a tumultuous song'
And cover the pale blossoms of your breast
22 With your ~~long~~ dim shadowy hair
And bid a sigh for this heart without rest
Trouble the twilight there.
And trouble with sighs for all hearts longing for rest
24 The rose-heavy twilight there
August 24th

Yeats slightly altered lines 8, 17, 21 and 23 before printing the poem in *The Saturday Review* on November 2, 1895. We can summarize Yeats's progress by working back from the finished poem. If we ignore changes in punctuation and spelling, Yeats finished in the form first printed lines 1, 12, 16, and 18 in MS. 1; lines 2, 3, 9, 10, and 15 in MS. 2; lines 4, 5, 6, 7, 11, 13, 14, 19, 20, 22, and 24 in MS. 3. The poem reached its final form in *The Wind Among the Reeds,* except for one word; Yeats changed the archaism "elder" introduced into line 7 back to "older" in *Collected Poems,* 1933.

These drafts show how very hard Yeats was working on his diction and meter. Indeed the style of most of the poems included in *The Wind Among the Reeds* was so finished that Yeats never revised them. He achieved this finish by dint of the scrupulous care we see him exercising here. In MS. 1, for instance, Yeats uses "piteous" in line 6 and again in line 19; in MS. 2 he revises line 6 to avoid this repetition. "O piteous candle flame" becomes "O heart like a thin flame," and then in MS. 3 "O hearts of windblown flame." The successive versions of line 13 read "mourning with love-pale face"/ "wander with love-lorn face"/ "hover with love-lorn face." Here the changes seem to result from Yeats's careful adjustment of his vowel sounds. In six successive versions of line 23 Yeats at once generalizes his meaning ("this heart/ all hearts/ all things") and makes a series of delicate metrical adjustments. The number of syllables in the line shifts from 10 to 12 to 11 to 13, and the sound pattern counterpointed against the ground base of the iambic foot grows increasingly complex:

And bid/ heave a sigh for all/ this heart without rest (MS. 1)
And heave a sigh for all hearts without rest (MS. 2)
And bid a sigh for this heart without rest (MS. 3)
And trouble with sighs for all hearts longing for rest (MS. 3)
And trouble with sighs for all hearts without rest (SR)
And trouble with a sigh for all things longing for rest (*Wind*)

More interesting than these illustrations of technical care are illustrations of what might be called a depersonalizing process through which Yeats put this poem and, I think, most of the poems included in *The Wind Among the Reeds*.[1] In the first draft two lovers are together. The man asks the woman "Draw down your long dim hair/ And make a twilight over your lips, and say" — he then puts the words of the long passage in italic into her mouth. In draft 3 the intimacy of the poem has been greatly reduced, indeed even the meaning of lines 4 and 5 becomes uncertain when Yeats changes them to read "Crush the rose in your hair/ And shed a twilight over your lips and say." In revising line 11 Yeats wrote successively "bridal curtains/ bridal beds/ battle curtains/ battle banners" which again restrains the definite if vaguely expressed sexual intimacy of the first draft. A ghost of this intimacy lingers at the end of the poem when Yeats writes

And cover the pale blossoms of your breast
With your dim shadowy hair
And trouble with sighs for all hearts longing for rest
The rose-heavy twilight there.

Surely this poem reflects Yeats's affair with Diana Vernon, yet Yeats in his successive drafts is intentionally making this fact less apparent.

Many critics of Yeats have discussed the point at which his art had arrived when he completed *The Wind Among the Reeds;* Thomas Parkinson, Richard Ellmann, and John Unterecker seem to me to have discussed it with most insight. I have little to add to what they have already said, but since Yeats's poetry is about to take a new direction it may be useful once again to say where we are before we take off in the new direction. The situation as it appears to Yeats's present-day readers and as it seems to have appeared to him can be stated simply: Yeats never wrote more finished poetry than he wrote in *The Wind Among the Reeds;* indeed it is hard to imagine how he might have gone further along this line. Yet this poetry is far less interesting to most of his readers than his later poetry.

The explanation is partly technical. For one thing Yeats's diction has not yet achieved the metaphysical penetration which is the special characteristic of his later style:

> Caught in that sensual music all neglect
> Monuments of unageing intellect.
>
> Solider Aristotle played the taws
> Upon the bottom of a king of kings.

It is also instructive to observe that Yeats has not yet begun to use the various stanza forms which he perfected for his greatest poems. He does use ballad stanzas in his early poetry, though even his ballad stanzas undergo a radical development in his later poetry. Rather in *The Wind Among the Reeds* Yeats's principal effort is to write his poem in a single sentence, to make the poetic unit and the grammatic unit coincide, as John Unterecker has noted; Yeats accomplishes this surprisingly often, albeit with a little cheating by the use of frequent semicolons. He has not yet mastered a form or a diction that would be suited to a poem such as "Byzantium" or to the quite different needs of "In Memory of Major Robert Gregory."

But a more adequate explanation of the relative inadequacy of the early poems can be found if we look back to the drafts of the three poems studied above; Yeats has not yet begun to invent the forceful personae of his later poems. "The Hosting of the Sidhe" really has no persona. The theme of the poem is the theme of *The Shadowy Waters:* the attraction of an imagined, more than mortal way of life, a theme that obsessed Yeats for many years. Here it is brightly but not urgently stated. Yeats does use a persona in "The Host of the Air"; he is first called MacMara, then O'Driscoll. I don't see that it matters what he is called, since he functions in the poem very passively. And yet his situation reflects Yeats's personal situation at the time of writing; he loses his bride because of her "desire for some impossible life," for the reason Yeats feared he would lose Maud Gonne.

In the first printing of "The Lover asks Forgiveness" the poem had the title "The Twilight of Forgiveness," had, that is, no named persona. Then in *The Wind Among the Reeds* Yeats changed the title to read "Michael Robartes asks Forgiveness." Michael Robartes is one of three imagined personae — the others are Aedh and Hanrahan — into whose mouths Yeats put many of poems included in *The Wind Among the Reeds*. Yeats's note on Michael Robartes in the original edition defined him as "fire reflected in water," as "the pride of the imagination brooding upon the greatness of its possessions, or the adoration of the Magi." All this hardly describes the voice of a man. Things became a little better in 1906 when Yeats gave the poem its present title: at least a lover is a man, not an abstraction. The trouble is that Yeats is saying what he has to say — here he is expressing his doubts and hesitations over beginning an affair with Diana Vernon while still obsessed by Maud Gonne — too tangentially, too unurgently.

Yeats has not yet solved for himself the problems of the artist's relation to his art, and to his reader. The man, W. B. Yeats, was always "involved"; at no time was he more involved than in the 1890's. But his art was not involved; it was, indeed, an antidote to rather than an expression of his own involvement. One proof of this is that none of these poems are occasional whereas most of his great poems are. One would be hard put to guess from this early poetry much of anything about the man who had contrived it, or about the political and social matrix that lay back of it. Yeats's breakthrough to a greater art, greater in all its aspects, came after he had developed the concept that poetry must be "personal utterance," though as was noted above this term needs to be carefully defined.

The earliest expression I have seen of the doctrine of "personal utterance" is found in an unpublished lecture Yeats gave in London on March 9, 1910.[2] Yeats's lecture was taken down as he spoke by an unidentified secretary; Yeats revised and corrected the manuscript produced by this secretary, part of which I quote:

One day I was at the Young Ireland Society in Dublin and took up an old newspaper, and in that old newspaper I read a ballad by some one of our obscure Irish poets. A returned emigrant was describing the first sight of the hills of his own country as he came back on shipboard. I found I was moved to tears. I said, "Why is this? It is very bad writing"; and the thought came to me, "It is because it is a man's exact feeling, his own absolute thought, put down as in a letter." I said to myself, "We have thrown away the most powerful thing in all literature — personal utterance. This poetry of abstract personality has taken the blood out of us, and I will write poetry as full of my own thought as if it were a letter to a friend, and I will write these poems in simple words, never using a phrase I could not use in prose. I will make them the absolute speech of a man."

Once the doctrine of personal utterance was worked out, Yeats's own involvements found their way into his poetry, to its great enrichment.

And yet I do not want to underrate Yeats's early verse, nor the importance of his apprenticeship. It is true that the world is largely absent from this early verse. Instead we dwell in an artistic construct, a kind of arcanum presided over by the symbolic rose. The air in this arcanum is heavy at times, the decoration sometimes over elaborate and rich. Still it is a very pleasant, not to say intoxicating place, albeit a little uncanny. Yeats took his construct very seriously; indeed, if I read "The Secret Rose" right, hoped that it would shortly displace the actual world. However this may be, Yeats worked hard at his writing then, and always. For me as for others, Yeats's revision of his early verse for *Poems*, 1895, marks the end of his apprentice years. From 1895 on his artistic means, so to speak, were adequate; he was able to express whatever he had to express, either in prose or verse, in a finished style. In a word, he was a writer, and on his way to becoming a great writer. To become one required as Yeats observed in "Reveries" that "good luck or bad luck make my life interesting." Certainly at the time Yeats thought the decade 1899–1909 a tissue of bad luck: theatre business, Maud Gonne's marriage, estrangement from Ireland, the death of Synge. Yet as Thomas Parkinson has fully demonstrated in *W. B. Yeats: Self-Critic*, Yeats's experience in the theater was the crucial event in his development as a poet. Yeats could not have entered just any business: it had to be "theatre business."

2

Words AND The Wild Swans at Coole

IN the years following the publication of *The Wind Among the Reeds* Yeats wrote very few lyric poems. During the decade 1899–1909 most of his energy went into the Irish dramatic movement. With others he founded the Irish Literary Theatre in 1899, became president of the Irish National Theatre Society in 1902, and after December 27, 1904 was at times almost immersed in the affairs of the Abbey Theatre. His own writing centered in an exploration of subjects derived from Irish heroic legend in a series of plays and narrative poems. Plays exploiting Irish legend included *Cathleen ni Houlihan* (1902), *On Baile's Strand* (1903), *The King's Threshold* (1904), and *Deirdre* (1907); narrative poems such as "The Old Age of Queen Maeve" and "Baile and Aillinn" make a somewhat different use of similar materials. Yeats also wrote much prose during these years; the expanded *Celtic Twilight* appeared in 1902, *Ideas of Good and Evil* in 1903, the rewritten *Stories of Red Hanrahan* in 1904, *Discoveries* in 1907. In December 1908 Yeats began the Journal from which he later extracted "Estrangement" and "The Death of Synge."

These activities caused Yeats early in 1909 to wonder seriously if he would continue to grow as a poet. It was on February 25 that he wrote the journal entry which he slightly revised in "Estrangement XXXVIII":

I often wonder if my talent will ever recover from the heterogeneous labour of these last few years. The younger Hallam says that vice does not destroy genius but that the heterogeneous does. I cry out vainly for liberty and have ever less and less inner life. . . . I thought myself loving neither vice nor virtue; but virtue has come upon me and given me a nation . . . Has it left me any lyrical faculty? Whatever happens I must go on that there may be a man behind the lines already written; I cast the die long ago and must be true to the cast.

At about the same time Yeats wrote in "All Things can Tempt me"

> All things can tempt me from this craft of verse;
> One time it was a woman's face, or worse —
> The seeming needs of my fool-driven land;
> Now nothing but comes readier to hand
> Than this accustomed toil.

Yeats's talent did recover from the heterogeneous. He emerged from these activities a capable manager of theater business, a successful propagandist, and a better poet. Why Yeats's engulfment in the heterogeneous had this last effect we shall perhaps never certainly know. The ways of genius are not entirely explicable, but it is clear that bad luck had made his life interesting which meant that Yeats had more to say, and it is also clear that a decade spent in writing largely for the theater had given him wide experience in developing and handling a seemingly colloquial style. Whatever the causes, shortly after writing the laments quoted above Yeats in 1909 began once more frequently to write lyric poems, now nearly always personal utterances. The man behind the lines was a changed man with a changed conception of the nature and purpose of art. During the years 1909–19 he was to write many of his greatest poems.

i

"Words"

I HAVE CHOSEN "WORDS," a simple, easily achieved poem, to show Yeats at work in 1909 because I believe that the record of its composition is fairly complete; the record includes the prose sketch or "subject," the drafts written on January 22, 1909, and the revisions of stanzas 2 and 3 made on January 23rd. Yeats wrote the poem in the Journal referred to above. The prose sketch of the poem forms section 10 of the Journal; the drafts sections 12 and 15:

Today the thought came to me that P.I.A.L. [Maud Gonne] never really understands my plans, or motives, or ideas. Then came the thought, what matter? How much of the best I have done and still do is but the attempt to explain myself to her? If she understood, I should lack a reason for writing, and one can never have too many reasons for doing what is so labourious.

1 I had this thought an ~~hour~~ while ago
× I thought of this a while
I suddenly thought an hour ago
2 My darling cannot understand
3 What I have done, or what would do
4 In this blind bitter land.
× And I was dashed to think of it
And I grew sorry thinking it
× I had grown sorry at the thought
Until my thought ~~grew clear~~ cleared up again
Remembering that the best I have writ
Was ~~but~~ writ to make ~~it~~ all plain.
9 ~~How~~ That every year ~~I've~~ I have ~~said~~ cried at length
~~She'll~~ She can but understand it all
11 Because ~~I've~~ I have come into my strength
12 And words obey my call
× ~~But~~ And had she done so — He can say
× Who shook me from his sieve
× If I'd have thrown poor words away
16× And been content to live
or else this verse
13× ~~But~~ ~~And~~ ~~How~~ That had she done so — ~~He~~ who can say
× ~~Who~~ But he that shook me from his sieve
× ~~Whether~~ If I'd have thrown poor words away
16× And been content to live.

13 That had she done so — who can say
14 What would have shaken from the sieve —
15 I might have thrown poor words away
16 And been content to live.

January 22

The next day Yeats wrote, "The second and third stanzas of poem written yesterday should read:

I had grown weary of the sun;
6 Until my thoughts cleared up again
7 Remembering that the best I'~~ve~~ have done
8 Was done to make it plain;

9 That every year I have cried 'At length
10 My darling understands it all
11 Because I have come into my strength
12 And words obey my call.' "

Comparison with the printed version shows that Yeats changed the poem very little. Once it was printed in *The Green Helmet and Other Poems,* he never revised it, though he did change the title from "The Consolation" to "Words" in *Collected Poems,* 1933. Here the process of composition was about as easy as it ever was for Yeats, perhaps because he only needed to elevate the colloquial a bit (note his careful handling of contractions) to control the very moderate heat rising from the tangential, hence self-limiting, intimacy of the poem. Colloquial language is, so to speak, one wall; arm's-length emotion is another. All Yeats had to do was to drive down the middle.

The persona is Yeats himself, the subject his own art and Maud Gonne's relation to that art. Yeats is speaking directly out of his personal situation and in his own voice. I do not see that he has much trouble here managing his I-persona. Perhaps

That had she done so — who can say
But he that shook me from his sieve

is slightly awkward because it interrupts the personal point of view by suggesting that God alone knows what might have happened.

That had she done so — who can say
What would have shaken from the sieve

is better and keeps our attention on the persona. Admittedly "Words" is a slight poem, but there has been a great increase in energy and directness of expression.

ii

"The Wild Swans at Coole"

THOUGH MANUSCRIPTS OF MANY POEMS included in *Responsibilities* (1914) have survived, they are for the most part late drafts, and I have seen no manuscripts of some of the finest poems in the volume, such as "September 1913," and "To a Shade." *Responsibilities* is remarkable for the appearance in it of poems concerned with public issues such as the *Playboy* crisis and the controversy over Sir Hugh Lane's offer to give a collection of pictures to Dublin if a suitable gallery were supplied for them. Through the rest of his life Yeats continued to write poems on men and events; taken together they are a splendid achievement and one almost unique in our time, since few other great poets of the twentieth century have commented so directly on our tragic history as it was being made. One could hardly deduce this history from the corpus of Wallace Stevens' poetry, and Eliot has largely confined himself to one aspect of it, the loss of traditional faith and his own efforts to regain it. Pound is occasional in his special way: he becomes occasional to denounce, with the result that he often seems to beat a dead horse. Yeats's stance is different from any of these. He addresses himself in work after work to the moral question how modern man is to act in typical situations, in the process powerfully asserting custom and ceremony and extracting from the traditions of western man all that is most viable. The poems in which he does this are the cause, I think, of the continuing popularity of Yeats. Whereas for the special student Yeats's art may well seem to culminate in such cryptic poems as "Supernatural Songs," the general reader will continue to prefer "Nineteen Hundred and Nineteen."

No complete run of drafts of any of the public-speech poems in *Responsibilities* has, so far as I know, survived. There is more material available for the study of "To a Wealthy Man" than for any other poem of its kind, but even this does not reward intensive study since it begins late in the total process of composing the poem. There are two manuscripts of the whole poem written December 24 and 25, 1912, and a corrected typescript in which the poem has reached its final form. Even the first surviving manuscript is, however, a late draft during which twenty-six of the poem's thirty-six lines were finished; most of the unfinished lines are well along toward their final wording.

The form has been set, the correlatives all assembled. Yeats has, that is, worked out his contrast of renaissance Italy and modern Dublin in all its detail.

The manuscripts of poems included in Yeats's next collection, *The Wild Swans at Coole* (1917), are likewise for the most part late drafts, and again there are not in Mrs. Yeats's collection any manuscripts at all of some of the finest poems, such as "In Memory of Major Robert Gregory" [1] and "The Double Vision of Michael Robartes." This is all the more to be regretted since beginning in 1915 and 1916, in poems such as "Ego Dominus Tuus," "The Wild Swans at Coole," and "Easter 1916," Yeats experienced a breakthrough to a greater art than he had hitherto created. Fortunately the manuscripts of "The Wild Swans at Coole" do show that poem in various stages of its creation.

Yeats's general mood, his cast of mind was reminiscent and nostalgic, though an Irish event like the revolution of 1916 could, as always, arouse his interest in an occasion. He had recently finished "Reveries over Childhood and Youth" and was continuing his autobiography in the manuscript known as "First Draft" which brings the story of his life up to 1898. It is natural that Yeats while meditating on his youth should begin his questioning of old age. This theme now moves into the very center of his poetry; in October 1916 Yeats finished "The Wild Swans at Coole," one of his greatest poems on old age. In this characteristic work Yeats uses what is nearest to him and most familiar, a walk along Coole Water, to express a universal state of mind and emotion. As he does this he achieves a diction and a rhetoric that can rightly be called noble.

Three successive drafts of the poem have survived. In all of them the order of the stanzas is as in the first printing of the poem with what is now the last stanza in the middle of the poem, following line 12. Draft A must have been written very early in the process of composition, since Yeats completed only four lines of his poem in this draft; draft B is transitional, that is it grows directly out of A and moves toward draft C; here Yeats completed thirteen lines and the whole of his original last stanza; by the end of draft C Yeats had nearly finished his poem. The three drafts are printed below.

Before he began work on draft A Yeats had established his stanza form, perhaps in still earlier drafts which have not survived. In this stanza three long lines — they range in the finished poem from eight to eleven syllables — alternate with three short lines of five, six, or seven syllables. The basic pattern seems to my ear to place four stresses against three with a variation of five against three at each fifth line and occasionally elsewhere. The stanza has the unusual rhyme scheme abcbdd. It has not occurred before in Yeats's poetry and does not exactly recur, though many years later Yeats used this rhyme scheme but not the pattern of line lengths in "Three Songs to the Same Tune" and the related "Three Marching Songs." The arrangement of the rhymes varies the ababcc pattern that was a favorite scheme with Yeats. The stanza pattern described above governs everything Yeats does in the drafts. In this A draft the last two stanzas of the poem (in their original order) are much less far along than the first three. The A draft was written on two sheets of paper; there is no indication as to their order. I have arranged the stanzas as they were first printed. In some of the drafts of "The Wild Swans at Coole" Yeats indents his short lines. Since this was not done consistently, I have brought all the lines out to a uniform left margin.

[A 1]

These/ The woods are in their autumn colours
But the Coole Water is low
× And all the paths are dry under
And all paths dry under the foot
In the soft twilight I go

The woods are in their autumn colours
× The lake narrow and bright
But the Coole Water is low
~~And all paths dry~~ The pathways hard under the footfall
× When in the twilight
× Night after night I go
Where I at twilight go
× Indolently among the trees and the stones,
× And number the wild swans.
Indolently ~~here and there among grey stones~~ among the shadow of the grey stones
And number the wild swans.

[A 2]

× It is now in the 19th autumn
× Since I first made my ~~tot~~ count
8 Since I first made my count

× And now we are in the 19th year
× Since the first I counted

[At this point WBY marked "It is now in the 19th autumn" stet]

~~Should they~~ Should I go nearer to the
And when I go too near the water
Suddenly they'd mount
× And beating
Scattering, wheeling in great broken rings
On their slow clamoring wings.

25 But now they drift on the still water
× I have Coole's fifty nine
26 Mysterious, beautiful.
Among what waters low build nests/ rushes laid their eggs
And by what stream or pool
Where ~~will they flee~~ they have fled when I awake some day
And find they have flown away

[A 3, the verso of A 1]

They're but an image on a lake
Why should my heart [?] be wrung
× When I first saw them I was young
The white white unwearied [?] creatures
Delighted me when young
When I first gazed upon them

× Why is [it] when I gaze upon them
× That my heart is wrung
× I found it pleasing [?] to love them
× When I

× Ah now when I do gaze on them
× My heart, my heart is wrung
× And yet the white and loving/ unwearied creatures
× Delighted me when young

× And were they to clamor overhead

[A 4, the verso of A 2]

The lovely white unwearied creatures
~~Delighted~~ Always when yet young

When they flew or clamored overhead
Gave me a lighter tread

Many conquests have they
× Their hearts have not grown cold
They have not grown old
× By passion and by conquest
× By lovingness and
For wander where they will
They are attended still
Passion and conquest wander where they will
24 Attend upon them still

In draft A 1 Yeats has brought together the materials of his first stanza: the trees in their autumn colors, the dry paths, the twilight, and contrasts with these emblems of old age and approaching death what seems the eternal beauty of the swans. One detail, the low water twice referred to, has been significantly changed in the finished poem where Yeats departs from the reality of the observed scene and places his swans on "brimming water." He has transferred the water, always a symbol of the sensual life in Yeats's poetry, from one set to another of the contrasting images in the stanza.

In this draft and the next Yeats introduces his I-persona, that is himself, into this stanza: "I at twilight go/ Indolently." Though beginning a poem in the first person is a frequent practice with Yeats, it would have been more frequent still had he not in instance after instance removed his I-persona from the onset of a poem late in the process of composing it. He will do this in the C drafts. Revisions of this sort are so common that we should ask what Yeats accomplished by them: many of Yeats's greatest poems begin with the setting of their symbolic scenes ("The Second Coming," the Byzantium poems, "Meditations in Time of Civil War," and "Vacillation" among others); then the persona arrives, so to speak, and when he does Yeats's meditative exploration of the scene begins. The result is that at the onset of these poems the scene itself and the themes it suggests have the reader's undivided attention. This does not happen when the persona is immediately present, for then we must divide our attention between the contemplator and what is being contemplated. Another way of putting this would be to say that the type of opening chosen involves the question whether Yeats wants the point of view to be controlling, or the view itself, or both equally. Yeats can accomplish marvels with all these strategems, but the marvels are of different sorts as one can see by comparing "The Wild Swans at Coole" with "The Tower." Shall Yeats begin as he eventually does here with youth/age, mortality/immortality, or with my age, my mortality, with the symbolic scene or with the masked man? Here too it seems to me that "indolently" introduces too much of Yeats's accidence, his state of being at the moment. When he cancels this in the B drafts we have a clear example of revision involving management of the persona.

The form of the stanza is set: even in these very early drafts Yeats never rhymes line 1 with line 3; he picks up his b rhyme at line 4 and goes on to his concluding couplet. In this draft four stress lines alternate with three stress lines except at line 5; in the finished poem line 3 has also five stresses. The rhyme words of the final couplet (stones, swans) are in place. Yeats has achieved very little of the diction of the finished poem: we note "autumn" and "twilight," but even that essential word "dry" has for the moment been dropped. The last line of this draft "And number the wild swans" will eventually suggest Yeats's title.

On sheet A 2 Yeats drafts his second and what was originally his third stanza. Yeats made more progress on stanza 2 than he had on stanza 1. The materials of the finished poem are all here; four rhyme words are in place (count, mount, rings, wings); line 8 is done, line 11 nearly done. Even the number of syllables in the various lines of the stanza are identical for lines 8–12 in this draft and in the finished poem: 6, 9, 5, 10, 7. The essential words are all here, though not always in their final form (scattering/ scatter, clamoring/ clamorous). Stanza 3 (now stanza 5) is as far along in its action, form and language. Here as in the finished poem the poet contemplates the drifting swans, "mysterious, beautiful," and fears that they will leave Coole Water. The line ends are in place for lines 25, 26, 28–30 (water, beautiful, pool, day, away); lines 25 and 26 are done; the pattern of line lengths is the same in the draft and the finished poem (9, 7, 8, 6, 10, 7). Most of the words found in the finished poem are here. The cancelled draft line "I have Coole's fifty-nine" will in the C drafts be effectively reworked to supply line 6.

The A 3 and A 4 drafts of the original fourth and fifth stanzas are not nearly so far along. Yeats uses all of A 3 and part of A 4 to work on his fourth stanza. Though the essential idea of the stanza, the poet's changing attitude toward the swans as he ages and they appear not to, is present, Yeats anticipates some of the material he will eventually use in his next stanza — the fact that the swans seem "unwearied," for example. No line is even near its final form. Three of the line ends are in place (creatures, head, tread), though "creatures" will be transposed to the first line of the stanza. Most of the essential words — brilliant, sore, twilight, bell-beat, trod — are still to be found. The first half of what was then Yeats's last stanza (lines 19–21) had still to be invented after these A drafts had been completed. Yeats does make good progress with the last three lines of the stanza; indeed by combining draft lines one can get

> Their hearts have not grown cold
> Passion and conquest wander where they will
> Attend upon them still.

In the A drafts Yeats has assembled most of his materials, he has established his stanza form, and found much of the diction of the finished poem. He has established eighteen line ends and completed lines 8, 25, 26, 24. He has brought stanzas 1, 2, and 3 much further toward completion than stanzas 4 and 5. In the B drafts which follow Yeats got very little further with his first three stanzas; he remade stanzas 4 and 5, indeed he completed stanza 5 in this draft. The B drafts are written on three sheets of punched paper; there are no page numbers. Yeats was undoubtedly working in a looseleaf notebook, and he seems to have followed his usual practice of writing first on the right hand page of an opening, reserving the left hand page for revising.

THE SWANS AT COOLE

[B 1]

The woods are in their autumn colours
But the lake waters are low
~~And all~~ The paths ~~dry~~ hard under the footfall
The pathways hard under the foot~~fall~~
~~And I when~~ In the pale twilight I [go]
× In the half dark I ~~will~~ go
× Indolently among the shadow of the grey stones
× And number the swans

× Indolently among the stones and number the swans
Among the shadow of grey stones, and number the swans
Floating among the stones.

We are now at the nineteenth autumn
8 Since I first made my count.
I make no sound for if they heard me
Suddenly they would mount
~~Scattering and~~ And wheel above the waters in great broken rings
And a slow clamor of wings.

25 But now they drift on the still water
26 Mysterious beautiful
Among what rushes will their eggs
× Where is the stream or pool

[B 2]

× All will have flown to
× All
Upon what stream or pool
Shall they in beauty swim, when I come here some day
To find them flown away

× They are but images on water
× Why should a heart be young
I turn away from the wat
Why do I turn from the water;
As though my heart were wrung
× At how those
× To gaze upon
To ~~gaze~~ look upon those brilliant creatures
I ~~did turn~~ always, when I was young
× As they came swinging by or clamored overhead
× I did not turn with this slow tread.
× When they ~~when~~ swung by or
When they came swinging by or clamored overhead
I had a lighter tread.

[From the opposite page (verso of B 1). I have arranged the drafts in what seems to me their proper order.]

~~I looked~~ To look upon those brilliant creatures
× Gaily when I was young
Always when I was young
If they swung by or clamored overhead
× I'd have a
I have trod with a lighter tread.

And yet when I was young
If they swung by, or clamored overhead
I had a lighter tread

I look upon the brilliant creatures
And am heavy and heartsore
Yet nine[teen] autumns from ~~the autumn~~ this [word undeciphered]
× I walking upon
I hearing upon this shore
17 The bell-beat of their wings above my head
18 Trod with a lighter tread

[B 3]

Many companions float around them
Their hearts have not grown cold
Their wings can carry them to where [they] please
Their bodies are not old
Passion and conquest dip in what stream they will
24 Attend upon them still

Companion by companion
× And beautiful and bold
The beautiful and the bold
Have crossed the skies and climbed the river
Their hearts have not grown cold
Passion and conquest, wander where they will
24 Attend upon them still.

[From the verso of B 2]

Ah nineteen years from now
And I am growing old
They drift there lover by lover
Their hearts have not grown cold

Passion and conquest, wander where they will
24 Attend upon them still.

[The three versions of this stanza printed just above have all been cancelled.]

I turn away — lover by lover
20 They paddle in the cold
21 Companionable stream, or climb the air
22 Their hearts have not grown old
Passion and conquest, wander where they will
24 Attend upon them still.

[Yeats returned to the bottom of sheet B 2 to write two versions of line 19, the second in final form.]

× Ah lover by unwearied lover
19 Unwearied still — lover by lover

STANZA 1. After setting an intermediate title at the top of the page, "The Swans at Coole," Yeats wrote a version of stanza 1 which develops directly from the A draft. He did not finish any of his lines, he did not even establish any additional line ends. He kept the description of the lake's low level, and his "I-persona." At line 5 in the phrase "pale twilight" he fell into a characteristic cliché of the 1890's: he tried "half-dark," but cancelled that and left his difficulty unresolved. He did drop "indolently," unfortunate because it involves us too much in his own state of mind, and reversed the order of lines 5 and 6.

STANZA 2. Here Yeats may perhaps be said to have gone backwards. He kept his finished eighth line, and the rhyme words already established for lines 10–12; but his pattern of line lengths is no longer so nearly that found in the finished poem. He did make one important change: in this draft the swans do not rise from the surface of the lake, "I make no sound for if they heard me/ Suddenly they would mount." He then went on in his original third stanza to describe the swans floating on the lake: "But now they drift on the still water." Perhaps we have here the explanation of Yeats's transposition of stanza 3 to the end of the poem. The two contrary actions in the finished poem, the swans' flight up from the water and their floating on the water, come too close together in the poem as first printed.

STANZA 3. Yeats copied the first two lines, finished in the A drafts. He made a slight change in line 3, and then went on to invent slightly new detail for the end of the stanza when he wrote.

> Upon what stream or pool
> Shall they in beauty swim, when I come here some day
> To find them flown away.

Again, no additional lines have been finished, no additional rhymes set.

STANZA 4. Yeats wrote four drafts of this stanza, and made great progress. At the outset he took over most of the language of the A draft; this he gradually cancelled as he achieved much of the splendid diction of the finished poem. For example, line 3 in the A draft ends with "unwearied creatures"; the swans now became "brilliant creatures" and their unweariable nature was reserved for stanza 5. Then in his fourth draft Yeats transferred "brilliant creatures" to line 1, where we find it still, and established his line ends. Here again Yeats makes a revision that involves management of his persona when he shifts from his state now at the imagined moment of the poem to his state when he first saw the swans. "I did not turn with this slow tread" involves us again in the accidence of the moment; Yeats cancels this and replaces it after several revisions by the statement that he, even nineteen years before, hearing

> The bell-beat of their wings above my head
> Trod with a lighter tread.

These lines are now in their final form.

STANZA 5. Yeats also made four drafts of these lines, and on his fourth try nearly finshed them. These drafts provide a study in emergence. In the A drafts the swans were emblems of youth and love; they were in complete contrast with the aging man who watched them. Yeats started with these ideas, kept his b rhyme and his closing couplet, though he tried a variant of line 23 when he wrote "Passion and conquest dip in what stream they will" before re-establishing the A reading. Yeats now introduced a new idea, the fact that the swans were a company while he was alone. This led eventually to the splendid beginning of the stanza. "Many companions float around them" became

"Companion by companion"; then this was dropped down to the third line and rephrased "They drift there lover by lover." Yeats then transposed "lover by lover" to line 1:

I turn away — lover by lover
They paddle in the cold . . .

A false start, one more change, then the lines were done:

× Ah lover by unwearied lover
Unwearied still — lover by lover.

While working toward his finished stanza Yeats explored and abandoned many details: should he describe the swans as "beautiful and bold"? Should he explicitly state his own age and loneliness? When the poem ended with this verse it had in some ways better balance, for we end as we will begin with the "I-persona" excluded from the first — this will happen in the C drafts — and from the final stanzas. In its original form the poem moved from the objective, to the subjective, back to the objective.

The C drafts of the poem were written on four unnumbered sheets. In this draft Yeats virtually finished his poem: twenty-two of its thirty lines are done and the others nearly done.

[C 1]

× The woods are in their autumn foliage
The trees are in their autumn foliage
The water in the lake is low
× The paths of the wood are
All pathways hard under the foot
× From stone to stone I go
In the pale twilight I go
Among the great grey stones I number the swans
Floating among the stones.

[On a page which I believe was originally to the left of this, which I designate C 2, WBY redrafted this stanza in nearly final form.]

The trees are in their autumn foliage
2 The woodland paths are dry
× The water ~~in~~ under the October twilight

3 Under the October twilight the water
4 Mirrors ~~the~~ a still sky
5 Upon the brimming water among ~~the stones~~ stones
6 Are nine and fifty swans

[Back to C 1]

We are/ I am now at the nineteenth autumn
× From the time of my
8 Since I first made my count
I make no sound for if they heard me
Suddenly/ All suddenly they would mount
Scatter and wheel in those great broken rings
With slow clamor of their wings

25 But now they drift on the still water
26 Mysterious, beautiful
× Among what rushes will their eggs
× Upon what shore or pool
× Swim, when
× Shall five and forty dream creatures play
× When they have flown away
× Shall they disport when I awake some day
× To find they have fled away

[From C 2]

× Among what reeds
Among what rushes do they build
28 By what lake's edge or pool
29 Delight men's eyes when I awake some day
30 To find they have flown away

Nineteen autumns ago
When

[C 3]

× In numbering the brilliant creatures
× I have numbered all the brilliant creatures
× And I am but heart sore

× I have counted five and forty two
× And I am more heart sore

I turn from all those brilliant creatures
Heavy and heart sore
× ~~And yet~~ Yet nine[teen] autumns from this evening
× I, hearing on/ upon this shore
17× The bell-beat of their wings above my head
18× Trod with a lighter tread

13 I have looked upon those brilliant creatures
14 And now my heart is sore
15 All's changed since I hearing at twilight
16 The first time on this shore
17 The bell-beat of their wings above my head
18 Trod with a lighter tread

[On the sheet opposite, that is on the verso of C 1, WBY did another version of stanza 2]

The nineteenth autumn has gone
Since that first time I counted
They heard when I had but half finished
And all suddenly mounted
And scattered wheeling in great broken rings
12 Upon their clamorous wings

[C 4]

19 Unwearied still — lover by lover
20 They paddle in the cold
21 Companionable steams or climb the air
22 Their hearts have not grown old
Passion and conquest wander where they will
24 Attend upon them still

STANZA 1. The C drafts begin with two versions of this stanza. In the first, most of the detail of the B draft recurs; in the second Yeats finished the stanza except for one word. In the first form of the stanza Yeats retained the observed detail of the low lake-water, the essential word "dry" was still missing, "pale twilight" came back, and Yeats was still very much with us as poet-protagonist. Then in the second draft the miracle occurred and the "poem comes right with a click like a closing box." To make it come right Yeats abandoned his b rhyme and wrote "The woodland paths are dry"; this had the further happy effect of taking "I go" along with it by forcing Yeats to write a new form of line 4. In place of "pale twilight" Yeats definitely established the time of the poem by writing "October twilight." He now neglected what he had observed; his imagination suggested the contrast of dry land with "brimming water" on which the swans might appropriately float. Since the "I-persona" had gone, the idea of counting the swans was dropped, and Yeats speaks instead of Coole's fifty-nine swans, a detail he had tried momentarily in draft A 2, though at another place in the poem. Yeats had still to replace "Autumn foliage" with "autumn beauty," easy to do since the line end was not involved in his rhyme scheme. The stanza is now magnificently balanced, with three autumnal images (autumn beauty, dry paths, October twilight) giving way to three images of the sensual life (water, brimming water, swans); its diction is superb.

STANZA 2. This stanza was recalcitrant, and after the C drafts were finished Yeats had still more work to do on it than on any other part of the poem. In the draft on C 1, which takes off directly from the B drafts. Yeats retains the idea of not disturbing the swans as they float on Coole Water. He made slight verbal rearrangements as when "And wheel above the waters in great broken rings" became "Scatter and wheel in those great broken rings." Then on the verso of C 1 Yeats tried another version. He dropped the idea of not disturbing the swans. Now instead of merely imagining what would happen if they were disturbed, he recalls their flight from the lake nineteen years before. For the moment he has phrased the stanza in the past tense: "heard," "mounted," "scattered." His principal revision changes these verbs to the present tense. Only line 12 is done, but lines 10 and 11 are nearly done. Line 8, the first line of the poem to be finished, has for the moment been changed.

STANZA 3. Here, as with stanza 1, Yeats made great progress. He began by copying out his finished opening lines (25, 26), then went on to explore detail that might fill out his stanza. The progressive versions of line 29 illustrate this exploration:

> Shall five and forty dream creatures play
> Shall they disport when I awake some day
> Delight men's eyes when I awake some day.

With the invention of the line just quoted, the stanza suddenly came right; all the lines save line 27 are done; that nearly done.

STANZA 4. Yeats began by slightly changing the action that takes place in this stanza in the B drafts, where Yeats looked at the swans. He now explored the idea of counting them again, then turning away from them, before he returned to a slight revision of B, "I have looked upon those brilliant creatures." When Yeats abandoned his second explicit reference to his condition now compared with his condition nineteen years before, the stanza came right. He has stated again the essential theme of the poem, the contrast of youth and age, but in more general terms:

All's changed since I hearing at twilight
The first time on this shore.

Yeats concluded the stanza with his already finished seventeenth and eighteenth lines.

STANZA 5. This has the same form as in the B drafts.

During the course of these three drafts Yeats completed lines 2–6, 8, 12–22, 24–26, 28–30, and his unfinished lines required only slight correction before reaching the form in which they were first printed. The final word in line 1 was changed from "foliage" to "beauty"; in line 23 "and" became "or"; the verb in line 27 was changed from "do" to "will." Stanza 2 was rewritten before it was printed. I place the manuscript version above the version printed:

The nineteenth autumn has gone
Since that first time I counted
They heard when I had but half finished
And all suddenly mounted
And scattered wheeling in great broken rings
Upon their clamorous wings

The nineteenth autumn has come upon me
Since I first made my count;
I saw, before I had well finished,
All suddenly mount
And scatter wheeling in great broken rings
Upon their clamorous wings.

Once printed, the text of "The Wild Swans at Coole" remained unchanged except for Yeats's decision to place what was originally his final stanza in the middle of his poem. This change first appeared in the Cuala Press edition of *Wild Swans*. We have already speculated about Yeats's reasons for making this change.

The doctrine of personal utterance is clearly operative both in "Words" and in "The Wild Swans at Coole," though the great difference in dimension and quality of the poems already suggests that a personal utterance should not be too personal. In both poems Yeats is writing of his own life, but perhaps only in the second has he made of it "something intended, complete," achieved that is the ideal stated in 1937 in "The First Principle." This achievement accounts for the increasing power of his verse. The breakthrough to controlled personal utterance came with "Adam's Curse" (written 1902, see *Letters*, p. 382) and affects all the poems printed with *The Green Helmet*, poems written in the years 1908–11, among them "Words." These are not Yeats's greatest poems, though "No Second Troy," "The Fascination of What's Difficult," and "Brown Penny" are fine poems, but with them we have clearly left behind the hermetic world of *The Wind Among the Reeds*. We hear of land agitation and the Abbey Theatre, we discover in "At Galway Races" the onset of lines of speculation that will engross Yeats for many years — the ideal relation of the poet and the man of action (the horseman) which will come with the dawn of a new age.

In *Responsibilities* a breakthrough to a larger audience is achieved when in "To a Wealthy Man" and "September 1913" Yeats writes the first of his great "public speech" poems. In *The Wild Swans at Coole* Yeats's mood seems meditative — seems because Yeats reserved for his next volume the poems inspired by the Easter Rebellion, all splendid examples of public speech and all written before the content of *Swans* was set in the volume Macmillan published in 1919. "The Wild Swans at Coole" is a typical and brilliant Yeatsean meditation, clearly a personal utterance from first to last which already avoids the danger that mere accidence may intrude into and spoil such an utterance. It illustrates the enlargement of Yeats's art which took place during these middle years, an enlargement that is intellectual as well as technical. A personal utterance becomes public speech in "Easter 1916" (as yet only privately printed); this mode of poetry was more and more to prevail.

3

Nineteen Hundred and Nineteen

THE years 1918–20 were particularly fruitful for Yeats. His personal life had settled into a satisfactory pattern at last. He was intellectually and emotionally stimulated by those strange experiences described in "A Packet for Ezra Pound." His playwriting, now that he had adapted the Noh form to his dramatic purposes, was going so well that in 1919 he was at last delivered from that succubus, *The Player Queen.* But his euphoria is most apparent in his poetry, which reaches now one of its greatest moments in poems such as "The Second Coming," "A Prayer for my Daughter," "All Souls' Night," and "Nineteen Hundred and Nineteen." Jon Stallworthy has printed and analysed the manuscripts of "The Second Coming" and "A Prayer for my Daughter" in *Between the Lines.* I have chosen "Nineteen Hundred and Nineteen" for study, even though the surviving drafts begin at a late point in the total process of the poem's creation, chosen it because of the greatness of the poem and because these surviving drafts do constitute a typical manuscript. These drafts include three manuscripts and a typescript which I have designated MS. 1, MS. 2, TS. 1, and MS. 3. MS. 1 was written on ten unnumbered sheets of unlined notebook paper; MS. 2 is a clean copy of MS. 1 written on seven sheets of the same paper, numbered by Yeats; TS. 1 is a transcript of MS. 2 on five sheets of standard typing bond, numbered and stapled; MS. 3 (containing further drafts of lines 9–32 only) is written on five sheets, four of letter and one of notebook paper, unnumbered, and without other external evidence of the order of drafts. I am responsible for the order in which MS. 1 and MS. 3 are printed.

Even in MS. 1 Yeats has already assembled most of his concourse of emblems and correlatives; he has worked out the intricate stanza patterns used in the various parts of the poem, with all their delicate shifts in line lengths, and stress and rhyme patterns; he has found most of the diction of the finished poem; the manuscript is carefully punctuated. It is undoubtedly a late draft, as the following table will further establish.

Part I. 29 lines are done as in the first printing; 14 lines have rhyme words established or virtually established; 5 lines have rhyme sounds established or virtually established. This accounts for all 48 lines.

Part II. Finished

Part III. All lines are finished save 69 and 79, and these require only the change of a single word.

Part IV. Finished

Part V. All lines are finished save 93, 103, and 107; these require only minor adjustments.

Part VI. Finished, save for a tense shift (weary/ wearied) in line 116.

NOTE. The substance and much of the language of the explanatory note to Part VI is found in the manuscript.

This table shows that only part I of the poem required much additional work.

From the drafts described above I print the whole of MS. 1, interesting even when it reaches final form because of the many verbal changes made; part I from MS. 2; and the whole of MS. 3.

[MS. 1, page 1]

THE THINGS ~~RETURN COME~~ THAT COME AGAIN

I

1 Many ingenious lovely things are gone
2 That seemed sheer miracle to the multitude;
Changeless and deathless; above the murdering moon
Above the insolence of the sun. There stood
Where many a gold and silver paten shone
6 An ancient image made of olive wood;

7 And gone are Phidias' carven ivories
8 And all his golden grasshoppers and bees.

9 We too had many pretty toys when young:
10 A law indifferent to blame or praise,
A speedy remedy for obvious wrong
No swaggering soldier on the public ways
Who weighed a man's life lighter than a song;
A general confidence in future days
In some great thing to come, because we thought
16 That the worst rogues and rascals had died out.

[Page 2]
And we would say if conversation turned
On ignorance and armies and such things
That all men soon would be both fed and learned;
That armies now that parliaments and kings
No more might covet what they had not earned
Existed for their drums and fiddle strings
And did the cannon sound 'twere but perchance
To make a guardsman's lazy charger prance

× But our good dream is spent, once
× That good dream has had its day
But now in place of comfortable dreams nightmare
~~Returns again~~ Can ride again, a drunken soldiery
27 ~~May~~ Can leave the mother murdered at her door
28 To crawl in her own blood and go scot free;
× Night shakes with terror as it shook before
29 The night can sweat with terror as before
30 We pieced our thoughts into philosophy
31 And planned to bring the world under a rule
32 Who are but weasels fighting in a hole.

× Henceforth let no man
× Who dare now fancy that his work will stand
× Whether ambition wrought or pure intent
× And whether work of mind or work of hand;
× And that he may keep pride of intellect
× Nor by vain hope nor by despair unmanned

× I'd give him one dear thought: all triumph would
40× But break upon his ghostly solitude

[Page 3]

33 He ~~would~~ who can read the signs, nor sink unmanned
34 Into the half deceit of some intoxicant
35 From shallow ~~brains~~ wits; who knows no work can stand
36 Whether health, wealth, or peace of mind were spent
× On work of ~~mind~~ intellect, or work of hand
× No passion leave a lasting monument
× Has but one comfort left: all passion would
40× But break upon his ghostly solitude.

37 On masterwork of intellect or hand
38 No ~~passion~~ honour leave ~~eternal~~ its mighty monument
39 Has but one comfort left — all triumph would
40 But break upon his ghostly solitude

[Page 4]

× For all the rest is but love's bitterest wound:
41 And other comfort were a bitter wound
× Hope set upon what fades and vanishes;
42 To be in love and love what vanishes;
43 Greeks were but lovers, all that country round
Who dared admit, if such a thought were his,
45 Incendiary or bigot could be found
46 To burn that stump on the Acropolis
47 Or break in bits the famous ivories,
48 Or traffic in the grasshoppers and bees.

[Page 5]

II

× When Loie Fuller's chinese dancers ~~enwound~~ unwound
× Suddenly that long ribbon of shining cloth
50× ~~Suddenly~~ A shining web, a floating ribbon of cloth
× It seemed a dragon of the air
× Had fallen upon them and turned them round and round
× Fallen upon their paths had turned them round
× Or caught them up on its own whirling path
× Or carried them off ~~on its~~ to its own whirling path

54× ~~The great~~ So the Platonic year
55× Whirls out new right and wrong
56× Whirls in the old instead
57× All men are dancers ~~and tread~~ and their tread
58× Goes to the barbarous clangour of a gong

II

49 When Loie Fuller's Chinese dancers enwound
50 A shining web, a floating ribbon of cloth
× It seemed a dragon of air
× Suddenly fallen had whirled them around
51 It seemed that a dragon [of] air
× Suddenly fallen had whirled them round and round
× Had fallen of a sudden and whirled them around
× ~~Had fallen~~ Suddenly fallen among dancers, whirled them round
52 Had fallen among dancers, had whirled them round
× Or swept them away to its own furious path
53 Or hurried them off on its own furious path;
54 So the Platonic Year
55 Whirls out new right and wrong
56 Whirls in the old instead
57 All men are dancers and their tread
58 Goes to the barbarous clangour of a gong.

[Page 6]

III

59 Some moralist or mythological poet
60 Compares the solitary soul to a swan;
61 I am content with that,
62 Contented that a troubled mirror show it
63 Before that brief gleam of its life be gone
64 An image of its state;
65 The wings half spread for flight
66 The breast thrust out in pride
67 Whether to play or to ride
68 Those winds that clamour of approaching night.

A man in his most secret meditation
70 Is lost amid the labyrinth that he has made

71 In art or politics,
72 Some platonist affirms that in the station
73 Where we should cast off body and trade
74 The ancient habit sticks
75 And that if our works could
76 But vanish with our breath
77 That were a lucky death
78 For triumph can but mar our solitude

The swan has leaped into a desolate heaven;
80 That ~~thought~~ ~~brings~~ image can bring wildness, bring a rage
81 To end all things, to end
82 What my laborious life imagined, even
83 The half imagined, the half written page;

[Page 7]

84 O but we dreamed to mend
85 Whatever mischief seemed
86 To afflict mankind but now
87 That winds of winter blow
88 Learn that we were crack-pated when we dreamed.

IV

89 We who seven years ago
90 Talked of honour and of truth
91 Shriek with pleasure if we show
× Weasel
92 The weasel's twist, the weasel's tooth.

[Page 8]

V

Come let us mock the great
94 That had such burdens on the mind
95 And toiled so hard and late
96 To leave ~~some~~ ~~that~~ some monument behind
97 Nor thought of the leveling wind.

98 Come let us mock at the wise;
~~With~~ For all those calendars, whereon
100 They fixed old aching eyes,

101 They never saw how seasons run
102 And now but gape at the sun

And after mock at the good
× That thought even goodness might be gay
× Who thought mere goodness might be gay
104 That fancied goodness might be gay
105 Grown tired of their solitude,
106 Upon some bran-new happy day:
Wind shrieks and where are they:

108 Mock ~~poets~~ mockers after that
109 That would not lift a hand maybe
110 To help good, wise, or great
× To shut the ~~north~~ bleak winds out for ~~we~~ ~~he~~ we
× Delight in mockery
× Are heartened by mockery
× Delight in mockery
× Love bitter mockery
× To ~~shut the foul storm out~~ shutter out the storm for we
× Traffic in mockery
111 To bar ~~that tempest~~ that foul storm out, for we
112 Traffic in mockery.

[Page 9]

VI

113 Violence upon the roads: violence of horses
114 Some few have handsome riders, are garlanded
115 On delicate sensitive ear or tossing mane
But weary running round and round in their courses
117 ~~They~~ All break and vanish and evil gathers head:
118 Herodias' daughters have returned again
119 A sudden blast of dusty wind and after
120 Thunder of feet, tumult of images
121 Their purpose in the labyrinth of the wind
122 And should some crazy hand dare touch a daughter
123 All turn with amorous cries, or angry cries
124 According to the wind for all are blind.
× But with the ~~settled~~ settling dust worse company
125 But now wind drops, dust settles; thereupon

× There lurches there his great eyes without thought
126 There lurches past his great eyes without thought
127 Under the shadow of stupid straw-pale locks
× Infamous Robert Artisson of Kilkenny
× There lurches by that infamous Robert Artisson
128 That insolent fiend Robert Artisson
129 To whom the love-lorn Lady Kyteler brought
130 Bronzed peacock feathers, red combs of her cocks

Note: The country people see at times certain apparitions whom they name now "fallen angels," now "the ancient inhabitants of the country," and describe as riding "with flowers upon the heads of their horses." I have assumed in the sixth poem that these comely apparitions, now that the times worsen, give way to worse. Robert Artisson was an evil spirit much run after in Kilkenny at the start of the fourteenth century. Are not those who travel in the whirling dust also in the Platonic Year?

WBY.

Further notes on MS. *1:*

Part I. Lines 3–5 were altered after MS. 2 was written, and before the poem was first printed. They reached final form in *The Tower*, 1928. Lines 9–26 were completed in MS. 3, printed below. Lines 41–43 have the form in which they were first printed; they also reached final form in *The Tower*, 1928. The remaining lines (1–2, 6–10, 16, 27–43, 45–48) have reached their final form.

Part II. The changes made in this draft improve Yeats's diction and phrasing. The pattern of the elaborate stanza must have been set in earlier drafts, and all the materials assembled.

Part III. Lines 61–62 reached final form in *The Tower*, 1928. In line 69 "most secret" became "own secret" and in line 79 "into a desolate" became "into the desolate" in MS. 2.

Part V. Yeats completed lines 93 and 103 when he decided to repeat three times the clause "Come let us mock at the." He finished line 93 in MS. 2, line 103 after MS. 2. In line 107 a shift of tense (shrieks/shrieked) occurs in MS. 2. The change from "Mock poets" to "Mock mockers" at line 108 particularly interests me. I suspect Yeats made it for doctrinal reasons. While Yeats thought that the man who was also an artist should be engaged, he thought that the artist *per se* should have no faith except a faith in works. He had quoted Balzac to that effect many years before in an essay dropped from *Discoveries*. The successive versions of lines 111 and 112 show two fine lines emerging from a series of characteristic changes in wording. Lines 105–6 reached final form in *The Tower*, 1928.

As was noted above, MS. 2 is little more than a clean copy of MS. 1. Yeats did finish one additional line of part I (44). I print part I from this MS. so that the record of its composition may be as complete as possible.

[MS. 2, part 1, page 1]

THOUGHTS UPON THE PRESENT STATE OF THE WORLD

I

1 Many ingenious lovely things are gone
2 That seemed sheer miracle to the multitude,
Changeless, deathless, above the murdering moon,
Above the insolence of the sun. There stood
Where many a gold and silver paten shone
6 An ancient image made of olive wood;
7 And gone are Phidias' carven ivories
8 And all his golden grasshoppers and bees.

9 We too had many pretty toys when young:
10 A law indifferent to blame or praise;
A speedy remedy for obvious wrong;
No swaggering soldier on the public ways
Who weighed a man's life lighter than a song;
A general confidence in future days,
In some great thing to come, because we thought
16 That the worst rogues and rascals had died out.

[Page 2]

And we would say, if conversation turned
On ignorance and armies and such things,
That all men soon would be both fed and learned;

That armies, now that parliaments and kings
No more might covet what they had not earned,
Existed for their drums and fiddle strings,
And did the cannon sound 'twere but perchance
To make a guardsman's lazy charger prance.

× But that good dream has had its day; nightmare
× Comfortable dreams are gone; nightmare
~~Can ride again~~ In place of comfortable dreams night-mare
Can ride our sleep; a drunken soldiery
27 ~~May~~ Can leave the mother, murdered at [her] door,
28 To crawl in her own blood and go scot free;
× Night shakes with terror as it shook before
× Night sweats with terror as those nights before
× And the night sweats with terror as before
29 The night can sweat with terror as before
30 We pieced out thoughts into philosophy
31 And planned to bring the world under a rule
32 Who are but weasels fighting in a hole.

× Who now dare fancy that his work will stand
× Whether ambition wrought or pure intent
× His passion find a lasting monument
× ~~And~~ Whether on work of mind or work of hand
× And that he may keep pride of intellect
× Health wealth or peace of mind were spent
× Nor mocked by hope nor by despair unmanned

[Page 3]

× This certainty remains: all triumph would
40× But break upon his ghostly solitude
× For all the rest is but love's bitterest wound:
× Hope set upon what fades and vanishes.
43× Greeks were but lovers; all that country round
× Who dared admit, if such a thought were his,

× Who now dare fancy that his work will stand?
× Whether health, wealth, or peace of mind were spent
× Upon some work of intellect or hand,
× Who thinks to leave a lasting monument
× Makes nothing but the devil's rope of sand;

× Let storm turn up the sand and be content
× With one dear thought of thoughts: all triumph would
× But break upon our ghostly solitude

× Makes but a devil's rope out of the sand
× For wind must gather what the wind has sent
× And may be that is well

33 He who can read the signs, nor sink unmanned
34 Into the half deceit of some intoxicant
35 From shallow wits, who knows no work can stand,
36 Whether health, wealth, or peace of mind were spent
37 On master work of intellect or hand,
38 No honour leave its mighty monument,
39 Has but one comfort left: all triumph would
40 But break upon his ghostly solitude.

[Page 4]

× For all the rest is but love's bitterest wound:
41 And other comfort were a bitter wound:
× Hope set upon what fades and vanishes;
42 To be in love and love what vanishes;
43 Greeks were but lovers, all that country round
44 ~~Who~~ None dared admit, if such a thought were his,
45 Incendiary, or bigot, could be found
46 To burn that stump on the Acropolis,
47 Or break in bits the famous ivories,
48 Or traffic in the grasshoppers and bees?

Stanzas 1, 2, and 3 (lines 1–24) are verbally identical in MS. 1 and MS. 2. MS. 2 is more carefully punctuated. Beginning with stanza 4, MS. 2 ceased to be merely a clean copy, for Yeats began to cancel lines and make verbal changes. He did little more, however, than explore the possibilities inherent in MS. 1. On pages 2 and 3 of the manuscript, he wrote and cancelled a series of versions of stanza 5 and the first half of stanza 6, but at the bottom of page 3 he reinstated verbatim the version of stanza 5 he had written in MS. 1. In the draft of stanza 5 found in the middle of page 3 Yeats explored two new details which might possibly serve as emblems of the transientness of works of art and intellect: the devil's rope of sand, and, in "For wind must gather what the wind has sent," possibly the Sibylline leaves. He abandoned both. In MS. 1 stanza 6 had been completed except for line 44. Yeats tried a slightly different wording of the first half of this stanza on page 3 of the manuscript, but cancelled this. On page 4 he reinstated the readings of MS. 1, but did finish line 44.

Save for lines 3–5 and 11–26 Yeats now had part I of his poem in the form he first printed it. I have seen no manuscript of Yeats's revision of lines 3–5, which were changed before first printing and again in *The Tower*, 1928. Below is MS. 3, a series of versions of lines 11–26. In the last of them these lines have their final form.

[MS. 3, page 1]

× And if we still had empire and such things

We dreamed, though we had empire and such things
Their teeth were drawn, their ancient tricks unlearned
What matter if no parliaments nor kings
Had made their guns be all to ploughshares turned
Women love shows. Mere drum and fiddle string
Unless some tons of gunpowder were burned
Had not made uproar great enough perhaps
To make some guardsman's drowsy charger prance.

9 We too had many pretty toys when young:
10 A law indifferent to blame or praise
To bribe or threat; all obvious wrong
× Melted like sun warmed wax
× Melted as it were wax in the sun's rays
Half melted down like wax in the sun's rays:
× A public conscience
13 Public opinion, ripening for so long
We thought it would outlast all future days:
15 O what fine thoughts we had because we thought
16 That the worst rogues and rascals had died out

[Page 2]

9 We too had many pretty toys when young:
10 A law indifferent to blame or praise,
To bribe or threat; all obvious wrong
Half melted down like wax in the sun's rays;
13 Public opinion ripening for so long
14 We thought it would outlive all future days;

15 ~~And~~ O what fine thoughts we had because we thought
16 That the worst rogues and rascals had died out.

We dreamed, though we had empires and such things,
Their teeth were drawn, their ancient tricks unlearned;
What matter if no parliaments nor kings
Had made their guns be all to ploughshares turned;
× Women love shows; mere drums and fiddle strings
× Women love shows — ~~yet~~ but drums and fiddle strings
× Women love shows; ~~yet drums and~~ how could mere trumpetings,
× Unless some tons of gunpowder were burned,
× Might not make uproar great enough ~~perhaps~~ perchance
× To make some guardsman's drowsy charger prance.

25× Now days are dragon ridden, the nightmare
× Riding our sleep: a drunken soldiery

Women love horses; though an army brings
Trumpet and kettle but no powder burned
The uproar is not great enough perchance
To make a guardsman's drowsy charger prance.
25 Now days are dragon ridden, the nightmare
Riding our sleep

[Page 3]

9 We too had many pretty toys when young:
10 A law indifferent to ~~praise or to~~ blame, or praise,
To bribe or threat; all obvious wrong
Half melted down like wax in the sun's rays;
13 Public opinion ~~ripened~~ ripening for so long
14 We thought it would outlive all future days;
15 O what fine thoughts we had because we thought
16 That the worst rogues and rascals had died out.

We dreamed, though we had empire and such things,
Their teeth were drawn, their ancient tricks unlearned;
What matter if no parliaments nor kings
Had made their guns be all to ploughshares turned;
× Women love shows
An army is for show and though it brings

Trumpet and kettle if no powder's burned
The uproar is not great enough, perchance,
To make a guardsman's drowsy charger prance.

25 Now days are dragon ridden, the nightmare
Is riding sleep: a drunken soldiery

[Page 4]

17 All teeth ~~are~~ were drawn, all ancient tricks unlearned
18 And a great army but a showy thing;
19 What matter that no cannon ~~has~~ had been turned
20 Into a ploughshare; parliament and king
21 ~~Think~~ Thought that unless a little powder burned
22 The trumpeters ~~may~~ might burst with trumpeting
23 And yet it lack all glory, and perchance
24 The guardsmen's drowsy chargers ~~will~~ would not prance

25 Now days are dragon ridden, the nightmare
× Is riding
Riding upon sleep

[Page 5]

9 We too had many pretty toys when young:
10 A law indifferent to blame or praise
11 To bribe or threat; habits that made old wrong
× Dissolve away like wax
12 Melt down, as it were wax in the sun's rays;
13 Public opinion ripening for so long
We thought it would outlast all future days.
15 O what fine thought we had because we thought
16 That the worst rogues and rascals had died out.

17 All teeth were drawn, all ancient tricks unlearned,
18 And a great army but a showy thing;
19 What matter that no cannon had been turned
20 Into a ploughshare; parliament and king
21 Thought that unless a little powder burned
22 The trumpeteers might burst with trumpeting
23 And yet it lack all glory; and perchance
24 The guardsmen's drowsy chargers would not prance.

25 Now days are dragon ridden, the nightmare
26 ~~Riding~~ Rides upon sleep: a drunken soldiery

On page 1 of MS. 3 Yeats began with a radical attack on stanza 3 (lines 17–24). He tried reversing the a and b rhymes used in MSS. 1 and 2 (the rhyme pattern of the stanza is abababcc), and explored possible new detail that could express man's social hope before World War I. Much of this he kept in his finished poem. His new detail included a reference to empire; the drawn teeth, the ancient tricks unlearned, and the swords beaten into ploughshares found in the finished poem; the notion that because women love shows powder must be burned so horses will prance. He has accumulated too many correlatives; in later drafts he dropped the reference to empire and to the women who love shows, though he did not drop this last detail until after it had caused him a great deal of trouble. Yeats didn't finish any of his lines, but he did make a new beginning. The draft of stanza 2 (lines 9–16) on the bottom of the same manuscript page was also a crucial draft. Lines 12 and 13 in MS. 2 read

No swaggering soldier on the public ways
Who weighed a man's life lighter than a song.

This is a specific reference to the Black-and-Tans and would have been recognized as such by Irish readers, a reference, that is, to the violence going on in the world as Yeats wrote his poem. But his subject in this stanza and the one that follows is the nonviolent civilization that had existed before 1914. Yeats replaced this anticipation of his thought in stanza 4 by the simile of wrong melting like wax, and went on to his reference to ripening public opinion. These changes cleared up the logical progression of the poem, and they enabled Yeats to finish lines 13 and 15, nearly to finish line 14.

Yeats began page 2 of these drafts by making a clean copy of the lines he had just written; while doing this he finished line 14 when he replaced "it would outlast" by "it would outlive." (He reinstated the earlier reading on page 5 of this MS.) He then did another version of lines 17–26, in which the a and b rhymes are still reversed. Most of his difficulties here grew out of his efforts to give poetic substance to the idea that because "women love shows" some powder had to be burned in order to make the chargers prance. While trying and cancelling line after line, Yeats did invent "trumpetings" to replace the "drum and fiddle strings" of earlier drafts. He went on to finish line 25 by introducing into it the phrase "dragon ridden," a preparation for the "dragon of air" in part II, which was already finished. This preparation for a coming central image is as characteristic of Yeats as it is of Proust. Though he cancelled the line after first writing it, he reinstated it at the bottom of the page. Just above this he tried another, more logical version of lines 21–24: now "women love horses," and it is the burning powder that makes the horses prance.

Page 3 begins with a further version of stanza 2, identical with that on the top of page 2. The rhymes are still reversed in the draft of stanza 3 which follows, but Yeats did give up here the attempt to make anything of the "women love shows" business. When he cancelled this and wrote "An army is for show" he has expressed the central idea of stanza 3 in the finished poem. On page 4 a characteristic miracle of organization occurs, and Yeats finishes stanza 3. He puts his a and b rhyme words back into the order they had had in MSS. 1 and 2. The crucial event occurred, I think, when Yeats established line 18

> And a great army but a showy thing;

the stanza took shape around this line. Every detail, nearly every word or phrase used has occurred somewhere or other during the course of many drafts, but Yeats till now had failed to fuse them together in their inevitable order. The clause "And yet it lack all glory" is likewise a new invention. It is instructive to note that both are general statements around which what had been a clutter of detail can logically accumulate. At the bottom of the page Yeats nearly finishes line 26.

On page 5 Yeats finished his second stanza. Here the crystallizing took place when Yeats invented the clause "habits that made old wrong/ Melt down." He went on to make a clean copy of stanza 3. At the very bottom of the page he got line 26 right when he changed to the present tense in "the nightmare/ Rides." This urgently states the contrast of past with present. Lines 19–26 were done at last, and one of Yeats's greatest poems, "Nineteen Hundred and Nineteen," done but for a little subsequent touching up.

We noticed that Yeats's difficulties here clustered around the phrase "women love shows," and that the offending lines did not come right until Yeats dropped this detail entirely. Again we have revision involving management of the persona. The persona of "Nineteen Hundred and Nineteen" is Yeats himself in the role of vatic poet commenting on events, though Yeats in the finished poem reserved the first person till section III where he shifts to direct commentary. The "women love shows" idea is destructive of this persona. How can it coexist with the mother murdered? Yeats's final idea that an army is a showy thing is appropriate to the voice that laments and speaks the poem. Here Yeats revises to build his persona.

4

The Tower, *Section iii,* AND Lullaby

i

"The Tower," Section III

THE SUCCESSIVE DRAFTS of some of the great poems Yeats wrote during the 1920's have survived; we are now able, perhaps for the first time with the poems studied in this book, to follow Yeats through the entire process of composing a poem. I have chosen part of section III of "The Tower" to illustrate this process because of the state in which the rough drafts have been preserved. Yeats composed them in a looseleaf manuscript cover. Occasionally, as in this instance, looseleaf workbooks have been preserved with drafts of various items of prose and verse still in them. Usually when Yeats had dictated from such drafts or had them transcribed, he withdrew the sheets and filed them in an envelope. A probable explanation of the few manuscript covers with drafts still in them is that Yeats had been given a new cover — manuscript covers and manuscript books were gifts he much appreciated — and abandoned the old one just as it stood.

Whatever the explanation, we can be fairly certain that the pages containing the early versions of section III of "The Tower" are preserved just as Yeats left them. Sometime after writing these early drafts of "The Tower," Yeats completed a manuscript of the entire poem on October 7, 1925. A typescript with two carbons was made of this manuscript, and Yeats made corrections on all three copies. Typescript 2, which has no manuscript revisions, was made from these corrected copies of TS. 1. In it the poem nearly reached the form in which it was first printed.

When writing in a manuscript book or looseleaf cover, Yeats normally started to work on the right hand page and used the facing page for revisions. So in the transcription printed below, I first give these right hand pages; then, below each of them, the facing page. When the facing page is blank, no "facing page" is given.

[Page 1]

× It is time give [?] I my testament
  [Undeciphered line]

× O
× Old men
× An old man makes his testament
× And I
× And this is mine

× Now will I write my testament
× And choose
× And choose once more for an heir
× Young men

  I write my testament being old
× And choose for an heir young men and tall
× And chose once, that tall young man
× Some tall young man shall be my heir
× Climbed a mountain stream in the cold
× Many dawns
× Climbing a mountain stream in the cold
  ~~Casts a fly~~ Drops a fly ~~under~~ in the cold
× Dawn light upon the bare

[Facing page 1]

  And choose a sunflecked man for an heir
× That can climb up a cold mountain
  ~~I choose a tall young~~ man for an heir
  ~~A man that fishes~~ That clambers up a cold
  Mountain stream on Ochte's bare [1]

Or Bulben's woody side, and at dawn ~~throws~~
× Throws a
× A fly under a fly under a froth
Throws a deft fly ~~among the froth~~ under the side
× Under a dark stone
× Under the edge of a dark stone
Of a great ~~foam~~ froth.

[Page 2]

× Morning
× Dawn light,
Mountain stream on Ochte's bare
× And
Or Bulben

I write my testament being old
I choose a stalwart man for my heir
× And
× Through him climbing a [?]
And summon him from a cold
Mountain stream upon Ochte's bare
Or Bulben's shaded side where at dawn
× He has dropped a fly
× He cast amid the eddying froth
× Even that
× He cast for
His trout fly dropped amid the froth
A young imaginative man
In rough grey Connemara cloth

[Facing page 2]

I choose ~~out~~ young outstanding men
× ~~Men~~ That climb up ~~the~~ little
× That climb up the rocks

[Page 3]

145 And I declare my faith
146 I mock Plotinus' thought
~~Declare~~ Aye, and in Plato's teeth
~~I cry in~~ And in Plato's teeth
× That the Greeks lied in the throat

× Declare that there had been naught
Cry that there was naught
× ~~But~~ ~~Until~~ Till ~~made~~ man has made the whole
149 ~~Made stock and~~ Till man made up the whole
× ~~Made~~ ~~Aye~~ Lock and stock and barrel
151 Out of his bitter soul
Made sun, and moon and stars all
And all that is under the sun
× I mock at Greek and Jew
Why could no Rabbi say

[Yeats has placed a line with a query beside the two lines above.]

That Eternal Man
Rested the seventh day
× That day by day we renew
I mock at Greek and Jew
And add to what I have said
Day by day we renew
The living and the dead

[Facing page 3]

~~Of~~ The bursting fruit, ~~or~~ ~~the falling~~ the sudden shower
× The moon full and high
× Out of a summer sky
Out of a sullen sky
The swan that in that hour
When he must fix his eye
141 Upon a fading gleam
~~And~~ Float ~~up~~ out up the long
× Glittering stretch of stream
× And there sing his last song
Last glittering stretch of the stream
144 And there sing his last song
~~Or the burst~~ Of bursting fruit, or the sudden shower
Out of a summer sky
Of the swan in that last hour
When he must fix his eye
141 Upon a fading gleam
And mount ~~his last~~ up a long

143 Last/ Reach of glittering stream
144 And there sing his last song

[The entire page above is cancelled]

[Page 4]

121 It is time that I wrote my will
122 I choose upstanding men
That climb to pool or rill
In mountain rocks and at dawn
Drop their fly at the side
Of a dripping stone. I declare
127 They shall inherit my pride
The pride of the people that were
Bound neither to cause or state
130 Neither to slaves that were spat on
131 Nor to the tyrants that spat
Those of the people of Grattan
133 That gave though free to refuse:
A pride like that of the morn
That lets the wild light loose
136 Or that of the fabulous horn
Or that of a sudden shower
138 When all streams are dry
139 Or that of the hour
140 When the swan must fix his eye
141 Upon a fading gleam
142 Float out upon a long
143 Last reach of glittering stream
144 And there sing his last song.

[Facing page 4]

That climbs the streams until
~~Rock~~ The weed grown rock, and at dawn
Drops a cast at the side
Of a dripping stone

[Page 5]

145 And I declare my faith
146 I mock Plotinus' thought
147 And cry in Plato's teeth

148 Death and life were not
149 Till man made up the whole
~~Aye~~ Made lock and stock and barrel
151 Out of his bitter soul
Aye sun and moon and stars all
153 And further add to that
× We ~~made~~ make who is born
We stretch beyond the tomb
And day by day create
Our

[From here on the page has been cancelled]

× [undeciphered line]
× And then I mock at the Jew
Because ~~he did so say~~ no Rabbi says
That the Eternal Man
Rested the seventh day
× And add to what I have said
~~I therein mock at~~ I have great scorn of the Jew
And add to what I have said
That day by day we renew
× The living and dead
× The blessed dream of the dead
The blessed life/ dream of the dead
With that we make and do
× Because their life is a dream
× For man and dreams at the last

[Facing page 5]

mind I have made
But ~~of late I have made~~
&
No further I add to that
× ~~That~~ ~~And~~ This mockery of the tomb
× That living men create
× Their own eternal home

F
And

When I go to my final rest
I shall

× For dead we are that we made [?]
× Or that we have done, and I

[Page 6]
× The blessed dream of the dead
× And mine [?] is almost ready
× The forms come crowding fast
× [undeciphered line]
× Man is a dream at the last
× I ~~make~~ [word undeciphered] ~~peace my peace~~ build my
learned peace
× Poets and saints and kings
× Of England Italy Greece
160× Poet's imaginings
161× And memories of love
162× Memories of the words of women
× All/ And all those things whereof
× ~~They make up their~~ The dead compose superhuman
× Mirror resembling dreams
~~So~~ And at the loophole there
167 The daws chatter and scream
And lay twigs layer upon layer
× That mount from the stone floor up
× To the narrow sill when abreast
× They will hollow and round the top
× When sill and top are abreast
× They will hollow the top
× And round it out a nest

[This page in two columns, left given above, right below.]

× I build my Eternal peace
× With old Italian things
× Or the old stones of Greece
160× Poet's imaginings

× I build my eternal peace,
× With stories of dead kings

× ~~The~~ In Ireland ~~Italy or~~ or in Greece
× Out of Italian Art
× Out of the sculpture of Greece

157 I have prepared my peace
With old Italian things
And the old stones of Greece
160 Poet's imaginings
161 And memories of love
162 Memories of the words of women
And all those things whereof
164 ~~The dead create~~ Man makes a superhuman
165 Mirror resembling dream

169 When they have mounted up
170 The mother bird will rest
Upon their hollow top
× And [word undeciphered] her [word undeciphered] nest
And round their wild nest

[Facing page 6]

And further add to that
× That even being made ["dead" intended?], we rise
× And from our acts create
× The second Paradise

~~That~~ We on the third
That being dead we
~~Men on the third~~ day rise
× And if they will
155 Dream and so create
A second Paradise

[Page 7]

Yes to young men I leave all
Pride and faith, to young men
That ride upon horses and climb the water course
In grey Connemara cloth
That cast fly [in] the eddying foam high up the mountain
Ready for trumpet or beckoning hand
Message or challenge

I leave them my pride and faith
× I leave to sanguine men
× Ready for
× That want a ~~beckoning~~ ~~hand~~ a summoning [?] blast
× And care not for a [word undeciphered]
× Or beckoning hand and blast
I leave to men that cast
A summoning blast or hand
The [word undeciphered] to sanguine men
[undeciphered partial line]

[Page 8]

I blow a trumpet blast
I raise a beckoning hand

× I make
× I have called with the sound
× And raised a beckoning hand
× To cast their flies at dawn

My musical notes are blown
My beckoning hand is raised

[Page 9]

To young and sanguine men
× That climb that climb the river
In grey Connemara cloth
That drop their flies at dawn
Among the eddying froth

× I leave

I have left faith and pride
× To young and sanguine men
× That climb the mountain side
× To men that near the dawn
The men that climb at dawn
The mountain's rocky side
To young and sanguine men
In grey Connemara cloth
× That drop a cast of flies
× In the eddy and the froth

That drop a cast of flies
Into the eddying froth

I leave to live vigourous men
× That ri climb the riv
That climb the river side
To young and sanguine men
That find ~~where the~~

[Facing page 9]

Young/ May young and sanguine men
× In grey Connemara cloth
That climb up near the dawn
To drop in eddying froth
A deft cast of flies
In a cleft mountain side
Under the cold skies
Inherit my faith and pride

To men who climb at dawn
The rocky river's source
To young and sanguine men
That find the river's source

[This page in two columns, left given above, right below.]

I left to vigorous men
Not sedentary as I
To

That climb the river course
× That they cast/ fling near dawn
That they stand at dawn
× Where the cold source
× Under the
To find their high source
× Under the
~~In~~ Under bursting dawn
In the cleft mountain side
To young and sanguine men
My faith and my pride

[Page 10]

They climb the river courses
In grey Connemara cloth
Up to where the source is
Amid its eddying froth
And cast a line as dawn
Breaks on the mountain side
× A vigourous healthy man
× I ~~bid~~ call these vigourous men
× Inherit
× To inherit faith and pride
I beckon to these men
And offer faith and pride

I ~~leave~~ have left ~~both~~ faith and pride
× To ~~vigourous~~ ~~sanguine~~ young vigourous
× To these upstanding men
175 That climb the mountain side
~~That~~ under the bursting dawn
That they may drop a fly
Being of like metal made
179 Till ~~Though~~ it was broken by
180 This sedentary trade

[Facing page 10]

That traverse/ tread the river courses
In grey Connemara cloth
Up to where the source is
Amid the eddying froth

× Many men
That climb the river courses
× Up the cleft mountain side
× And tell us where the source is

They tread
~~Men climb~~ the river courses
In grey Connemara cloth
dawn
side
men
pride

And cast their lines ~~at~~ as the dawn
~~In the cleft~~ Breaks on mountain side
Young and sanguine men
Inherit my ~~pride~~ faith and pride

Section III of "The Tower" grows out of these lines in section I:

It seems that I must bid the Muse go pack,
Choose Plato and Plotinus for a friend
Until imagination, ear and eye,
Can be content with argument and deal
In abstract things; or be derided by
A sort of battered kettle at the heel.

The general subject of section III is Yeats's refusal to take the course of action here anticipated. Instead he chooses for his heirs men like the "freckled man" he had imagined as being an ideal audience in "The Fisherman," and then composes a poetic last will and testament in which he leaves his heirs the Anglo-Irish pride he has himself embodied. He goes on to reject Plato and Plotinus —

I mock Plotinus' thought
And cry in Plato's teeth —

before declaring his own esoteric faith. Then, amusedly aware, perhaps, of the somewhat ramshackle nature of this "faith" as compared with Judaism and Christianity, he composes the delightful image of the daw's nest — a daw's nest is a mere heap of trash which yet serves life's obscure purpose well enough. He leaves this faith to his imagined heirs and then claims kinship with them.

Presumably Yeats had this general arrangement in mind when he started to write, though not the exact relation of the parts. Once he establishes relation, the floundering on pages 1, 2, and 3 becomes a sudden assurance on page 4. He had also decided to use a metrical pattern different from those used in sections I and II. Section I is in five stress lines which rhyme alternately; section II uses the elaborate stanza which Yeats had earlier used in "Prayer for my Daughter" and "In Memory of Major Robert Gregory," and was to use again in "Byzantium"; section III returns to the rhyme scheme of I, but the stresses have been reduced to three. In the earliest drafts there is some hesitation between four stress and three stress lines ("Under a dark stone/

Under the edge of a dark stone"), but soon the metrical pattern Yeats kept emerges.

In manuscript pages 1 and 2 Yeats has immense difficulty with the lines describing the heir or heirs he has chosen, and his difficulties return with his heirs' return at lines 173–80. I will consider possible explanations of these difficulties when we get to these lines, but want to deal with one part of the problem here. Part of the trouble comes, I think, because Yeats returns to "The Fisherman" to find the kind of man he wants for heir. I have noticed time after time how difficult it was for Yeats to make a new beginning; prose subjects and early drafts of poems are frequently haunted by echoes of work already finished. An example of this is found in the "Creed" on which "Under Ben Bulben" was based (see part i of introduction to "Poems"). Section II of this "Creed" shows that Yeats considered using the image of Sato's sword once again, an image he had already used many times. While composing lines 122–26 and 173–80 of "The Tower" Yeats considered direct references to, and verbal echoes of "The Fisherman": "And chose once, that tall young man"; "sunflecked," and "grey Connemara cloth." In the final versions of both passages Yeats has reduced his allusions to the earlier poem to a pleasant echo. While adjusting this difficulty, Yeats also generalized his setting by abandoning references to Ben Bulben and Ochte. The difficulty of making a beginning is shown by the fact that at the end of the second page Yeats has not written any lines he will keep, and has only one line end in place ("dawn," line 124).

In the drafts Yeats now goes on to his declaration of faith; the idea of stating his own and Anglo-Irish pride and willing it to his heirs developed later. The many drafts of this declaration of faith (lines 145–65) are of great interest, for they show that in the 1920's although Yeats was questioning Christian doctrines as he had questioned them before ("The Magi") and would again in many poems which culminate in "Supernatural Songs," he was not questioning them very openly. "Two Songs from a Play" seem an exception, but perhaps Yeats felt these poems were so gnomic and learned they would not offend. I see, perhaps fancifully, in these revisions an effort to spare Irish sensibilities, which, given the whole record, seems rather odd. Perhaps Yeats remembered that an Irish senator was writing "The Tower," perhaps he is simply conscious of the fact that he is directly addressing an Irish audience. On manuscript page 3 it is not the God of Genesis who rested on the seventh day of the creation, but "Eternal Man." As the drafts proceed Yeats softens his statements that man has created this world and the next by enveloping them in a kind of esoteric fog. Here he even drops all reference to Jewish tradition, which he once rejected along with the Greek. In these early drafts of his declaration of faith Yeats develops a line of thought he was to keep, makes a good start at establishing his rhyme[2] sounds, and composes four lines that still stand (145, 146, 149, 151).

Then on the facing page Yeats begins work on his statement of Anglo-Irish pride (lines 126–44). He gropes his way, as it were, towards the images he will use to characterize this pride: the shower and swan images are in place, and "bursting fruit" perhaps anticipates the "fabulous horn" of the finished poem. Eight rhyme sounds and seven rhyme words are in place; three lines are finished.

On manuscript page 4 Yeats puts the fisherman and his legacy of pride together, thereby getting the first twenty-four lines of section III pretty well organized, though he later improved them greatly by verbal revision. All the rhyme sounds are in place, and all save one of the rhyme words (line 123); fourteen lines are in final form. It was at this point, no doubt, that Yeats cancelled the page facing 3.

On manuscript page 5 and on the facing page Yeats returns to his declaration of faith and gets lines 145–53 into shape. It was while working on this draft, apparently, that Yeats decided to cut his references to Jewish tradition and Eternal Man. All the rhyme words are established, and seven lines are finished. The words he needs to state the esoteric doctrine of lines 154–56 continue to elude Yeats, perhaps because he is not quite sure what his "faith" about the life after death is.

On the sixth manuscript page, after another abortive try at lines 154–56, Yeats continues the poem with a first draft of lines 157–72. Yeats has written all over this page. From internal evidence I deduce that he wrote the material in this order: the lines in the left column were composed first, and in order; the right column was used for rewriting, but the material there is not in the order of composition. The five lines "I build my eternal peace . . . Out of the sculpture of Greece" were written before the lines just above them "I build my Eternal peace . . . Poet's imaginings." Then, still in the right column, beginning "I have prepared my peace," Yeats drafted lines 157–65 in nearly final form; he picked up the three uncancelled lines in the left column beginning "And at the loophole there," and completed his draft of lines 166–72 in the right column. If one reads only the uncancelled lines on this manuscript page, he will discover that Yeats has this part of the poem pretty well shaped up. He has written the same number of lines he will use in the finished poem, the rhyme sounds are all in place, and nine lines are finished. Yeats appears to have achieved the happy image of the daw's nest very quickly and directly.

On the manuscript page facing 6 Yeats has a final try at lines 154–56. While doing this, he states another heresy, this one quickly abandoned. Earlier he had assigned to creative man God's role in Genesis; here he equates creative man with Christ when he writes:

> Men on the third day rise
> Dream and so create
> A second Paradise.

This certainly is a clearer statement of doctrine than the ultimate lines

> That, being dead, we rise,
> Dream and so create
> Translunar Paradise.

Manuscript pages 7, 8, 9, and 10, along with such facing pages as Yeats wrote on, were all used to draft what are now lines 173–80. Yeats makes many false starts; he has some trouble managing his persona, for he sounds pompous and affected when he writes

> I blow a trumpet blast
> I raise a beckoning hand.

He has more trouble reintroducing his fisherman heir than he had introducing him earlier in the drafts. When Yeats got stuck during the process of composition, he really got stuck. There are always signs of such trouble, one of them being the physical appearance of the writing. On page 7, for instance, the writing trails off into an indecipherable scrawl, as though Yeats knew while writing that he wasn't getting anything he could use. Finally on page 10 Yeats breaks through the impasse after a series of attacks and very nearly achieves the lines he was to keep.

One can only speculate why these lines and lines 122–26 proved so difficult. I should like to start by observing a marked similarity between section III of "The Tower" and "Under Ben Bulben." Both contain declarations of faith; both are addressed to Yeats's spiritual heirs. In theme the poems are very much alike, but in tone very unlike. In "Under Ben Bulben" Yeats invites all forthcoming poets, sculptors, and painters to

> Bring the soul of man to God,
> Make him fill the cradles right.

Later in the poem he is more particular when he writes:

> Irish poets, learn your trade. . . .
> Cast your mind on other days
> That we in coming days may be
> Still the indomitable Irishry.[3]

Here Yeats knows precisely who his heirs are (artists who come after him), and he knows precisely what he wants them to do: they are to carry on the tradition in art within which he himself has worked. In "The Tower" Yeats has a very difficult time deciding what qualities he wants in his heirs. They are not as in "Under Ben Bulben" to be artists who will succeed him: we conclude rather from the allusions to "The Fisherman" that they are to form an imagined ideal audience for his own work. By the time he finishes Yeats has decided that they are to be men of action rather than men of thought, hence the fishing and mountain climbing; they are to embody his and Irish pride derived from intellectuals and patriots of that eighteenth-century Ireland which Yeats was making into a myth; they are to be men who can receive his here vaguely stated non-Christian faith.

If we assemble the successive versions of lines 122 and 174, we will be able to pinpoint Yeats's difficulties:

122 And choose for an heir young men and tall
And chose once, that tall young man
Some tall young man shall be my heir
And chose a sunflecked man for an heir
I choose a tall young man for an heir
I choose a stalwart man for my heir
I choose young outstanding men
I choose upstanding men

174 Yes to young men I leave all
I leave to sanguine men

To young and sanguine men
I leave to live vigourous men
May young and sanguine men
I left to vigourous men
To young and sanguine men
A vigourous healthy man
I call these vigourous men
To vigourous sanguine [men]
To young vigourous [men]
To these upstanding men
Young and sanguine men
To young upstanding men

[This last line is from the MS. dated Oct. 7, 1925.]

The drafts of line 122 show, I think, that in trying to conceive of his valid heirs Yeats was far from sure just what qualities he wanted them to have. Should they merely be young men of good physique, or should they have certain moral qualities, and, if so, what moral qualities? Yeats starts with the merely physical. "Young men and tall" has no real content, and so it is eventually rejected for the visual, the primitive "sunflecked." Despite "The Fisherman" this fails to suggest the kind of continuity Yeats seeks for himself. Physical and ethical qualities combine in "stalwart," but the word is far too hackneyed for serious poetry, so Yeats backs off from it into something worse, the Rotarian "young outstanding." The sound of this suggests a solution. "Upstanding" works, after a fashion, for it does combine the physical and ethical (*OED* "of open, honest or independent bearing" "having an erect carriage, well set up"), and it is not hackneyed. In the drafts of line 174 Yeats explores the possibility of using three other adjectives — "sanguine," "vigourous," "healthy" — again rather hackneyed ones, but finally decides to stick with "upstanding." While "upstanding" beautifully characterizes Yeats's own and Anglo-Irish pride, it fails to suggest either the effects or ends of that pride. Since it does so fail, Yeats seems in these passages neither to know himself nor his heirs; "upstanding" is a merely verbal solution. In short, I suggest that the difficulty Yeats experienced in composing these lines grew out of his uncertainty about what he wanted to say. Section III of "The Tower" excels in rejecting, in mocking Plotinus' thought and crying in Plato's teeth. But its characterization of Anglo-Irish pride sounds a little strident until Yeats gets to images, and he narrowly escapes the hackneyed, even the maudlin, when he chooses and describes his heirs and his own relation to them.

Hard as all this was, one of Yeats's best lines, "This sedentary trade," seems to have come quite easily. The word "sedentary" first appears in the right column on the page facing 9 where Yeats writes "Not sedentary as I." Then, at the bottom of page 10, Yeats struck off his splendid line without any more experimenting.

When he had finished these drafts, Yeats was well on his way to finishing section III of "The Tower." We can follow his progress further in a manuscript of the entire poem which Yeats finished October 7, 1925, and in TS. 1 and TS. 2. In the manuscript section III goes as follows:

121 It is time that I wrote my will:
122 I choose upstanding men
123 That climb the streams until
× ~~The reed grown~~
124 ~~The last~~ The fountain leap and at dawn
125 Drop their cast at the side
Of a dripping stone. I declare
127 They shall inherit my pride:
128 The pride of the people that were
Bound neither to cause or state
130 Neither to slaves that were spat on
131 Nor to the tyrants that spat
× Those of the people of Grattan
John Synge and those people of Grattan
133 That gave though free to refuse,
134 Pride like that of the morn
Casting its strange light loose
136 Or that of the fabulous horn
Or that of a sudden shower
138 When all streams are dry
139 Or that of the hour
140 When the swan must fix his eye
141 Upon a fading gleam
142 Float out upon a long
143 Last reach of glittering stream
144 And there sing his last song.

145 And I declare my faith:
146 I mock Plotinus' thought
147 And cry in Plato's teeth
148 Death and life were not
149 Till man made up the whole
Made lock and stock and barrel
151 Out of his bitter soul
Aye sun and moon and stars all,
153 And further add to that
154 That being dead we rise
155 Dream and so create
A second Paradise
157 I have prepared my peace
158 With learned Italian things
159 And the proud stones of Greece
160 Poet's imaginings
161 And memories of love
162 Memories of the words of women
And all those things whereof
164 Man makes a superhuman
165 Mirror resembling dream;
I have left faith and pride
174 To young upstanding men
175 That climb the mountain side
That under the bursting dawn
177 They may drop a fly,
178 Being of that metal made
179 Till it was broken by
180 This sedentary trade.
Sept Oct 1925

At this point Yeats has altered the end of the poem by omitting the extended simile of the daw's nest. On October 7 he decided to reinstate that passage. He cancelled lines 173–80 and added another page to his MS. which goes as follows:

166 And at the loophole there
167 The daws chatter and scream
168 And drop twigs — layer upon layer
169 When ~~it has~~ they have mounted up

170 The mother bird will rest
171 ~~Upon~~ On their hollow top
And warm her wild nest.

173 I leave both faith and pride
174 To young upstanding men
175 That climb the mountain side
176 That under bursting dawn
177 They may drop a fly;
178 Being of that metal made
179 Till it was broken by
180 This sedentary trade.

WBY. ~~Sept~~ Oct 7 1925

When this version of section III is compared with the earlier drafts, we find that Yeats has completed lines 123–25, 128, 134, 154, 158–59, 166, 171, 173–74, 176–78. None of the changes is substantive; they involve minor adjustments of diction and meter. Section III of "The Tower" in TS. 1 is verbally identical with the MS. just printed. Yeats corrected a carbon copy of TS. 1 and made the following changes in wording:

John Synge and those people of Grattan
That of those people of Grattan
132 The people of Burke and of Grattan

and

Casting its strange light loose
135 When the headlong light is loose.

All Yeats's lines are now in the form first printed except lines 126, 129, 137, 150, 152, 156, 163, and 172; these require such slight changes as the dropping or adding of a single syllable, as in line 172 where

And warm her wild nest

becomes

And so warm her wild nest.

There is evidence in this same copy of TS. 1 that Yeats was still not satisfied with the end of the poem, for he has cancelled lines 173–80. These lines are omitted from TS. 2, where Yeats has added lines

181–95 with which the poem we know ends. No manuscript versions of these new lines have been found, so I cannot trace the history of their composition. Apparently Yeats completed them in 1926, the date he gave the finished poem. All the lines of "The Tower" section III which are included in TS. 2 are in the form first printed except line 156. Before Yeats printed the poem he returned lines 173–80 to its text.

ii

"Lullaby"

YEATS WROTE THE EARLY DRAFTS of "Lullaby," and many other poems included in "Words for Music Perhaps," in the Rapallo Notebook inscribed "Diary of Thought begun Sept 23. 1928 in Dublin." Yeats was in Rapallo when he wrote the poem, away from his Dublin study. Very often when Yeats was away from home he used a bound manuscript book as a workbook, as in this instance. "Lullaby" is a different kind of poem from those we have been studying. Yeats deeply loved the poem and lavished on it, I think, even greater care than usual.

[Draft A]

[Page 1, left-hand page of first opening]

sleep
alarms
deep
bed
arms

Thus sang
× A mother sang her child asleep
Thus a mother sang to sleep
× The child that lay upon her breast
× Sleep and as deep

~~That~~ Thus a mother sang asleep
The child her breast had fed
Sleep beloved and as deep
As daring Paris did

Sleep beloved sleep
The breast where [you] have fed
× ~~Protects~~ Must guard you from all ha

Sleep where you have fed
Forget the world's alarms

Sleep upon my breast
As

[Page 2, right-hand page of first opening]

As Paris slept
That first night
In his Helen's arms

The sleep that Paris found
Towards the break of day
Under the slow breaking day
That first night in Helen's arms

That first night on Helen's bed

× That first
× Sleep the sleep
The sleep that dreaming Paris
× When that morning broke
That first dawn
That first sleep that Paris found

[Page 3, left-hand page of second opening. Yeats cancelled this page.]

Sleep beloved sleep
Sleep where you have fed
Forget the world's alarms

Sleep beloved, ~~lie~~ sink asleep
On the breast where [you] have fed
× Forgetful of the world's alarms

× Sleep beloved
× Sleep, beloved and

Beloved may you sink as deep
× As far from fright [?]

× Sleep beloved sink in sleep

Put away the world's alarms
Sink into a rest as deep

[Page 4, right-hand page of second opening. Yeats divided the page by drawing a line.]

× That sank upon the golden bed
× When the dawn broke in ~~Helen~~'s arms

1 Beloved may your sleep be sound
2 ~~On the breast where you have~~ That have found it where you fed
What were all the world's alarms
To that great Paris when he found
Sleep upon the golden bed
6 That first dawn in Helen's arms?

— — — — — — — — — — — — — — — —

Sleep beloved with such a sleep
~~As that~~ As on the hunter Tristram fell
× When beloved night had gone
× When the potion's work was done
× At the end
× When the last
× When at
When the birds began to stir
And all the potion's work was done

Sleep beloved the sleep that fell
On Tristram the famed forester
When all the potion's work was done

[Yeats wrote the next two lines on the bottom of page three.]

Sleep beloved with such sleep
As the hunter Tristram got

[Page 5, right-hand page of third opening. The drafts on this page are earlier than those on the facing left-hand page.]

7 Sleep beloved such a sleep
As Tristram that famed forester felt
× When the potion ~~had its will~~ will was done
× Found when
Found when the potion's work ~~was~~ being done
× When the birds began
× Found when birds began to stir

× When the deer began to
× When

× And bird could sing and nestling cheep
× And stag
× Birds could sing and
Birds could warble, deer could leap
The oak leaf and the beech leaf stir
And the world begin again

[Page 6, left-hand page of third opening. Yeats has divided the page by drawing a line.]

× Lie beloved fast asleep
7 Sleep beloved such a sleep
As Tristram that famed forester
× Found when the potion's work was done/ being done
Found when the potion's work being done
× Birds could sing, and
The birds could sing, the deer could leap
The oak bough and the beech bough stir
And the world begin again

— — — — — — — — — — — — — — — —

Found the potion's work being done
When birds could sing and deer could leap

bank swan

sank bank
love ~~limbs~~

swan sank
dims care

limbs

[Page 7, right-hand page of fourth opening. Yeats used the left-hand page for rewriting. Passages from the left-hand page have been worked into the drafts where they seem to belong. Yeats worked on stanzas 2 and 3 on this page, perhaps simultaneously. I have separated them.]

Such sleep, as on Eurota's bank
× Did the famous Leda guard
× Where
× Did the king of heaven guard

[From the left-hand page.]

× Such sleep as Leda tried to guard
× When upon Eurota's bank
bank
where
length
sank
care

[Continues on the right-hand page.]

~~Sleep~~ Belovéd such a sleep as fell
14 ~~On~~ Upon Eurota's grassy bank
15 When the holy ~~swan~~ bird that ~~swan~~ there
16 Accomplished ~~the~~ his predestined will
17 From the limbs of Leda sank
18 But not from her protecting care

[From the left-hand page.]

Such a sleep as Leda saw
When upon Eurota's bank
where
care

[Continues on the right-hand page.]

× Lie beloved ~~fast asleep~~ in such a sleep
7 Sleep belovéd such a sleep
8 ~~Such~~ As did that wild Tristram know
9 When the potion's work being done
~~The~~ Birds could sing ~~the~~ and deer could leap
The beech bough sway and the oak bough
And the world begin again

Stag could run ~~crop~~ and hares could leap
Birds could sing and stags could leap
× And pheasants crow upon the bough
× For the world began again
The beech bough sway by the oak bough
And the world begin again

[Draft B]

LULLABY

I

1 Beloved may your sleep be sound
2 That have found it where you fed
What were all the world's alarms
× To that great Paris when he found
× What to Paris when he found
To mighty Paris when he found
Sleep upon the golden bed
6 That first dawn in Helen's arms

II

7 Sleep beloved such a sleep
8 As did that wild Tristram know
9 When the potion's work ~~was~~ being done
~~Stage~~ Stag could run and ~~hares~~ roe could leap
The beech bough sway by the oak bough
× And the world begin again
Stag could leap and roe could run

III

Beloved such a sleep as fell
14 Upon Eurota's grassy bank
15 When the holy ~~swan~~ bird that there
16 Accomplished his predestined will
17 From the limbs of Leda sank
18 But not from her protecting care

March 1929

[Yeats wrote another draft of this poem on a separate sheet; here the poem reaches the form in which it was first printed in *The New Keepsake*.]

[Draft C]

~~CRADLE SONG~~
LULLABY

1 Beloved may your sleep be sound
2 That have found it where you fed.
3 What are all the world's alarms?
4 What were they when Paris found

5 Sleep upon a golden bed
6 That first dawn in Helen's arms.

7 Sleep beloved such a sleep
8 As did that wild Tristram know
9 When, the potion's work being done,
10 Roe could run or doe could leap
11 Under ~~the~~ oak and ~~the hazel~~ beechen bough,
12 Roe could leap or doe could run;

13 Such a sleep, and sound as fell
14 Upon Eurota's grassy bank
15 When the holy bird, that there
16 Accomplished his predestined will,
17 From the limbs of Leda sank
18 But not from her protecting care.

Yeats has his usual trouble getting "Lullaby" started; as the drafts continue he proceeds more and more surely until he accomplishes a finished draft of stanza three the first time he attempts it. Yeats seems from the first to be working toward a six line stanza, though he does experiment with different rhyme schemes and line lengths. He seems also to have his three extended allusions to the love stories of Paris, Tristram, and Zeus established in his mind.

Yeats begins his work on stanza 1 by listing five possible rhyme words. These are not arranged in the scheme he eventually adopted (abcabc), but he does use three of the five — alarms, bed, arms — in the finished poem. Then Yeats sets the scene, so to speak, by writing

Thus a mother sang to sleep
The child that lay upon her breast.

On page 1 of the drafts he drops this indirect approach in favor of having the whole poem a song when he writes

Sleep beloved sleep
Sleep where you have fed.

In the drafts on pages 1, 2, and 3 the third line is addressed to the child as it again will be in the C draft, and it is put through many revisions while being transferred to sleeping Paris on page 4. Yeats then goes on to work out his comparison of the sleeping child with Paris asleep on Helen's bed after their first night together. On page 2 this is stated simply:

As Paris slept
That first night
In his Helen's arms

Then Yeats remembers that though the world speaks of lovers sleeping together that is not what the world means, so he immediately changes his expression to a more accurate one:

The sleep that Paris found
Towards the break of day
That first night on Helen's bed.

By the end of page 2 Yeats has not finished any lines, and he has not certainly established his rhyme scheme; though five rhyme words are in place they are not in final order (fed, alarms, found, arms, bed).

The draft on page 3 is still hesitating and uncertain, Yeats does not make much progress. Then on page 4 the first stanza takes shape. Yeats finishes lines 1, 2, and 6 and nearly finishes the others. The slight but wonderfully effective changes Yeats makes can be seen by comparing this draft with the latest forms of the various lines in the preceding drafts:

1 Beloved may you sink as deep
Beloved may your sleep be sound
2 On the breast where [you] have fed
That have found it where you fed
3 Put away the world's alarms
What were all the world's alarms
4 That first sleep that Paris found
To that great Paris when he found
5 That sank upon the golden bed
Sleep upon the golden bed
6 When the dawn broke in Helen's arms
That first dawn in Helen's arms?

The revision of line 1 helps Yeats develop his persona, the imagined mother who sings the lullaby: "Beloved may you sink as deep" is truer to the object; "Beloved may your sleep be sound" is truer to the persona, since it expresses her wish rather than merely an observation.

On the lower half of page 4 Yeats begins work on stanza 2, continuing on 5 and the top half of 6; his progress is much faster. Yeats selects and arranges the detail which will convey Tristram sleeping in the waking forest after the consummation of his love. Line 7 reaches final form on page 5; in the drafts of line 8 "hunter Tristram" becomes "Tristram that famed forester." Line 9 throughout these drafts has the same content, but goes through many verbal changes: "When beloved night had gone/ When the potion's work was done/ And all the potion's work was done/ When all the potion's work was done/ When the potion's will was done/ Found when the potion's work being done." In the drafts of lines 10–12 Yeats introduces these dawn sounds: stirring, singing, and then warbling birds; leaping deer; stirring oak and beech leaves. At the end of page 5 Yeats has completed line 7 and set the rhyme words for lines 9 and 10. The draft of this stanza on the top of page 6 shows some advance. The birds are now content to sing, and the leaves have become boughs.

On the lower half of page 6 Yeats experiments with rhyme words for stanza 3, and in his right-hand column sets three of the words he will use in the finished poem — bank, sank, care. In the drafts of stanza 3 on page 7 Yeats's attack is both quick and sure. He explores his details a bit, and then writes the stanza off in a single draft, essentially as it appeared in *The New Keepsake*. Yeats then returns to drafts of stanza 2. He finishes lines 7–9; lines 10–12 do not yet come right. Rhyming "done" and "again" seems daring even for Yeats. The dawn birds, who will shortly disappear, are giving trouble.

Draft B, dated March 1929, is little more than a clean copy of the A drafts. Yeats did make changes in lines 4, and 10–12. At line 4 "To that great Paris" becomes "To mighty Paris"; at lines 10–12 Yeats begins to work his way toward his final readings. At the bottom of page 7 of the A drafts lines 10–12 read:

> Birds could sing and stags could leap
> The beech bough sway by the oak bough
> And the world begin again.

Now Yeats banishes the birds, rephrases line 10, cancels line 12 and replaces it by repeating the image used in 10, slightly changing the order of the words:

Stag could run and roe could leap
The beech bough sway by the oak bough
Stag could leap and roe could run.

Yeats has found the strategy though not the words used in the finished poem. A general statement "And the world begin again," summing up the content of the preceding images, is dropped in favor of a refrain-like repetition of one of those images. When this happens the slight consonance of *done/ again* becomes full rhyme in *done/ run.* In Yeats's poetry such summary statements of the content of his images as the one here dropped occur frequently:

Mere anarchy is loosed upon the world

for example, or

Those masterful images because complete
Grew in pure mind, but out of what began?

Yeats must have felt that such a statement was not necessary in this simple poem; perhaps too it had the effect of somewhat removing our attention from the sleeping lovers.

In draft C "Lullaby" reached the form in which *The New Keepsake* first printed it in November 1931. Here Yeats changes the wording of lines 3, 4, 10–12, and 13.

What were all the world's alarms
To mighty Paris when he found

3 What are all the world's alarms?
4 What were they when Paris found

Stag could run and roe could leap
The beech bough sway by the oak bough
Stag could leap and roe could run
10 Roe could run or doe could leap
11 Under oak and beechen bough,
12 Roe could leap or doe could run

Beloved such a sleep as fell
13 Such a sleep, and sound as fell

Here line 3 again becomes a question asked of the sleeping child, a form of it I like, though Yeats eventually reverted to the reading found in the B draft. Line 4 in its new wording introduces the first allusion neatly and avoids "mighty Paris," which rather jars on the ears of readers of the *Iliad*. The changes in the second stanza accomplish several things: they introduce what is to my ear a very insistent internal rhyme; they soften the sound by deleting "stag" — there is now a ripe interplay of soft consonants and open vowels; they change the boughs from a correlative to the mere setting of a correlative — they had been one of the images set to show us the reawakening forest, now they describe the place where the deer leap and run. The new form of line 13 was invented, I think, to avoid a third repetition of "beloved"; Yeats achieves a more subtle variation of line 1 when he drops "beloved" and picks up "sound."

As was noted above the draft just discussed is exactly that first printed in *The New Keepsake*. It would be easy enough to move from this first printing to the final text of the poem which was established in Macmillan's *Winding Stair* in 1933. It would only be necessary to say that in 1933 Yeats reverted to the form lines 3 and 4 had in draft B, keeping the rest of the poem as it had been printed. But between these two printings came the version printed in the Cuala Press's *Words for Music* in November 1932. Since I propose to discuss this version in detail, I print it below:

LULLABY

Beloved may your sleep be sound
That have found it where you fed.
What were all the world's alarms
To mighty Paris when he found
Sleep upon a golden bed
That first night in Helen's arms.

Sleep beloved such a sleep
As did that wild Tristram know
When, the potion's work being done,
Stag could run and roe leap
Under oak and beeches bough,
Stag could leap and roe could run.

Beloved such a sleep as fell
Upon Eurotas' grassy bank
When the holy bird that there

Accomplished his predestined will
From the limbs of Helen sank
But not from her protecting care.

I shall first describe the relationship of the three earliest printings, and then speculate concerning their relationship. I assume that the following Cuala Press readings are misprints which I may ignore: line 11 "beeches bough," line 17 "From the limbs of Helen sank"; and further that "Eurota's" in line 14 of the *New Keepsake* text derives from the copy Yeats supplied and that the change to the correct form in the Cuala Press version need not be further discussed. If these assumptions are allowed, then the three versions have identical forms of lines 1, 2, 5, 7–9, 11, 14–16; *New Keepsake* and Macmillan identical forms of lines 6, 10, 12, 13; Cuala Press and Macmillan identical forms of lines 3 and 4.

Now for speculation. The Cuala Press text of "Lullaby" seems to me very poor for several reasons. First, because of the misprints already noted: "Under oak and beeches bough" is bad enough, but the confusion of Helen with Leda in line 17 quite spoils the poem. Then the form line 6 has in the Cuala Press printing

That first night in Helen's arms

reintroduces a reading Yeats had abandoned on page 2 of the A drafts, abandoned, that is, very early in the process of composing the poem. Not only does the reading "first dawn" wonderfully set the stage for stanza 2 by a typical Yeatsean preparation for the emergence of a new correlative, it is also more accurate and avoids the initial but here unwanted association most readers will have with the phrase "first night," namely a first production of a dramatic work.

It is difficult to imagine how such a version got into print a full year after a satisfactory text had appeared. One must, I think, conclude that Cuala printed from very poor copy, from some early and superseded version of the poem, perhaps from a typescript which Yeats had not corrected. Since the poem had been virtually finished in March 1929, there were undoubtedly many copies of it about in 1932. One would go on to conclude that when Yeats prepared copy for Macmillan he kept the *New Keepsake* readings for all lines except 3 and 4; for these he preferred the Cuala Press readings. The poem in its final form is, then, a corrected, eclectic text.

Whether Yeats's art was greatest in the 1920's or the 1930's is a question like the question whether Burgundy is better than claret, Rhine better than Mosel; and we, Yeats's readers, are in the position of the French judge who, when asked to adjudicate between Burgundy and claret, replied that he was willing to spend his life examining the evidence, but that he did not expect to reach a conclusion. It is impossible, I think, to do more than prefer "Nineteen Hundred and Nineteen" to "Supernatural Songs," or "Supernatural Songs" to "Nineteen Hundred and Nineteen." In the 1920's the prevailing mode in Yeats's poetry is the "public speech" mode; he then wrote many poems in his role of vatic poet commenting on men and events in a rhetoric that is traditional, noble, and in some degree forensic. In the 1930's the prevailing mode is metaphysical in the philosophic sense of that word; typical poems are concerned with final things, and Yeats's rhetoric is often fantastic ("Supernatural Songs") and even at times outrageous ("News for the Delphic Oracle"). Yet the prevailing modes barely prevail; Yeats wrote metaphysical poems in the 1920's ("Two Songs from a Play"), public speech poems in the 1930's ("Lapis Lazuli"). Both sorts of poem are now in their different ways usually personal utterances. Yeats found this approach congenial and, once he had established it, rarely tried another.

Both sorts of poem are more and more concerned with Yeats's central doctrine, Unity of Being; they are, so to speak, variations on this theme. The doctrine, Unity of Being, developed so slowly that it is difficult to set a date when it was clearly enough formulated to be operative in Yeats's poetry. The year 1919 will do as well as any; in that year Yeats wrote in "If I were Four-and-Twenty" [first printed in *The Living Age,* Oct. 4, 1919, p. 33]:

When Dr. Hyde delivered in 1894 his lecture on the necessity of 'the de-anglicization of Ireland,' to a society that was a youthful indiscretion of my own, I heard an enthusiastic hearer say: 'This lecture begins a new epoch in Ireland.' It did that, and if I were not four-and fifty, with no settled habit but the writing of verse, rheumatic, indolent, discouraged, and about to move to the Far East, I would begin another epoch by recommending to the nation a new doctrine, that of unity of being.

By one of those pleasant ironies which abound in Yeats's career, he did not move to the Far East; he ignored his rheumatism, indolence, discouragement; he spent the next twenty years recommending the new doctrine.

5

POEMS
WRITTEN IN THE 1930's

i

"The Mother of God"

ON NOVEMBER 23, 1930, Yeats made the first entry in a new manuscript book, by far the largest and most sumptuous he ever used. He continued to work in this book into the summer of 1933. In it he composed drafts of many of the poems included in *The Winding Stair,* among them "The Mother of God" and "Vacillation." Yeats was staying at Coole during most of the fall and winter of 1931–32, in order to be with Lady Gregory during her final illness. Both poems were composed during these months.

The subject of "The Mother of God," along with the subject of "Remorse for Intemperate Speech" and some notes on Cowley's rhymes, is found in this same book, near the end of a manuscript draft of *The Resurrection.* One would like to conclude from this that the idea of the poem occurred to Yeats while he was at work on the play, and possibly this happened. The question whether Christ was man, or God, or both man and God is the substance of the play. Mary's attitude towards Christ's divinity is discussed in it. But Yeats seldom used his bound manuscript books methodically, starting on page 1 and going to the end; indeed his use of this particular book was decidedly unmethodical. Since it is certain that the items in the book do not occur in order of their composition, it seems more probable that Yeats skipped a page while composing draft 3 of *The Resurrection,* and filled it in later with various notes, including the subject of "The Mother of God." Certainly the poem was written after Yeats completed draft 3 of *The Resurrection;* indeed the finished play was being printed by the Cuala Press at the very time he wrote the poem. Since Yeats usually went on to compose a poem rather soon after writing its subject, I am inclined to think that the subject as well as the poem itself is later than *The Resurrection.*

Here is the subject:

The Virgin shrinks from the annunciation. Must she receive "the burning heavens in her womb"? Looks at the child upon her knees at once with love and dread.

The quotation marks Yeats placed around the phrases "the burning heavens in her womb" and "with love and dread" no doubt indicated that he intended to use them in the poem. He found a place for the first at the end of stanza 1, the last line of which, in all the drafts as in the finished poem, reads "The Heavens in my womb." The second phrase so marked was not used, but it does express the central idea of the poem. Neither the subject nor the drafts of "The Mother of God" found in the manuscript book are dated. A manuscript on a detached sheet is dated "Sep 3 1931." Mrs. Yeats has dated the composition of the poem September 3–12, 1931. Yeats was at work on the poem before September 3, since the version with that date is clearly later than some of those found in the manuscript book.

When composing a poem in a manuscript book, Yeats often established a center, so to speak, and then worked out from it in both directions. He did this when composing "The Mother of God." The earliest drafts of the poem found in the manuscript book were written in ink. I have arranged these in what I believe to be the order of their composition and called them MS. 1.

[MS. 1]

× Threefold the terror that upon me came
× The terror of the dove in the room
× The terror that smote me through the ear

× Terror of the voice out of the air,
× Terror of the dove in the room,

× Terror of that that smote me through the ear
× Terror of the dove in the room

× Terror of what smote me through the ear
× Terror of that voice in the air
× Terror of a dove in the room
× Terror of all terrors that I bear
5× The heavens in my womb

× Past terror
× Three terrors — the

× A three fold terror — the light shining there
× The shaft that struck me in the ear
× ~~That burst into~~ Bursting through the hollow of an ear
× The terror of the dove/ Pinions beating about the room
Terror of all terrors that I bore
5 The heavens in my womb

A threefold terror — ~~the great star~~'s ~~dying~~ that star's fallen
flare
Entering through the hollow of an ear
Some strange bird/ Those wings beating about the room
4 The terror of all terrors that I bore
5 The heavens in my womb

Yeats continued with a single draft of his second stanza, and multiple drafts of his third.

× I loved what everybody does or knows
× Toil and the sound of friendly shoes
How beautiful are common sights and shows
Voice face footfall that one knows
~~Carpenter bench~~ Chimney corner and garden walk
That rocky cistern where we tread the clothes
10 And gather all the talk

× He is all mine I bought him with my pains
× All mine, that my own milk sustains

× I call that mine
× All mine is He that my milk sustains

× I bore him [in] my bodily pains
× But my heart seems to stop

× What horror comes amid my body's pains
× Have [I] not bought that body with my pains
× What is that mouth that my milk stains
× ~~What~~ Suddenly my heart seems to stop

× May I not call that mine by body's pains
× Bought, or that my breast sustains
× I cry but my heart seems to stop
× And something shakes a chillness through my veins
× And the hair of my head stands up.

What could I more than buy him with my pains?
His mouth is mine that my milk stains?
What can have made my heart's blood stop
What can have struck the chill into my veins
What makes my hair stand up

Yeats wrote another version of "The Mother of God" on a detached sheet, and dated it. It is printed below:

[MS. 2]

THE MOTHER OF GOD

I

~~A three-fold~~ ~~Love that is~~ A three-fold terror — that star's fallen flare
Entering through the hollow of an ear
~~Wings that beat about~~ ~~Those wings beating~~ ~~These~~ strange wings beating in the room
Terror of all terrors that I ~~bear~~ bore
5 The heavens in my womb.

II

× How beautifully a common ~~morning~~ evening goes
× How beautiful are common sights and ~~sounds~~ shows
How pleasantly the daylight comes and goes
× Voice, face footfall that one knows

Nothing there but what one knows
8 Chimney corner, garden walk
That rocky cistern where we tread the clothes
10 And gather all the talk

III

× Have I not bought him with my pains
× What could I more than buy him with my pains?
× His mouth is mine that my milk stains
× But what has made my heart's blood [stop]?
× What can have struck the chill into my veins?
× What makes my hair stand up?

× Mine; my heart's blood seems to stop
× ~~Something has struck~~ And something strikes a chill into my ~~veins~~
× The hair of my head stand up.
× And makes my hair stand up.

Mine, mine my body purchased with its pains
A body that my milk sustains
Mine: my heart's blood seems to stop
Something has struck a chill into my bones
And made my hair stand up.
W. B. Y. Sep 3 1931

Typescript I is an uncorrected carbon of a clean copy of the above. It seems to have been transcribed from the MS., for there are many blanks, and it is not very accurate. Yeats returned to his manuscript book and continued work on the poem in a series of drafts written in pencil. I have called these MS. 3 and MS. 4:

[MS. 3]

I
Threefold terror of love: a fallen flare
Etc. etc
that I bore
Etc.

II

× How
× Pleasantly the morning goes
× Nothing there but what
× P

common daylight shows
How pleasantly the daylight comes and goes
Nothing but what one knows

II

× I had
6 Had I not found content among the shows
7 Every common woman knows
8 Chimney corner, garden walk
9 ~~Cis~~ Or rocky cistern where we tread the clothes
10 And gather all the talk

× ~~Although~~ Though my common
× But that I purchased with my body's pains
× That my mother's milk sustains
× The

III

× My/ Mine, mine, my body purchased with its pains
× A body that my milk sustains
× ~~But~~ Mine but what has made my heart's blood stop
× And what has struck the chill into my bones
× And made my hair stand up

III

11 What is this flesh I purchased with my pains
12 This fallen star my milk sustains
13 This love that makes my heart's blood stop
14 Or strikes a sudden chill into my bones
15 And makes my hair stand up

In the next draft Yeats made a clean copy of his poem, revising as he went along; when he had finished the poem was nearly done.

[MS. 4]

~~THE ANNUNCIATION~~ MARY VIRGIN

I

Threefold terror of love; a fallen flare
2 ~~Entering~~ Through the hollow of an ear;
3 ~~Those~~ Wings beating about the room;
4 The terror of all terrors that I bore
5 The heavens in my womb

II

6 Had I not found content among the shows
7 Every common woman knows
8 Chimney corner, garden walk,
9 Or rocky cistern where we tread the clothes
10 And gather all the talk.

III

11 What is this flesh I purchased with my pains
12 This fallen star my milk sustains
13 This love that makes my heart's blood stop
14 Or strikes a sudden chill into my bones
Or makes my hair stand up

In TS. 2, printed below, "The Mother of God" reaches its final form. The change of "makes" to "bids" in the final line suggests that TS. 2 may have been part of the copy for Macmillan's *Winding Stair*, for this change was first printed there. It may, that is, be later than the Cuala Press's *Words for Music*.

[TS. 2]

THE MOTHER OF GOD

I

1 The three-fold terror of love; a fallen flare
2 Through the hollow of an ear;
3 Wings beating about the room;
4 The terror of all terrors that I bore
5 The Heavens in my womb.

II

6 Had I not found content among the shows
7 Every common woman knows,
8 Chimney corner, garden walk,
9 Or rocky cistern where we tread the clothes
10 And gather all the talk.

III

11 What is this flesh I purchased with my pains,
12 This fallen star my milk sustains,
13 This love that makes my heart's blood stop
14 Or strikes a sudden chill into my bones
15 And ~~makes~~ bids my hair stand up?

One of the last entries in the manuscript book Yeats had used to write several versions of "The Mother of God" has to do with that poem. It was Yeats's habit when he thought of a correction for one of his finished poems to record the correction in whatever manuscript book he was using at the moment. These particular corrections were never introduced into the printed text.

corrections in "Mother of God"
Love's threefold terror — that star's fallen flare
In the hollow etc.
and further down
"That star" not "This star"
July 13, 1933

These drafts show that Yeats had the plan of "The Mother of God" fully worked out before he began to write. He had decided that the poem was to be a dramatic monologue; in the drafts as in the printed poem Mary is speaking, and in both she begins with the terrors of the annunciation, then goes on to contrast her peaceful past with her present state now that she has borne God. Once the drafts are underway, Yeats establishes his stanza pattern quickly, which combines the rhyme scheme aabab with lines using a varying number of stresses, 5, 4, 4, 5, 3.

In MS. 1 Yeats makes Mary's terror at the annunciation threefold from the outset; he then goes on to experiment with a series of lines all beginning with the word "terror" which state in varying ways the events that filled her with fear. One source of terror, a "voice out of the air," Yeats soon abandons, settling on the fallen star that strikes Mary through the ear, the presence of the Paraclete in the form of a dove, and her fear of impregnation by the divine. All of this comes very quickly, as do the rhyme sounds and even the rhyme words that Yeats will use in the finished poem. Two of these — room and ear — he finds in the very first draft, in reverse order; at his third essay he turns these around, and in his fourth shapes up his entire first stanza, getting line 5, adapted from the prose version of the poem, in final form. In his sixth draft, Yeats adds detail, and with it the poem takes on an immediacy it has lacked hitherto: "The shaft that struck me in the ear" becomes "Bursting through the hollow of an ear": "The terror of the dove in [the room]" becomes "Pinions beating about the room." Yeats then nearly completes his fourth line by changing "bear" to "bore." Mary speaks this poem after the birth of Christ, and because she does the rhyme "ear / bear" must be abandoned and the "a" rhymes in stanza 1 reduced to the slight consonance of the r-sounds. The stanza is nearly finished in Yeats's seventh draft. Yeats almost achieves his eventual first line when he writes "A threefold terror — that star's fallen flare"; he finishes line 4. As was usually true with Yeats, the thought is more directly, more obviously expressed in this version than in the printed poem. Yeats names the star, for instance; eventually he will merely allude to it. Apparently he became too allusive, for he added a note about the star when he reprinted the poem in *The Winding Stair*.

Yeats quickly roughs in his second stanza before going on to the third. In the drafts of lines 6 and 7 he clearly isn't trying very hard; whatever is amiss can be set right after the more interesting problems posed by stanza 3 are solved. Even in this hasty draft he does establish four rhyme words (knows, walk, clothes, talk) and completes line 10.

Yeats begins the drafts of stanza 3 in declarative statement; then in the third draft he changes to interrogative statement. These are partial drafts. In the fourth draft Yeats attempts his entire stanza, establishing the general movement of his thought and placing four rhyme words. In this draft lines 11 and 12 are interrogative, lines 13–15 declarative. In the fifth draft Yeats uses questions throughout, in fact there is excessive insistence on the questioning in the "what" repeated four times as the first word in lines 11, 13, 14, and 15.

At the end of these first drafts "The Mother of God" would have read as follows had Yeats assembled a clean copy:

A threefold terror—that star's fallen flare
Entering through the hollow of an ear
Those wings beating about the room
4 The terror of all terrors that I bore
5 The heavens in my womb

How beautiful are common sights and shows
Voice face footfall that one knows
Chimney corner and garden walk
That rocky cistern where we tread the clothes
10 And gather all the talk

What could I more than buy him with my pains?
His mouth is mine that my milk stains?
What can have made my heart's blood stop
What can have struck the chill into my veins
What makes my hair stand up

Yeats has made good progress, but there are many rough spots in the diction, and the draft notably lacks the metrical subtlety of Yeats's later poetry where every possible variation of a basic iambic pattern can usually be found. Manuscript 2 develops directly from MS. 1, indeed Yeats copies out most of the readings found there before experimenting with others. In stanza 1 he makes slight alterations in lines 3 and 4: line 3 becomes "Strange wings beating in the room"; in line 4 the initial "The" is dropped. In the draft of stanza 2 Yeats explores new detail to express Mary's content with her earlier lot: the beauty of the evening, the pleasantness of daylight — beautiful and pleasant because they are known. Manuscript 2 ends with two complete and one partial draft of stanza 3. At the close of MS. 1 this stanza had been a series of questions. In MS. 2 Yeats begins in the interrogative, then in the partial and complete drafts that follow shifts to the declarative. In the last version found here Mary insists that Christ is her child by a three-fold repetition of "Mine," and she insists he is a mortal child "my body purchased with its pains/ A body that my milk sustains." She then goes on to admit her fear of the supernatural. Yeats has shifted from present to past tense.

Manuscripts 3 and 4 are exercises in refinement. In stanza 1 the revision of the first line is particularly incisive. The phrase "terror of love" which Yeats here invents is the perfect beginning of the poem. Not only does it state the theme and establish the mood of the poem, it also states a paradox; introduces, that is, an ideational element into Mary's monologue which has the important effect of slightly altering her role. The participant is in the process of becoming participant-observer. By the time these revisions are finished this more complex conception of Mary's role has been established. In line 4 Yeats confirms an earlier decision to use the past tense "I bore"; he decides, that is, to abandon rhyme in favor of consonance. This will affect the revision of line 14.

Yeats had left stanza II in a very rough state, especially lines 6 and 7. Now he explores briefly various details from MS. 2, then writes off the stanza in its finished form. I feel that the decision that led so quickly to a final draft was the decision to use "shows" (line 6) as a noun instead of as a verb. The rest of the changes grow out of that one.

There are three drafts of the last stanza, the first partial, the second and third complete. In the first the principal change is the use of "purchase" in place of "buy": one does not "buy" the child one bears, though one may properly "purchase" him, that is acquire him by effort. In the second draft Yeats experiments again with combining declarative statement and question. In the fourth draft in MS. 1 Yeats had made lines 11 and 12 a question, then gone on to declaration; in MS. 2 he had used declarative statements throughout his latest version; now lines 11 and 12 declare while lines 13–15 question. In MS. 1 Yeats had used the present tense; he had shifted to the past tense in MS. 2; this he keeps in MS. 3 for his first and second drafts. The revision of line 14 shows Yeats's solution of a technical problem. Yeats has reduced the "a" rhyme in stanza 1 at line 4 to a slight consonance — flare, ear, bore — while in stanza 2 line 9 rhymes exactly with lines 6 and 7 — shows, knows, clothes. When Yeats changes "chill in my veins" to "chill in my bones" the a rhymes in stanza 3 conform with the pattern of stanza 1. In the third draft Yeats achieves the lines he first printed. He shifts back to the present tense, bringing Mary out of her recollective mood into the terror and immediacy of the passing moment, and he again, as in the fifth draft in MS. 1 and the first draft in MS. 2, makes the entire stanza a series of questions. This rush of questions on the nature of God, now phrased with ultimate refinement, completes the process of making Mary both participant in and observer of the birth of Christ. The poem gains power and interest as Mary's role acquires an aspect in which both poet and reader can participate. Finally, Yeats changes line 12 by writing "The fallen star my milk sustains" in place of "A body that my milk sustains." This echo of line 1 ties the poem together into a completely articulated unit; it should have made unnecessary the explanation Yeats wrote for *The Winding Stair*.

Yeats now copied his poem out clean in MS. 4. He tried two titles, "The Annunciation" and then "Mary Virgin," neither of which he kept. He eventually returned to the fine title found at the head of MS. 2. Yeats made slight improvements in stanza 1; for stanzas 2 and 3 he merely copied versions he had already completed. The second line of stanza 1 had read "Entering through the hollow of an ear"; Yeats deleted "entering," no doubt to make his line conform with the second lines of his succeeding stanzas, each of which has four stresses. Yeats first wrote "Those wings beating about the room," derived from MS. 1; he now deleted "those" to make his third line begin with an unmistakably strong accent after the long pause marked by the semicolon at the end of line 2. During the process of this draft he gave more attention to his pointing than hitherto, but he has by no means finished punctuating his poem.

Yeats had now essentially the version of the poem he would shortly print. At some later time Yeats softened the beginning of his poem by writing "The threefold terror of love." Then, after the poem had appeared in the Cuala Press's *Words for Music Perhaps*, Yeats made one more textual change, that recorded in TS. 2. The last line had read "And makes my hair stand up"; Yeats raises the intensity of his drama to the ultimate pitch possible when he changes this to read "And bids my hair stand up."

Yeats very early came to believe that an age begins with the birth of its god. Altogether he wrote four poems which concern the actual or imagined beginnings of new ages: "The Secret Rose" 1896, "The Second Coming" 1919, "Leda and the Swan" 1923, and "The Mother of God" 1931. "The Secret Rose" is apocalyptic; it foresees the death of an old order and the birth of a new and better, a new order presided over by the tutelary symbol of the Rose. "The Second Coming" records the death of the hopes Yeats had expressed in "The Secret Rose": a new age has indeed dawned, but its deity is not the Rose, but rather the stony, enigmatic sphinx. Then while at work on *A Vision* Yeats wrote magnificently of the incarnation which began the Classical age in "Leda and the Swan." Finally, in the poem we have been studying, he wrote of the beginning of the Christian era.

Yeats created one of his finest and most objective personae in "The Mother of God," and because he did he is able to realize and express attitudes toward the birth of Christ which he did not share. Yeats was no admirer of Mary, and he did not consider Christianity a satisfactory religion. He has told us so in many places, as in the second of the "Supernatural Songs" where Ribh denounced Patrick explicitly for maintaining that the Eternal begat Christ on a virgin. Yeats expressed his attitude even more sharply in a phrase near the end of entry XXXI of *Pages from a Diary Written in Nineteen Hundred and Thirty* (1944). In manuscript the passage reads:

> Yet I must bear in mind that an antithetical revelation will be less miraculous (in the sense of signs and wonders) more psychological than a primary which is from beyond man and mothered by the void (Mary Virgin).

It is Yeats's sense of Mary, the persona who speaks the poem, that enables him here to control material that we would not expect him to be attracted to; it is precisely this persona that makes the material useable. The event is instructive. It was argued above that the relative weakness of much of Yeats's early verse comes from the weakness of his personae, the narrative voices invented for those poems, and that Yeats's strong style developed only after he had posited, so to speak, first person personae who are in some sense always Yeats, direct or antithetical. In the good poems this is a Yeats completely contained in his phantasmagoria, which is to say that the observation or biographical event which is often the starting point of a poem has been made "intended, complete" when the poem is done. One can go even further and claim with some confidence that with all of Yeats's male personae — Ribh, Old Tom, Malachi Stilt-Jack, John Kinsella — the principal thing involved is the degree of disguise that the mask chosen provides.

I do not think this is true of Yeats's women personae except in the literal sense that Yeats created all of them: they are by no means always Yeats and with them from very early on Yeats was able to achieve great objectivity, indeed an increasing objectivity which perhaps culminates in "The Mother of God." From Moll Magee on all the way to Crazy Jane these women are a great crew, and when Yeats uses them to speak his poems the problem of controlling his own accidence seems seldom to arise. "A Woman Young and Old" is a case in point: This sequence gave Yeats a great deal of trouble and was underway for many years (Yeats once thought it would be ready for inclusion in *The Tower*), but when it was done it was done (intended, complete) to a greater degree than "A Man Young and Old" where biographical accidence is not always controlled.

I can offer only probable explanations for this; no doubt Yeats himself might have found it difficult to explain. Doesn't the creative act, the imagined stance have built into it a necessary degree of objectivity when a writer who is a man undertakes to speak as a woman? Surely Molly is less Joyce than either Stephen or Bloom, though neither Stephen nor Bloom are Joyce involved in accidence, which is not to say that Molly is a greater creation, and surely the mother who speaks "Lullaby" and Mary who speaks "The Mother of God" are less Yeats than Ribh and John Kinsella not to speak of the "I" of "Byzantium." Yeats is more present in "Lullaby" than in "The Mother of God" for it seems unlikely that any actual mother ever thought of comparing the sleep of her child who has finished nursing with the sleep that overcame the world's great mythic lovers following consummation. The idea is daring, typical of Yeats, and it makes his "Lullaby" unique in the language. Such material would be immediately attractive, whereas much of the material in "The Mother of God" would not be (although Yeats might have seen in the woman with God in her belly a dark conceit of the artist, and he wrote in "A Packet for Ezra Pound" — first printed in 1929, this became part of *A Vision* in 1937 — of his own terror in the presence of the supernatural, a terror which he had just presented in other terms in *The Resurrection*).

Whatever the reason, none of Yeats's customary irritation with the nullity of virginity creeps into "The Mother of God." Rather he first imagines and then beautifully states how a simple peasant woman might have felt when caught up in these ponderous events; as she concludes her sililoquy she is no longer a simple peasant, but truly the Mother of God.

ii

"Vacillation," Section VIII

YEATS BEGAN "VACILLATION" at Coole in November 1931, and worked on it for several months. Some twenty-four of the very large pages of the manuscript book used while composing "The Mother of God" are filled with drafts of "Vacillation." The entire process of Yeats's creation of this splendid poem can be followed in the sheets of the manuscript book, but this was so complex that to do so would require a long monograph. Richard Ellmann has reproduced and analysed many of the drafts of section VII; I have chosen section VIII for study. Here is Yeats's first draft:

My teacher is not Von Hugel ~~though~~ I ~~scarce~~ ~~less~~ ~~than~~ ~~he~~
although both he and I
Accept the miracles of the saints, honour their sanctity
× Seventy or eighty years ago St. Teresa's tomb
That St. Teresa's body lies undecayed in the tomb
~~Moistened~~ ~~by~~ ~~strange~~ Bathed in miraculous oil, or that sweet
odours from it come
× Has once
× Does not astonish me
× Is not more
× Is not more strange than sights that I have seen
× Cannot ~~more~~ astonish more
Does not seem more strange than sights that I have seen—
Perchance
× Those learned hands
× Hands that prepared the Pharaoh's
× Learned fingers that prepared the Pharaoh's sacred mummy once
× Now mummify the saints
The hands that ~~made~~ ~~ready~~ readied for the tomb, the Pharaoh's
sacred mummies once
Now mummify the saints
× Bathed in miraculous oil or that
× Bathed in sweet
That it exudes miraculous ~~fragrant~~ sweet oil, or that perchance/
those hands

~~The hands that readied for the tomb~~ Turned into a mummy the Pharaohs' mummies once
Now mummify the saints. I ~~hold~~ think ~~things~~ well worthy of belief.
And that the examples of their lives ~~can~~ might bring ~~the~~ my heart relief
And set me on the heavenly [?]; and yet declare that I
× And yet I sw
× Yet swear to god that I
× And sanctify the soul, and yet I swear to god that I
× With fierce unchristened heart shall live in Homer's company
× ~~And set the soul by heaven's path~~ ~~my feet in heaven's way~~ ~~the feet in heaven's way~~ And set me upon heaven's way, and yet I swear that I
× With fierce unchristened heart ~~must~~ shall live in Homer's company
Must keep heart unchristened and walk in Homer's way
× And cast my soul upon the wind
× And turn my breast
× And lean my breast upon ~~the~~ that bitter wind
× Turn my breast toward the wind, my feet upon the way
× And
× Turn only what the fierce heart sang
The ~~lion's jaw the honey comb~~ Honey and the fierce animal, what was it Scripture said
~~I renounce~~ ~~So~~ I therefore shut Von Hugel but with blessing on his head
And set my feet on heaven's path and yet declare that I
Must keep my heart unchristened, like Homer live [and] die
Honey and
The lion and the honey comb what was it

The second draft went as follows:

× Von Hugel's ~~is~~ not my teacher and yet both he and I
Must we part Von Hugel, though alike in this that we
Accept the miracles of the saints, honour their sanctity.
80 The body of St Teresa lies undecayed in ~~the~~ tomb;
~~Exudes miraculous oil~~ ~~Miraculous oil exudes from it~~ Bathed in some miraculous oil; sweet odours from it come,

× ~~The kings rule and the saints rule~~ Kings have ruled and saints may rule; those ghostly hands perchance
× That altered Pharaoh's body to a sacred mummy once
× Have mummified Theresa. Might find relief
× In study of lives like hers, belief like her belief
× And all such things delight me, and yet I swear that I
× Must keep my heart unchristened, like Homer live and die.
88× The lion and the honey comb what has scripture said:
× I have shut Von Hugel though with blessings on his head.
82 Healing from its lettered slab; ~~those phantom hands~~ ~~the ghosts of those~~ ~~those very hands~~ those selfsame hands perchance
That altered Pharaoh's body to a sacred mummy once
Now mummify the saints; but I though heart might find relief
If I became/ Had/ Did I become a Christian man, or ~~chose~~ ~~choose~~ ~~chose~~ choose for my belief
86 What seems most welcome in the tomb, ~~play a different part~~ ~~play out my chosen part~~ play a predestined part.
Make Homer my example and his unchristened heart
88 The lion and the honeycomb what has scripture said:
× ~~I have~~ There, I have shut Von Hugel though with blessings on his head.
So get you gone Von Hugel though with blessings on that head.

Here is the third draft:

78 Must we part Von Hugel, though ~~alike in this that~~ much alike for we
79 Accept the miracles of the saints and honour sanctity.
80 The body of St. Teresa lies undecayed in tomb
81 Bathed in miraculous oil, sweet odours from it come
82 Healing from its lettered slab. Those self same hands perchance
× That ~~altered~~ scooped out Pharaoh's body to a sacred mummy once
× Now mummify the saints.
83 Eternalised the body of a modern saint that once
Had scooped out Pharaoh's mummy. But I, though heart might find relief
85 Did I become a Christian man and choose for my belief
86 What seems most welcome in the tomb, play a predestined part

Make Homer my example and his unchristened heart
88 The lion and the honey comb what has scripture said
89 So get you gone Von Hugel though with blessings on your head

Before Yeats began to write section VIII of "Vacillation," he had the plan of the poem clearly in mind and had decided on his metrical pattern. The pattern he picked uses long seven- and eight-stress lines rhymed in couplets, a pattern which he used to great effect in his later years. A comparison of this poem with Book III of *Oisin*, likewise written in long lines, will show how far Yeats had travelled toward complete mastery of the means of his art in forty-five years of constant writing. In the 1889 version the end of *Oisin* went as follows:

I will pray no more with the smooth stones: when life in my body has ceased —
For lonely to move 'mong the soft eyes of best ones a sad thing were —
I will go to the house of the Fenians, be they in flames or at feast,
To Fin, Caolte, and Conan, and Bran, Sgeolan, Lomair.

It seems hardly possible that one poet could have come all the way from this to "Vacillation," where Yeats uses such a variety of metrical patterns with such complete command that the poem is a kind of set piece, so to speak, of metrical virtuosity.

The objects and situations used in the poem have also been fully assembled. The opening and closing allusions to Von Hügel, the allusion to the miraculously preserved body of St. Teresa, the reference to the doctrine of multiple existences in the account of the embalmer, the rejection of Christianity in favor of Homer's Paganism, the allusion to Sampson's riddle — all of these things are present in the first draft and in the order they will have in the finished poem. In short, a large part of the work of composition had been done before Yeats began to write; the drafts show his search for expression.

An examination of the first draft shows that ten of the twelve rhyme sounds are in place (all except those used in lines 86 and 87), and nine of the rhyme words finally used (two of these "belief/ relief" will be inverted). These drafts are another example of how tenaciously Yeats clung to his rhyme words once he had established them. In draft 1 Yeats does not finish any of his lines, though line 88 is nearly finished: "The lion and the honey comb, what was it Scripture said."

One of the most skillful things in the finished poem is Yeats's management of person and number. There he begins with "we" — that is, himself and Von Hügel ("Must we part, Von Hugel"). The parting predicted in the opening question takes place in lines 84–86 when Yeats writes "I . . . play a predestined part," shifts, that is, from the first person plural to the first person singular. He then goes on to contrast his faith and Von Hügel's and to bid Von Hügel farewell. Yeats invented this artful management slowly. The first draft is in the first person singular throughout. While working on his second draft Yeats discovered the arrangement he was to keep, wherein the syntax itself reflects the parting that is the subject of the poem.

The use of the first person singular throughout the first draft involved Yeats in another difficulty which, again, he avoided in the second draft. The use of "I" brought too much of Yeats's personal accidence into the poem, brought, for instance, a reference to Yeats's own experience of the supernatural in the first draft of lines 80–82:

> That St. Teresa's body lies undecayed in the tomb
> Bathed in miraculous oil, or that sweet odours from it come
> Does not seem more strange than sights that I have seen —

Yeats revised this to read

> The body of St. Teresa lies undecayed in tomb
> Bathed in some miraculous oil; sweet odours from it come
> Healing from its lettered slab.

All accidence is gone from this revised version.

Yeats near the end of this first draft writes in three different ways of his own heart as unchristened:

> I swear to god that I
> With fierce unchristened heart shall live in Homer's company
> Must keep heart unchristened and walk in Homer's way
> Must keep my heart unchristened, like Homer live [and] die

In the second draft "unchristened heart" is transferred to Homer with happy results. Yeats bids loving farewell to Christianity in section VIII of "Vacillation"; poses and answers the question with whom shall the poet walk, Von Hügel or Homer? A drama of spiritual vacillation is unfolding, but when Yeats writes of his own "fierce unchristened heart" he has unfolded it before the climax. Since the phrase "unchristened heart" is too good to lose, Yeats transfers it appropriately to Homer, one of Dante's virtuous Heathen and Yeats's own forebear in the eternal world of art. This change like the others noted shows Yeats's highly skilled management of the "I-persona" here and throughout his later poetry.

This first draft is a remarkable achievement. Perhaps the happiest stroke in the finished poem is Yeats's allusion to Sampson's riddle; it would have spoiled the poem to quote "Out of the strong cometh forth sweetness." Yeats has so arranged things that the reader supplies this essential thought and is charmed by its ironic aptness to the situation of the unchristened artist. Yeats took this allusive approach even in his first draft. The cancellations make an interesting study. Most of the cancelled lines were dropped because Yeats immediately found better expression, but some of them again reflect his artful management of the "I-persona." This is especially apparent in the cancellation of such a line as, "And lean my breast upon that bitter wind."

In the second draft Yeats established all his rhyme words in final position, and finished four lines (80, 82, 86, 88). The best thing that happened in this second draft, aside from the shift from the first person singular already described, was Yeats's decision to make his poem an imagined conversation with Von Hügel rather than a mere consultation of Von Hügel's book. This more dramatic approach seems to have occurred to Yeats at the outset, where he cancels the first line adapted from draft 1 and writes, "Must we part Von Hugel, though alike in this that we." During the course of his work on this draft Yeats also made two adjustments noted above, that is he dropped the reference to his own experiences of the supernatural and transferred "unchristened" to Homer. He also accomplished some miraculous improvements in meter and wording. His revision of line 80 illustrates improved meter:

> The body of St. Teresa lies undecayed in the tomb —
> The body of St. Teresa lies undecayed in tomb.

It is hard to explain why the omission of "the" does so much for this line. Part of the improvement comes from the excision of the soft anapest. But part of the greatness of Yeats's later poetry comes from his paring away of everything that can be pared away, revealing by that paring the stark, inevitable outline. This is an example of such paring. Yeats greatly improved his diction as well as his sound and rhythm when he changed "play a different part" to "play a predestined part." In a religious discussion no word could be more highly charged than "predestined." Here some of the charge comes from the ironic fact that Yeats plays a predestined part in rejecting the very Christianity where doctrines of predestiny were once avidly discussed.

In the third and final draft Yeats finished ten of his twelve lines and nearly completed his work on the other two (84, 87). The most important change was the revison of lines 83–84. In the second draft these had read

> That altered Pharaoh's body to a sacred mummy once
> Now mummify the saints.

Yeats achieved his far more vivid lines in draft 3, on a second attempt.

> × That ~~altered~~ scooped out Pharaoh's body to a sacred mummy once
> × Now mummify the saints.
> Eternalised the body of a modern saint that once
> Had scooped out Pharaoh's mummy.

Here it is not too much to say that in the contrast between "eternalized . . . saint" and "scooped out" Yeats achieves the maximum tension possible among the realms of discourse.

Two things are finally striking about this run of drafts. The first is the extent of the improvement Yeats achieves within a single draft. This is characteristic of his late prose as well as his late verse. The second is the increased freedom of statement regarding religious belief. In 1932, when he finished the eighth section of "Vacillation," Yeats was taking full advantage of retirement from public life.

iii

"Ribh considers Christian Love insufficient"

YEATS WROTE THIS REMARKABLE POEM along with most of the other "Supernatural Songs" in a bound manuscript book which he began to use in 1934. There are no dates in the drafts of the poem, but it is based on an experience which occurred in October 1933, in the trance-speaking of Mrs. Yeats. Yeats recorded the experience on October 17:

Oct. 17
George three nights ago lit incense — I did not ask why nor perhaps did

she know. Presently she went into trance and Dionastes came, giving sign. He insisted on being questioned. I asked about fifteenth multiple influx. He said "Hate God." We must hate all ideas concerning God that we possess, that, if we did not, absorption in God would be impossible. . . . Later on George went two or three times into momentary trance and always to repeat "hatred, hatred" or "hatred of God." I was, the voice once said, "to think about hatred."

What seems to me the growing hatred among men has long been a problem with me. [Transcribed from the MS.]

The drafts of "Ribh considers Christian Love insufficient" occur in the manuscript book between the drafts of "The Four Ages of Man" and "He and She"; Yeats sent drafts of these to Olivia Shakespear in letters written in August 1934. I feel reasonably certain that the poem was written, at least finished, at about that time. All the drafts of "Supernatural Songs" are extremely difficult to decipher; Yeats did not form the ends of his words, and his cancellations are unusually heavy. Yeats, then, wrote approximately as follows:

[Draft 1]

× Hatred I seek
× Love is of God and comes unsought
I c

I cannot study love that is of God
3× I ~~hatred~~ study hatred with great diligence

× I can stu
× I do not seek for love love comes unsought

I do not seek for love nor study it
It comes unsought and passes human wit
× Because it comes from God
I seek to study with great diligence
× Hatred for that is in my own control
Those passions that I know and may control

[Parts of the next three lines are obscured by a blot]

× The only thing that [is] in my control
~~Is hatred that~~ Those [?] hatred that are purges of the soul
× Hatred; but in purging [?] of the soul

× [undeciphered line]
× Must leave it nothing but bare mind and sense
~~That leaves~~ me I would have nothing there but mind and sense

[From the side of the page]

Hatreds that are a besom to the soul
And leave it nothing but bare mind and sense [1]

7 Why do I hate man woman or event
Hatred delivered from the false lips lent
By terror shows that they are alien [?]
~~When native to my soul~~ ~~Which native to the soul~~ Dare dark distress, age shows at last
× What things are native to my soul at last
How that shall walk when all such things are past
~~Or how it~~ ~~How that has~~ Or how it walked before such things began

There on a darker scene I must learn
From all my thoughts of God in loathing turn
× All thoughts of God
15 From every thought of God mankind has had
~~The~~ Such thoughts are garments and the soul's a bride
That cannot in such trash and tinsel hide
× By hating God it
By hating Him it creeps more near to God

[two cancelled lines undeciphered]
Thereon must I through darker study learn
I must leave the scene and in hatred learn
~~The core of hatred and in~~ To touch the core and in my hatred turn
15 From every thought of God mankind has had
Thoughts are but garments, and the soul's a bride
And cannot in such trash and tinsel hide
× By hating God it creeps more near to God
~~In hatred of God~~ By hating God it creeps more near to God

In that last dark the soul cannot endure
20 A bodily or mental furniture
But just as he with his own hands shall give

× How look
× How can
What can she know unless he bid her know
× How look above her till he makes the show
× How live till in her
× How live till he in all her blood shall live
Where can she look until he makes the show
24 How can she live till in her blood he live.

[Draft 2]

RIBH'S SECOND POEM AGAINST PATRICK

1 Why should I seek for love or study it
2 It is of God and passes human wit;
× I seek to study with all diligence
3 I study hatred with great diligence
4 For that's a passion in my own control
5 A sort of besom that can clear the soul
Of everything that is not mind and sense.

7 Why do I hate man woman or event?
× Hatred delivered from the false light lent
× By terror shows what things are alien
8× That is a light my jealous soul has sent
× A light of terror deception free; it can
× Show dirt dust decay, show at last

7× Why do I hate man woman or event
× Hatred of man, thought, woman or event!
7 Why do I hate man woman or event?
8 That is a light my jealous soul has sent;
9 From terror and deception freed it can
Show dirt, dust decay, show at last
How soul shall walk when all such things are past
Or how ~~it~~ soul walked before such things began
× Then must I through deeper study learn
× To touch the centre and in hatred turn
× The apple's core and in my hatred turn
13 Then my delivered soul herself shall learn
14 A ~~deeper~~ darker knowledge and in hatred turn

15× From every thought of God ~~mankind~~ ~~has~~ ~~had~~ —
× my soul has had
15× mankind has had
15 From every thought of God mankind has had
Thoughts are but garments and the soul's a bride
17 That cannot in that trash and tinsel hide
~~In~~ ~~hatred~~ ~~of~~ ~~Through~~ ~~hating~~ In hating God she creeps more near to God
19 At stroke of midnight soul ~~shall~~ ~~not~~ cannot endure
20 A bodily or mental furniture
× But such as he has given or shall give
× What can she take until her master gives
What ~~can~~ shall she take until ~~his~~ ~~hand~~ ~~can~~ [her] master give
× But what his hand has given, ~~or~~ ~~shall~~ ~~give~~ what it gives.
22 Where can she look until he ~~makes~~ make the show?
What can she know until he ~~bid~~ bids her know?
24 How can she live till in her blood he ~~lives~~ live?

"Ribh considers Christian Love insufficient" was nearly finished in this second draft, and Yeats made unusual progress toward his finished poem in the first. This raises the question whether these were all the drafts he made. I cannot answer with certainty, but think it possible that the poem was accomplished in these two drafts. Yeats's statement here is unusually clear and direct; he uses very few images until he develops the extended metaphor at the end, where the soul after death is seen to approach God as the bride approaches the bridal bed and the waiting bridegroom. When Yeats's later poetry is difficult, it is often because he is saying something he has said before, because he is stating, say, the doctrine of Unity of Being yet once more. Then he must find some new and often enigmatic way of speaking. Here the thought is at once fresh, striking, and intrinsically poetic. If my dating is correct and some ten months separated the eruption of these thoughts in Mrs. Yeats's trance and the writing of the poem, then Yeats had surely thought long and deeply before he began to write. This too would help to explain the speed and assurance with which he worked. I would like, in short, to suppose that the drafts of "Ribh considers Christian Love insufficient" show that some times Yeats was able largely to arrange a poem in his head before taking to pen and ink.

If there is anything to the case stated above, if there were no earlier drafts of the poem, then draft 1 is a remarkable accomplishment. The thought develops through the four stanzas as it will develop in the finished poem; Yeats finds many of the words and images he will retain. In the drafts of stanza 1, he makes three false starts, then writes a draft of the whole stanza during the course of which he puts all of his eventual rhyme words in place. The ironically incongruous metaphor wherein hatred becomes a broom that will sweep accumulated trash out of the soul, an idea which Yeats develops in stanza 2 of this draft, is invented after Yeats explores in two draft lines the possibility of making hatred a purge. Only line 3 is finished (Yeats has cancelled it), but the stanza pattern is set, the theme of the poem stated, the line ends established.

Yeats goes on to a single draft of stanza 2. He begins by writing down line 7 as it will appear in the finished poem. He continues with what seems to me a recollection of Dionastes' voice speaking through Mrs. Yeats's trance: "Hatred delivered from the false lips lent/ By terror." In the "Introduction" to *A Vision* Yeats speaks of the terror that often accompanied these inexplicable experiences. The old age theme erupts momentarily. All in all there is too much accidence here, too much that is directly personal. We will see Yeats retrench this accidence in draft 2. In draft 1 Yeats finishes line 7, and gets all of his rhyme sounds and four of his rhyme words into place.

There are two draft versions of stanza 3, neither of them cancelled — indeed in his later manuscripts Yeats cancelled far less systematically than in his earlier. In the drafts of line 13 the transition to "the other life" is stated with increasing force and clarity: "There on a darker scene I must learn/ Thereon must I through darker study learn/ I must leave the scene and in hatred learn." The second form of line 14 "To touch the core and in my hatred turn" will lead to an image in draft 2, one quickly abandoned. Yeats explores with great assurance the striking metaphor with which the stanza ends, wherein the soul once delivered from the body becomes a bride who creeps to God, the bridegroom, in the nakedness of the bridal surrender. By the end of these drafts Yeats has finished line 15 and all his rhyme words are in place.

Stanza 4 takes shape quickly. At the end of a single draft two lines are done (20 and 24), the rhyme words are all in place (Yeats will reverse lines 22 and 23 in the next draft), and Yeats is experimenting with the strong interrogatives (What, Where, How) which begin lines 21–24.

A clean copy of this first draft will help us compare it with the second:

I do not seek for love nor study it
It comes unsought and passes human wit
I seek to study with great diligence
Those passions that I know and may control
Hatreds that are a besom to the soul
And leave it nothing but bare mind and sense

7 Why do I hate man woman or event;
Hatred delivered from the false lips lent
By terror shows that they are alien
Dare dark distress, age shows at last
How that shall walk when all such things are past
Or how it walked before such things began

I must leave the scene and in hatred learn
To touch the core and in my hatred turn
15 From every thought of God mankind has had
Thoughts are but garments, and the soul's a bride
And cannot in such trash and tinsel hide
By hating God it creeps more near to God

In that last dark the soul cannot endure
20 A bodily or mental furniture
But just as he with his own hands shall give
What can she know unless he bid her know
Where can she look until he makes the show
24 How can she live till in her blood he live.

In draft 2 Yeats finishes his first stanza except for a single word (line 6 "mind and sense/ mind or sense"). Each of the finished lines is implicit in the lines of draft 1, but each is transmuted, as it were, to a higher level of expression. Yeats now begins with a question, strikingly phrased, then in lines 3–6 returns to the declarative pattern of draft 1. The improvement of line 2 is almost a miracle: "It comes unsought and passes human wit/ It is of God and passes human wit." In his cancelled third line Yeats reworks draft 1, then rewrites the line, lifting "hatred" out of line 5 to establish his love/ hate contrast at the very beginning of his poem. Yeats used the space opened in line 5 by the removal of "hatreds" to phrase his ironic comparison (hatred/ besom) more fully: "Hatreds that are a besom to the soul/ A sort of besom that can clear the soul."

Yeats left stanza 2 full of his accidence; now in two drafts he cuts this back severely. In the first draft of line 8 he alludes less directly to the supernatural source of his meditation on hatred, then he omits it entirely:

> Hatred delivered from the false light lent/
> That is a light my jealous soul has sent.

In the drafts of line 10 Yeats tries naming those things — dirt, dust, decay — that the besom hatred can sweep out of the soul. The draft line is metrically awkward and needs rewriting, yet the image is sharper than the "Discover impurities" of the finished poem, and it once tied stanza 2 strongly to stanza 1. (The image also anticipates the rag-and-bone shop of "The Circus Animals' Desertion.") The new forms of lines 11–12 show how much clarity and emphasis can be gained by replacing pronouns by nouns. In draft 1 "that" and "it" are used to refer back the "soul" in line 5; Yeats now replaces them with "soul." Lines 7–9 are done, line 10 will be revised; lines 11–12 are nearly done.

In the drafts of stanza 3 Yeats first tries a more allusive statement of the transition from life to death; he also momentarily develops "core" into an image — he is going to learn the very core of the apple of knowledge of good and evil. He cancels this and replaces it with the direct statement of the finished poem:

> I must leave the scene and in hatred learn
> To touch the core and in my hatred turn [Draft 1]
>
> Then must I through deeper study learn
> To touch the centre and in hatred turn
> The apple's core and in my hatred turn
>
> 13 Then my delivered soul herself shall learn
> 14 A darker knowledge and in hatred turn.

The rest of the stanza is carried over from draft 1 with very little change. Line 18 as first printed was very close to this draft:

In hating God she creeps more near to God
In hating God she may creep close to God. [*Poetry*, December 1934]

Yeats introduced the present reading in *A Full Moon in March*. Lines 13–15 and 17 are done, lines 16 and 18 nearly done.

In revising stanza 4 Yeats replaced "In that last dark" by the more immediate "At stroke of midnight" in line 19. He copied out line 20, and then went on to clear up the rhetorical form of the four ponderous questions with which the poem ends. A cancelled version of line 21 is closer to the final form of the line than the version Yeats allowed to stand in this draft, "What can she take until her master gives." I think that Yeats reversed lines 22 and 23 to avoid beginning two successive lines with "what," at least "what, where, what, how" is to my ear far better than "what, what, where, how." When Yeats rewrote "What can she know unless he bid her know" to read "What can she know until he bids her know," he decided to risk the obstinate repetition "until, until, until, till" which accounts for a large part of the sheer rhetorical strength of lines 21–24. When Yeats finishes his draft, his final stanza is nearly done.

iv

"The Gyres"

I HAVE CHOSEN "The Gyres" to show Yeats at work on one of *New Poems* (1938) because its successive drafts are still to be found in the looseleaf manuscript cover where Yeats wrote them, I think in the order in which he composed.[2] In addition to the drafts of "The Gyres," this manuscript book contains other very late poems, a scrap of dialogue from *Purgatory*, the "Creed," already quoted, on which "Under Ben Bulben" is based, and a trial table of contents for *New Poems*. Yeats dated the final draft of "The Gyres" "April 9." He did not add the year. Mrs. Yeats has dated the poem 1937, and I agree with this dating, since the contents of the book make it certain that Yeats was using it in 1937 and 1938. The drafts of "The Gyres" which I transcribe are items 6, 8, and 10 in this manuscript book. Item 7 is the scrap of dialogue from *Purgatory*, item 9 the table of contents of *New Poems*.

Item 6 is a draft of what is now stanza 3 of "The Gyres." I believe that Yeats wrote this first, and that the whole poem grew out of the comforting idea with which the finished poem ends, that the gyre of history will bring around again those human types that he most admired, "the workman, noble and saint." I suggest that Yeats invented the first two stanzas to stage, so to speak, the thought of the third stanza with which he began.

[Item 6]

× And even as these three to meet it all again
× Search the country sides and find the three
× But then the joy

× When all is broken
Though all be broken, all may yet be whole
× Rocky face [?], if [you] can find these three
× If you

Old rocky face if you can find the three
That can perfect ~~the~~ a work ~~the~~ a life the soul,
× Go seek among the ruined valleys
× Somewhere between the polecat and the owl
× ~~Under~~ Go seek the cobwebs of ~~old~~ dead villages
× Or else between the polecat and the owl
× They may be hidden in old villages
Somewhere among the abandoned villages
Or skulking between the polecat and owl
Upon a mountain among storm tossed [?] trees
Say these all [word undeciphered] or say that we repeat
~~Bring in~~ But bring the craftsman the noble and the saint

[There is another page of jottings for this stanza which I cannot transcribe. Item 8 consists of working drafts of stanzas I and II. These pages have been cancelled entire.]

WHAT MATTER

I

× What matter — wrinkled rocky face look forth
× What's thought too long can be no longer thought

[From the facing page.]

× What's thought? What's thought? Old rocky face look forth
× What's thought too long must be no longer thought

[At this point Yeats marked lines 1 and 2 "stet."]

And blood's irrational streams must wet the earth
Those/ The three perfections ~~have been~~ must be blotted out;
~~But~~ Or here's a metaphor that has more pith
7 Hector is dead and there's a light in Troy
8 We that look on but laugh in tragic joy

II

What matter ~~if~~ that the topless glories drop
Into the mire and blood and take ~~its~~ ~~their~~ the stain
× Or that those sweaty gangsters live on top
× Or that base gangsters ~~are~~ clamber on the top,
× A greater and more gracious time has gone
× For greater and more gracious times have gone

[The next five lines are from the facing page.]

× That all the sweaty gangsters ride on top;
× ~~A~~ For greater and more gracious ~~time has~~ times have gone
What matter if the ~~gangster~~ base man is on top
And blood and mire our ancient [?] glory stain
11 What matter heave no sigh let no tear drop

[Back to original page.]

I sighed for bust or boxes of make up
~~From~~ In ancient tombs and shall not sigh again
What matter — out of the cavern comes a voice
× And that has but a single word rejoice
× And one sole word it cries rejoice.
And all commandment's in that word 'rejoice.'

[Yeats then made three more drafts of his first stanza. He cancelled all of them.]

WHAT MATTER

What's thought too long — old rocky face look forth
What's thought too long can be no longer thought
× And blood's irrational streams must wet the earth
× Those lineaments must all be blotted out

× But here's an image of more pith and worth
Beauty of beauty dies and worth of worth
~~All~~ Then the old lineaments are blotted out
The/ And the irrational ~~stream of blood has wet~~ blood stream wets the earth
For the great gyres have tumbled us about
7 Hector is dead and there's a light in Troy
8 We that look on but laugh in tragic joy

~~What matter~~, ~~what matter~~ Old cavern man, old rocky face look forth
2 Things thought too long can be no longer thought
And beauty dies of beauty, worth of worth
~~Then the old~~ The ancient lineaments are blotted out
× For the irrational blood stream wets the earth
× The irrational stream of blood was wetting earth
The irrational blood stream wets the earth
× For the great gyres have tossed us all about
The ancient/ A furious gyre has tumbled us about
7 Hector is dead and there's a light in Troy
8 We that look on but laugh in tragic joy

1 The gyres! The gyres — old Rocky face look forth
2 Things thought too long can be no longer thought
3 ~~And~~ For beauty dies of beauty, worth of worth
4 ~~The~~ And ancient lineaments are blotted out
The irrational blood stream ~~has wet all~~ begins to wet the earth
Empedocles has tumbled us about
7 Hector is dead and there's a light in Troy
8 We that look on but laugh in tragic joy

[Item 10 is a dated draft of the complete poem.]

I

1 The gyres, the gyres — old rocky face look forth
2 Things thought too long can be no longer thought
3 For beauty dies of beauty, worth of worth
4 ~~All~~ And ancient lineaments are blotted out
5 Irrational streams of blood are staining earth
6 Empedocles has thrown ~~our~~ all things about

7 Hector is dead and there's a light in Troy
8 We that look on but laugh in tragic joy

II

× What matter if blind ~~Fate~~ fury rides ~~on~~ upon the top

[The next line from the facing page.]

What matter though numb nightmare ride on the top
× And blood and mire the [word undeciphered] glory stain

[The next two lines from the facing page.]

× And blood and mire ~~all the rivers~~ the broken buildings stain
10 And blood and mire the sensitive body stain
11 What matter heave no sigh let no tear drop
~~For~~ A greater and more gracious time has gone
~~I sighed for~~ For painted bust or moxes of make up
14 ~~From~~ In ancient tombs I ~~shall not sigh~~ sighed but not again
15 What matter — out of ~~the~~ cavern comes a voice
× And all commandment's in the word rejoice
16 And all it knows is that one word rejoice

III

× Perfection of the work, the life the soul!
Come lineaments of work, conduct and soul
~~Orders that to old~~ Those lovers that to rocky face are dear
Those lovers of horses and of women shall
Out of ~~the~~ some stark oblivion disinter
Dark between the polecat and the owl
Or from the ruined [?] marble sepulchre
~~Artist~~ Workman noble and saint and all ~~things~~ shall run
24 ~~On~~ ~~Round~~ On that unfashionable gyre again.
April 9

Yeats finished "The Gyres" in two typescripts. In TS. 1 stanzas 1 and 2 are exact copies of those stanzas in the dated MS. printed just above. Stanza 3 is a later version than that found in the MS.; perhaps it copies a manuscript which I have not seen. Yeats corrected stanza 3 of TS. 1, but not stanzas 1 and 2. Stanza 3 from TS. 1 is given first as typed and then as corrected, and the same stanza as corrected in TS. 2:

[TS. 1, stanza 3, as typed]

Come lineaments of work, conduct and soul
From dark and bright that Rocky Face holds dear
19 Lovers of horses and of women shall
The Saint, the Noble, Workman, disinter;
Darkness between the pole cat and the owl
Bright marble of a broken sepulchre
Bridles upon the horses, women; all shall run
Upon that old forgotten gyre again.

[TS. 1, stanza 3, as revised]

17 Conduct and work grow coarse and coarse the soul;
From dark and bright that Rocky Face holds dear
19 Lovers of horses and of women shall
The Saint, Noble, and Workman, disinter;
Darkness between the pole cat and the owl
Bright marble of a broken sepulchre;
23 The Workman, Noble and Saint; and all things run
24 On that ~~old~~ unfashionable gyre again

[TS. 2, stanza 3, with Yeats's manuscript revisions]

17 Conduct and work grow coarse and coarse the soul,
18 What matter! ~~Some~~ Those that ~~old~~ Rocky Face holds dear,
19 Lovers of horses and of women, shall
20 From marble of a broken sepulchre
21 Or dark betwixt the polecat and the owl,
22 Or any rich, dark nothing disinter
23 The workman, noble and saint, and all things run
24 On that unfashionable gyre again.

Item 6, the early draft of what became Yeats's third stanza, shows, I believe, how fragmentary, inchoate even, the beginnings of Yeats's poems often were even at the end of his career. There is one slight bit of external evidence for my belief that here indeed is the germ from which the poem grew, the fact that it once stood first in the manuscript book. Since Yeats was working in a looseleaf manuscript cover, and since even when working in a bound manuscript book he often moved both back and forward from the sheet on which he began to write, this fact should be weighted rather lightly. The internal evidence is stronger, however. The whole idea of the poem is stated in the draft lines

> Though all be broken, all may yet be whole
> Old rocky face if you can find the three
> That can perfect a work a life [a] soul

The draft goes on with Rocky Face (in Mrs. Yeats's annotated copy of *Last Poems* Rocky Face is glossed as "Delphic Oracle") searching for the craftsman, noble and saint amid the ruins of civilization so that he may establish them again. Furthermore there is one line in the draft of stanza 1 in item 8 that makes it almost certain that Yeats composed item 6 before he composed item 8: "The three perfections must be blotted out." These bits of evidence, taken together, have led me to believe that Yeats began "The Gyres" by imagining some happier day when the process of history would bring back "the craftsman the noble and the saint," that he began where he now ends.

Item 8 begins with working drafts of stanzas 1 and 2 under the title "What Matter"; it continues with three successive drafts of stanza 1 during the course of which Yeats finishes that stanza. In these drafts both the poetic form and the progression of images Yeats will use in the finished poem emerge. In this draft of stanza 1 and in the draft of stanza 2 that follows, Yeats is experimenting with a seven line stanza with three rhymes. He has not certainly established the pattern of his "a" and "b" rhymes, but has decided to end the stanza with a couplet. The rhyme scheme of stanza 1 is ababacc, of stanza 2 abaabcc; if Yeats had allowed a cancelled line, "For greater and more gracious times have gone," to stand in the drafts of stanza 2 as the fourth line, he would have achieved his eventual ottava rima scheme, abababcc.

Yeats sets a title, then picks up the words of the title, "what matter," to begin his poem. He fills in his decasyllable line with "wrinkled rocky face look forth," where the "r," "c," and "f" sounds form a rather cacophonous pattern. Furthermore, though skin wrinkles, does rock? Yeats cancels this, then tries a daring repetition of "What's thought":

> What's thought? What's thought? Old rockyface look forth
> What's thought too long must be no longer thought.

Yeats cancels this, and marks the lines first written "stet"; he has, however, written a metrical equivalent of the first line of his finished poem and found in "old" the epithet he will retain for "rocky face." We will see Yeats invent his present third line in a later draft; now he uses an early form of line 5 as his third line, "And blood's irrational streams must wet the earth." He continues with the line commented on above, "The three perfections must be blotted out." Perhaps Yeats came to feel that this said too much, that he could achieve a more dramatic statement if he retained the three for his last stanza. Yeats's fifth line seems to take us inside the writing process, so to speak, "Or here's a metaphor that has more pith." Yeats then struck off without blotting a word the couplet with which the first stanza still ends.

The allusion to the burning of Troy at the end of his first stanza brought to mind Marlowe's description, so Yeats begins his second stanza "What matter that the topless glories drop/ Into the mire and blood and take the stain." The echo of Marlowe is followed here by an echo of Yeats's own "Byzantium." No doubt Yeats felt that this was too literary, for when he returned to these lines later in this same draft, he cut the echo of Marlowe. He did this while exploring the possibility of making the American gangster top dog in the age he so disliked. (We have all seen so many gangster movies that it is a relief when this folk myth disappears after several experiments.)

> Or that those sweaty gangsters live on top
> Or that base gangsters clamber on the top
> That all the sweaty gangsters ride on top
> What matter if the ~~gangster~~ base man is on top

While playing with the gangster, Yeats drafts three forms of what is now line 12; he cancels all of them, with the result that a seven line stanza again emerges with a rhyme scheme slightly different from that of the first draft of stanza 1. Yeats continues by writing off his eleventh line in final form. Lines 13–16 fall into place quickly; Yeats will adjust their diction and meter, but their substance is set. Yeats's progress with his second stanza has been remarkable. He has established the progression of images he will retain while cutting out those he does not want, his rhyme words are all in place, he has drafted a line with a "b" rhyme which he will be able to use when he decides on ottava rima form, he has finished line 11.

The first of the three successive drafts of stanza 1 which follow is the crucial one. During the course of this draft Yeats establishes his eight-line stanza, he rearranges his images and adds to them. Yeats composes five lines which come directly from the preceding draft, making a significant change in his fourth draft line when "The three perfections must be blotted out" becomes "Then the old lineaments are blotted out." This says much the same thing in a more suggestive and allusive way, while reserving "the three" for the final stanza; it also uses one of Yeats's favorite words, derived from Blake, rather differently from the way he had used it in writing of Maud Gonne. And when Yeats says in effect that the ancient bodily forms have been blotted out, is he not already on his way to poems and prose works concerned with eugenic reform? He continues with a new form of the line he had invented to introduce his closing couplet, "But here's an image of more pith and worth." It must have been clear to Yeats from the first that he would eventually cancel this line; he does so now, but makes it serve his purposes, for out of it he evolves his third line, which here reads, "Beauty of beauty dies and worth of worth." He then rewords lines 4 and 5 before inserting the gyres in line 6, "For the great gyres have tumbled us about." Their absence up to this point from a poem about the gyres has been rather surprising. Yeats finishes the draft by copying out the couplet which closed the stanza in draft 1.

In the second of these drafts Yeats is still experimenting with his first line. He tries his key words "what matter," which stood at the beginning of stanzas 1 and 2 in an earlier draft, then replaces these by "Old cavern man." He finishes line 2, and gets rid of the inverted syntax in line 3 when he writes "and beauty dies of beauty, worth of worth." In line 4, "Then the old lineaments" becomes "The ancient lineaments"; in line 6, "great gyres have tumbled" becomes "great gyres have tossed" and then "A furious gyre has tumbled us about." Again, there is no change in the concluding couplet.

In the third draft Yeats nearly finishes his first stanza. He makes a final and crucial change in the progression of his images when he moves the gyre from line 6 up to line 1, and repeats it. He has not yet added the title, but that is implied, surely, in this change. His poem will begin with "the gyres" three times repeated. Both the rhetoric and meter of this line repeat a beginning which Yeats tried and abandoned in his earliest draft, where the title "What Matter" was followed by a first line beginning "What's thought? What's thought?" Yeats finishes lines 1–4, revises line 5, and then introduces Empedocles into the space vacated by the gyre, no doubt moved to do so both because of the marvelous sound of the name and because he thought of Empedocles as an exponent of the cyclic tradition.

Item 10, a dated draft of the whole poem, is typical. Yeats finishes stanza 1; he makes good progress toward the final form of stanza 2; he leaves stanza 3, with which he had begun, far from finished. Very often in manuscript versions of Yeats's poems the various parts of a single poem are in various states of finish. The first four lines of stanza 1 had been finished in the preceding draft. Yeats copies these out, then makes an important change in line 5 when he changes "The irrational blood stream begins to wet the earth" to "Irrational streams of blood are staining earth." The revision knocks out two syllables from what had been an awkward thirteener, and the introduction of "staining" provides a link with line 10 of stanza 2. The change in line 6 — "Empedocles has tumbled us about/ Empedocles has thrown all things about" — was made, I feel, to get rid of "us"; the change helps the reader to move easily from the bloodstained present to the statement in the final couplet that such violence is recurrent, hence eternal.

The changes made in stanza 2 will be seen more clearly if we begin by looking at a clean copy of the first draft, with its cancelled fourth line put in place:

> What matter if the base man is on top
> And blood and mire our ancient glory stain
> What matter heave no sigh let no tear drop
> × For greater and more gracious times have gone
> I sighed for bust or boxes of make up
> In ancient tombs and shall not sigh again
> What matter — out of the cavern comes a voice
> And all commandment's in that word 'rejoice.'

In line 9 "Fate," "fury," and finally "numb nightmare" replace the "base man"; "numb nightmare ride on the top" is a powerful, an almost furious phrase, and the line is done except for the excision of "the" from "on the top." In line 10 Yeats introduces an almost miraculous improvement when he replaces "our ancient glory" with "the sensitive body"; the metaphor was weak because an abstraction like "ancient glory" cannot really be stained. Yeats copies out his finished eleventh line and then establishes and slightly changes line 12. In recasting lines 13–14 Yeats introduces an inverted sentence; this is contrary to his usual practice of putting inverted sentences into normal order while revising. I think Yeats made the change primarily to avoid the repetition of "sigh," though it also opened a place for the effective epithet "painted." I suppose that Yeats changed "bust" to "forms" before printing the poem because in Egyptian tombs opened in the 1920's the painted figures were forms. Line 15 is finished when Yeats strikes out "the." Yeats first copies out line 16 from the preceding draft, changing one word; then he recasts the whole line, perhaps because "commandment's" is an awkward elision.

In the draft of stanza 3 that was once item 6 in Yeats's manuscript book, Yeats directed Rocky Face to find the three "That can perfect a work a life [a] soul," either among the abandoned villages of an old culture or from the mountain where they are "skulking between the polecat and the owl." Find them where he might, Rocky Face was to "bring the craftsman the noble and the saint." This roughly expresses the thought of stanza 3 in the finished poem, toward the expression of which Yeats moved in a series of four consecutive drafts. During these drafts Yeats dropped some correlatives (villages, a mountain), he invented a series of new correlatives (broken sepulchre, rich dark nothing, unfashionable gyre), and he provided Rocky Face with agents (lovers of horses and of women) to disinter "the three."

He starts to do this in the draft found at the end of the manuscript dated April 9. First he writes and cancels a line that grows directly out of a line found in the earlier draft: "That can perfect a work a life [a] soul." This now becomes "Perfection of the work, the life the soul!" Since "the three" are notably absent from the two stanzas Yeats has completed, stanzas in which he has magnificently stated the historical and cultural situation which requires the return of "the three," the meaning of this new line is enigmatic. It is enigmatic because it looks too far forward. Not until we finish the stanza do we know that we can achieve the three perfections only if lovers dear to Rocky Face disinter the workman we admire for his work, the noble we admire for his life, and the saint we admire for his soul. Yeats expresses his meaning somewhat more clearly when he writes, "Come lineaments of work, conduct and soul." The repetition of "lineaments" takes us back to line 4: "And ancient lineaments are blotted out," and because it does serve as a useful link between the last stanza and the first. Since "lineaments" as used in this poem clearly means "bodily forms," Yeats is now saying "may the bodily forms associated with right work, right conduct, and right soul come again"; this prepares us for the action described in the remaining lines.

Yeats now largely invents lines 18–23 wherein the lovers dear to Rocky Face "shall disinter" the workman, noble, and saint from a "stark oblivion" foreshadowed by the "dead villages" of the earlier draft. Lines 21 and 22 particularize this stark oblivion. The earlier draft had ended by naming the three; [3] now Yeats names them in line 23, and invents in final form the last line which rounds out his poem by naming the new gyre which will replace the unsatisfactory gyre now operative. At the end of this draft Yeats has finished line 24 and set all his line ends, though in his final draft he will transpose "sepulchre" and "disinter."

Yeats completed stanza 3 in TS. 1 and 2. The three drafts to be discussed are particularly fascinating because in them Yeats reworks the stanza radically without altering any of his line ends. It is as though a terrific disturbance in the center of a pool took place without disturbing the waters on its circumference, or as if a painter completely rearranged the center of a picture while leaving its outer portion unchanged. This is a final proof of Yeats's extreme unwillingness to alter a form he had once set.

In the typed words of TS. 1 Yeats changes the order of his correlatives and slightly changes his meaning. In the dated manuscript Yeats had filled out his form by using "Those lovers" in lines 18 and 19:

> Those lovers that to rocky face are dear
> Those lovers of horses and of women shall;

He had also spread wide the main elements of his clause (lovers shall disinter workman noble and saint). Yeats gets rid of the tautology by slightly changing his detail:

> From dark and bright that Rocky Face holds dear
> Lovers of horses and of women shall . . .

He tightens his spread syntax by inclosing his direct objects ("The Saint, the Noble, Workman") between the two parts of the verb "shall disinter." His solution does not work: the brightness here introduced to contrast with the dark distorts Yeats's meaning; the transposition of "the three" from line 23 to line 20 leaves a gaping hole in line 23 which Yeats fills up anyhow by writing "Bridles upon the horses, women." While trying to fix lines 17–20 Yeats ruins lines

21–24, even in their detail, as when in line 24 he replaces "unfashionable gyre" with "old forgotten gyre."

Yeats accomplishes some of the necessary repairs in his revision of TS. 1. He begins these by inventing a new seventeenth line which still stands: "Conduct and work grow coarse and coarse the soul." This at once summarizes the situation described in stanzas 1 and 2, and points toward the need to disinter "the three" who will demonstrate right conduct, work, and soul. Yeats then tries the effect of naming the three both at line 20 and line 23, with very awkward results. His syntax no longer works, but he has somehow got the three back into his penultimate line where they need to be. A few more changes, the most important being the return to the text of the felicitous epithet "unfashionable," and lines 23 and 24 are done. Yeats has still to rework his syntax and further adjust lines 18, 20, 21, and 22.

In the revised TS. 2 Yeats solves all his remaining problems. He first writes a new and final eighteenth line which begins by repeating the phrase "what matter" for the fourth time. He drops the "dark and bright that Rocky Face holds dear" and fills out the line with "those that Rocky Face holds dear," a reworking of line 18 in the dated manuscript. He finishes lines 20–22 by spreading open still further the two parts of his verb "shall disinter" so that they now frame these lines. Within this frame Yeats rearranges his detail: he revises what had been line 22 to make his now finished twentieth line, and invents new matter for line 22, matter which further describes the enigmatic dark from which "the three" are to be disintered. Stanza 3 is done; the poem is done save for a little touching up of stanza 2.

V

"The Circus Animals' Desertion"

YEATS WROTE the first complete draft of "The Circus Animals' Desertion" in London during November 1937. In this manuscript the first four stanzas are very like the poem we know, save that the key or theme word of the poem, "heart," does not occur at lines 4, 13, and 27. The fifth stanza is quite different from that found in the finished poem. A typescript was made from this manuscript, and though this was corrected the poem remained pretty much as in the manuscript until September 1938 when Yeats went to work on it again and created the poem we know. It was among the last to be finished of his major poems and shows Yeats at work during his last year. The drafts show that Yeats's discipline, his ability to keep at a poem until it came right never deserted him. Since this whole study of Yeats at work on poems is a record of his craftsmanship, a demonstration that he did not write his poems in a trance though some of them began in dream visions, an analysis of the composition of "The Circus Animals' Desertion" brings it to an appropriate close.

Below is a list of the drafts of "The Circus Animals' Desertion," arranged in what I believe to be the order they were written.

MS. 1*a*. An early draft of stanza 1 and part of stanza 2.
MS. 1*b*. Another draft of stanza 1.
MS. 1*c*. Another draft of stanza 2.
MS. 2. A manuscript of the whole poem, dated "London November 1937."
MS. 3. Another draft of stanza 5, later than MS. 2 but earlier than TS. 1.
TS. 1. A transcription of MSS. 2 and 3, with corrections in WBY's hand.
TS. 2. A copy of the corrected TS. 1, with further manuscript corrections. Either WBY or George Yeats has written on it, "corrected Sept. 15."
TS. 3. A transcript of TS. 2 as corrected, with new and very important manuscript changes.
TS. 4. Another copy with further manuscript corrections, and a draft of a new fifth stanza in Yeats's hand. WBY has dated it "corrected Sept 23," and opposite the new draft has written "insert slip X."
MS. 4. Has the heading "Slip X." Two further drafts of stanza 5.

All of these drafts are printed below, and I follow each of them with my comments.

[MS. 1*a*]

× For some
I have sought a theme and sought for it in vain
And sought for it daily for some five weeks ~~now~~ or so
× I that/ perhaps
I am too old — old men alter
× Something resembling happiness they know

× If not happiness itself a show
× Of happiness because do not show
As much of happiness as a man can know
× Their minds are full and they no longer strain
× Like drowning men and [two words undeciphered] strain
× Their minds are too full now for pain and strain
× They have no [two words undeciphered] but the care to sow
For their full minds ~~have~~ may put off pain and strain
And all poetic themes are plants that grow
Out of the necessity of a mind
That were they lacking were but burning sand

[From the verso of this sheet the beginnings of stanza 2.]

A poem that no matter where it ~~goes~~ seems
Is ~~but an allegory~~ allegorical like those ancient shows
Of wretched life, but I set Usheen ride
× And I starved for the bosom of his bride
16 ~~And~~ I starved for the bosom of his faery bride.

[MS. 1*b*]

[From the back of one of the pages of the MS. of "The Municipal Gallery Revisited."]

I have sought a theme and sought for it in vain
I have [sought] it daily for five weeks or so
Perhaps I shall not find it an old man
Perhaps I am [at] last too old a man
~~And~~ I must be ~~content~~ satisfied with fact although
Last winter dream or theme before me ran
~~My~~ As traveling circus all ~~the~~ my beasts on show
× Giraffe and men on stilts or in a chariot
× Woman and lion and the Lord knows what
Giraffe, men on stilts, a high chariot
Giraffe, men upon stilts, or a high chariot
Lion and woman and Lord knows what

[MS. 1*c*]

[Another page of jottings for the second stanza.]

Through those three isles that are in all men's dreams

Through those three ~~islands~~ isles, or ~~allegoric dreams~~ ~~three perfect dreams~~ or allegoric dreams
× A journey dance insatiable [?] blows
× Peace ending wretchedly
Of insatiable [?] joy, insatiable [?] blows
Insatiable [?] peace, ~~three allegoric themes~~ one of those themes
The middle ages put into their shows
Or so I think that set on the ride

[All the above cancelled.]

Yet images were more than life it seems
10 First that sea rider Usheen led by the nose
11 Through three ~~allegorical~~ enchanted islands, allegorical ~~dreams~~
Of the emptiness of joy, battle and repose
× One of those
A summing up of life — one of those themes
The middle ages put in songs and shows
Or so I thought [that] set him on to ride
Starved for the bosom of his faery bride.

Manuscript 1 is, I believe, a very early draft, indeed it may be Yeats's first draft. It resembles other first drafts in its not quite certain exploration of materials and structure, in consisting mostly of cancelled lines, and in being extremely difficult to decipher. Already the stanza pattern of the poem has been determined (ottava rima) and governs what Yeats writes. He has set the a and b rhyme sounds of the finished poem (vain, strain; so, know, show), though only "vain," "so," and "show" persisted. Yeats later abandoned the c rhyme used here (mind, sand). Of the matters explored in the finished first stanza we find only the search for a new theme and Yeats's fear that he is too old to find one. The circus animals are notably absent. In their place we find a statement that poetic themes grow out of the necessity of a mind, which without such growth would be a veritable desert. In the draft on MS. 1b Yeats makes definite progress. The circus animals arrive: Yeats has assembled his materials, and he fills out, though in places rather hurriedly, his intended form. Seven line ends are in place (vain, so, man, although, show, chariot, what), and although no lines are quite finished 1, 2, 3, 7, and 8 are nearly so. Two details in this draft interest me particularly. The first is Yeats's statement that he must be satisfied to have "fact" replace his amazing emblems; it was not until very late in composing the poem that Yeats came to say he must be satisfied with feeling (heart) rather than with the emblems into which he had earlier translated this feeling. The second is the phrase "men upon stilts," both because of the sea-change it undergoes in the later drafts, and because of its anticipation of that rollicking poem, "High Talk."

On the verso of MS. 1a Yeats began work on his second stanza, here telescoped, so to speak, the form not completely filled out. Yeats has decided that the subject of the stanza will be *The Wanderings of Oisin* and his own human situation, that is his longing for love, at the time he wrote it. Yeats has set his rhyme sounds, and the ends of lines 13–16 are in place. Line 16 is done, though Yeats will try other forms of it before finally establishing this form. In MS. 1c Yeats wrote a partial and then a full draft of stanza 2. Yeats now began his stanza by briefly summarizing the action of *Oisin*, and by comparing his allegory with allegories "The middle ages put into their shows." In the full draft Yeats completed his stanza form, set six of his line ends, and completed lines 10 and 11. His preliminary work on this stanza was done.

Manuscript 2, the first surviving draft of the whole poem, has first and second stanzas derived from the drafts just studied. No preliminary drafts of stanzas 3, 4, and 5 seem to have survived, but stanzas 3 and 4 are here more nearly finished than stanzas 1 and 2. It therefore seems certain that earlier drafts of these stanzas, and probably of stanza 5, were made. Though stanza 5 is in this draft more worked over than the others, it contains nothing that Yeats will keep. Yeats tried another draft of this stanza, MS. 3, before having the poem typed.

[MS. 2]

~~TRAGIC TOYS~~
THE CIRCUS ANIMALS' DESERTION

I

1 I sought a theme and sought for it in vain
I have sought it daily for six weeks or so
3 Maybe at last being but ~~an aged~~ a broken man
I must be satisfied with life although ~~contented with this heart~~

[WBY has struck "satisfied with life" then marked it stet.]

5 Winter and summer till ~~this decline~~ old age began
6 My circus animals were all on show,
7 Those stilted boys, that burnished chariot,
8 Lion and woman and the Lord knows what.

II

× Those images ~~were more grand than~~ outglittered life it seems
× For all things counted more than life
× ~~And every toy was~~ Those tragic toys were more than life it seems
9 What can I but enumerate old themes
10 First that sea rider Usheen led by the nose
11 Through three enchanted islands, allegorical dreams
Vain exaltation, battle and repose
A summing up of life ~~one of those themes~~ or so it seems
14 That might adorn old songs or courtly shows
15 ~~Or so I thought~~ But what cared I that set him ~~up~~ on to ride
16 I starved for the bosom of his fairy bride

III

17 And then a counter truth filled out its play
18 *The Countess Cathleen* was the name I gave it
19 She pity crazed had given her soul away
20 But masterful heaven intervened to save it
21 I thought my dear must her own soul destroy
22 So did fanaticism and hate enslave it
23 And this brought forth a dream and soon enough
The dream itself had all my thought and love

IV

And then while Fool and Blindman stole the bread
26 Cuchulain fought the invulnerable sea
Great mysteries there and yet when all is said
28 It was the dream itself enchanted me:
29 Character isolated by a deed
30 To engross the present and dominate memory.
The players and the painted stage took all my love
32 And not those things that they were emblems of.

V

× Why brood upon old triumphs? Prepare to die
× For all those burnished chariots are in flight.
× O hours of triumph come and make me gay;
× Even at the approach of/ For even on/ For on the edge of
~~the~~ unimagined night
× Man has the refuge of his gaiety;
But lonely to the lone; ~~the~~ tents blown away
Women and stilts and chariots all in flight
Man makes a refuge of his gaiety
~~Mocks the approach~~ Even at the approach of unimagined
night
O hour of triumph come and make me gay
A dab of black enhances every white
Tension is but the vigour of the mind,
Cannon the god and father of mankind.
London
November 1937

[MS. 3]

[On a separate sheet WBY wrote another draft of the final stanza which is later than the complete MS. but earlier than TS. 1.]

Why brood upon old triumphs, prepare to die
× Renounce immortality learn to die
The burnished chariot is wheeled ~~away~~ from sight
O hour of triumph come and make me gay
× For though the black velvet of unimagined night
× Comes I have still my gaiety
Even at the approach of unimagined night
Man has the refuge [of his] gaiety
A dab of black enhances every white
Tension is but the vigour of the mind
Cannon the God and father of mankind

Yeats made several interesting changes in this draft of stanza 1 and nearly completed his first eight lines. In line 2 "five weeks" becomes "six weeks," perhaps an indication that draft 1b had been written some days before. Line 3 was greatly improved:

MS. 1b Perhaps I am [at] last too old a man
MS. 2 Maybe at last being but a broken man.

In line 4, when Yeats wrote and cancelled "contented with this heart," he began to explore the central theme of the finished poem, but for some reason backed away from it. "Satisfied with life," which Yeats allowed to stand, is an advance over "satisfied with fact." Line 5 in MS. 1b read

Last winter dream or theme before me ran

when Yeats finished line 5 here he has generalized his statement, removed the accidence of the moment from it

Winter and summer till old age began.

The diction of line 6 has improved amazingly:

MS. 1b As travelling circus all my beasts on show
MS. 2 My circus animals were all on show.

Knowing that the "stilted boys" of line 7 derived from "men upon stilts" adds a new dimension to the meaning of Yeats's epithet. Oisin and Forgael walk upon stilts, so to speak, but they are also stilted in the more usual, metaphoric sense. Lines 1, 3, 5–8 are done, line 2 nearly done, all the line ends are established.

In stanza 2 Yeats also made great progress. In line 9, "more than life" (1c) becomes "more grand than life," then "outglittered life," "counted more than life," "Those tragic toys were more than life." It was no doubt after he had written the phrase "tragic toys" that Yeats tried at the head of this draft the title "Tragic Toys." Yeats finally dropped all of these descriptions of his emblems in order to express again his lack of a new theme. The line, "What can I but enumerate old themes," is a happy introduction to section 2 of the poem. At line 14 the reference to the Middle Ages in the earlier drafts is absorbed in the epithet "old." All the line ends are set; three additional lines are finished (9, 14, 15); line 16 has again the form of the 1a draft.

Since no earlier drafts of stanzas 3 and 4 have come to light, no study of Yeats's progress is possible. Stanza 3 is finished save for one word in line 24; stanza 4 nearly as far along. I have marked line 26 finished, for I feel certain "Cuchulain fought the invulnerable sea" is the reading Yeats intended. His manuscript is unusually clear at this point; there can be no doubt that he wrote "invulnerable." [4] It is inconceivable that Yeats would consciously back off from this into "ungovernable," though that does fill out the meter and works after a fashion. His typist made the mistake, and Yeats may never have noticed it, given the eye's uncanny ability to see what it expects rather than what is on the page. Here and elsewhere, as I show, Yeats's text could be considerably improved by a study of his manuscripts.

Neither in MS. 2 nor 3 does Yeats achieve even an adumbration of his splendid final stanza. In MS. 2 he recapitulates details from earlier parts of the poem, then goes on to introduce a recollection of "Lapis Lazuli" in the play on "gay" and "gaiety." One is reminded by this typical event of how "The Fisherman" haunted section 3 of "The Tower" many years before. Yeats's anticipation of his own death is too baldly expressed, and the last two rather cryptic lines add little to what he has said elsewhere about the role of violence in human life. In MS. 3 Yeats slightly rearranged his materials and even his lines (3 to 5, 5 to 3), but makes no significant progress. He still has trouble managing his persona, and he has not got rid of echoes from earlier poems.

Typescript 1 was transcribed from MSS. 2 and 3. Then Yeats corrected it, particularly the pointing, in his own hand. I print below this characteristic TS. as corrected.

[TS. 1]

THE CIRCUS ANIMALS' DESERTION

1 I sought a theme and sought for it in vain,
2 I ~~have~~ sought it daily for six weeks or so.
3 Maybe at last being but a broken man
I must be satisfied with life, although
5 Winter and summer till old age began
6 My circus animals were all on show,
7 Those stilted boys, that burnished chariot,
8 Lion and woman and the Lord knows what.

9 What can I but enumerate old themes,
10 First that sea-rider Oisin led by the nose
11 Through three enchanted islands, allegorical dreams,
12 Vain ~~exaltation~~ gaiety, vain battle, ~~and~~ vain repose,
A summing up of life, or so it seems,

14 That might adorn old songs or courtly shows;
15 But what cared I that set him on to ride;
16 I, starved for the bosom of his faery bride.

17 And then a counter truth filled out its play,
18 "The Countess Cathleen" was the name I gave it,
19 She, pity-crazed, had given her soul away
But masterful heaven intervened to save it.
21 I thought my dear must her own soul destroy
22 So did fanaticism and hate enslave it
23 And this brought forth a dream and soon enough
The dream itself had all my thought and love.

And then when Fool and Blind Man stole the bread
26 Cuchulain fought the [ungovernable] sea;
Great mysteries there, and yet when all is said
28 It was the dream itself enchanted me:
29 Character isolated by a deed
30 To engross the present and dominate memory.
The players and the painted stage took all my love
32 And not those things that they were emblems of.

× Why brood upon old triumphs, prepare to die
× For all those burnished chariots are in flight,
× What if burnished chariots are put to flight,
× O hour of triumph come and make me gay.
O hour of triumph come and make me gay.
If burnished chariots are put to flight
Why brood upon old triumph; prepare to die
Even at the approach of un-imagined night
Man has the refuge of his gaiety,
A dab of black enhances every white,
Tension is but the vigour of the mind,
Cannon the god and father of mankind.

Yeats finished lines 2 and 12 by correcting TS. 1; the change in line 12 from "exaltation" to "gaiety" is certainly a preparation for stanza 5 of this version. The slight rearrangement of the first three lines of stanza 5 was written out by Yeats and cued into its proper place. Typescript 2 is a copy of TS. 1 as corrected, except that again Yeats has written out the revised beginning of stanza 5 and cued it into place, evidence that those lines were changed after TS. 2 was typed. There is one other manuscript correction: in line 25 "And then when" becomes "And when." With the cancellation of "then" line 25 is finished. More important than these minor changes is the annotation "corrected Sept. 15," probably by George Yeats. (I don't remember Yeats ever putting a period after the abbreviation of a month.) This must mean that TS. 2 represents the state "The Circus Animals' Desertion" had reached in September 1938, ten months after MS. 2 was written.

In TSS. 3 and 4 and in MS. 4 Yeats finished his poem. In TS. 3 Yeats introduces the modal or thematic word of his finished poem when he makes the following changes in his own hand:

4 "satisfied with life" becomes "satisfied with my heart"
13 "A summing up of life" becomes "Themes of the embittered heart" (Yeats first tried another phrase, which I cannot decipher.)
27 "Great mysteries there" becomes "Heart mysteries there"

Yeats then went on to cancel stanza 5, an event for which these changes prepare. He wrote one line of a possible substitute stanza:

Animals and chariots ~~are~~ be still poetic themes.

He also inserted Roman numerals I and II before stanzas 1 and 2 where they are still to be found. Lines 4, 13, and 27 are now finished.

Yeats wrote all the changes noted above into another copy of the poem, which I call TS. 4. At the head of the sheet he experimented further with his title. He cancelled "The Circus Animals' Desertion"; wrote and cancelled "Despair"; wrote "On the Lack of a Theme" and let that stand. He finished line 31 by cancelling "the" before "players" and "painted." He again cancelled stanza 5, wrote a new version of it into the margins of the sheet, and dated it "corrected Sept 23." Here is the new version of stanza 5:

× The faery woman, Cathleen, Fool and Blind Man
× Their cousins and their brothers because complete
33 ~~These processional forms~~ Those masterful images because complete
34 Grew in pure ~~mind but out of what began?~~ intellect but how began
~~Out of~~ From the inanimate sweepings of the street,

Bits of old newspaper, that broken can?
× Or from old rag and bone, that raving slut
From rag and bone, that raving slut
Called Heart and Company. My ladder's gone
And I lie down where all the ladders start
40 In the foul rag and bone shop of the heart.

I think Yeats had invented his splendid final line before he began this draft; the handling of detail in the middle of the stanza seems to point toward it unmistakably. He began by direct allusions to stanzas 2, 3, and 4, then decided to remind his readers of them by two phrases which begin with the demonstrative "those": "Those processional forms/ Those masterful images." No English poet after Spenser has used the allegorical procession so frequently as Yeats; such processions flourish in his poetry from beginning to end. The phrase does evoke *Oisin,* so full of processions, more clearly than *Cathleen* or *On Baile's Strand,* and this may account for the changed reading. Yeats hesitates between "mind" and "intellect" to state the contrast between art and its emotional source, then goes on to explore detail that may be used to describe the rag and bone shop, a process he continues through two later drafts. Yeats in this first draft involves the heart in the rag and bone shop less successfully than later, but his "that raving slut/ Called Heart and Company" does explain what I should have guessed but never had, that the heart keeps the till in the heart's rag-and-bone shop. The ladder that follows, apparently struck off at white heat, is one of Yeats's more complex images. Surely the ladder stands for the pure mind or intellect, the fusing-all-to-one imagination, the faculty which invents the art work. Yeats's splendid final couplet reminds him and us that this art, though a product of pure mind, began of necessity in the accidence of feeling.

Typescript 4 had become so written over that Yeats put in the margin "insert from slip X." I next print Slip X, containing the two final drafts of stanza 5.

[MS. 4]

SLIP X

III

33 Those masterful images because complete
34× Grew in pure mind, but out of what began?

Grew in pure intellect, but ~~where~~ from what began?
~~In this and that~~ ~~Old orange peel~~, ~~dirt~~ Dirt, orange peel, the sweepings of the street
~~Bits of old~~ Old bits [of] newspaper, a broken can,
37 Old iron, old bones, old rags, that raving slut
38 Who keeps the till. Now that my ladder's gone
39 I must lie down where all the ladders start
40 In the foul rag and bone shop of the heart

[WBY cancels the above entire.]

III

33 Those masterful images because complete
34 Grew in pure mind but out of what began?
35 ~~Dirt~~, ~~orange peel~~ A mound of refuse or the sweepings of ~~the~~ a street,
36 Old ~~whiskey bottles~~ kettles, old bottles and a broken can
37 Old iron, old bones, old rags, ~~that~~ the raving slut
38 Who keeps the till. Now that my ladder's gone
39 I must lie down where all the ladders start
40 In the foul rag and bone shop of the heart.

In these final drafts Yeats's progress seems inevitable. He hesitated still between "pure mind" and "pure intellect," finally deciding on "pure mind." He decided also that a general statement followed by detail would put the rag-and-bone shop before us most vividly, and finished line 35 when he wrote "A mound of refuse or the sweepings of a street," then went on to selected detail. He prepares us for the final line by "old bones, old rags," which will be reversed in "rag and bone shop," a device Yeats uses very frequently, and his poem is done except for one word. In line 24 "The dream" became "This dream" sometime before the poem was printed. The new stanza is free of unwanted echoes of his recent work, and Yeats now manages his I-persona in such a way that our thought is transferred from the man Yeats to a phantasmagoric Yeats.

We began to watch Yeats at work upon his poems in 1893; we end in the fall of 1938. In 1893 Yeats's apprenticeship was nearly over; he meticulously completed it shortly after when he reworked his early verse for *Poems*, 1895. Yeats's poetic powers were still as brilliant as ever in September 1938 when he completed "The Circus Animals'

Desertion," though the circle of his activities had necessarily grown narrower.

Yeats was already fully equipped for his sendentary trade when he wrote *The Wind Among the Reeds*, and he never allowed his equipment to rust unused. Early and late he worked at his art strenuously. It is this continued faith in works that in part distinguishes him from lesser poets, that and an unusual ability to stay at a poem until it came right. Yeats himself put it nicely when he quoted from Balzac's *Les Comédiens sans le Savoir* in a little essay which he omitted from *Discoveries:*

Here in Paris, only too often will some artist, seeking Fame that he may have Fortune, seek out some royal road and think to enlarge his stature by identifying himself with some cause, or advocating some system. . . . But while opinion cannot give talent, this mentality spoils it. An artist's opinion ought to be a faith in works.

Such a faith in works Yeats never lost; he made an intense effort, an almost unnatural effort, always to write well.

PART TWO

Plays

AN INTRODUCTION

YEATS'S EARLIEST PUBLICATION was a dramatic poem, The Island of Statues printed in 1885; his creative work closed with his last play, The Death of Cuchulain. Yeats was at work on plays, then, during the whole of his long career; there are twenty-six titles in his Collected Plays, and some have not been collected. In addition to writing these plays, Yeats devoted himself for years to the work of the Abbey Theatre, reading manuscripts, rehearsing and producing plays, raising money, managing. Yeats was, in short, among other things a man of the theater; he had far more practical experience of the theater than any other major writer of our time.

Yeats's apprenticeship as a playwright was long drawn out and exceedingly strenuous. I think it ended in 1910 when Yeats published The Green Helmet. I pick this year because, except for the trifling A Pot of Broth (1904), The Green Helmet is the first of Yeats's plays which was never radically revised after first publication. He reached in The Green Helmet that moment of relative textual stability which he had reached in his poems with The Wind Among the Reeds. Granted that Yeats's texts were never more than relatively stable, still after 1899 he rarely rewrote his poems after their first printing, and the poems he did rewrite were his less important *ones ("*The Hour Before Dawn*"); after 1910 he rarely rewrote plays. He did continue, as everybody knows, to tinker interminably with his early verse, and by 1910 he had not yet put all of his early plays into the form in which we know them. By 1910, however, many of his early plays had been rewritten, and he nearly completed their recasting in the 1913 version of* The Hour-Glass; *after this rewriting the texts of Yeats's early plays except* The King's Threshold *remained reasonably stable. After 1913 Yeats only twice (in* The Resurrection *and* A Full Moon in March) *recast a play after its first printing as he had rewritten nearly all his early plays. Yeats wrote of his plays in* The Bounty of Sweden *"I have altered them so many times that I doubt the value of every passage." But this statement simply is not true of most of his later plays, beginning with* The Green Helmet.

In this study I have avoided the early plays for practical reasons. The textual development of most of the earlier plays through successive printings is extraordinarily complex, and it cannot be fully studied until Colonel Russell Alspach publishes his variorum edition. Furthermore, many of these early plays are so long that a study of their genesis and development would proliferate endlessly, and for many of them, in addition to the successive printed versions, there is a vast accumulation of manuscripts. Manuscript versions of The Countess Cathleen *filled a file drawer when they were in Mrs. Yeats's collection (she has given the manuscripts of Yeats's plays to the National Library of Ireland), and the manuscripts of* The Shadowy Waters *and* Deirdre *are nearly as formidable. When the creative process was so long drawn out as it was with these plays it simply defies description.*

Yeats became a playwright while writing and rewriting a group of plays based largely on Irish legends. These are not particularly original either in form or language. Rather they carry on the efforts of such poets as Browning and Tennyson to write plays based on historic and legendary material, though I think Yeats's plays, at least in their final form, are far more viable theatrically than those of his predecessors. Yeats begins to move toward a dramatic form at once more lyric and more personal with the 1906 version of On Baile's Strand *and the 1907 version of* The Shadowy Waters, *both essentially the versions that we know. Then in 1910 with* The Green Helmet, *which Yeats described as "an heroic farce," he invented a* highly original dramatic form. He used this form with great success on two later occasions for The Player Queen and The Herne's Egg, both farces and both heroic. Between 1910 and 1916 Yeats wrote no new plays, though he did revise four of his old ones (The Countess Cathleen, The Land of Heart's Desire, Cathleen ni Houlihan, 1912; The Hour-Glass, 1913). In the winter and spring of 1916 he wrote and produced At the Hawk's Well; in this play for dancers Yeats invented his most characteristic and original dramatic form.

I begin my study with At the Hawk's Well; continue with The Words upon the Window-pane, written 1930; The Resurrection, written 1925–31; A Full Moon in March, written 1934–35; and Purgatory, written 1938. These plays are among the best Yeats wrote and they are of different sorts, illustrating the range of his dramatic talent. In At the Hawk's Well Yeats adapted the Noh drama to his own special purposes; in The Resurrection, with great difficulty he dramatized a philosophical question; in The Words upon the Window-pane he explored the realistic mode. In A Full Moon in March and Purgatory Yeats reached the height of his powers as a dramatist. With the plays as with the poems, my choice of texts has to an extent been governed by the manuscripts available; for example The Dreaming of the Bones (1919) seems to me a better play than At the Hawk's Well, but there are only a few partial manuscripts of it at the National Library of Ireland.

i

The process Yeats followed in writing a play was similar to the process he followed in writing a poem. Yeats first wrote out the subject of a poem in prose; he then elaborated this subject in successive drafts until he had created a poem that satisfied him. When working on a play he began with what he called a "scenario." These are always in prose and are usually very roughly written. Yeats had a visionary mind, and his scenarios record visions of a dramatic action, sometimes intense visions. Yeats sees in his mind's eye, as it were, a dramatic action unfolding before him in a theater. Some of the scenarios are short; this is true of those of The Resurrection and A Full Moon in March. Others, for example the scenarios of The Words upon the Window-pane and Purgatory, are longer and fully develop the plays that grew out of them. Just as Yeats's subjects for poems sometimes do not fully anticipate the poems that will develop out of them, so too his scenarios do not always accurately forecast the play. This is notably true of the two scenarios for The Resurrection. When Yeats had trouble with a play, he would start again by writing new scenarios; many quite different scenarios of The Player Queen have survived. A successful scenario states the theme of the play, begins to develop the principal characters, outlines the action, suggests the staging, and sometimes begins to develop the dialogue.

Once he had written a scenario that satisfied him, Yeats would begin to draft his play. First drafts were usually in prose even though Yeats intended the finished play to be in verse. Again, these first drafts are roughly written; many words are omitted and the text is very lightly punctuated. In them Yeats begins to develop the action and the characterization, to work out the staging in some detail, and to invent the language of the finished play. Sometimes Yeats wrote more than one prose draft even of a play that he intended to put into verse; there are two prose versions of A Full Moon in March, the second so finished as to suggest that Yeats had not yet decided to make this a play in verse. Usually with plays in verse Yeats began his versification with the second draft; he did this while writing At the Hawk's Well. The extent to which the words of the prose draft are used in the verse differs markedly in two of the verse plays studied below: Yeats uses much of the prose draft of At the Hawk's Well in his verse, relatively little in A Full Moon in March.

In early drafts Yeats usually worked out the central action of his play and did not interrupt his work on this to compose any contrasting lyrics he may have intended to use. He will often indicate where a lyric is to occur, but he usually composed these separately, at the end of his manuscript or elsewhere. In later drafts Yeats slowly assembled his play, so to speak, and continued to refine his language and enlarge his stage directions. He wrote draft after draft until he had produced a manuscript that was a satisfactory dramatic statement of his subject in language suited to the voice of the actor and the ear of the listener.

Yeats then had his play typed and, if its subject was not too outrageous of Irish sensibilities, produced. During rehearsals he frequently made changes in his text; a record of the changes made during the rehearsals of At the Hawk's Well will be found in the discussion of that play. Some fifteen of Yeats's plays were produced *before they were printed, a certain indication that Yeats whenever possible wished to see his plays before completing his revision of the text. Rather soon after production Yeats would have his plays printed, often in a magazine or in whatever book was being planned by the Cuala Press at that moment. Few of the later plays were drastically revised after first printing. Rather Yeats would touch them up and include them in collections such as* Four Plays for Dancers *(1921),* Plays and Controversies *(1923), and* Wheels and Butterflies *(1934). In such collections he provided many elaborate commentaries that have wholly disappeared from* Collected Plays. *These discuss the staging of the play, its meaning, or its relation to Yeats's System. For many of the dance plays, Yeats had special music composed. This he would include in such collections.*

6

At the Hawk's Well

DURING the years 1913–16 Yeats spent part of each winter at Stone Cottage with Ezra Pound — their association is pleasantly reflected in Canto LXXXIII. Pound was editing Ernest Fenollosa's translations of certain Noh plays, and he introduced Yeats to the Noh drama. This was an event of great moment in the development of Yeats's dramatic work, for after study of the Noh drama Yeats invented a new dramatic form, the play for dancers. Yeats worked out this form while writing and producing *At the Hawk's Well* during the winter and spring of 1915–16. His excitement over his invention is reflected in the essay he wrote in April 1916 (*Essays and Introductions,* p. 221) for Pound's *Certain Noble Plays of Japan:* "With the help of Japanese plays 'translated by Ernest Fenollosa and finished by Ezra Pound,' I have invented a form of drama, distinguished, indirect, and symbolic, and having no need of mob or press to pay its way — an aristocratic form." Indeed Yeats's essay, written while he was rehearsing *At the Hawk's Well* and having it produced on April 2 and 4, 1916, is as much concerned with his own venture as with the Noh drama. He felt that after years of experiment he had finally found what he liked to call "the theatre of beauty."

Most of Yeats's plays written after 1916 are either plays for dancers, or make use of some of the devices found in the plays for dancers. In a play for dancers the few main characters are masked; they are involved in a highly symbolic action; the climax of the play is expressed by a dance; a chorus of two or three musicians, not involved in the action, will sing or chant commentaries to a simple musical accompaniment and sing or speak lyrics at the opening of the play, at intervals in its action, and at its close; they open and close the play by unfolding and folding a cloth. The other plays for dancers — *The Only Jealousy of Emer* (1919), *The Dreaming of the Bones* (1919), and *Calvary* (1921) — use all of these devices, though the dance is incidental in *Calvary* and is replaced by choreographic movements around the stage in *The Dreaming of the Bones*. Three of Yeats's later plays, *The Cat and the Moon* (1924), *The King of the Great Clock Tower* (1934), and *A Full Moon in March* (1935) are essentially plays for dancers, though in each of them the form invented for *At the Hawk's Well* is slightly modified. The First Musician takes part in the action of *The Cat and the Moon*, and Yeats does not begin or end these plays with the unfolding and folding of a cloth. Elements of the play for dancers are found in *The Player Queen* (masked actors, lyric interludes, dance), *The Herne's Egg* (choreographic movements, dance), and *The Death of Cuchulain* (the climax of the play is expressed by a dance, three musicians close the play). Indeed of Yeats's later plays only *The Words upon the Window-pane* and *Purgatory* show no influence of the play for dancers. In *At the Hawk's Well* Yeats made a new beginning as a playwright.

The materials available for study of the composition of this play are unusually complete, though no scenarios have survived. They include the following manuscripts and typescripts, which taken together constitute MS. 8773 at the National Library of Ireland. I have arranged these materials in what I believe to be their progressive order and numbered them. They are not in this order at the National Library. All of the manuscripts are in Yeats's hand.

- MS. 1. A prose draft of the play, with the title "The Well of Immortality."
- MS. 2. A verse draft based directly on MS. 1, with the same title.
- MS. 3. Drafts of lyrics and an expanded version of the climax.
- TS. 1. The author's prompt copy, with Yeats's manuscript revisions, and with annotations by Allan Wade, Edmund Dulac, and Ezra Pound.
- MS. 4. (Mixed MS. and TS.) Further revision of TS. 1.
- TS. 2. A revision of the opening speeches of the Musicians, labelled "Second version."
- MS. 5. Another revision of these opening speeches.

It is possible by studying these manuscripts to reconstruct most of the process Yeats went through in composing *At the Hawk's Well:*

He wrote, in prose, a draft of the central action of the play, that is of the cheating of the Old Man and Cuchulain (MS. 1); he turned this into blank verse (MS. 2); he wrote the lyrics to be inserted in the dialogue and an expanded version of the climax of the play (MS. 3); he had the play typed and began to rehearse it, during rehearsals he made changes both in the text and the action (TS. 1); he made further revisions of the opening of the play, of the Old Man's description of the woman of the Sidhe, and of the end of the play (MS. 4); he composed two more versions of the opening of the play, which he rejected in favor of the version found in MS. 4 (TS. 2 and MS. 5).

If TS. 1 and MS. 4 are combined, the resulting text is almost word for word that published by the Cuala Press in November 1917 in *The Wild Swans at Coole*. Though this version was published after the play had appeared in *Harper's Bazaar* (March 1917) and *To-day* (June 1917), it is the earlier version and Yeats introduced new revisions into the *Harper's Bazaar* text. No manuscripts of these revisions have survived. Subsequent printings of *At the Hawk's Well* are all based on the *Harper's Bazaar* text.

i

Manuscript One

ALTHOUGH NONE SEEM TO HAVE SURVIVED, Yeats must have written one or more scenarios for *At the Hawk's Well*, for in the prose draft of the play which follows the characters have been invented, the action entirely determined, and Yeats has decided to use a chorus of musicians. The play had been fully planned, that is, before Yeats began to write MS. 1. In writing first a prose draft of a play Yeats, as we have seen, is following his usual practice. The manuscript printed below is typical of such first drafts, being roughly written and wordy. I have edited it by supplying obvious omissions, by putting the stage directions in italics and the speakers' names in small caps, and by supplying most of the punctuation.

[MS. 1]

THE WELL OF IMMORTALITY

Chorus (2) spreads black cloth. When it is taken away Girl is sitting by square cloth to show where well is.

CHORUS. (*Singing*) The night is coming on; the mountain side is darkening. The leaves of the hazel have fallen, driven by the autumn [winds], and half choked up the dry bed of the well. And too weary with her work clearing the well, the guardian of the fountain sits alone upon the stone margin. Nearby, stirred by the falling wind, the dry leaves rustle the green, and the great heap stirs and flutters. She sits with heavy eyes, looking upon the ground. (*Change by the singer*) Now comes the Old Man, he who has for so many years sought the well [of] immortal life in vain, with a bundle of sticks to light his fire, to warm him in the cold night. He too is weary, he is some tired man, and he [is] shivering at the chilly wind that blows from the distant sea. Now that he has set the sticks in order he makes a light, whirling his fire stick, and now the tinder catches, and now the fire leaps up. Soon now it will cast its light upon rocks, and upon the edge of the empty well.

OLD MAN. So you have not a word. You do not say 'are you tired of gathering all those sticks? Have they made your fingers very cold?' No, not a word out of you. Yesterday you spoke three or four times. You said 'the well was full of leaves; that the wind was from the west; or that if it rained there would be mud.' Today you do not speak at all. (*Looks at her*) Your eyes are dazed and heavy today. If the Sidhe must have a guardian of the well to keep the cattle from making it dirty and the leaves from filling it, why do they not choose somebody who would talk and be pleasant, if it were only once in the week. Do you know anything? Your eyes had just that glassy look last [time] the water ran in the well. (*Shakes her*) You will not answer. My God, none of them know anything. Speak – not a word. Ah, there is someone coming. I can see him on the path below. How can he hope to see the bubbling of the water and to dip down his head and drink, when I have never seen it and drunk, who have been waiting here for so long.

CHORUS. A beautiful young man climbs the hill. He comes up as from the sea, and he carries a spear in his hand. His clothes are strange. Surely he comes from over sea. The wind blows in his hair, the wind out of the sea. Is he a man as we are, [or] one of the Sidhe who haunt this mountain side?

Cuchulain enters

OLD MAN. Who are you who come to this unlucky place? By your clothes, by the gold upon your head and upon your feet, I judge not one of those who have found the world evil.

CUCHULAIN. Cuchulain, son of Sualtim.

OLD MAN. That violent and turbulent man. What then has brought you across the sea from Ireland? Men say that you are mad [?] after the shedding of blood, and after women. Here are no fair women.

CUCHULAIN. If you are a native of these parts, as it seems, you perhaps can lead me to the place I seek. There is a well in this country, I have been told, sacred to the Sidhe, and he who drinks of that well remains young forever. It lies, they say, under hazel trees and great stones, and is guarded over [by a] young girl.

OLD MAN. Are there not hazel trees before your eyes, and great stones, and yonder is a young girl?

CUCHULAIN. But here is no well — nothing but a hollow place among the stones half full of withered leaves.

OLD MAN. Did you think that so great a gift was found so easily, that all you need do was to cross the sea and climb a mountain side? Oh folly of youth. Maybe for you as for me it will be always dry.

CUCHULAIN. Is there then some moment when it fills?

OLD MAN. Yes, a secret moment; only the Sidhe know that moment and it [is] soon over.

CUCHULAIN. I will stand here and wait. Why should the luck of Sualtim's son desert him now? Never have I had long to wait for anything.

OLD MAN. No, go from this accursed place. This place belongs to me, that girl there, and to the Sidhe, deceivers of men.

CUCHULAIN. Who are you who speak against the holy Sidhe? May their name be blessed.

OLD MAN. One whom the Sidhe have always cheated. Fifty and more years ago I came hither, as young as you are, my hair upon my shoulders and a spear in my hand. The well was dry and I sat down and waited. I knew — one had told me as [I] tell you — that it filled at some secret hour. I waited a long while, never going out of sight of the well, snaring birds for my food and making my fire with the sticks of the hazel. Once when I woke from sleep I found the stones wet — the hour had passed. Again I waited, and after many months I was sitting on that stony rim and fell asleep at broad noon sitting bolt upright, and while I slept it bubbled. Then I knew it was the malice of the Sidhe. It was they who put sleep upon me. Since then I have seen [it] dry and seen the stones wet many times, but always it is dry while I am awake. But I still watch, hoping they will relent, or that I can defy them and keep my lids open, and live forever.

CUCHULAIN. They will not put me asleep. If I become drowsy, I will drive this spearhead into my foot.

OLD MAN. Do not do that. The foot is very quick to feel pain. Better go away and leave the well to me. It belongs [to] the old and all that is withered.

CUCHULAIN. Have I not said I stay?

Guardian gives the cry of a hawk

There is that bird again.

OLD MAN. There is no bird near.

CUCHULAIN. I had thought I heard the cry of a hawk. As I came up the mountain side from the sea, a great hawk swept down suddenly out of the skies. It was larger than any hawk in the house where I keep my hawks — I have never had upon my wrist so great a bird. It swept by close to my head as though to strike me, but I drove it off. It flew a little way, and then in the midst of a smooth place lit upon a rock. I threw a stone at it and it flew off, and then lit upon another rock. I followed it, but found it was leading me away from the path. If I had followed longer, night would have come on before I had found this place.

OLD MAN. That was the terrible [one] — the woman of the Sidhe herself. She is always flitting upon the mountain side. Go before she has you in her power. She will cast a curse upon you. Year after year misfortune will come upon you. Perhaps it will be never to love a woman and not lose her; perhaps she will kill your children. You will find them dead, with the mark on them through which the beak of a hawk has torn them, or perhaps she will turn your own hand against them.

CUCHULAIN. Have you made a bargain with her to drive all who come away? You are so dried up — as dry as these leaves — you do not seem to belong to life. (*Cry again*) There is that cry again. It was that women who made [it]. Why does she cry like a hawk?

OLD MAN. No no — it was the terrible one herself, through the woman's mouth. Now I know why all day she has been so stupid. Look how she begins [to] shiver. Her eyes are dazed. The terrible [one] is taking possession of her. Three times have I seen her like that before, and afterwards she knew nothing about it. Thought she had been asleep. Awoke suddenly, and began sweeping the leaves out of [the] well, but the leaves were wet. The water had come. The water will come now in a moment. I am an old man. If I do not drink it now, I shall not live till it comes again. Maybe there will not be enough for two.

CUCHULAIN. Do not fear old man. I will dip my helmet in the water, and even if there are but a few drops we share them with one another. I will drink [?] my half and then I will give you the helmet.

OLD MAN. I know you will drink it. Will you swear to let me drink first? But believe me, it is better for you to go away. You are young, you can come again some other year. O do not look at her. I will cover my eyes, I cannot bear it. It is not the girl's eyes that are looking at me. (*He covers his face, and is soon asleep*)

CUCHULAIN. Why do you look at me with the eyes [of] a hawk? Goddess, or bird or woman you shall not draw me from this. (*He sits down by well*) Dance on, you are like the lapwing who would draw the hunter from her nest, but I shall not leave this place till, bird, I am immortal as you are.

Chorus describes first part of dance

CUCHULAIN. (*Who has risen slowly to his feet*) Hawk, hawk, you shall be perched upon this wrist whether you will or no. Some that were perched upon it were called queens.

Chorus continues description of dance. How they go from rock to rock on the mountain side. Is it hate or is it love? Sometimes she leads him near the fountain, and then away. The fountain bubbles. At that moment the woman [four words undeciphered] *breaks from him and runs out. He goes half way to the fountain, then hears the cry of the hawk and runs out after the woman. The Old Man gets up and goes to well.*

OLD MAN. Again, again I am cheated. The well is empty again. It came and emptied while I slept. Oh accursed Sidhe, accursed Gods — so you have deluded me all my life long.

CUCHULAIN. (*returning*) She has fled from me; she has hidden herself somewhere among the rocks.

OLD MAN. Fool, she has led you from the fountain. Look, the stones and the leaves are dark where the water has been, and yet there is not a drop to drink.

CUCHULAIN. What is that sound upon the hill — those cries, those crashing spears?

OLD MAN. She is rousing against you the fierce women of the hills, they that carry shield and sword. Eofe and all her troop. Never till you lie in your grave will you know rest.

CUCHULAIN. Again the clash of arms, the wild cries.

OLD MAN. Do not go. The mountain is accursed. I do not deceive you now — I have nothing more to lose. Stay here with me.

CUCHULAIN. I will face whatever fate is before me. I come, Cuchulain, son of Sualtim, comes. (*He goes out.*)

The Chorus sing while they place the cloth before Old Man and well.

CHORUS. Accursed the life of man. Between passion and emptiness what he longs for never comes. All his days are a preparation for what never comes.

At the end of the manuscript Yeats wrote a draft of part of the song which eventually was used to open the play:

I sing of the desolate places
And men that have their fair share
The palour of ivory faces
Their lofty desolate air
Have travelled until they die.
At the day's close they but find
A well long choked up and dry
And boughs long stripped by the wind.

The stripped leaves fall from the tree

The manuscript breaks off at this point.

In this prose draft Yeats fully works out his central action: Whether one pursues wisdom actively, or passively awaits its coming, whether he tries with Cuchulain to force fate or tries with the Old Man to endure it, the result is the same — frustration and pain. Yeats has invented a fable to express once again an idea that haunted him all his life, "All [man's] days are a preparation for what never comes." The characters too — Yeats would have thought of them as "persons"

— are fully worked out; they are emblems of the "passion" (Cuchulain) and "emptiness" (Old Man) between which man "longs for . . . what never comes." Already they are partly characterized by the speech assigned them: the Old Man is wordy and garrulous, surely by intention, whereas Cuchulain speaks more directly.

The form of the play has been planned. A Chorus of two musicians open and close the play by covering the acting area with a cloth. At the close of the play they sing while doing this, and Yeats has suggested the thought of the lyric they will sing: "Accursed the life of man. Between passion and emptiness what he longs for never comes. All his days are a preparation for what never comes." The musicians describe the setting and the characters, and at the climax of the play describe the symbolic dance.

And yet much remains to be done. The language of the prose draft is very flat in places and needs to be revised: "If you are a native of these parts, as it seems, you perhaps can lead me to the place I seek" and at the climax of the play "I will face whatever fate is before me." As the drafts progress Yeats reduces Cuchulain to a universal role to such a degree that I have always doubted whether *At the Hawk's Well* should be thought of as one of the Cuchulain plays. He becomes simply "Young Man" in the speech tags of the finished play; though he names himself twice, he there approaches the anonymity of the "Old Man." The masking of the principal characters completes this universalizing. Unfortunately the surviving manuscripts do not show just when Yeats decided to mask his characters, for the fact that the principal characters wear masks (we know from Wade's *Bibliography* that they did in the original production — see Item 119) is not stated in any of the texts preceding the one printed in *Harper's Bazaar*. This taken together with Yeats's uncertainty how the dance is to be used — is it to be staged or merely described by the Chorus? — suggests that his collaboration with Edmund Dulac who made the masks had not yet begun, and that he did not know Michio Ito would be available to perform the dance.

ii

Manuscript Two

YEATS HAD TRANSLATED THIS PROSE into verse by the time he wrote the draft printed below, which strikes me as much too finished to be Yeats's first draft in verse. Though many of the lyrics are still missing, the dialogue between Cuchulain and the Old Man is virtually done; indeed 161 of its lines are in the first printed form. One noticeable thing about this draft is the extent to which the words of the prose version appear in the verse. To call attention to this I have italicized several passages where the verbal correspondence is particularly striking.

[MS. 2]

THE WELL OF IMMORTALITY

Chorus enters with black cloth

FIRST VOICE. The dry leaves fall from the tree
18 The sun goes down in the west
SECOND VOICE. But the heart knows all that shall be
The heart beats on without rest.
FIRST VOICE. 21 Night falls
22 The mountain side grows dark
23 The withered *leaves of the hazel*
24 *Half choke the dry bed of the well*
25 The *guardian of the* well is sitting
Upon the old gray stones at its side
27 Worn out from raking its dry bed
28 Worn out from gathering up the leaves
Her head is bowed — her heavy eyes
29 Know nothing or but look upon stone
31 The wind that blows out of the sea
32 Turns over the heaped-up leaves at her side
33 They rustle and diminish.
[SECOND] VOICE. 39 That old man climbs up hither
40 Who has been watching by this well
41 These fifty years.
42 He is all doubled up with age
43 The old thorn trees are doubled so
44 Among the rocks where he is climbing
He has a *bundle of* dry *sticks*
45 He has made a little heap of leaves
46 He lays the dry sticks on the leaves
Shivering with cold he has taken up
Fire Stick and socket from its hole

49 He whirls it round to get a flame
And now the dry sticks catch the fire
51 *And now the fire leaps up* and shines
52 Upon the hazels and the *empty well*

BOTH TOGETHER. 'I alone cannot sleep' the heart cries
36 'And the wind, the salt wind, the sea wind
We alone under the skies
We alone — being blind.'

53 O wind, O salt wind O sea wind
Let me sleep cries the rocky gray steep (the gray rocks of the steep)
Let me sleep cries the heart and the mind
I am old and would sleep

OLD MAN.
57 Why don't you speak to me. Why don't you say
58 'Are you not weary *gathering those sticks,*
59 Are not your *fingers cold.*' You have not one word
60 While *yesterday you spoke three times.* You said
61 '*The well is full of* hazel *leaves,*' you said
62 '*The wind is from the west,*' and after that
63 'If there is rain — it's likely there'll be mud.'
64 Today you are as stupid as a fish
65 No worse, worse being less lively and as dumb

Goes near

Her eyes are *dazed and heavy — if the Sidhe*
67 *Must have a guardian* to clean out the well
And drive the cattle off — they might choose someone
69 That can be pleasant and companionable
70 Once in the day. Why do you stare like that?
71 You had that *glassy look* about the eyes
72 Last time it happened. Do you *know anything?*
73 It is enough to drive an old man crazy
74 To look all day upon these broken rocks
And ragged thorns, and at one stupid face
76 And speak and get no answer.

CUCHULAIN. Then speak to me
77 For youth is not more patient than old age
78 And I have trod the rocks for half a day

79 Nor found what I am looking for.

OLD MAN. Who speaks

80 Who comes so suddenly into this place

81 Where nothing thrives — If I may judge by the gold

Upon head and feet, and glittering in your dress

83 You are not of those that hate the living world.

YOUNG MAN. 84 I am named Cuchulain — I am Sualtim's son

86 I have an ancient house beyond the sea.

OLD MAN. I have [heard] that name about a shepherd's fire

What mischief brings you hither, for they say

That you are crazy to shed the blood of men

And crazy after women.

YOUNG MAN. A rumour brings me

A story told over the fire towards dawn

91 I rose from table, found a boat, spread sail

92 And with a lucky wind under the sail

93 Crossed waves that have seemed charmed and found this shore

OLD MAN. 94 There is no house to sack among these hills

Nor women to be carried off

CUCHULAIN. *If you are native* here, and that rough tongue

97 Matches the barbarous spot — you can it may be

98 Lead me to what I seek, a well wherein

99 Three hazels drop their nuts and withered leaves

100 And where a solitary girl keeps watch

101 Among gray boulders. He who drinks, they say,

102 Of that miraculous water lives forever.

OLD MAN. And are there not before your eyes at this moment

104 Gray boulders and a solitary girl

105 And three stripped hazels?

CUCHULAIN. *But there is no well*

OLD MAN. 106 Can you see nothing yonder

CUCHULAIN. I but see

107 A *hollow among stones half full of leaves*

OLD MAN. And do *you think so great a gift were found*

109 By no more toil than spreading out a sail

110 And climbing a steep hill — *Oh folly of youth*

111 Why should that hollow place fill up for you
112 Are you a better man than I who have lain in wait
113 For more than fifty years to find it empty
Or but to watch the stupid wind of the sea
115 Drive round the perishable leaves.

CUCHULAIN. So it seems
There is some moment when it fills with water

OLD MAN. A *secret moment* that the Holy Sidhe
118 That dance upon the desolate mountain know
119 And not a living man, and when it comes
120 The water has scarce plashed before it is gone

CUCHULAIN. 121 *I will stand here and wait — why should the luck*
122 *Of Sualtim's son desert him now, for never*
123 *Have I had long to wait for anything.*

OLD MAN. 124 *No go from this accursed place — this place*
125 *Belongs to me, that girl there* and those others
126 *Deceivers of men.*

CUCHULAIN. And who are you who rail
127 Upon those dancers that all others bless

OLD MAN. 128 One whom the dancers cheat — I came like you
129 When young in body and mind, and blown
130 By what had seemed to me a lucky sail
131 *The well was dry _I sat* upon its edge
132 I waited the miraculous flood. I waited
133 While the years passed and withered me away
134 I have *snared the birds for food* and eaten grass
And drunk the rain, neither in dark or shine
136 Wandered too far away to have heard the plash
137 And yet the dancers have deceived me — thrice
138 I have awakened from a sudden sleep
139 To find the stones were wet.

CUCHULAIN. My luck is strong
140 It will not leave me waiting nor will they
141 That dance among the stones *put me asleep*
142 If I grow drowsy I can pierce my foot.

OLD MAN. No do not pierce it — the foot is tender
144 It feels pain much, but find your sail again
145 And *leave the well to me* for it belongs

146 To *all that's old and withered.*

CUCHULAIN. No, I stay

(*Girl gives cry of a hawk*)

147 There is that bird again.

OLD MAN. *There is no bird.*

CUCHULAIN. 148 It sounded like the sudden *cry of a hawk*
149 But there's no wing in sight. As I came hither
A hawk *swept down out of the sky*
151 And though I have good hawks, the best in the world
I fancied I have none so big — it flew
153 As though it would have torn me with its beak
154 Or blinded me, smiting with that great wing.
155 I had to draw my sword to drive it off
156 And after that it flew from rock to rock
157 I pelted it with stones a good half hour
158 And just before I had turned the big rock there
159 And seen this place, it seemed to vanish away.
160 Could I but find the means to bring it down
161 I'd hood it.

OLD MAN. *The woman of the Sidhe herself*
The mountain witch, the unappeasable one
In one or another shape, now hawk or wolf
Or panic striken deer, as her mood takes her.
163 *She is always flitting upon this mountain side*
To allure or to destroy — Go from this place
Before she takes you in her grip, before
She has put a lifelong curse upon you.
172 Those that have long to live should fear her most
173 The old are cursed already — That curse may be
174 Never to win a woman's love and keep it
175 Or always to mix hatred in the love
176 Or it may be that she *will kill your children*
177 That you will find them, their throats torn and bloody
178 Or you will be so maddened that you kill them
179 With *your own hand.*

CUCHULAIN. Have you been set down there
180 To threaten all who come and scare them off

181 You seem as *dried up as the leaves* and sticks
182 As though you had no part in life
(*Girl gives hawk cry.*)
That cry
183 There is that cry again — *that woman made it*
184 But *why does she cry out as the hawk* cries.
OLD MAN. 185 It was her mouth and yet not she that cried
The terrible one cried out behind her mouth
187 And *now I know why she has been so stupid*
188 All the day through and had such heavy eyes.
Look at her shivering, the terrible one
190 Is slipping through her veins — she is possessed.
191 Who knows whom she will murder or deceive
192 Before she awakes in ignorance of it all
193 And gathers up the leaves? But they will be wet
194 The water will have come and gone again.
195 That shivering is the sign. O get you gone
At any moment now I will hear it bubble
197 If you are good you will leave it. I am old
198 And if I do not drink it now will never.
199 I have been watching all my life and maybe
200 Only a little cupful will bubble up.
CUCHULAIN. I'll *dip my helmet in* — we shall both drink
202 *And even if there are but a few drops*
203 Share them.
OLD MAN. But swear that I may drink the first
204 The young are greedy and if you drink the first
You'll drink it all. Why do you look at her?
206 She has felt your gaze and turned her eyes on us
207 I cannot bear her eyes — they are not of this world
They are no girl's eyes — they are the terrible one's.
(*Covers head*)
CUCHULAIN. *Why do you look at me with the eyes of a hawk*
210 I am not afraid of you, bird, woman, or witch
(*He goes and sits down by well which the girl has left.*)
And do what you will *I shall not leave this place*
212 *Till I* have grown immortal like yourself.

(*Chorus and dance*)

Hawk, hawk you shall be perched upon this wrist
Whether you will or no — Some that perched there
Have been *called queens.*

(*Dance and chorus*)

[OLD MAN.] The *well is empty* yet the stones are wet
232 The water flowed *and emptied while I slept*
Again I have been deluded — accursed ones
233 *You have deluded me my whole life* through
234 Accursed dancers you have stolen my life

CUCHULAIN. (*entering*)
236 *She has fled from me* and hidden in the rocks

OLD MAN. 237 She has but *led you from the fountain* — Look!
238 *The stones and leaves are dark where* it has flowed
239 *Yet there is not a drop to drink.*

CUCHULAIN. What are those cries
240 What is the sound that runs along the hill
241 Who are they that beat a sword upon a shield.

OLD MAN. 242 She has roused up the *fierce women of the hills*
243 *Eofe and all her troop,* to take your life
244 And never till you are lying in the earth
245 Can *you know rest.*

YOUNG MAN. *The clash of arms again.*

OLD MAN. 246 O *do not go — the mountain is accursed*
247 Stay with me I have nothing more to lose
248 *I do not now deceive you.*

YOUNG MAN. I will face them
249 He comes, *Cuchulain, son of Sualtim comes.*

(*He goes out.*)

Yeats made few changes in the matter of the play while casting prose into verse. He does not begin with the song composed at the end of MS. 1, which in revised form opens the finished play; the play now opens with four lines of a new song. The opening description is followed by a lyric which the two voices speak together, and Yeats indicates where he will introduce further lyrics at the climax of the play when both the Old Man and Cuchulain miss drinking the water that will make them immortal. Yeats omits the description of Cuchulain climbing the mountain found in MS. 1, perhaps because he was planning to speak of it in the opening song, and has him enter without preparation. Cuchulain's brief description of his voyage and the Old Man's comment after it that neither plundering nor rape is possible on this barren mountain are both new. Yeats is beginning to depersonalize Cuchulain: on four occasions his speeches are assigned to "Young Man." The most interesting additions are the designations of the Sidhe as "dancers." The Old Man speaks of the "holy Sidhe/ That dance upon the desolate mountain." Cuchulain asks "who are you who rail/ Upon those dancers"; the Old Man says "One whom the dancers cheat," adding "the dancers have deceived me"; Cuchulain says that the dancers will not put him asleep. Then at the end of the play the Old Man says "Accursed dancers you have stolen my life." The dance and the dancer formed part of Yeats's "phantasmagoria" from early till late, though their symbolic content changes. Here they are part of a whole cluster of images and correlatives in Yeats's earlier work which symbolize some impossible way of life for which the soul longs; in Yeats's later work the dancer is often a symbol of Unity of Being, as in "Among School Children."

But these slight changes in content are not so important as the sea change the language undergoes when Yeats casts his play into verse. Yeats's plays in verse, or in verse and prose, written before *The Green Helmet* (1910) are in that dramatic blank verse which he "loosened, almost put out of joint" for *The Countess Cathleen.* He writes in the introduction he prepared in 1937 for the proposed Dublin Edition that he had become dissatisfied with that meter [*Essays and Introductions,* pp. 523–25]:

> When I wrote in blank verse I was dissatisfied; my vaguely mediaeval *Countess Cathleen* fitted the measure, but our Heroic Age went better, or so I fancied, in the ballad metre of *The Green Helmet.* There was something in what I felt about Deirdre, about Cuchulain, that rejected the Renaissance and its characteristic metres and this was the principal reason why I created in dance plays the form that varies blank verse with lyric metres.

Yeats forgot one thing in this description of the evolution of his dramatic verse. When he rewrote *The Hour-Glass* in 1912, he developed a verse form for the Wise Man with lines of irregular length. Here, to illustrate, is the Wise Man's final speech:

> Be silent. May God's will prevail on the instant.
> Although His will be my eternal pain.
> I have no question:
> It is enough, I know what fixed the station
> Of star and cloud.
> And knowing all, I cry
> That whatso God has willed
> On the instant be fulfilled,
> Though that be my damnation.
> The stream of the world has changed its course,
> And with the stream my thoughts have run
> Into some cloudy thunderous spring
> That is its mountain source —
> Aye, to some frenzy of the mind,
> For all that we have done's undone,
> Our speculation but as the wind.

The description that opens *At the Hawk's Well* in MS. 2 uses a similar verse pattern. Though most lines have eight syllables, they range in length from two syllables to twelve. The basic verse pattern is certainly not iambic tetrameter; rather Yeats, perhaps under the influence of Pound, seems almost to be experimenting in free verse. (In TS. 2 and MS. 5 Yeats does two further drafts of this opening speech. These he rejected in favor of the version found in MS. 2.) This opening description provides a metrical contrast to the blank verse used in the dialogue between the Old Man and Cuchulain.

When we compare the prose and verse drafts of *At the Hawk's Well* we discover first of all a general tightening of the syntax and phrasing. For example, the Old Man's description of his fifty-year wait at the well of immortality in MS. 1 contains 193 words; the corresponding passage in MS. 2 is 100 words long, even though Yeats has added such details as "eaten grass/ And drunk the rain." The second MS. is also far more vivid. MS. 1: "OLD MAN. Yes, a secret moment; only the Sidhe know that moment and it [is] soon over." MS. 2: "OLD MAN. A secret moment that the holy Sidhe/ That dance upon the desolate mountain know/ And not a living man, and when it comes/ The water has scarce plashed before it is gone."

The style and tone of MS. 2 evoke a greater emotional response from the reader than the style and tone of MS. 1; this is immediately apparent when we compare the opening descriptions:

[MS. 1]

CHORUS. (*Singing*) The night is coming on; the mountain side is darkening. The leaves of the hazel have fallen, driven by the autumn [winds], and half choked up the dry bed of the well. And too weary with her work clearing the well, the guardian of the fountain sits alone upon the stone margin. Nearby, stirred by the falling wind, the dry leaves rustle the green, and the great heap stirs and flutters. She sits with heavy eyes, looking upon the ground.

[MS. 2]

FIRST VOICE. Night falls
The mountain side grows dark
The withered leaves of the hazel
Half choke the dry bed of the well
The guardian of the well is sitting
Upon the old gray stones at its side
Worn out from raking its dry bed
Worn out from gathering up the leaves
Her head is bowed — her heavy eyes
Know nothing or but look upon stone
The wind that blows out of the sea
Turns over the heaped-up leaves at her side
They rustle and diminish.

The repetition "worn out from raking," "worn out from gathering" is especially effective, as is also the last line, "They rustle and diminish."

Finally, the economy Yeats shows in turning prose into verse is often rather startling: MS. 1: "But here is no well — nothing but a hollow place among the stones half full of withered leaves." MS. 2: "I but see/ A hollow among stones half full of leaves."

MS. 1: "Hawk, hawk, you shall be perched upon this wrist whether you will or no. Some that were perched upon it were called queens." MS. 2: "Hawk, hawk you shall be perched upon this wrist/ Whether you will or no — Some that perched there/ Have been called queens."

MS. 1: "Fool, she has led you from the fountain. Look, the stones and leaves are dark where the water has been, and yet there is not a drop to drink." MS. 2: "She has but led you from the fountain — Look!/ The stones and leaves are dark where it has flowed/ Yet there is not a drop to drink."

iii

Manuscript Three

YEATS FINISHED HIS PLAY in its first form by inventing new songs, and in one place slightly modifying his dialogue. I have collected these drafts together and called them MS. 3. They include the final revision of the first verse of the opening song begun at the end of MS. 1 — as we shall see Yeats did not invent the second verse of this song until after TS. 1 had been typed — and the songs for the unfolding of the cloth at the end of the play. The song beginning "Come to me, human faces" is in the form found in TS. 1, printed below, so I do not reproduce it here. The draft of the song with which the play now ends is not in final form. The draft goes as follows:

265 The man that I praise
266 Cries out the empty well
Has lived all his days
Where the clang of a bell
Can gather the cows
To the door of his ancient house
For who but a crazy would praise
The dry stones of a well

273 The man that I praise
274 Cried out the leafless tree
275 [Has] married and stays
By the hearth side and he
277 On naught has set store
278 But the children and dogs on the floor
For who but a crazy would praise
280 A withered tree.[1]

Before TS. 1 was prepared, Yeats also did an expanded version of the climax of the play, beginning with the line "The madness has laid hold upon him" and continuing through the Musicians' song that ends "Among his children and friends." Except for the song this expanded version is nearly identical with the text found in TS. 1, below. There are two draft versions of the song in MS. 3, neither of which agrees with TS. 1, where the song has been finally revised. They go as follows:

Better to have mild death
By his own hearth side and his lass
228 An old dog's head on his knees
Among children and wife
Better to have mild death

Ah that a moment could wrest
All joy from a man's heart
All content from his life
Who might have grown old at his ease
228 An old dog's head on his knees
Among children and wife.

When the various odds and ends that I have called MS. 3 are put with MS. 2, they make up together manuscript versions of nearly all the lines found in TS. 1.

iv

Typescript One and Manuscript Four

YEATS'S PROMPT COPY of *At the Hawk's Well* is one of the most interesting items in the collection of manuscripts and typescripts of Yeats's plays at the National Library of Ireland. Yeats has made extensive manuscript revisions of the text, and in addition to his annotations there are, according to a note by Mrs. Yeats, notes by Edmund Dulac on the musical accompaniment, notes by Allan Wade on the movements of the actors, and a few notes by Ezra Pound. In the transcription printed below I reproduce the typed words in roman, and Yeats's manuscript revisions in italic. We know from Allan Wade's discussion of *The Well of Immortality* (item 119) that the play was revised during rehearsals; probably most of the changes written into Yeats's prompt copy were made then. This corrected prompt copy does not provide a complete text of *At the Hawk's Well*, but when the revisions made in MS. 4 are put with it the result is a complete text.

It seems probable that these MS. 4 revisions had been incorporated into the play at the time of its first production.

[TS. 1]

AT THE HAWK'S WELL, OR WATERS OF IMMORTALITY

Enter Chorus, they are musicians and each has some kind of small instrument; they carry a black cloth, it is stretched between them so as to fall perpendicularly. It has upon it the image of a hawk. They stand so that the black cloth hides the part of the room selected for the stage. While they are doing this they sing:

BOTH MUSICIANS (singing)

1 I call to the eye of the mind
2 A well long choked up and dry
3 And boughs long stripped by the wind,
4 And I call to the mind's eye
5 Pallor of an ivory face
6 Its lofty dissolute air,
7 A man climbing up to a place
8 The salt sea wind has swept bare

[Both the opening stage direction and the song have been deleted]

FIRST MUSICIAN (*singing*)

× Dry leaves fall from the tree,
17 *The boughs of the hazel shake,*
18 The sun goes down in the West.

SECOND MUSICIAN (*singing*)

× But the heart knows all that shall be,
× The heart beats on without rest.
19 *The heart would be always awake,*
20 *The heart would turn to its rest.*

(They now go to one side of the stage, rolling up the cloth. A girl has taken her place by a square blue cloth representing a well. She is motionless.)

FIRST MUSICIAN

21 Night falls
22 The mountain side grows dark,
23 The withered leaves of the hazel

24 Half choke the dry bed of the well.
25 The guardian of the well is sitting
26 Upon the old gray stone at its side,
27 Worn-out from raking its dry bed,
28 Worn-out from gathering up the leaves,
29 ~~Her head is bowed~~, her heavy eyes
30 Know nothing, or but look upon stone.
31 The wind that blows out of the sea
32 Turns over the heaped-up leaves at her side.
33 They rustle and diminish.

[This speech was deleted, then marked "stet"]

SECOND MUSICIAN

34 I am afraid of this place.

BOTH MUSICIANS (singing)

× "I alone cannot sleep," the heart cries,
35 "*Why should I* sleep," the heart cries,
36 "~~And~~ *For* the wind, the salt wind, the sea wind"
× "We alone under the skies,"
37 "*Is beating a cloud through the* skies,"
× "We alone being blind."
38 "*I would wander always like the wind.*

FIRST MUSICIAN (speaking)

39 That old man climbs up hither
40 Who has been watching by this well
41 These fifty years,
42 He is all doubled up with age.
43 The old thorn trees are doubled so
44 Among the rocks where he is climbing.

[This speech was deleted, then marked "stet"]

(An old man enters through the audience from the other side, he crouches down a little way from the well, moving his hands as if he were making a fire. He has, however, nothing in his hands.)

FIRST MUSICIAN (speaking)

45 He has made a little heap of leaves.
46 He lays the dry sticks on the leaves.
47 And shivering with cold he has taken up

48 The fire-stick and socket from its hole.
49 He whirls it round to get a flame,
50 And now the dry sticks take the fire,
51 And now the fire leaps up and shines
52 Upon the hazels and the empty well.

MUSICIANS (singing)

53 "O wind, O *salt* wind, O sea-wind
× "Let me sleep," cry the gray rocks of the steep,
54 *Cries the heart "it is time to sleep,*
× "Let me sleep," cries the heart to the mind,
55 *Why wander and nothing to find,*
× "I am old and would sleep."
56 *Better grow old and sleep."*

OLD MAN (speaking)

57 Why don't you speak to me? Why don't you say
58 'Are you not weary gathering those sticks?
59 Are not your fingers cold?' You have not one word,
60 While yesterday you spoke three times, you said
61 'The well is full of hazel leaves.' You said:
62 'The wind is from the West.' And after that:
63 'If there is rain it's likely there'll be mud.'
64 Today you are as stupid as a fish,
65 No, worse, worse, being less lively and as dumb.

(He goes nearer.)

66 Your eyes are dazed and heavy. If the Sidhe
67 Must have a guardian to clean out the well
68 And drive the cattle off, they might choose somebody
69 That can be pleasant and companionable
70 Once in the day. Why do you stare like that?
71 You had that glassy look about the eyes
72 Last time it happened. Do you know anything?
73 It is enough to drive an old man crazy
74 To look all day upon these broken rocks,
75 And ragged thorns, and that one stupid face,
76 And speak and get no answer.

YOUNG MAN (who has entered through the audience during the last speech)

Then speak to me

77 For youth is not more patient than old age

78 And I have trod the rocks for half a day
79 Nor found what I am looking for.

OLD MAN

Who speaks?

80 Who comes so suddenly into this place
81 Where nothing thrives? If I may judge by the gold
On head and foot and glittering in your coat
83 You are not one of those who hate the living world.

YOUNG MAN

84 I am named Cuchulain, I am Sualtim's son.

OLD MAN

85 I have never heard that name.

YOUNG MAN

It is not unknown.

86 I have an ancient house beyond the sea.

OLD MAN

87 What mischief brings you hither, — you are like those
88 Who are crazy for the shedding of men's blood,
89 And for the love of women?

YOUNG MAN

A rumour has led me,

90 A story told over the wine towards dawn.
91 I rose from table, found a boat, spread sail,
92 And with a lucky wind under the sail
93 Crossed waves that have seemed charmed, and found this shore.

OLD MAN

94 There is no house to sack among these hills
95 Nor a fair woman to be carried off.

YOUNG MAN

96 You should be native here, for that rough tongue
97 Matches the barbarous spot. You can, it may be,
98 Lead me to what I seek, a well wherein
99 Three hazels drop their nuts and withered leaves,
100 And where a solitary girl keeps watch
101 Among gray boulders. He who drinks, they say,
102 Of that miraculous water lives forever.

OLD MAN

103 Are there not before your eyes at the instant

104 Gray boulders and a solitary girl
105 And three stripped hazels?

YOUNG MAN

But there is no well.

OLD MAN

106 Can you see nothing yonder?

YOUNG MAN

I but see
107 A hollow among stones half-full of leaves.

OLD MAN

108 And do you think so great a gift is found
109 By no more toil than spreading out a sail,
110 And climbing a steep hill? O, folly of youth,
111 Why should that hollow place fill up for you?
112 Are you a better man than I who have lain in wait
113 For more than fifty years to find it empty,
114 Or but to find the stupid wind of the sea
115 Drive round the perishable leaves.

YOUNG MAN

So it seems
116 There is some moment when the water fills it?

OLD MAN

117 A secret moment that the holy shades
118 That dance upon the desolate mountain know,
119 And not a living man, and when it comes
120 The water has scarce plashed before it is gone.

YOUNG MAN

121 I will stand here and wait. Why should the luck
122 Of Sualtim's son desert him now? for never
123 Have I had long to wait for anything.

OLD MAN

124 No! Go from this accursed place! This place
125 Belongs to me, that girl there and those others,
126 Deceivers of men.

YOUNG MAN

And who are you who rail
127 Upon those dancers that all others bless?

OLD MAN

128 One whom the dancers cheat. I came like you

129 When young in body and in mind, and blown
130 By what had seemed to me a lucky sail.
131 The well was dry, I sat upon its edge,
132 I waited the miraculous flood, I waited
133 While the years passed and withered me away.
134 I have snared the birds for food and eaten grass
And drunk the rain, and neither for dark or shine
136 Wandered too for away to have heard the plash,
137 And yet the dancers have deceived me. Thrice
138 I have awakened from a sudden sleep
139 To find the stones were wet.

YOUNG MAN

My luck is strong
140 It will not leave me waiting, nor will they,
141 That dance among the stones put me asleep.
142 If I grow drowsy I can pierce my foot.

OLD MAN

143 No, do not pierce it for the foot is tender,
144 It feels pain much. But find your sail again
145 And leave the well to me, for it belongs
146 To all that's old and withered.

YOUNG MAN

No, I stay
(The GIRL gives the cry of the hawk)
147 There is that bird again.

OLD MAN

There is no bird.

YOUNG MAN

148 It sounded like the sudden cry of a hawk,
149 But there's no wing in sight. As I came hither
150 A great gray hawk swept down out of the sky.
151 And though I have good hawks, the best in the world
152 I had fancied, I have not seen its like. It flew
153 As though it would have torn me with its beak
154 Or blinded me smiting with that great wing.
155 I had to draw my sword to drive it off,
156 And after that it flew from rock to rock.
157 I pelted it with stones a good half hour,
158 And just before I had turned the big rock there

159 And seen this place, it seemed to vanish away.
160 Could I but find a means to bring it down
161 I'd hood it.

OLD MAN

The woman of the Sidhe herself,
162 The mountain witch, the unappeasable shadow:
In one or another shape, now hawk, or wolf
Or panic stricken deer as the mood takes her,
163 She is always flitting upon this mountain-side,
To allure or to destroy. Go from this place
Before a beak or claw is in your flesh,
Before she has put a life-long curse upon you.
172 Those who have long to live should fear her most,
173 The old are cursed already. That curse may be
174 Never to win a woman's love and keep it
175 Or always to mix hatred in the love,
176 Or it may be that she will kill your children,
177 That you will find them, their throats torn and bloody
178 Or you will be so maddened that you will kill them
179 With your own hand.

YOUNG MAN

Have you been set down there
180 To threaten all who come, and scare them off,
181 You seem as dried up as the leaves and sticks,
182 As though you had no part in life.

(GIRL gives hawk cry again)

That cry
183 There is that cry again. That woman made it,
184 But why does she cry out as the hawk cries?

OLD MAN

185 It was her mouth, and yet not she, that cried.
186 It was that shadow cried behind her mouth,
187 And now I know why she has been so stupid
188 All the day through, and had such heavy eyes.
189 Look at her shivering now, the terrible life
190 Is slipping through her veins. She is possessed.
191 Who knows whom she will murder or deceive
192 Before she awakes in ignorance of it all,
193 And gathers up the leaves. But they will be wet,

194 The water will have come and gone again.
195 That shivering is the sign. O get you gone!
196 At any moment now I shall hear it bubble,
197 If you are good you will leave it. I am old
198 And if I do not drink it now will never,
199 I have been watching all my life and maybe
200 Only a little cupful will bubble up.

YOUNG MAN

201 I'll ~~dip my helmet in~~ *take it in my hands*. We shall both drink
202 And even if there are but a few drops
203 Share them.

OLD MAN

But swear that I may drink the first,
204 The young are greedy and if you drink the first
You'll drink it all. Why did you look at her?
206 She has felt your gaze and turned her eyes on us,
207 I cannot bear her eyes, they are not of this world,
208 Nor moist nor faltering; they are no girl's eyes.

(He covers his head)

YOUNG MAN

209 Why do you gaze upon me with the eyes of a hawk?
210 I am not afraid of you, bird, woman, or witch.

(He goes to the side of the well which the GIRL has left)

211 Do what you will, I shall not leave this place
212 Till I have grown immortal like yourself.

(He has sat down, the GIRL has begun to dance, moving like a hawk. The OLD MAN sleeps. *The dance goes on for some two minutes.*)

× MUSICIANS (singing)

× The horror of unmoistened eyes
× Slips by me with side-long head
× From stone to stone, or half flies
× The unappeasable gray wings spread.

FIRST MUSICIAN (singing or half singing the first three lines then speaking)

213 O God protect me
214 From a horrible deathless body
215 Sliding through the veins of a sudden

To fling itself out of a sudden
Leaving me lost
In the stupidity of human life.

× MUSICIANS (singing)

× The horror of unmoistened eyes
× Slips by me with side-long head
× From stone to stone, or half flies
× The unappeasable gray wings spread

(*The dance goes on for some two minutes.* CUCHULAIN rises slowly)

FIRST MUSICIAN

216 The madness has laid hold upon him now
× Ah, she has stirred him now and he grows pale,
217 *For* he grows pale and staggers to his feet.

YOUNG MAN

218 Run where you will,
219 Gray bird you shall be perched upon my wrist,
220 Some were called queens and yet have been perched there.

(*The dance goes on for some two minutes*)

× MUSICIANS (singing)

× The horror of unmoistened eyes
× Slips by me with side-long head
× From stone to stone, or half flies
× The unappeasable gray wings spread.

× FIRST MUSICIAN (speaking)

× Keep me from dancing feet and terrible eyes,
× Two feet seeming like two quivering blades,
× Eyes long withered and yet seeming young
× Keep from me — How should I bear those eyes.

× (They cover their faces with their hands. The dance goes on to the instruments alone)

(*The* HAWK *goes out*)

MUSICIANS (speaking)

221 I have heard the water plash, (uncovering their faces) it comes, it comes
× The stones are covered by a glittering pool.
223 ~~He heard the plash,~~ Look, he has turned his head.

× (The GIRL rushes out giving cry of hawk followed by CUCHULAIN. OLD MAN wakes during following song and creeps up to well.)

MUSICIANS (singing)

224 He has lost what may not be found
225 Till men heap his burial mound
226 And all the history ends,
227 He might have lived at his ease,
228 An old dog's head on his knees
229 Among his children and friends
(The OLD MAN creeps up to the well)

OLD MAN

230 *The accursed shadows have deluded me*
231 ~~The well is empty~~, ~~yet~~ The stones are dark,
and yet the well is empty
232 The water flowed and emptied while I slept,
× Again I have been deluded. Accursed,
233 You have deluded me my whole life through.
234 Accursed dancers, you have stolen my life.
235 *That there should be such evil in a shadow.*

YOUNG MAN (entering)

236 She has fled from me and hidden in the rocks.

OLD MAN

237 She has but led you from the fountain. Look!
238 The stones and leaves are dark where it has flowed,
And yet there is not a drop to drink.
(A cry and the sound of a sword struck on a shield. Off)

YOUNG MAN

What are those cries?
240 What is that sound that runs along the hill?
241 Who are they that beat a sword upon a shield?

OLD MAN

242 She has roused up the fierce women of the hills,
243 Eofe, and all her troop, to take your life,
244 And never till you are lying in the earth,
245 Can you know rest.

YOUNG MAN

The clash of arms again!

OLD MAN

246 O do not go. The mountain is accursed,

247 Stay with me I have nothing more to lose,
248 I do not now deceive you.

YOUNG MAN

I will face them.

(He goes out ~~calling~~ *no longer as if in a dream, but shouldering his spear and calling*)

249 He comes! Cuchulain, son of Sualtim, comes!

(The CHORUS stand up, one ~~of them crosses over the stage, screening it with the black cloth~~ *goes to centre with folded cloth. The others unfold it.* While they do so they sing. During the singing the OLD MAN goes out taking the well with him. ~~The chorus follow, singing~~)

250 Come to me human faces,
251 Familiar memories,
252 I have found hateful eyes
253 Among the desolate places,
254 Unfaltering, unmoistened eyes.

255 Folly alone I cherish,
256 I choose it for my share,
257 Being but a mouthful of air,
258 I am content to perish,
259 I am but a mouthful of sweet air.

260 O lamentable shadows,
261 Obscurity of strife,
262 I choose a pleasant life,
263 Among ~~the watered~~ *indolent* meadows,
264 Wisdom must live a bitter life.

A comparison of MSS. 2 and 3 with TS. 1 shows that Yeats made the following revisions before the typed version was assembled. All the stage directions in TS. 1 are new, and they have been greatly expanded. Yeats will expand them still further in the *Harper's Bazaar* version of his play. He has inserted from MS. 3 the first verse of the song that opens the play. Then MS. 2 and TS. 1 are nearly identical through the opening speech of the First Musician. Here Yeats inserts a new line, "I am afraid of this place," and has the Musicians sing the first verse of the song beginning " 'I alone cannot sleep' the heart cries" from MS. 2 before the First Musician describes the Old Man. This speech is identical in MS. 2 and TS. 1, save that Yeats adds a syllable to two of its lines. It is followed by the second verse of the song, which now frames the description of the Old Man. Manuscript and typescript are again nearly identical up to the point where Cuchulain, now uniformly called "Young Man" in the speech tags, names himself. The Old Man says he has never heard of him; this is new, for in all the earlier drafts the Old Man recognizes Cuchulain's name. This change makes necessary some minor adjustments in the speeches that follow. From this point up to the climax of the play, which is marked by the beginning of the dance, Yeats changes a word here and there, but on the whole the two versions are remarkably alike. The nature of the changes made can be seen by comparing the two versions of the Old Man's speech about the woman of the Sidhe who has taken the form of a hawk. In MS. 2 Yeats writes: "Go from this place/ Before she takes you in her grip, before/ She has put a life long curse upon you." In TS. 1 this becomes: "Go from this place/ Before a beak or claw is in your flesh/ Before she has put a life-long curse upon you."

There are no early drafts of the Musician's song beginning "The horror of unmoistened eyes"; we encounter it here for the first time as well as the First Musician's speech beginning "O God protect me." Yeats then inserts from MS. 3 the passage describing the filling of the fountain, beginning "The madness has laid hold upon him now" and ending "look, he has turned his head"; he adds a new and final version of the Musicians' song of comment, beginning "He has lost what may not be found." The final exchange between Cuchulain and the Old Man is almost identical in MS. 2 and TS. 1. Yeats closes the play by inserting the lyric "Come to me human faces" from MS. 3.

In summary, when preparing copy for TS. 1 Yeats made very few changes in the dialogue between the Old Man and Cuchulain which he had drafted in MS. 2. He did insert several lyric interludes, probably all of them drafted elsewhere, and he began to elaborate his stage directions. The changes made in the text of the play as typed, Yeats's manuscript revisions printed in italic, are more substantive and interesting.

To begin, TS. 1 as revised in its margins is not complete. The opening of the play has been cancelled, for example; so has the crucial stage direction which has Cuchulain follow the Girl out just as the miraculous waters flow. Yeats did not intend to cancel this exit, for a moment later Cuchulain returns. Then too the expanded stage direction marking Cuchulain's last exit, "He goes out no longer as if in a dream, but shouldering his spear and calling," clearly implies a revised stage direction describing Cuchulain's previous exit. Finally, the corrected stage direction at the end of the play indicates that the use of the cloth which screens the acting area was changed while the play was in rehearsal. In the cancelled initial stage direction and the unrevised final stage direction the cloth is stretched between two musicians; they do not unfold and fold it.

Several pages of corrections clearly later than those written into TS. 1 have survived; they fit into TS. 1 perfectly and supply all the missing parts of the play. I have called these MS. 4, though they are only partly in manuscript. I print these corrections before discussing the details of Yeats's revision of the play as typed in TS. 1. First, a revised opening, which has the play begin with the unfolding and folding of the cloth, and which adds for the first time the second stanza of the opening song, the stanza which anticipates the man "With sixty or more winters on his head" found in "Among School Children." I believe that this passage took the place of the opening deleted in TS. 1.

[MS. 4]

AT THE HAWK'S WELL

SCENE: *The stage is any bare place in a room against a wall. Against the walls are placed before the play begins a drum, cymbals, and a stringed instrument. The three musicians enter slowly. One carries a black cloth. He stands in the middle of the space. The others stand on either side and slowly unfold the cloth until a part of the stage is hidden. As they unfold it they move backward and outward so that the cloth makes an angle with one musician at the apex. Hid by the cloth a girl enters and crouches on the ground.*

The musicians sing while the cloth is being unfolded

1 I call to the eye of the mind
2 A well long choked up and dry
3 And boughs long stripped by the wind,
4 And I call to the mind's eye
5 Pallor of an ivory face,
6 Its lofty dissolute air,
7 A man climbing up to a place
8 The salt sea wind has swept bare.

(*They fold up the cloth singing*)

9 I have dreamed of a life soon done,
10 Will he lose by that or win?
11 A mother that saw her son
12 Doubled over a speckled shin,
13 Cross-grained with ninety years,
14 Would cry, 'How little worth
15 Were all my hopes and fears
16 And the hard pain of his birth!'

(*The musicians sit down near the wall*)

FIRST MUSICIAN (*singing*)

17 The boughs of the hazel shake,
18 The sun goes down in the West.

SECOND MUSICIAN (*singing*)

19 The heart would be always awake,
20 The heart would turn to its rest.

The next revision is a sheet with MS. and TS. versions of this passage:

SECOND MUSICIAN

34 I am afraid of this place

MUSICIANS (*singing*)

35 "Why should I sleep" the heart cries
36 "For the wind, the salt wind, the sea wind,
37 Is beating a cloud through the skies.
38 I would wander always like the "wind."

The revision printed above, except for its punctuation, is no more than a clean copy of the passage as corrected in TS. 1. There is no record in TS. 1 of the next revision, a changed version of the Old Man's description of the woman of the Sidhe. Again MS. and TS. versions are found on the same sheet:

164 When she has shown
165 Herself to the fierce women of the hills
166 Under that shape, they offer sacrifice
167 And arm for battle; and there falls a curse
On all that have looked on that unmoistened eye
169 So get you gone while you have that proud step
And confident voice — for there's no man alive

171 Has so much luck that he can play with it —
Before she has put a life long curse upon you

The last corrections are of the end of the play. They incorporate the manuscript revisions in TS. 1 and add others:

(*He has sat down. The girl has begun to dance, moving like a hawk. The old man sleeps. The dance goes on for some two minutes*)

FIRST MUSICIAN. 213 Oh God protect me
214 From a horrible deathless body
215 Sliding through the veins of a sudden.

(*The dance goes on for some two minutes.* CUCHULAIN *rises slowly*)

216 The madness has laid hold upon him now
217 For he has grown pale and staggers to his feet

(*The dance goes on*)

YOUNG MAN. 218 Run where you will
219 Gray bird, you shall be perched upon my wrist
220 Some were called queens and yet have been perched there

(*The dance goes on*)

MUSICIANS. 221 I have heard the water plash (*the* HAWK *goes out*) It comes it comes
It glitters among the stones. He has heard the plash
223 Look he has turned his head.

(CUCHULAIN *drops his spear as if in a dream and goes out as if in a dream. The* MUSICIANS *sing*)

224 He has lost what may not be found
225 Till men have heaped his mound
226 And all the history ends.
227 He might have lived at his ease
228 An old dog's head on his knees
229 Among his children and friends

(*The* OLD MAN *creeps up to where the well is supposed to be*)

OLD MAN. 230 The accursed shadows have deluded me,
231 The stones are dark and yet the well is empty;
232 The water flowed and emptied while I slept.
233 You have deluded me my whole life through,

234 Accursed dancers, you have stolen my life.
235 That there should be such evil in a shadow!

When TS. 1 and MS. 4 are put together, the resulting text is almost word for word that which Yeats printed in *The Wild Swans at Coole*. I believe that this was also the text used in production, since the prompter's copy as corrected is incomplete and inconsistent.

Yeats and his collaborators made the following changes in the play during its rehearsal: They added a third musician, and invented the unfolding and folding of the cloth at the beginning and end of the play, perhaps to give all three musicians something to do. Since the cloth was now unfolded and folded, the opening song was given a second stanza. Perhaps the song "The Well and the Tree," found in MS. 3, was used at the end of the play, though the fact that Yeats published it separately in Macmillan's *Responsibilities* may indicate that he had decided to leave it out of the play.

The songs which frame the description of the scene and of the Old Man at the beginning of the play were all reworked. The revised versions are more directly phrased and have a more precise meaning. In the TS. 1 version of the song the restless heart and the sea wind cannot sleep. The rocks ask the wind to let them sleep; the heart asks the mind to let it sleep. The effect is decidedly busy. In the revised song the waking heart that desires rest is disturbed by the sea wind; it tells the wind to sleep.

The MS. 4 version of the part of the Old Man's speech describing the woman of the Sidhe accomplishes two things: Yeats cut the song the Musicians sang during the hawk dance, beginning "The horror of unmoistened eyes." He now puts the unmoistened eyes into his description of the woman of the Sidhe. The passage as revised also prepares for the end of the play, where Cuchulain goes out to fight "the fierce women of the Hills."

The revision of the climax of the play shows that during rehearsals Yeats became convinced that Michio Ito's dance could adequately express the fatal attraction of the immortal woman, for he cut the thrice repeated song

The horror of unmoistened eyes
Slips by me with side-long head
From stone to stone, or half flies
The unappeasable gray wings spread.

He cut two other passages and tidied up the verse and the stage directions. The second of the cut passages describes the dance; no doubt the dance itself made the words seem inaccurate or redundant.

> Keep me from dancing feet and terrible eyes,
> Two feet seeming like two quivering blades,
> Eyes long withered and yet seeming young
> Keep from me — How should I bear those eyes.

Taken together the revisions indicate a fuller dependence on the dance as an expressive means.

V

Typescript Two and Manuscript Five

IN TS. 1 PARTS OF THE OPENING of the play were deleted and then marked "stet." Typescript 2 is a variant opening of the play headed "Second version." Perhaps it was added during rehearsal in place of the deleted passages. These were eventually preferred, for they appear in all printed versions of the play. In this "Second version" the meaning is unchanged. Yeats is experimenting with diction and meter, especially with a shorter and still less regular pattern of line lengths. The tone of the passage is more colloquial ("he fumbles about") than the version Yeats came to prefer.

[TS. 2]

SECOND VERSION

The guardian of the well
Is sitting on an old gray stone
Worn out from raking its dry bed
Worn out from gathering up the leaves
Her heavy eyes
See nothing but the gray stones
The wind that blows out of the sea
Is turning over the heaped up leaves at her side,
They rustle and diminish

SECOND MUSICIAN I am afraid of this place.

(*singing as before*)

FIRST MUSICIAN *speaking*

That old man climbs up hither

Who has been watching by this well
These fifty years
Being chilly with old age
He has been gathering sticks,
He is all doubled up
A thorn tree among rocks.
(*stage direction as before*)

FIRST MUSICIAN

He has made a little heap of leaves,
He lays dry sticks on the leaves,
Now shivering with cold
He fumbles about to find
The fire-stick and the socket.
He whirls it round
And now the dry leaves take the fire
And now the fire leaps up.
And now it shines upon the empty well.

Manuscript 5 is a still later version of the same passage, later because in it Yeats retains most of the changes made in TS. 2 and adds others. Here Yeats tries even shorter lines. He reduces four lines by a single syllable, one line by two syllables, one line by four. The four syllable cut forces Yeats to draft a new line "Beside the ancient well."

[MS. 5]

Night falls
The mountain side grows dark
The withered leaves of the hazel
Half choke the dry bed of the well

The guardian of the well
Is sitting on an old gray stone
Worn out from raking its bed
Worn out from gathering the leaves
Her heavy eyes
See nothing but gray stone
The wind that blows from the sea
Is turning over the heaped up leaves at her side
They rustle and diminish

I am afraid of this place

That old man climbs up hither
Who has kept watch
These fifty years
Beside the ancient well
Being chilly with old age
He has been gathering sticks
He is all doubled up
A thorn tree among rocks

He has made a heap of leaves
He lays dry sticks on the leaves
Now shivering with cold
He fumbles about to find
The fire stick and the socket
He whirls it round
And now the dry leaves catch
And now the fire leaps up
And now it shines upon the empty well

One wonders why Yeats eventually preferred the TS. 1 version of this passage to the MS. 5 version. This to my ear reads very well. It has been stripped to the essentials; it is direct and powerful. Further, the last version is much less dominated by the iambic pattern, so nearly inescapable in English verse, than the TS. 1 version. The deletions in TS. 1 strongly suggest that one or both of the variants reproduced above were tried in rehearsal; the "stet" marks there prove that the original version came to be preferred. Perhaps the variants sounded too stark, too heavily accented. One also wonders whether Ezra Pound had anything to do with these experiments. We know from Mrs. Yeats's note on TS. 1 that he reviewed it; unfortunately I was unable to distinguish his hand from Yeats's own.

vi
The Printed Texts

IN 1917 YEATS PUBLISHED *At the Hawk's Well* in two rather different texts. I am convinced that the latest text Yeats prepared was the first to be printed, that found in *Harper's Bazaar* for March. Yeats also included the play in *The Wild Swans at Coole* published by the Cuala Press in November. This text is almost word for word the revised TS. 1 text with the corrections made in MS. 4 substituted for the corresponding passages in TS. 1. I have argued above that MS. 4 must be combined with TS. 1 to produce a full text of the play, and suggested that this was probably the version produced in 1916. The Cuala Press text is not in the line of subsequent textual descent, for all later printings of the play are based on the *Harper's Bazaar* text.

In the *Harper's Bazaar* text Yeats has added a list of "Persons of the Play"; he has revised most of the stage directions and expanded them, adding for the first time the crucial fact that the principal players are masked; he has made a few changes in wording. Nearly all of these changes appear in later printings of the play, which, according to Mr. Saul (*Prolegomena*, p. 48) reached nearly final form in 1921 in *Four Plays for Dancers*. The nature of the changes made can be illustrated by following the evolution of the Old Man's speech describing the woman of the Sidhe:

[TS. 1]

The woman of the Sidhe herself,
The mountain witch, the unappeasable shadow:
In one or another shape, now hawk, or wolf
Or panic stricken deer as the mood takes her,
She is always flitting upon the mountain-side,
To allure or to destroy. Go from this place
Before a beak or claw is in your flesh,
Before she has put a life-long curse upon you.

[*Wild Swans*]

The woman of the Sidhe herself,
The mountain witch, the unappeasable shadow,
She is always flitting upon the mountain side
To allure or to destroy. When she has shown
Herself to the fierce women of the hills
Under that shape, they offer sacrifice
And arm for battle; and there falls a curse
On all who have looked on that unmoistened eye;
So get you gone while you have that proud step
And confident voice — for there's no man alive
Has so much luck that he can play with it —
Before she has put a lifelong curse upon you.

This passage reached final form in the *Harper's Bazaar* printing: "and there falls" became "there falls" — "looked on that unmoistened eye" became "gazed in her unmoistened eyes" — "for there's no man alive" became "for not a man alive." The line "Before she has put a lifelong curse upon you" was omitted. This passage was the most changed of any in the play, which indicates a textual stability truly remarkable when we recollect what happened to the texts of many of Yeats's earlier plays.

In Yeats's unpublished dialogue "The Poet and the Actress," also written in 1916 according to the date on the envelope in which the manuscript is filed, a poet urges upon an actress the need for an "unreal theatre," a theater wherein "the battle with reality itself" may be staged. The poet continues with a passage that seems to describe *At the Hawk's Well:*

Is not all comedy a battle — a sham fight often — but still a battle? Now the art I long for is also a battle but it takes place in the depths of the soul, and one of the antagonists does not wear a shape known to the world or speak a mortal tongue. It is the struggle of a dream with the world. It is only possible when we transcend circumstances and ourselves, and the greater the contest the greater the art.

In *At the Hawk's Well* and generally in the plays for dancers Yeats does create a successful nonrealistic theater wherein plays which transcend circumstances and ourselves can be effectively staged.

In a play for dancers drama has been stripped to its bones. No stage is required, no special lighting effects. The dramatic situation — it can hardly be called a plot — has been reduced to its essentials. In *The Dreaming of the Bones,* for example, when Yeats has the young Aran Islander who has fought in the Easter Rebellion encounter the ghosts of Diarmuid and Dervorgilla, who have first called the English to Ireland, he telescopes the seven centuries of English dominion and Ireland's long struggle against it. The few characters in a dance play are not people, but rather timeless persons — a Young Man, a Stranger, a Swineherd, a Queen. They are usually masked, their movements are formal, unimitative, so that in spite of the intimate nature of Yeats's theater a great aesthetic distance is achieved. Every effort is made to avoid an empathic response between audience and actors.[2]

This aesthetic distance is increased by the use of song, music, and dance, ancillary arts associated with the theater from its beginnings but banished from the realistic stage. A chorus of musicians or attendants fills some of the functions of the chorus in Greek drama by commenting on the action taking place or providing a lyric interlude, but Yeats uses the chorus tangentially, so to speak; it is less involved in the action than is the chorus of a typical Greek play, and though the songs it sings are thematically related to the dramatic action they echo this indirectly. The chorus has only two or three members; like everything else in the dance play it has been reduced to small dimensions, and yet it provides an effective contrast to the words and actions of the principals. *At the Hawk's Well* demonstrates Yeats's impatience with every aspect of the popular theater of his time, and for that matter of our's— its sheer size, its noise and bustle, its realism, its dependence on lighting and spectacle. It did not seem possible to him to turn the dramatic action inward upon the soul while using such a dramatic medium. And of course the words of the dramatist, even Shakespeare's words, had been for a long time nearly lost in the sheer exuberance of production — a situation hardly tolerable to a great poet.

These plays for dancers seem very strange to an audience accustomed to the realistic theater, less a drama than an anti-drama. Large claims have been made for them by Eric Bentley and others, and those who have seen them staged as they should be staged have found the experience memorable; Dubliners still talk of a production of *The Dreaming of the Bones* in Yeats's drawing room at 82 Merrion Square. It seems to me that in his plays for dancers Yeats has created the first successful poetic drama since the seventeenth century. These plays are an original and remarkable accomplishment; their action does indeed "take place in the depths of the soul." In *At the Hawk's Well* Yeats made a new beginning as a playwright.

7

The Words upon the Window-pane

AFTER completing and producing *At the Hawk's Well*, Yeats wrote three other plays in much the same form (*The Only Jealousy of Emer, The Dreaming of the Bones, Calvary*) which he collected in 1921 in *Four Plays for Dancers*. He also completed *The Player Queen* (on the stocks since 1908) and had it produced in 1919. During the early years of the 1920's Yeats seems either consciously or unconsciously to have turned away from writing new plays, though perhaps the mass of other work in which he was involved is a sufficient explanation. His involvement in the political affairs of his country became more intense than at any time since the 1890's when he accepted membership in the Irish Senate in 1922; much of his time went to the composition of *A Vision*, so much indeed that Mrs. Yeats feared for his poetry; he was collecting, rearranging, revising (sometimes rewriting) his early work for the collected edition that Macmillan was issuing; he was continuing his *Autobiographies*. The preparation of two volumes for this collected edition, *Plays in Prose and Verse* (1922) and *Plays and Controversies* (1923), no doubt served Yeats as a kind of summing up of what he had done as a playwright beginning back in the 1890's with *The Countess Cathleen*. For whatever reason, and since Yeats seems always to have found time to write what he had to write we may at least suspect that the reason was in some sense psychological and internal, related to the no doubt partly subconscious sense of the development of his whole *oeuvre*, he did not undertake a new major play until he began work on *The Resurrection* in 1925 or 1926. He published an early version of this play in 1927, but this did not please him and he put the play aside until late in 1930. While *The Resurrection* was lying fallow, Yeats wrote one of his best plays, *The Words upon the Window-pane*, finished at Coole in October 1930.

My own conclusion is that not all the manuscripts of this play have survived, but enough have to make it possible for us to watch Yeats working on a play in prose which employs to great effect dramatic conventions quite different from those he had adapted for his plays for dancers, to study another aspect of Yeats's methods of dramatic composition. My study of the composition of *The Words upon the Window-pane* is based on the following manuscripts: In the Rapallo Notebook labelled "E" there are two scenarios, one of the whole play and one of the opening of the exposition, a list of the persons in the play, a draft of the opening speeches, a draft of the entire exposition down through the beginning of the séance, and a draft of Corbet's speech to Mrs. Henderson after the séance is broken off. Yeats's final manuscript, signed and dated from Coole Park, is at the Houghton Library. I reproduce and discuss the material from Rapallo Notebook "E" in the order in which it is found there.

The scenario of the whole play is one of the longest Yeats wrote and one of the most detailed; as we read it we observe Yeats working out a play step by step. Aside from its length and detail, it is a characteristic scenario, though an unusually successful one for by the time he completed it Yeats had roughed out the play we know. I have edited the scenario by italicizing stage directions and, when Yeats assigns speeches, giving the names of the speakers in small caps. When Yeats writes a passage of continuous dialogue, I print it in conventional dramatic form. I have not transcribed any cancelled passages, nor corrected miswritten titles or mistaken allusions.

Yeats begins by establishing his setting, a room in a Dublin house where lines from Stella's birthday poem to Swift have been scratched upon a window-pane. Yeats has not yet decided to base his title on this circumstance; the scenario is called "Jonathan Swift." The "young man" and "old man," who will eventually become Dr. Trench and John Corbet, enter, and, after saying that they have come to attend a séance, immediately discuss Swift, whom the young man opposes to Rousseau.

JONATHAN SWIFT

SCENARIO

I

A large room in a Georgian house near Dublin. Two men enter, one a young Englishman, the older man a Dublin man. The old man says, "We held our first meeting on Nottingham [?] Street. Mrs. Patterson is so well known that we had to get a larger room." THE YOUNG MAN. "A wonderful room for a lodging house." [OLD MAN.] "This was somebody's town house— not that it was exactly in the town — up to some eighty years ago. Swift used to visit here, and if you will come over here I will show you some lines he is supposed to have scratched on the pane with a diamond. But you can't read in this light." YOUNG MAN. "What were the lines?" OLD MAN. "To tell you the truth, I never looked to see; something cynical I suppose. I wonder what he would have thought of our séance tonight? Not too unfavorably, perhaps. Is not there something of the kind in Gulliver?" YOUNG MAN. "The magicians' island. Gulliver was told he could call up whom he pleased. He chose seven men, half-a-dozen old Romans and then Sir Thomas Moore; he declared the world could not add an eighth." OLD MAN. "But only one of the seven was a Christian. What a pagan he was." YOUNG MAN. "No, no, no. He was a deeply religious man, but he despised ordinary men. Those seven men, Cato, Brutus, and the rest, were martyred because they saw more than their followers. He calls the Houyhnmhnms the perfection of nature — nature made perfect by intellect. He thought nature bred and bound and disciplined something the Roman Senate had in its great days. Rousseau, who was the opposite in everything, preferred some sort of untutored savage or primitive man to the Roman Senate." OLD MAN. "What a lot you read. I read Swift when I was young, but have not time to read anything now." YOUNG MAN. "But it does not need any great reading to see how different they were. Rousseau did not call up seven to whom the world could not add an eighth, but the uneducated mob, all that is satirized in *Gulliver* and *The Tale of the Tub*."

[In the next section of the scenario the various persons who will attend the séance assemble, and Yeats, after stating the young man's skepticism (he is now Mr. S), makes a somewhat random exposition of certain aspects of spiritism: the re-enaction of the death scene when a spirit is first summoned; the condition of spirits in the spirit world; deceiving spirits.]

People have been coming in. Old Man introduces Mrs. L. "Here is a young friend of mine, Mr. S. from Oxford. Thinks it all some kind of juggling, but we all have to make a beginning." [MRS. L] "O Mr. S., I have had curious proof. My husband was killed in a flying accident two years ago. I nearly died of grief, and then somebody took me to Mrs. P. Mrs. P. did not even name my name, and my husband came at once. At first it was very terrible, for all the death condition came back. The breaking of something — knowledge that he was falling, but it [was] only at first." OLD MAN. "Yes, that is often the way at first; they re-enact the death scene." MRS. L. "Presently he called me by my Christion name, and then he told me things only known to us two. Now I come to see him constantly and ask his advice about everything. Our son is with him. He died when he was a little boy, but he has grown up there. He looks, my husband tells me, as if he was thirty years old. He will never grow any older than that." YOUNG MAN. "Do you all come here to séances to meet somebody who is dead?" MRS. L. "That old man sitting by the door had no religious belief, he thought the grave ended everything. He had a horror of death. Now he wants to die. He told me the other night that there are horse races there. Says Silver Cloud told him that." OLD MAN. "I don't believe Silver Cloud said anything of the kind. He has lost a lot on horses, but when he gets there he will win it all back. (YOUNG MAN *laughs.*) Hush, he may hear you." MRS. L. "O no, he is very deaf." OLD MAN. "He is deaf enough to have mistaken what Silver Cloud was saying." MRS. L. "There are deceiving spirits. That is the disappointing thing, Mr. S. We get the most convincing evidence, then something goes wrong and there is nothing but deception. After all, that is natural. A liar does not cease to be a liar because he is dead." OLD MAN. "A good control like Silver Cloud should be able to select. May I introduce Miss X, our secretary?"

[The scenario continues with a statement that two previous séances have been spoiled by a "horrid spirit"; this leads to an explanation of earth bound spirits. The medium enters, briefly explains her mediumship, and the séance begins with the singing of a hymn.]

II

Old man says the people are late tonight. As he is speaking younger woman says they are before their time. It is only just eight thirty. Is introduced to young man. It is his first séance. He asks questions. She describes usual procedure. He is skeptical, but she says natural at first. Sometimes they get good discipline, etc. Describes sitters. Lately horrid spirit has upset things for Mrs. P. Says connected with house perhaps. Discussion of similar cases. She tells of Abraham Willage [?] and the gambler. But it is not always the moment of death. There are spirits who go over and over again the events of their past lives. Old Man says why all bad? They have suffered so much that they are drawn back, as it were, must repeat some action, just as we [look] back upon things that made us suffer. Young Man gives example from Homer, Achilles in a black cloud. Young woman is convinced this spirit is bad. Spoilt two séances. He would do nothing but pour out a lot of abuse, abusing some woman. He said the most awful things. Two of their members resigned.

While they have been talking various persons, half-a-dozen, perhaps more, have come and taken seats. The young woman says, "Ah, there is Mrs. Patterson," and goes over [to] quite old medium. Medium says "Now my dear friends we will begin. There [are] some strangers among us. I want to explain that I do [not] call up spirits. I make the right conditions, that is all, and they come. I do not know who is going to come; they decide that. The guides do their best, but they cannot always succeed just at once. I say to each one of you that if you want to speak to some dear one who has passed on, they will find [him] for you if you have patience. If they do not find [him] tonight, they may the next time. Now we will begin. You need not hold hands, but nobody should cross their legs, that interferes with the magnetism [?]. Now Miss X, a hymn please. The same verse we had last time will do. All who can should join. It does not matter if you cannot sing very well. A hymn is always a great help."

(HYMN)

[The medium goes into trance, and her control, Silver Cloud, a little American Indian girl, speaks. Almost immediately the spirit of Swift dominates the séance, and the terrible scene between Swift and Vanessa unfolds.]

MISS X. "She always snores like that when she is going off; she will be in trance in a moment." CHILD SPIRIT SPEAKS: "Glad to see you, friends. Good evening, everybody." MISS X says "That is her child [control], Silver Cloud." CHILD: "There is somebody for the lady by the door." Is recognized. Says "Drive that old man away" then, "ill, he is not old. But I say that he is a horrid old man. Nobody wants him here. Thank you, thank you." MISS X [says] "That's the spirit I told you of. She could not get rid of him last time." Silver Cloud goes on. Another description. She again interprets. Description recognized and message received. Then comes somebody not recognized.

Suddenly Swift's voice, speaking through medium: "You have written to her. What if she and I are married? What right have you to ask questions?" MISS X. "That is the spirit that spoils everything." [SWIFT'S VOICE.] "I found you an ignorant little girl, without intellectual or moral ambition, and that I might teach you I have left great men's houses. How many times did I not stay away from my Lord Treasurer, neglect affairs of the greatest moment, that we might read Plutarch together? I taught you to think in every situation of life not what Hester Vanhomrigh should do in that situation, but what Cato would and Brutus would, and now you peep and peer like any common slut, a common slut, I say a common slut. A common tavern slut her ear against the keyhole."

YOUNG MAN. Did you catch the name, Hester Vanhomrigh, that of the woman he called Vanessa?

MEDIUM (*in* VANESSA'S *voice*). Why did you make me love you? Why did you let me spend hour after hour in your company?

YOUNG MAN. That old woman wants us to believe that Vanessa is there too, speaking through her mouth.

SWIFT'S VOICE. My God, do you think it is easy to me? I am a man in whom [passion] is strong, and I swore that I would never marry.

VANESSA'S VOICE. If you are not married, Cadenus, why should we not live like other men and women? You came to my mother's house and began to teach me. I loved you from the first moment. I thought it would just [be] enough to be near you and speak to you. I followed [you] to Ireland five years ago, and I can bear [it] no longer. It is not enough [to] see you. It is not enough to see enough, not enough to see and speak to you, not enough to see and speak and touch your hand when we meet and part. Cadenus, Cadenus, I am a woman. Were the women Cato and Brutus loved any different? (*The* OLD WOMAN *stands up*.)

SWIFT'S VOICE. I have that within me no child must ever inherit. Do you recall that day in London when I got dizzy? I had to hold on to the bookcase, I almost fell. Dr. Arbuthnot — you remember the wise old man — I told of these attacks and other things, worse things. It was him who explained. Pope knew. You remember that line of his that great wit is allied [to madness]? He wrote that because I told him.

VANESSA'S VOICE. "Great wit is unto madness near allied." But Cadenus, if we had children, my blood would make them healthy. Give me your hand, let me lay [it] upon my heart, upon the Vanhomrigh blood, blood that has been healthy for generations. (OLD WOMAN *stands up.*)

[SWIFT'S VOICE.] What if it be healthy, what if [it] make mine healthy, or I add to all that common crowd called to till the fields?

VANESSA'S [VOICE.] Look at me Swift. It is your arrogance [?] that keeps you from me. Give [me] your hand, I say, give me both your hands. I would put then here upon my breast. O, it is white, white as are the gambler's dice, the little ivory dice. It is the uncertainty that brings them to the table. A mad child, perhaps — perhaps not, perhaps not, Cadenus. What does intellect matter with its loaded dice? I am the common ivory dice — white — white — white ivory. (OLD WOMAN *rises and then sinks back again.*) It is not my hands that pull you back, Cadenus. You love and I love. You are growing old. Do you want to grow old without children? Old people are very solitary. Their friends that remain are old too and solitary. They turn toward the young, but only their children or the children's child will endure an old man. But you are not yet old, Cadenus, and you love — white dice, white ivory dice. (*The* OLD WOMAN *gets up tottering.*)

SWIFT'S VOICE. O God, hear my prayer. Grant to Jonathan Swift, that afflicted man, that he may leave to posterity nothing but the intellect that came to him from Heaven. (*Comes to door.*) Who shut this door? (*Beats at door.*) My God, I am shut in with my enemy, with Vanessa who hates my soul. (*Crouches at door.*)

VOICE OF SILVER CLOUD. Bad old man. Big chief once. Bad old man, [does not] know he is dead. Don't let him back. Used up power and Silver Cloud can do nothing. Cannot find dear ones — fathers, husbands, sons that have passed over — if no power. (*Some one leads* OLD WOMAN *back to her chair.*) Have another verse of hymn. Everybody sing. Bring good influence. (*Verse sung.* OLD WOMAN *begins to speak during singing. Singing falters and stops.*)

SWIFT'S VOICE.

[In this scenario Yeats did not work out the contrasting scene with Stella. He merely outlined it, and then went on to the closing scene of the play.]

The following scene is what Swift speaks to Stella, quoting her poem. He has not wronged her? He asks her assurance. But no, he has her poem. She has had no children, but she has her intellect. Many friends. If she had married, what would she be now? Would her face give so much light? He begs [her] to outlive him, to close his eyes. His life has been always solitary but for her. Many friends and yet solitary. Begs her to the end. Repeats her poem. Yes, that is right and true to her soul.

*

[VOICE OF] SILVER CLOUD. Power all gone. Silver Cloud can do nothing more tonight. Goodby friends. Silver Cloud very sorry. Bad old man.

*

Miss X says "We're not [disappointed], you did your best." Puts down money. Old Woman says cannot accept it after a séance like that. "No, no, you must. Whether séance is good or bad it exhausts you just the same." People who had put down money take it up again. "No, put it down." They go out door. Young Man says "I thought it a wonderful séance, Mrs. P. You know, I get my doctorate by an essay on Swift. That is what brought me to Dublin." OLD WOMAN. "I should not take your money. I should not, really. I will not take anything." He says, "Look, I have given you twice as much as your regular fee. Now I will make it three times as much. They are all gone now. Won't you tell me how you know so much about Swift? Hardly anybody knows anything about the poem by Stella, and it is the best woman's poem in the language. Don't you think it like Donne in places? Then the begging of one could have explained events. [I am very uncertain of the transcription of the preceding sentence.] I wonder [what] she read? Then too that about his madness. I never could accept the idea so many people hold that he treated Stella and Vanessa as he did because of what the biographers call a physical defect. It is dead against the old Dublin tradition. Do you remember the story about the negress?" "Who are you talking about, Sir." "Why about Swift, of course." OLD WOMAN. "I don't know anybody called Swift." "O yes you do." "Nobody of that name here — but in Glasgow, I am a Glasgow woman, a great many people come to the séances. Or is it somebody who has passed on?" "Swift, Jonathan Swift, the spirit that was here tonight. You gave a wonderful impersonation." "What, that man, that dirty old man. Don't talk of him, it's not lucky to talk of him. Don't think of him, a bad spirit like that. To talk of them or think of them brings them." YOUNG MAN. "O well, I see you are very tired. We will have our talk some other day. Good night. You are certainly a genius." (*Exit. She lowers the lamp or blows out the candles. Puts on kettle.*) SWIFT'S VOICE. "Harley gone, Bolingbroke gone, the Duke of Ormonde, Godolphin gone" — *counting on fingers* — "five great ministers, ten great ministers that I have known. I have not fingers enough to count up the great ministers that I have known and that are gone." (OLD WOMAN *wakes with a start, takes down teapot and cup and goes to fire to arrange kettle better.*) SWIFT'S VOICE. "Perish the day on which I was born etc."

In this scenario of *The Words upon the Window-pane* Yeats has worked out his play much more completely than he usually did in scenarios. The reason for this may be that his materials were all thoroughly familiar. He had experienced the drama of the séance room hundreds of times; Swift had become the central figure in a kind of classic Anglo-Ireland Yeats was in the process of constructing. Yeats says in his "Introduction" to the play in *Wheels and Butterflies*, "Swift haunts me; he is always just around the next corner." Even a visitor can find Swift curiously present still in modern Dublin, especially in those parts of Dublin around St. Patrick's. Then too the Irish memory is so very long that Cromwell's brutal pacification seems to have happened only yesterday, Swift's long deanship to have been more recent still.

In fact the scenario version of the exposition of the play shows that the drama of the séance room, the doctrine of earth bound spirits, and so on, were too familiar to Yeats. He assumes too much knowledge in his audience. His initial exposition is very rapid; he has not yet invented the character Abraham Johnson whose wish to exorcise the spirit disturbing the séances leads Dr. Trench to explain earth bound spirits. In addition to this major change, Yeats will make many minor changes in his exposition. He has still to invent the character names he will use. He will change some incidents; Mrs. Mallet's husband will drown rather than die in a flying accident. Mrs. Henderson's control is here, and through several drafts of the exposition remained, Silver Cloud, a little American Indian girl. Yeats noted in an unpublished manuscript, "Leo Africanus," that the "controls" of many mediums were similar — a man with a deep voice, an American Indian girl, a child — all possessed of speech characteristics easy to imitate. No doubt Yeats made the change to avoid the jargon of the stage Indian;

when Silver Cloud calls Swift a "big chief" she is unintentionally funny at a point in the play where verbal humor is hardly in order.

But the central action of the play has been worked out in the scenario; the contrast of Swift with Rousseau has been stated; the scene between Swift and Vanessa very fully realized, even to much of the language that Yeats will retain. He has roughed in the contrasting scene with Stella; he has only to expand and finish this sketch. The scenario ends much as the finished play ends, and the final line "Perish the day on which I was born" is in place. We will find when we examine the drafts of *Purgatory* that its final line also occurred to Yeats early and persisted through many drafts. In spite of some contradictory stage directions and slips of memory, as when Yeats attributes Dryden's line "Great wits are sure to madness near allied" to Pope, the work of planning the play has largely been done.

Yeats continued work on *The Words upon the Window-pane* by writing a list of his *dramatis personae,* a summary of the exposition, then two drafts of this exposition, the second of which he carries down to the beginning of the séance, that is to the point where the scenario begins to anticipate the action of the finished play very closely. My editing of these drafts is more radical than usual, because I have frequently had to choose between trial locutions all left uncancelled, and to decide just where Yeats intended to begin and to end his cancellations. Again, as with the scenario, I have not transcribed any cancelled passages, except in the list of characters.

The list of characters and brief scenario which follow were written on a single page:

CHARACTERS

John ~~Lefanu~~ McKenna	man of ~~sixty~~ seventy
John Corbet	man of 25
Mary Duncan	between 27 and 30. not married
Rev. Simon Mallet	man of 35
Mrs. Henderson	sixty, stout and common
Mrs. James	woman of 45

SCENARIO

Lefanu and Corbet. Discuss room and Swift's character. Mallet and Mrs. Duncan come in to complain of annoying spirit. Mallet wants an exorcism. Lefanu objects. Explains what spirits are. Lefanu introduces

Corbet to Miss Duncan. Skeptical conversation. She thinks spirits are transference fed by telepathy, but he thinks it all juggling. Medium comes in.

Here Yeats establishes four of the character names he will keep, though he will transfer the name MacKenna to the secretary, here called Mary Duncan, and the name Mallet to the woman here called Mrs. James. Cornelius Patterson, only referred to in the scenario, is omitted both from the list of characters and the summary outline of the exposition. This outline shows that Yeats was planning the fuller explanation of earth bound spirits found in the finished play. On the next page of his manuscript book Yeats began a draft of his exposition. He broke off his draft after eight speeches, then started again and carried through to the beginning of the séance. I have placed the partial first draft alongside the second draft to make the detail of Yeat's changes clear.

[Draft 1]

A large room. CORBET *and* MACKENNA'S *voices heard at first outside the door in what follows.*

MACKENNA: Through a glass darkly seems old fashioned now as Uncle Silas reads as well as ever.

CORBET: Her making the one good influence on Uncle Silas a Swedenborgian shows where her interests lay.

MACKENNA: Yes, that kind of thing runs in my mother's family. Sheridan Lefanu was her uncle. If you had heard the talk I have heard from my mother and from my old aunt, you would understand how in after life such things become an obsession. I have worked at my business and have done well, and yet I can honestly say that it has had very little of my

[Draft 2]

SWIFT

PETER TRENCH *and* WILLIAM CORBET *enter*

PETER TRENCH: We have no good mediums in Ireland, and we are so few that we can seldom afford to bring a medium from the other side. Mrs. Henderson has come from Glasgow. We all give what we can; she lives very economically and does not expect a great deal. This is her third séance. This is the first of her séances that I have been able to attend, but I thought. My great interest in life has been what people call apparitions — all that relation between man and the supernatural which philosophy and the church ignores. Though my study has been mainly theoretical, for there are no good mediums in Ireland, and there are so few to share the expense that we can very seldom get one from across the water. Mrs. Henderson has come from Glasgow at her own risk; we are all to give her what we can. She lives very economically and does not expect a great deal. Help me with these chairs; they should be nearer that arm chair.

CORBET: A wonderful room for a lodging house.

saw a great deal of the movement as a young man. I knew Home, the Fox sisters, Eglinton — all the great mediums. That is why they have made me chairman of the Dublin Spiritualistic Society.

CORBET: I have [never] been to a séance.

TRENCH: And think it all juggling?

CORBET: Yes.

TRENCH: I thought the same, but one soon gets over that. If you get nothing tonight, you must come again. Several is little evidence. Sometimes a séance is spoiled. Mrs. Henderson's séances have been a good deal spoiled — a disturbing influence of some kind. She is a trance medium. If all goes well, you may get some evidence for it, or even recognize some mannerism, some trick of phrase, or even of movement, though that is rare.

CORBET: A wonderful room for a lodging house. (*During what follows two or three people enter,*

MACKENNA: It was a private house until about forty years ago. It was not so near the town in those days. There are quite large stables at the back. It was an important place in the eighteenth century. Yes, I think that should be enough. I do not expect many people. In the early eighteenth century this house belonged to friends of Swift — it's mentioned in the Journal to Stella several times. Stella used to play cards here and Swift chaffed her about her losses.

CORBET: How exciting. I am hoping to get my doctorate in Oxford by an essay on Swift and Stella. That is what brought me to Dublin.

MACKENNA: There are some lines from a poem of Stella's cut on that window with a diamond. I wonder what Swift would think of our work tonight?

CORBET: Not much, I think.

but remain near the door as if listening to what is going on outside.)

TRENCH: This was a private house until about fifty years ago. It was not so near the town in those days. There are quite large stables at the back. People of some importance lived here in the eighteenth century. It once belonged to friends of Swift — it is mentioned in the Journal to Stella several times. Stella used to lose small sums at cards and Swift chaffed her about them. Somebody cut with a diamond two lines from a poem of hers on the window-pane. Tradition says Swift, but that is not likely, and he never [wrote] anything that was not bitter or satirical. Here they are, but you can hardly read them in this light. (*They stand at window.* TRENCH *points out the exact spot.* CORBET *stoops down to see.* JOHNSON *and* MISS MACKENNA *enter.*)

Yeats broke off his first draft at this point. The two drafts make an interesting contrast. In the second Yeats has changed to the character names he will keep, inventing a new name for Trench and transferring the name Mackenna to the secretary. In draft 1 the opening speeches don't accomplish anything; Yeats starts hares he has no intention of pursuing. In draft 2 Peter Trench says everything essential to be known in his first, much shorter speech. Yeats then goes on to present

Corbet as a skeptic neophyte, a man to whom explanations such as the audience needs would be in order. Trench immediately starts these explanations when he talks of Mrs. Henderson's séances being spoiled and of the nature of her mediumship. Just before Yeats broke off draft 1, he had Corbet present himself as a Swift expert. This is far more effectively represented in the continuation of draft 2 when Corbet shows himself to be a Swift scholar by recognizing the lines from Stella's poem.

Draft 2 continues:

JOHNSON: Where is Mrs. Henderson?

MACKENNA: She is upstairs. She always rests before a séance.

JOHNSON: I must see her before the séance. We must get [rid] of the evil influence which has disturbed the last two séances. I know what has to be done.

MACKENNA: If you speak to her you will upset her nerves, and then there will be no séance at all.

JOHNSON: Where is Mrs. Mallet? She is, I am told, an experienced spiritualist. I will consult [her]. (*A bell rings or knocker sounds.*)

MISS MACKENNA: There she is now, and she has probably brought old Rogers. You can bring him into the smoking room. (*Her voice is heard "We are so glad to see you, Mrs. Mallet; there is something, etc."*)

CORBET: I know those two lines well. They are from a poem she wrote for his birthday. They might [be] out of some seventeenth century poet — Donne or Crashaw. (*He quotes*)

['You taught me how I might youth prolong
By knowing what is right and wrong,]

She was a much better poet than Swift.

TRENCH: I have shown that writing to several people and you are the first to recognize those lines.

CORBET: I am writing an essay on Swift and Stella. It is for my doctorate at the university. He would not think much of our occupation tonight.

TRENCH: Is there something in *Gulliver* about an island where [they] could call up any of the great dead they had a mind for?

CORBET: There is.

TRENCH: A kind of séance.

CORBET: The magicians' island. It comes in the second voyage.

TRENCH: Something like our séance tonight.

CORBET: Gulliver was told that he [could] call back from the dead anybody he liked, and asked for Brutus, Cato, Sir Thomas Moore, seven men, and except for Sir Thomas Moore, all Greek or Roman worthies — men to whom, as Swift says, the world could not add an eighth. If we could call up such men and give proof that they really came, your movement would conquer the world.

TRENCH: So Gulliver called up seven men, the seven men out of all history most admired by Swift, and there was only one Christian among the seven. What a pagan Swift was. The power of the spiritualist movement, considered not as a science but as a religious movement, is that it enables ordinary people to speak across the great barrier to other ordinary people whom they have known and loved. In the first phase of the movement a great many people thought they could call up just such spirits as Gulliver called up on the magicians' island. They ran into every kind [of] absurdity and delusion.

CORBET: Swift hated the ordinary man. "I hate lawyers, I hate doctors," he was accustomed to say, "though I love judge so-and-so and doctor so-and-so." He calls the Houyhnmhnms his ideal people, the perfection of nature, meaning by that nature bred, trained and disciplined, nature made perfect by intellect. He thought the Roman Senate had it in its great days. I hope to prove in my essay that in Swift's day Europe had reached its highest point of intellectual achievement. I can prove from Swift's every work that he foresaw the ruin to come, Democracy, Rousseau, the French Revolution. That is why he hated ordinary men, that is why he wrote *Gulliver,* that is why he wore out his brain, that where he got *saeva indignatio,* that is why he sleeps now under the greatest epitaph in history. You remember how it runs, "He has gone where fierce indignation can lacerate his heart no more." (JOHNSON *returns and comes up to* TRENCH, *followed by* MISS MACKENNA *and two or three other persons.*)

JOHNSON: Something will have to be done, Mr. Trench, to drive away the influence that has been disturbing the séances. I have come here at considerable expense week after week. I am from Belfast. I am by profession a minister of the gospel. I do a great deal of work [among] the poorer classes, and often produce as great [an] effect by my singing as by my preaching, and my great hope is that I shall be able to communicate through some medium with the great revivalist preacher, Mr. Sankey. I want to ask him to stand by me upon the platform and help me with his influence. A woman in Belfast, a fortune teller who has a great gift with the cards, a woman in every way comparable to one of the ancient sybils, told [me] that I would be able to speak to Mr. Sankey if I came to Dublin. But I have got nothing.

MRS. MALLET: What Mr. Johnson says is quite true. The last two séances have been completely spoiled by a spirit which says a lot of unintelligible [things] and does not pay the slightest attention to what we say. For after the séance has begun, the spirit begins talking, though there are, as I think, two spirits. There is a long unintelligible quarrel. And poor Mrs. Henderson is lost to those here and this in the most horrifying way.

TRENCH: Did this spirit, or these spirits, say the same things each night?

MRS. MALLET: Yes, just as [if] they were characters in a play, a very horrible play.

MR. TRENCH: We spiritualists do not admit there are any evil spirits. The spirits are just ordinary people like ourselves. We do not permit the spirits that come to us to be driven away with curses, or violence of any kind. Some spirits are what we call earth bound. They think they are still living and go over and over some action of their lives. We cannot help dwelling on our past actions, and if they were bad actions the thought is very painful. After we are dead we do not merely think of the past action, but re-enact [it]. When a spirit comes back through a medium for the first time, it re-enacts the pains of death.

MRS. MALLET: When my husband came first, he seemed to gasp and struggle as [if] he were drowning. As the medium had to do the same it was most painful to watch.

TRENCH: But sometimes, and most ghosts are of this kind, the spirit re-enacts some painful or passionate moment of its life. The murderer repeats his murder, the robber his robbery, the lover seems to make love once more, the soldier to hear the word of command. We write *requiescat in pace* on the tombs, but they cannot rest. If I were a Catholic I would say such spirits were [in purgatory]. Such spirits do not often come to séances unless those séances take place in the house where the event re-enacted took place. This spirit who speaks unintelligible words, who does not answer when spoken to, if it was such a spirit, we can help it by patient and friendly thoughts. It wears out its remorse or passion by re-enacting it.

JOHNSON: I am convinced that the spirit which has spoiled the last two séances is an evil spirit. You will not object, I conclude, if I pray that the séance may be protected from evil spirits?

TRENCH: Such prayers are unnecessary. Every good medium is protected by his controls, and Silver Cloud, Mrs. Henderson's principal control, is very able and experienced.

JOHNSON: I will not pray aloud, I will pray in my own mind.

TRENCH: Pray that the spirit may be at rest — that can do no harm. (*He sits down and begins moving his lips.* MRS. HENDERSON *enters and during what follows all take their places, turn up the gas, arrange the chairs, etc.*)

TRENCH: Mrs. Henderson, may I introduce Mr. Corbet, a young man from Cambridge. He is a skeptic, but we were all that once, and here is Miss Mackenna, our secretary.

MISS MACKENNA: I am glad you are a skeptic, Mr. Corbet. I have been at all Mrs. Henderson's séances, and I do not know what to think.

CORBET: (*In a low voice*) Is it not all just conjuring and play acting?

MISS MACKENNA: Mrs. Henderson's somnambulism is perfectly genuine, but I sometimes think that there is nothing that cannot be explained by thought transference. Mrs. Henderson's trance personality may draw upon the thoughts of those present. What Mrs. Mallet and old Rogers call the "summer land" [?] is just the kind of paradise some people desire. Everything they do here they expect to do there. Old Rogers lost every penny he had on horses, and expects to find a breed [of] dogs and horses in the grave where he can win back his money.

CORBET: I prefer the heaven of Bottecelli [?].

MISS MACKENNA: But old Rogers and Mrs. Mallet don't want [to] be Bottecelli [?] angels, or anything different from what they are.

CORBET: You think that spiritualism gets its pupils because it professes to prove the existence of a heaven, of an utterly impossible and preposterous heaven?

MISS MACKENNA: Sometimes I think that and then I don't mind, but at other times I think just as Mr. Trench does, and then I am terrified. You remember the words of Job, "A spirit passed before my face, and the hair of my head stands up."

CORBET: You say you are glad I am a skeptic?

MISS MACKENNA: It makes me feel safer. I came here rather terrified, as if something might happen tonight.

Yeats broke off his draft at this point, or carried it on elsewhere on loose sheets which have not survived. We observed earlier that from this point on the scenario anticipates almost exactly the action of the rest of the play, and it may be that it gave Yeats sufficient guidance for the remainder. There is in this same manuscript book a draft of Corbet's final speech to the medium, Mrs. Henderson:

You have excited me beyond words. Were they actually spirits, or did you, as I prefer to think, create it all, whether awake or asleep? I would like to compliment your scholarship. Your explanation of Swift's celibacy [is] an explanation which I proved in my essay for my doctorate as the only plausible explanation. But there is something that I want to ask. Swift was the chief representative of the intellect of his epoch, that intellect arrogant [in] its triumph over superstition; he foresaw its collapse. Did he refuse to beget children out of dread of the future? Was Swift mad, or was it the intellect itself that was mad?

The draft of the exposition reproduced above has faults exactly opposite from those of the corresponding parts of the scenario. I suspect from this example and from others in unpublished works that whenever Yeats began to write on esoteric subjects he tended to become expository and prolix, to make a kind of Shavian exhortation on his very un-Shavian subject.

In this draft all the names that Yeats will use are established, except for Cornelius Patterson who is here referred to as old Rogers, and the exposition develops along the lines of the exposition of the finished play. When the play opens in the draft, Corbet and Trench are alone. They talk about Mrs. Henderson's mediumship, Corbet's skepticism, and then go on directly to discuss the room where the séance is to be held. The device of formal introduction used in the finished play, where Miss Mackenna lets them in, is neater. When Miss Mackenna leaves them in the finished play, Trench explains trance mediumship and describes more fully than in the draft the hostile influence that has intruded on the earlier séances; both are needed to explain the séance that follows. At this point in the finished play they begin to discuss the room, and while they are reading the words scratched on the window-pane, Johnson and Mrs. Mallet enter. From their entry to the point where Corbet reads out the words of Stella's poem the draft and the finished play are very similar. The draft continues with the account of the magicians' island from the third book of *Gulliver's Travels.* In the finished play this has been cut entirely, and in place of it Corbet makes a brief exposition of the relations of Swift, Stella, and Vanessa. Again, something not needed has been cut out, something needed put in. The draft continues with Trench's account of the usual view of spiritualists towards the "other life" — that it will be just like this life only more so. Again, Yeats cuts this from the finished play, along with Miss Mackenna's extension of the same line of thought a little further down. Instead he puts into Corbet's mouth his own view of Swift's position: here the substance of the draft and the finished play are the same. In both versions Corbet has just Englished Swift's epitaph when Johnson and the others enter. Save for the excision of Mrs. Mallet's and Cornelius Patterson's ideas of heaven, draft and finished play are much alike down to the entrance of Mrs. Henderson: Johnson proposes the exorcism, Trench explains earth bound spirits, there is further discussion of Corbet's skepticism. The draft breaks off at the point where the séance begins. Certainly the exposition in the finished play is admirably neat and concise, and better yet seems natural and uncontrived, something that cannot be said of the exposition in the draft, though even here Yeats has advanced a long way beyond the scenario. Yeats's happiest device in draft and finished play is to make Corbet a skeptic and a neophyte, a character to whom explanations would necessarily be made. The draft of Corbet's speech to Mrs. Henderson after the séance is very like the finished play.

The only other manuscript of *The Words upon the Window-pane* that I have seen is Yeats's final manuscript, signed, and dated from Coole Park, October, 1930. In this manuscript the play has reached final form; indeed I know of no other manuscript by Yeats so nearly like the work printed from it. Perhaps lack of a secretary caused Yeats in this instance to carry on in manuscript work which he usually did on typescripts. I do not know whether there were intermediate drafts which I have not seen, but I am inclined to believe that Yeats made such drafts. At least he did not usually make so much progress on a play between successive drafts as we would have to suppose he made here if his final manuscript grew directly from the versions we have been studying.

The Words upon the Window-pane combines several of Yeats's favorite subjects — Swift, Anglo-Ireland in the 18th century, an earth bound spirit — and exploits the drama of a séance. The result is a fine play, though hardly a typical one. In his plays Yeats seldom ventured into the contemporary world: the young Aran Islander in *The Dreaming of the Bones* who is making his way home following the Easter

Rebellion is the only other certain instance, though a play like *Purgatory* is timeless and Yeats's production note indicates that he thought of it as happening in the present: "The destruction is taking place all over Ireland today." And though in various plays Yeats used some aspects of the realistic mode, this is the only play in which he used all of them. Indeed David R. Clark has shown in a fine essay not yet published that in *The Words upon the Window-pane* Yeats borrowed Ibsen's dramaturgy entire to express a subject very unlike Ibsen's usual subjects. I suspect Yeats derived a certain wry amusement from doing this, perhaps not unlike the amusement Shakespeare must have felt when he made *The Tempest* conform to the Unities. Certainly Yeats's play demonstrates that it was not any inability to handle the realistic mode that caused him to spend his life perfecting nonrealistic modes. And Yeats's view of Swift, although it will hardly please recent Swift scholars, does make a crucial point: namely that Swift's *saeva indignatio* cannot be adequately explained by his dislike of Walpole's government or the desperate condition of Ireland, rather that he did indeed foresee what was from his point of view, that of a Christian humanist, (and Yeats's different point of view) "the ruin to come." [1]

8

The Resurrection

YEATS began *The Resurrection* in 1925 or 1926, long before he began *The Words upon the Window-pane,* but he did not finish until after the Swift play had been successfully produced. Yeats had the same kind of difficulty with *The Resurrection* that he had with certain of his early plays, with *On Baile's Strand,* for example, which he re-wrote within three years of its first publication. Only two of Yeats's later plays were printed in radically different versions, *The Resurrection* and *The King of the Great Clock Tower,* rewritten as *A Full Moon in March.* The first printed version of *The Resurrection,* which appeared in *The Adelphi* for June 1927, Yeats later described as a "chaotic dialogue"; he seemed to know that the play was not done, for he did not print it in any of the books he published between 1927 and 1931 when he included it in *Stories of Michael Robartes and His Friends,* published in 1932.

Since the manuscript record of *The Resurrection* is complex, it may help us to study it with understanding if we begin with speculations why it took Yeats so long to complete the play. It was certainly not because the ideas expressed in it were new or had not been elsewhere explored: Yeats wrote out a paraphrase of Heraclitus' words with which the play ends in a slightly different form in a Journal begun in December 1908. (The entry is not dated; the next dated entry was written April 15, 1909.) In his Journal Yeats wrote: "The immortals are mortal, the mortals immortal, each living the other's death and dying the other's life. Heraclitus." Another basic idea found in the play was expressed in "The Second Coming" (1919) — the shock of Christ's incarnation to the classical world — and nearly all the themes of the play are explored in the "Dove or Swan" section of *A Vision* finished according to Yeats's dating at Capri in February 1925.

Part of the explanation why it took Yeats so long is that *Calvary* got very much in his way. In the economy of Yeats's art, as we have seen before, an earlier work using material to which he wished to return in a later work frequently stood in the way of the new work. Here this was particularly true of the use of Judas in the earlier play. Judas does not appear in *The Resurrection*, but Yeats was not finally able to exorcise discussion of him from the new play until he revised his third manuscript. And yet I cannot see that the discussion of Judas contributed anything to the new play at any time. It was excess baggage from the start.

A better explanation of the delay is, I believe, the sheer difficulty of the playwriting task which Yeats had set himself in *The Resurrection:* he undertook to dramatize a theological argument about Christ's nature — was he all man, was he all God, was he both man and God? Part of the answer how to do this was easy, give each point of view a spokesman, and Yeats arrived at it easily for he has already done this in manuscript one. But the answer to the problem of making these bones live was more difficult to arrive at. It is easy enough to say that one makes an abstract argument theatrically viable by clothing it in effective symbolic detail, but to do this is another matter. For what detail is effective? A piece of Odysseus' oar, an unhatched egg of Leda? The manuscript record shows that Yeats did indeed experience serious difficulty in selecting effective symbolic detail, difficulty more serious than he had had at any time since his long struggle with *The Player Queen.*

Then too problems which all dramatists must face seem to have caused Yeats more trouble while composing *The Resurrection* than they usually did: getting one's exposition done quickly and in an orderly way without making your audience too aware that you are making an exposition; achieving an effective dramatic style, and so on. The search for a solution to these problems, combined no doubt with others — was Yeats really sure he wanted to come up with so Christian an answer? — may explain why it took Yeats five or six years to write this play.

The genesis of *The Resurrection* is found in two scenarios, different from each other and quite unlike either the 1927 or 1931 versions. Then Yeats wrote two manuscript versions of the play before its first printing; the second manuscript is very like the *Adelphi* text. He returned to the play in 1930 and wrote two more manuscript versions of it. In the fourth manuscript he nearly finished the play as we know it. Manuscripts 1 and 2 are at the National Library of Ireland; the rest of the manuscript material quoted is in Mrs. Yeats's collection.

i

The Scenarios

THE DATING OF THE SCENARIOS and the first draft of *The Resurrection* is a problem typical of Yeats scholarship, so I will present the conflicting evidence briefly, leaving the problem unsolved: The scenarios are dated either "~~Sunday~~ Jan ~~20~~ 21 & 22" or "~~Sunday~~ June ~~20~~ 21 & 22." (Yeats often wrote "Jun" for June, and his "a" and "u" are nearly identical.) Yeats dated the flap of the envelope in which MS. 1 is filed "June 1925." Hone reports (p. 417, English ed.) that the play was read out at 82 Merrion Square in 1925, writing as though he had been present at the reading. To the contrary, Lady Gregory reports that Yeats composed the second stanza of the "Song for the unfolding and folding of the curtain" on May 24, 1926 (*Journals*, p. 263). There is an early draft of this stanza on the back of the last sheet of MS. 1, the MS. filed in the envelope dated by Yeats "June 1925." June 20, 1926 did fall on a Sunday, and was the only June *or* January day so to fall in the mid-twenties. Summary: Yeats and Hone, both notoriously unreliable about dates, favor 1925; Lady Gregory, notoriously reliable about dates and the fact that June 20, 1926, was Sunday, favors 1926.

The manuscript of the scenarios of *The Resurrection* was written on loose sheets of paper. When I examined it, it had been placed with the final manuscript of the play (MS. 4), written in 1930–31 in the Rapallo Notebook labelled "E." The manuscript of the scenarios, very roughly written, is quite different from any drafts of the play.

~~RESURRECTION~~

DANCE PLAY

Musician comes [in] as in my dance plays. Curtained place. Enter two men. The men go through movement of rolling back stone, which a musician describes. Figure of Christ enters in long spiral garment and stands in middle. Women enter and go through movements of unwinding grave clothes. Probably they sing both while rolling back stone and when unwinding. Christ stands motionless. Song in which one voice says "Saul said why have you troubled me" and the other speaks "Coming forth from the tomb." Christ does not at first remember who or where he is. He vaguely remembers the crucifixion. Then they say "Yes, you died for men, and so on." This recalls all. Question and answer are in such form as to bring out the essential facts. Then Christ says, "I have taken away the sins of men," and asks who they are. They tell their deaths. Each has died for man. When he questions, Buddha says "No, I died of eating too much pork." Other interrupts. His sacrifice was the worst of all—he was not put to death. He renounced heaven to be always with mankind. Christ [cries] out in agony again, "The endless sin and misery of men, for whom the gods die in vain." All the others steal away except three women who kneel at his feet and Buddha who says, "This is your mother and two friends." The three Maries. And Christ hesitates and then says, "I am the way and the life."

Or musicians could be left out — orchestra takes their place. In which case the two figures who roll away stone should describe scene instead of musicians doing so.

Or it could be made a dance play for ordinary theatre as follows: Two black-clothed men. Hats to suggest fairly modern tall hats. They look at the heavens and say, "The moment has come to roll back the stone, the constellations are rightly placed." They roll away stone which is represented, not suggested merely. They discuss and describe. Christ comes from tomb still, except for feet, wrapped in grave clothes. Some women approach, friends of the god who has died, the men say. These women who wear clothes of no period with some tone to suggest the hospital nurse, dance, slowly unwinding the grave clothes. Christ when unwound does not know where he is. Has a vague memory, growing in intensity, of the crucifixion. The two men speak like doctors to a patient — all will be well in a moment, he should not think of such dreams, etc. Presently he bursts out that it was no dream, he remembers all now. He has taken away the sins of men. He speaks in exultation. He asks who these are who question. One is Dionysus, who describes his death; one is Buddha. There is perhaps a third. The son of the great Mother, perhaps, crucified in a pine tree. He asks Buddha, "Did you also die for the people?" Buddha says, "No, I died sitting under a tree from eating too much pork." The other says they never question him, his sacrifice was too great. He did not die, he refused heaven that he might be near mankind. "It is a tragedy to men to die, and to the gods to be born." Then Christ sees many persons coming. He asks "Who are these" and is told "Gods who have died for men." He is about to kneel, but Buddha stops him. He answers "I am still a man." Buddha says [?] "Only the god who suffers lives, or only the act is divine — in that we put on divinity; now one, now another as the turning heavens decree." They pass singing before him and bow as they pass. Their song is "Why have you troubled me said Saul" enlarged to a stanza or chorus, and verses about the risen Christ. They pass out and the women pass out, all but three. Christ bursts out about the eternal sins of man, his vain suffering. Buddha, who alone of the men remains, says, "Look, they kneel to you — Mary your mother, the other Maries, chief of all your worshippers." Christ spreads out his arms. "I am the life and the way."

Apparently Yeats never tried to work either of these sketches up into a play; indeed he largely gave up the idea of making *The Resurrection* a dance play. He used the central idea of the scenarios, that the death and birth of God recurs eternally, in his opening lyric, and also expressed it in the play when he treated the resurrection of Christ and Dionysus as parallel events. The rather odd idea of having Christ's spirit participate in the "dreaming back" of the dead described in *A Vision* and elsewhere Yeats abandoned entirely. The spirally wound grave clothes or mummy cloths is one form of a symbol that recurs frequently in poems written in the 1920's, but this does not appear in any draft of *The Resurrection.* The last lines of the finished play are anticipated in scenario 2 when Yeats writes "It is a tragedy to men to die, and to the gods to be born," though Yeats's, as was noted above, had first paraphrased Heraclitus in 1909. Neither scenario strikes me as very promising: the unwinding of Christ's grave clothes by dancing women in scenario 2 reminds one of a maypole dance; giving Christ a speaking part would surely embarrass production; there are far too many gods.

ii

Manuscript one

THE EARLIEST MANUSCRIPT of "The Resurrection" is a draft which appears to have been written rapidly. Already the theme of the play is established, that the death and rebirth of the gods occurs in cycles and that the essential difference between the Christian myth and earlier myths is that Christ was very man as well as very God, that he did indeed die, and that he was reborn in his double nature.

Manuscript 1 opens with the Greek and Hebrew on stage. There is no song for the unfolding and folding of the cloth. A draft of the first stanza of this is attached at the end of the manuscript on an unnumbered sheet; there is a rough draft of the second stanza, the stanza Lady Gregory heard Yeats composing, on the back of the last numbered page of the manuscript. The Greek and Hebrew begin the play by discussing Judas, seeking an explanation why he betrayed Christ and why he has hanged himself. They tell us they are guarding the Apostles, who are taking a simple meal in an inner room. The Hebrew then expresses his doubt of Christ's divinity, which he thinks Judas had doubted long ago. The Greek expresses the gnostic view he was to continue to express in all versions of the play, that Christ was a phantom, that all gods have been phantoms. The Hebrew doesn't share this view of Christ's nature, and insists that the Apostles don't either. For them it must be "complete light or complete darkness." The Greek and Hebrew return to the discussion of Judas. He betrayed Christ because he doubted Christ's divinity, and because he had expected Christ to found a temporal kingdom. The Greek insists that Christ was never interested in politics. The Hebrew says that Christ first deceived himself by coming to believe in his divinity, then he deceived others. They discuss Christ's miracles. To the Hebrew these can be explained; after all, other men have worked miracles. He is rather glad it is all over: "I know a wine shop where there are girls." The Greek returns to his phantom theory, but the Hebrew wants his savior to be both god and man, and feels he has been deceived. He hears the sound of the Dionysian revel, which is now described. The sacrifice of the kid by the priests of Dionysus is seen as a travesty of the communion. Dionysus' death is described. Then the Syrian returns with the news that Christ's tomb is empty. He wants to tell the Eleven, but the Greek and Hebrew refuse to let him. Then in MS. 1 the end of the play goes as follows:

THE HEBREW If we told them, they would think as I do, but Peter's misery would be deepened. I have been with them longer than you, and I know what would happen. Peter would remember that the women did not flinch; and that their dream showed that they had loved their master as he did not; and after that he would imagine that John was looking at him and he would turn away and bury his head in his hands.

THE GREEK He is right, we should [not] bring them any story unless we ourselves are certain that it is true.

THE SYRIAN But why should it not be true; a moment ago I passed the priests of Dionysus; and all over Asia Minor and even Rome when they worship Attis there are priests who represent such death and resurrection. But why should not God himself turn ceremony into reality at last?

THE GREEK That is to say God himself has been crucified. I think that you are right.

THE SYRIAN He became flesh.

THE GREEK You were right when you said God has been crucified, but when you said God became flesh you said what is nonsense. How could the creator of the world enter into the body of a woman and be born from a woman, and be washed and fed by women?

THE SYRIAN I thought just now as I came down the mountain, we have all suffered, one man for this, another for that; and we are all discontented and humiliated; but if God himself has suffered, and all for my sake, I will not be discontented and humiliated any more.

THE GREEK To think that God who is all purity could be mixed into the indignity of the human body is the most terrible blasphemy. Nor is it possible that God suffered, for being God, he is perfect and therefore entirely happy.

THE SYRIAN Then what did Mary of Galilee nurse [upon] her knees?

THE GREEK The thought of children makes women mad, and even a thaumaturgist could make women believe that they carried upon their knees the master of the world. Christ was never laid in the tomb, and so no wonder it is now empty. The women have seen Christ, and he's today as he has always been. The childhood in Galilee, the preaching, the crucifixion, the seeming dead body, the figure on the mountain side are phantoms. He but seemed to show [?] in condescension to our weakness.

THE SYRIAN He was a god, he was a man.

THE GREEK God, pure god, god only.

THE HEBREW He was a man and he is dead. There are the priests of Dionysus again, but at the other side of the house. They carry their image through all the streets of the city calling upon it to awake, and every year they do that. They make god live and die as they please, and all is but a lunatic phantasy. Listen to them now, "God has arisen" they cry — poor lunatics, drunk with their imaginary joy. "God has arisen." Look at them, look how they roll their painted eyes; did ever men show such abandon in the expression of a real emotion as they in their histrionic phrensy? But the ears of the dead are not as sensitive as ours. (*A loud sound of rattles and drum strokes*) Why are they suddenly silent? They raise their hands above their heads and cry out "He has arisen; he has arisen from the dead." That is what they cry.

THE GREEK There is someone in the house.

THE HEBREW Where?

THE GREEK I do not know but I thought I heard someone breathing.

THE HEBREW There is no one here. Nobody could have got in without our knowing. Look, the door is still fastened.

THE GREEK The curtain over there is moving.

THE HEBREW No, it is quite still; and besides there is nothing behind that curtain but a blank wall.

THE GREEK Look, look.

THE HEBREW Yes, it has begun to move.

THE GREEK My god, there is someone coming through it. (*They have turned away. The figure of Christ comes through curtain*) It is the form [of] our master. Why are you afraid? Seeing that he never was crucified and never was buried — never a reality — it is natural that he should appear. But there is nothing there but an appearance, a form, a phantom. There is no flesh and blood. Look, because I know the truth [I am] so little afraid that I will touch it. (*He does so, and then cries out*) The heart of the phantom is beating! The heart of the phantom is beating! (*He shrinks back. The Figure passes through to inner room, the other two passing in before it.*) Something terrible [has] happened. I thought that my hand would have passed through it. He is standing in [the] midst of them now. Some of them are afraid — Peter and James and John. Thomas is saying something. The phantom is speaking; it has parted the grave clothes from its side and shows the wound. Thomas has put his hand into the wound. Now they are all gathering round, and the phantom is speaking again. Something terrible has happened. Those out there in the street are standing perhaps as they were a moment [ago] with their arms lifted. Yes, they are standing and they look as if they knew nothing. And there are the Galilean women, Mary the mother of Jesus and Mary the mother of James and the rest coming from the mountain. They know; they are coming to say what they [have] seen. Hitherto we have had the dead or the quick, now we have the dead and the quick. Never before did the heart of a phantom beat. It is very terrible. (*Then with a loud* [*voice*]) Hear, all you men of Jerusalem, know now all men whether men of Rome, of Alexandria, or of Athens. The heart of a phantom is beating.

The MS. 1 version of *The Resurrection* shows a considerable advance over the scenarios: the excess gods have been cut away, and Yeats now centers his action on the similarities between Christ and Dionysus. The play ends strongly when the Greek feels Christ's heart beating; indeed except for improvements in language the end of the play was little changed in the successive versions. But the play is almost dominated by discussion of Judas and continued to be until Yeats cut all this out in a revision of MS. 3. The exposition of the three views of Christ's nature — that he was a man, that he was a god, that he was both man and god — takes far too long and its presentation is talky and undramatic. Yeats did not solve this problem until he revised MS. 4. The style is often flat, without tension: Yeats uses these words in the Greek's final speech, "It is very terrible."

iii

Manuscript two

MANUSCRIPT 2 is a careful revision of MS. 1, which it considerably improves. In MS. 2 Yeats brings *The Resurrection* very close to the version printed in *The Adelphi* in June 1927. The opening lyric is now in place, though it has not quite reached its final form. The Greek has become an Egyptian from Alexandria. The play opens with a bit about sending the Syrian to see if Jesus' body is still in the tomb. The discussion of Christ's nature, of Judas' betrayal, and of the situation of the disciples follows, much as in MS. 1 except for inevitable verbal revision. The description of the myth of Dionysus is considerably enlarged, and then Yeats goes on specifically to contrast the Greek and Jewish religions. The Hebrew tells of a visit to Sparta where he saw in a temple a piece of an oar used by Odysseus and an unhatched egg of Leda.

THE EGYPTIAN An egg of Leda, did you say? And unhatched? What frustrated destiny!

THE HEBREW From another of her eggs came Helen. Helen and Odysseus will give the Greeks mastery of the human race forever, for even I, at sight of that old piece of an oar and that egg, could hardly keep from prostrating myself before the altar. What phantom can prevail against the treasure of Sparta! Paris found a beating heart in Helen's breast.

THE EGYPTIAN Odysseus and Helen died; Christ only seemed to die.

THE HEBREW What have you in your head now? Is it that we may see him again? That being but dead in seeming, he may show himself again. But no, no, I will not let you put such thoughts into my head.

THE EGYPTIAN What did you say about a heart — a beating heart? (*The Hebrew has gone to the door and is listening*) But it is the heart, the flow of blood that separates mankind from divinity. What is the heart but corruption, change, death? It is gloomy, dark, terrible.

[At this point the Syrian returns with his report of the miracle. Here is the end of the play.]

THE HEBREW If you tell them your story they would think of it as I do, but Peter's misery would be increased. I have known him longer than you and I know what would happen. Peter would remember that [the] women did not flinch, that not one amongst them denied her Master, that this dream but proved their love and faith. Then he would think that he had lost both, and he would imagine that John was looking at him, and he would turn away and bury his head in his hands.

THE EGYPTIAN I believe your story. Before you came I was about to say that Christ might appear again at any moment. I contrasted him with Helen and Odysseus, who can never so appear.

THE SYRIAN Suddenly it came into my head — even while I was running — those priests of Dionysus had just passed with all [their] noise — that all over Greece, all over Asia Minor and Magna Grecia, from generation to generation, men have celebrated the death and resurrection of Attis or Adonis, or Dionysus, of God under some name or other, and now God himself, out of mercy, and that he might, as it were, sanctify man's tragedy, has turned all those songs and dances into prophesy, and that which we but dreamed has been accomplished, and God has become flesh.

THE EGYPTIAN God has form but not body and, therefore, he is neither visible nor tangible, but God can communicate with mankind through an illusionary body, such a form as sculptors in my city make for Alexander the Great — no beating, suffering heart, all stone or bronze, as it were, perfect — exactly six feet high, neither more nor less — nothing can be added, nothing taken away, and perfect maturity. Now Christ when he began to preach was exactly thirty years old.

THE SYRIAN If Christ were but a phantom, whom was she I met but now and heard called Mary, the Mother of Jesus?

THE EGYPTIAN God made her believe that she had carried him upon her knees, that we might not discover the truth till the right time had come. This Jew said a moment ago that women will believe anything.

THE SYRIAN But . . . .

THE EGYPTIAN Listen to me. There can be no contact, Hermes, the Thrice Great has said, between the corruptible and [the] incorruptible, and to suggest that he was born from a woman, that he lay in her womb, that she fed him upon her breast, that she washed him as other children are washed, is the most terrible blasphemy.

THE SYRIAN You mean that God has not really died for us?

THE EGYPTIAN A God cannot die.

THE SYRIAN (*To the Hebrew*) You will understand me; this Egyptian cannot because he is almost a Greek. We are all humiliated by life; we think that we are nothing and that it is no use behaving well. But what if God said to himself, "I will share all their humiliation and let them know that I have done it out of love. If I do that they will no longer think [that] they are nothing." What if he came down for that reason and was born and died, not in seeming but in reality? Why should I care for a phantom or a shadow which only seemed to suffer?

(*Drum taps and rattle*)

THE EGYPTIAN But what you say is impossible, but how can I make myself understood with all that noise outside.

THE HEBREW One is as impossible as the other. You with your phantom that appears from nowhere. You with your god that needs to be fed and washed. There is only one sensible thing to say; he deceived himself and us, maddened by too great love perhaps, and now he is dead. The priests of Dionysus are at the other side of the house, but they have hidden the image of the dead man. So they have begun their lunatic cry "God has arisen, God has arisen!" They will cry that through every street of the city, making their god live and die as they please. But why are they silent — is it because they [are] hoarse that [they are] dancing silently, or is it some part of the play, poor effeminate crack-pated men, to seem at last speechless with their imaginary joy? They are coming nearer and nearer, dancing all the while to some kind of ancient step, like steps of an old Syrian dance. Look how they roll their painted eyes as the dance grows quicker and quicker. Did ever men show such abandon in the expression of a real emotion? They are almost under the window now.

THE DRUNKEN MAN'S SONG

By dreaming on a crazy drum
By an odour of spilt blood
Time's great measure is reversed
God is drummed out of the tomb.

(*Low sound of drum and rattle*)

THE HEBREW Why are they all suddenly silent and raise their arms above their heads and stand motionless, all their unseeing eyes turned upon this house?

THE EGYPTIAN There is someone in the room.

THE HEBREW Where?

THE EGYPTIAN I do not know but I thought I heard someone breathing.

THE HEBREW There is no one here. No one could have got in without our knowing, and the door is still fastened.

THE EGYPTIAN The curtain over there is moving.

THE HEBREW No, it is quite still, and, besides, there is nothing behind the curtain but a blank wall.

THE EGYPTIAN Look! Look!

THE HEBREW Yes, it has begun to move!

THE EGYPTIAN O gods of Egypt! There is someone coming through it! (*They cower away from curtain, the Syrian towards the door to inner room. The figure of Christ enters from curtain.*)

THE HEBREW It is the ghost of our master.

THE EGYPTIAN It is his form. Why are you afraid? Seeing that he was not buried or crucified in reality, it is natural that he should appear. But there is nothing but an appearance, a phantom — there is no flesh, there is no blood. Because I know the truth I am not afraid — look, I will touch it. It may be hard under my hand, I [have] heard

of such things, or my hand may pass through it, but there is no blood. (*He goes up to the phantom slowly and touches it, then cries out.*) The heart of the phantom is beating — the heart of the phantom is beating! (*He shrinks back as the phantom passes and goes into the inner room, the Syrian passing in before it. The Hebrew is cowering against the back of the stage.*) Something terrible has happened; I thought my hand would have passed through it. He is standing in the midst of them now — some of them are afraid — he looks at Peter and James and John and he smiles. Thomas is saying something and he answers. He has parted the grave clothes from his side and there [is] a wound, a great wound in his side — Thomas has put his hand into the wound. Now they are all gathering round. He speaks again, and there in the street the priests of Dionysus are still standing, perhaps, with their arms lifted. (*Going to window*) Yes, they are still standing and they look up in a kind of stupor, and that drunkard is still dancing, turning round like a top, and they know nothing. And there are the Galilean women, Mary, the mother of Jesus, and Mary, the mother of James, and the rest coming from the mountain to tell what they have seen — they know, but they do not know how terrible it is. Never before did the heart of a phantom beat. How very terrible! Reason itself is dead. (*In a loud voice*) Rome, Greece, Egypt — it has come, the miracle, that which must destroy you, irrational force. The heart of a phantom is beating!
[The play ends with the first stanza only of what is now the closing lyric.]

In MS. 2 the thought of *The Resurrection* has been expanded beyond MS. 1; and there has been a considerable gain in dramatic circumstantiality. The kinds of change Yeats made can be shown in a comparison of the two versions of the end of the play. In MS. 1, for instance, the Syrian after his return claims credence for his account of Christ's rebirth by saying that what was ceremony in the worship of Attis has become reality. In the MS. 2 version he expands this thought:

all over Greece, all over Asia Minor and Magna Grecia, from generation to generation, men have celebrated the death and resurrection of Attis, or Adonis, or Dionysus, of God under some name or other, and now God himself out of mercy and that he might, as it were, sanctify man's tragedy, has turned all those songs and dances into prophesy, and that which we but dreamed has been accomplished, and God has become flesh.

This same kind of expansion or filling in is illustrated by comparing the accounts of Christ's physical perfection, or the account of Mary's belief that she is the mother of God. In MS. 1 the Greek simply says "being God, he is perfect and therefore entirely happy." In MS. 2 "perfect" is expanded into a description of God's illusionary body: "— no beating, suffering heart, all stone or bronze, as it were, perfect — exactly six feet high, neither more nor less — nothing can be added, nothing taken away, and perfect maturity." In MS. 1 the Syrian asks "Then what did Mary of Galilee nurse upon her knees," and the Greek replies that even a thaumaturgist could have made Mary believe that her son was master of the world; in MS. 2 he argues much more fully that God's body is phantasmal, referring to the doctrines of Hermes Trismegistus. The description of Dionysian revelers which follows is likewise expanded in MS. 2. In many places, MS. 2 is more sharply phrased. Manuscript 1 ends "Hear, all you men of Jerusalem, know now all men whether men of Rome, of Alexandria, or of Athens. The heart of a phantom is beating." The second ends "Rome, Greece, Egypt — it has come, the miracle, that which must destroy you, irrational force. The heart of a phantom is beating!"

In spite of these undoubted improvements, the MS. 2 version of *The Resurrection* is still not a satisfactory play. The contrast of the Greek and Jewish religions, for instance, along with other parts of the play, sounds like something from *A Vision* put into dialogue. It is far too talky. Worse yet, when Yeats during this contrast says that it is the beating heart of mankind that separates man from God, he robs the end of the play of its dramatic surprise. Before Yeats printed the play in *The Adelphi,* he touched up the dialogue and rewrote "The Drunken Man's Song." After this printing he left it alone for more than three years. He returned to the play late in 1930, not to the printed version found in *The Adelphi,* but to MS. 2. He wrote to Olivia Shakespear on December 27, 1930: "At the moment I am putting the last touches to a play called *The Resurrection* — young men talking, the apostles in the next room overwhelmed by the crucifixion. Christ newly arisen passes silently through. I wrote a chaotic dialogue on this theme some years ago. But now I have dramatic tension throughout."

iv

Manuscript three

YEATS USED SOME FORTY FIVE PAGES of a large vellum-bound manuscript book to make a new draft of "The Resurrection" (MS. 3). He first made a series of notes, apparently with MS. 2 open before him; at least the page number given after the eighth note corresponds to the correct page in MS. 2. Here are the notes:

Judas.
Why they are on guard.
Apostles described.
They doubt, that is why they are miserable.
Are we more certain?
They are different.
Judas not a bad man.
So far little change (to page 7).
Can they hear?
How many times did you hear him?
Three times. Sure he was Messiah.
Only once. ~~Sure he was a phantom~~. Hebrew mocks Egyptian. Yet it is natural at times like this to believe anything.
How many times did apostles see him? They are simple men.
The gods are never flesh and blood.
Thought him a god, etc.
Thought on death leading up to Dionysian procession.
Syrian comes. Says tomb is empty.
Hebrew refuses to accept idea. Syrian and Greek unite [?]
Listen, I have more to say. He's met women etc.
Hebrew refuses to believe what the women say.

Following these notes, which do not anticipate all the changes Yeats was going to make, the working draft begins. The Egyptian becomes a Greek from Alexandria, as he had been in MS. 1. Yeats got the opening scene of the play, down to the Hebrew's remark that the disciples were intended to be saints, into pretty much its final form, though he achieved this only after many cancels and revisions. These seem to have been made at different times. Manuscript 2 begins with a bald statement by the Hebrew that he has heard that the body of Jesus has been taken from the tomb, and that he has sent the Syrian to find out if the report is true; the Hebrew and the Egyptian then go on to discuss Judas' death. In MS. 3 Yeats begins with the Dionysian revel, and the Greek does not say what he has sent the Syrian to do. Yeats first expanded their discussion of Judas, and then cut it entirely, thereby greatly improving the unity of the play. In MS. 3 the dialogue between the Hebrew and the Greek on Christ's nature, which follows, was in a transition state between the MS. 2 version and final version. In MS. 2 they open the subject, interrupt its discussion to describe the followers of Dionysus, then return to it. In MS. 3 Yeats puts the two parts of their discussion together, goes on to describe the Dionysian revel, then has the Syrian enter almost immediately with his news that Christ's tomb is empty. Their discussion of Christ's nature, however, is stated far less dramatically than in the finished play, and far less succinctly.

Beginning with the Hebrew's speech "It was always foretold that he would be born of a woman" and continuing to the end of the play, Yeats got pretty much what he wanted, but he did not get it all at once. The next six speeches, down to the Hebrew's "What I have described is what I thought until three days ago" are very close to the final version. They were followed by a long passage discussing Christ's nature which Yeats included in MS. 4 in an expanded version. Some time after the completion of MS. 4, Yeats cut this out and replaced it by the dramatic statement, made by the Greek while pointing to Calvary, that Christ was all god, a phantom, and the Hebrew's counter statement that Christ was only a man.

After the Greek's speech "I think there is nothing in the tomb," MS. 3 goes along more smoothly, though there are still many cancelled passages. In one of these the Hebrew and the Greek talk about what they will do now that they are no longer followers of Christ: the Hebrew is going to become a horse trainer; the Greek is going to Athens to found a school for young men. The description of the followers of Dionysus achieved pretty much its present form in MS. 3, save that Yeats did not stop to compose the song "Astrea's Holy Child!" He merely indicated "A song to Moon" and went on. He composed the song at the end of the manuscript, using for its subject a rather tedious prose account of Dionysus' murder told by the Egyptian-Greek in MS. 2. The Greek's long comment following the song was worked out in this same manuscript book as a separate item and inserted in place in MS. 4. As MS. 3 continues, the Syrian enters almost immediately, and for some sixteen speeches Yeats follows MS. 2 more closely than in any other part of the revised play. From there to the end of the play the two versions differ radically.

Here is the end of the play from MS. 3:

THE HEBREW If you told them your story, they would think of it as I do, but Peter's misery would be increased. I have known him longer than you; I know what would happen. Peter would remember that the women did not flinch, that not one amongst them denied her master, that this dream but proved their love and faith. Then he would [remember] that he had lacked both, and he would imagine that John was looking at him, and he would turn away and bury his head in his hands.

THE GREEK I said that we must all be convinced [of] it. There is another reason why you must not tell them anything. Somebody else is coming. I am certain that Jesus Christ has never had [a] human body, that being but a phantom he can pass through walls, that he will come, that he will pass through this room, that he himself will speak to the apostles.

THE SYRIAN He is no phantom. We put a great stone over the mouth of the tomb, and yet the women say it has been rolled aside.

THE HEBREW The Romans heard yesterday that some of our people had planned to steal the body, and put abroad a story that Christ had arisen. Very likely they have stolen it to escape the shame over rebirth.

THE SYRIAN [The] Romans put sentries at the tomb, but the women say they found the sentries asleep. He had put them asleep that they might [not] see him move the stone.

THE GREEK A hand without bone, without sinew could [not] move a great stone.

THE SYRIAN It contradicts all human knowledge. (*Laughs as he speaks*) Another Argo seeks another fleece, another Troy is sacked.

THE GREEK Why are you laughing? The knowledge that keeps the roads from this to Persia free of robbers, and built the beautiful humane cities, that has made the modern world, that stands between us and [the] barbarian.

THE SYRIAN But what would happen if there were something it could not explain, and if that something became more important than everything else?

THE GREEK You mean that the barbarian would come back.

THE SYRIAN What if there is always something that lies outside knowledge, outside order. Always at the moment when order seems finally established, everything finally explained, that something appears. (*He begins to laugh.*)

THE HEBREW Stop laughing. The Greek laughed when Christ's body was being nailed to the cross, and now you laugh.

THE GREEK He has lost control of himself.

THE HEBREW Stop, I tell you. (*Rattle and drums*)

THE SYRIAN But I am not laughing. It is the people out there who are laughing.

THE HEBREW No, they are shaking rattles and drums.

THE SYRIAN And I thought they were laughing. How horrible. (*He covers his face with his hands and stands near the curtain to the inner room.*)

THE GREEK (*Looking out over heads of audience*) The worshippers of Dionysus are coming this way again. They have hidden their image of the dead man and now begin their lunatic cry, "God has arisen, god has arisen." (*These words have been sung by the musicians in faint voices to faint drum taps.*) They will cry that through every street in the city, making their god live and die at their pleasure. But why are they silent? They are dancing silently. They are coming nearer and nearer, dancing all the while, using some kind of ancient step unlike anything I have seen in Alexandria. They are almost under the window now.

THE HEBREW They have come to mock us because their god arises every year while our god is dead forever.

THE GREEK How they roll their painted eyes as the dance grows quicker and quicker. They are under the window. Why are they all suddenly motionless? Why do they raise their arms above their heads and remain motionless? Why are all those unseeing eyes turned upon this house? Is there anything strange about this house?

THE HEBREW Somebody has come into the room.

THE GREEK Where?

THE HEBREW I do not know, but I thought I heard someone breathing.

THE GREEK No one could have got in without our knowing. The door is still closed.

THE HEBREW No, there is no one here.

THE GREEK The curtain over there is moving.

THE HEBREW No, it is quite still, and besides there is nothing behind it but a blank wall.

THE GREEK Look, look.

THE HEBREW Yes, it has begun to move.

THE GREEK There is someone coming through it. (THE HEBREW *cowers back from the moving curtain. The figure of* CHRIST *enters from the curtain.* THE SYRIAN *draws slowly back the curtain that shuts off the room where the apostles are.*) It is the phantom of our master. Why are you afraid? He has been buried, crucified, but only in semblance, and is among [us] once more. But there is nothing here but a phantom. It has no flesh and blood. Because I know the truth I am not afraid. Look, I will touch it. It may be hard under my hand, I have heard of such things, or my hand may pass through it, but there is no blood. (*He goes up to the phantom slowly and passes his hand over its side.*) The heart of a phantom is beating. O — O — O. (*The figure of* CHRIST *passes into the inner room where the apostles are.*) He is standing in the midst of them now. Some are afraid. He looks at Peter and James and John, and he smiles. He has parted the grave clothes from his side and there is a great wound in his side. Thomas has put his hand into the wound, he has put his hand where the heart is. Greece, Egypt, Rome, something has come to destroy you. The heart of a phantom is beating. Man has begun to die, for your words are clear to me at last, O Heraclitus, god and man die each other's life, live each other's death.

Yeats did not copy out the first stanza of the song for the unfolding of the cloth at the end of the play, which he had composed years earlier. After several pages of redrafts, which Yeats has cued into the manuscript, he did write a version of a new second verse. Before he finished he had this in final form.

Everything that man esteems
Endures a moment or a day
Love's pleasure drives his love away
The painter's brush consumes his dreams
The herald's cry, the soldier's tread
Exhaust his glory and his might
What ever flames upon the night
Man's own resinous heart has fed.

It was in MS. 3 that Yeats turned a chaotic dialogue into a play; what he states in MS. 2 he dramatizes in MS. 3. A comparison of the two versions of the end of the play, quoted above, will show this clearly. In MS. 2, for example, the Egyptian-Greek says that Christ may "appear again at any moment"; in MS. 3 he says "he will come . . . he will pass through this room . . . he himself will speak to the apostles." The Syrian says why he believes in Christ's resurrection far more dramatically in MS. 3. In MS. 2 he cites Mary's belief that she had borne a god; now he cites the miracle of the stone that has been rolled back, and goes on to say that a new cycle is beginning with the resurrection: "Another Argo seeks another fleece, another Troy is sacked," picked up from the opening lyric. An attempt to adduce proof has been replaced by a statement of certainties. When the followers of Dionysus return to witness the miracle of Christ's rebirth, they are described more vividly, more terribly; the song of the drunken priest, inappropriate at such a moment, is cut away. Both versions end with the actual appearance of Christ. Perhaps the best illustration of the change Yeats achieved is a comparison of the Greek's two comments on this event:

> Something terrible has happened; I thought my hand would have passed through it. He is standing in the midst of them now — some of them are afraid — he looks at Peter and James and John and he smiles. Thomas is saying something and he answers. He has parted the grave clothes from his side and there [is] a wound, a great wound in his side — Thomas has put his hand into the wound. Now they are all gathering round. He speaks again and there in the street the priests of Dionysus are still standing, perhaps, with their arms lifted. (*Going to the window.*) Yes, they are standing and they look up in a kind of stupor, and that drunkard is still dancing, turning round like a top, and they know nothing. . . . And there are the Galilean women, Mary, the mother of Jesus, and Mary, the mother of James, and the rest coming from the mountain to tell what they have seen — they know, but they do not know how terrible it is. Never before did the heart of a phantom beat. How very terrible! Reason itself is dead. (*In a loud voice.*) Rome, Greece, Egypt — it has come, the miracle, that which must destroy you, irrational force. The heart of a phantom is beating!

He is standing in the midst of them now. Some are afraid. He looks at Peter and James and John, and he smiles. He has parted the grave clothes from his side and there is a great wound in his side. Thomas has put his hand into the wound, he has put his hand where the heart is. Greece, Egypt, Rome, something has come to destroy you. The heart of a phantom is beating. Man has begun to die, for your words are clear to me at last, O Heraclitus, god and man die each other's life, live each other's death.

V

Manuscript four

BEFORE COMPARING THE FINISHED PLAY with the *Adelphi* version, I should like to consider MS. 4, which was written out in the Rapallo Notebook labelled "E." In MS. 4 Yeats put the various parts of his play in order, he polished his dialogue, and sharpened the dramatic tension. This manuscript is very close to the printed play down through the Hebrew's comment on the Apostles, "They are unfitted for anything else." Manuscript 4 then continues with an account of Christ's nature and of the personal relations the Hebrew and Greek had with Christ. This was cut from the play before it was printed. Yeats cancelled much of this in MS. 4, but he did not compose his revision in this manuscript book, and I have not seen a manuscript of it. The new material begins with "What makes you laugh" (*Collected Plays*, English ed., p. 582) and continues to "I say there is nothing in the tomb" (p. 584). The content of this passage is essentially the same in MS. 4 and the printed play, but the final version is far more dramatic. In the finished play Yeats has the Greek point out of the window toward Calvary, and then the Greek and Hebrew state their conflicting views of Christ's nature — that he was all God, that he was all man — while looking at the three crosses.

From "I think there is nothing in the tomb" on, MS. 4 is remarkably close to the finished play. This can be seen by comparing the end of the play, quoted below, with the printed text. There has been little change from MS. 3; such revisions as Yeats made in MS. 4 are largely verbal and stylistic. The passage paralleling those already quoted from earlier versions is included to complete the record of revision.

THE HEBREW If you told your story, they would no more believe it than I do, but Peter's misery would be increased. I know him longer than you do, and I know what would happen. Peter would remember that the women did not flinch; that not one amongst them denied her master; their dream proved their love and faith. Then he would remember that he had lacked both and imagine that John was looking at him. He would turn away and bury his head in his hands.

THE GREEK I said that we must all be convinced, but there is another reason why you must not tell them anything. Somebody else is coming. I am certain that Jesus Christ never had a human body; that he is a phantom and can pass through that wall, that he will so pass, that he will pass through this room; that he himself will speak to the apostles.

THE SYRIAN He is not phantom. We put a great stone over the mouth of the tomb, and the women say that it has been rolled back.

THE HEBREW The Romans heard yesterday that some of our people planned to steal the body, and put abroad a story that Christ has arisen and so escape the shame of our defeat. They probably stole it in the night.

THE SYRIAN The Romans put sentries at the tomb. The women found the sentries asleep. Christ had put them asleep that they might not see him move the stone.

THE GREEK A hand without bones, without sinews could not move a stone.

THE SYRIAN What matter if it contradicts all human knowledge. Another Argo seeks another fleece, another Troy is sacked. (*Laughing as he speaks*)

THE GREEK Why are you laughing?

THE SYRIAN What is human knowledge?

THE GREEK The knowledge that keeps the road from this to Persia free of robbers, that has built the beautiful humane cities, that has made the modern world, that stands between us and the barbarian.

THE SYRIAN But what if there is something it cannot explain, something more important than anything else?

THE GREEK You mean the barbarian would come back.

THE SYRIAN What if there is always something that lies outside knowledge, outside order? What if at the moment when knowledge and order seem complete, that something appears? (*He begins to laugh.*)

THE HEBREW Stop laughing.

THE SYRIAN What if the irrational return, what if the circle begin again?

THE HEBREW Stop. He laughed when Christ's body was nailed to the cross, and now you laugh.

THE GREEK He has lost control of himself.

THE HEBREW Stop, I tell you. (*Drum and rattles*)

THE SYRIAN But I am not laughing. It is the people out there who are laughing.

THE HEBREW No, they [are] shaking rattles and beating drums.

THE SYRIAN I thought they were laughing. How horrible.

THE GREEK (*looking out over heads of audience*) The worshippers of Dionysus are coming this way again. They have hidden their image of the dead god, and have begun their lunatic cry "God has arisen, God has arisen." (*While he has been speaking, the musicians have been crying "God has arisen," but in low voices as if it were from some distance. They fall silent.*) They will cry "God has arisen" through all the streets of the city. They can make their god live and die at their pleasure, but why are they silent? They are dancing silently. They are coming nearer and nearer, dancing all the while, using some kind of ancient step unlike anything I have seen in Alexandria. They are almost under the window now.

THE HEBREW They have come back to mock us, because their god arises every year whereas our god is dead forever.

THE GREEK How they roll their painted eyes as the dance grows quicker and quicker. They are under the window. Why are they all suddenly motionless? Why are all those unseeing eyes turned upon this house? Is there anything strange about this house?

THE HEBREW Somebody has come into the room.

THE GREEK Where?

THE HEBREW I do not know, but I thought I heard a step.

THE GREEK [I thought] that some one had come.

THE HEBREW There is no one here. I shut the door at the foot of the stairs.

THE GREEK The curtain over there is moving.

THE HEBREW No, it is quite still, and besides there is nothing behind it but a blank wall.

THE GREEK Look, look.

THE HEBREW Yes, it has begun to move. (*During what follows he backs in terror towards the lefthand corner of the stage.*)

THE GREEK There is someone coming through it.

(The figure of CHRIST *wearing a recognizable but stylized mask enters through the curtain.* THE SYRIAN *slowly draws back the curtain that shuts off the inner room where the apostles are. The three young men are towards the left of the stage. The figure of* CHRIST *is at the back towards the right.)*

THE GREEK It is the phantom of our master. Why are you afraid? He has been buried and crucified, but only in semblance, and is among us once more. (THE HEBREW *kneels.*) But there is nothing here but a phantom. It has no flesh and blood. Because I know the truth I am not afraid. Look, I will touch it. It may be hard under my hand like a statue. I have heard of such things. Or my hand may pass through it, but there is no flesh and blood. (*He goes slowly up to the figure and passes his hand over its side.*) The heart of a phantom is beating. O, O, O. (*The figure of* CHRIST *crosses the stage, and passes into the inner room.*)

THE SYRIAN He is standing in the midst of them. Some are afraid. He looks at Peter and James and John. He smiles. He has parted the grave clothes from his side. There is a great wound there. Thomas has put his hand into the wound. He has put his hand where the heart is.

THE GREEK Something has come to destroy you. The heart of a phantom is beating. Man has begun to die. Your words are clear at last, O Heraclitus. God and men die each other's life, live each other's death. (*The musicians rise, one or more singing the following words. They unfold the curtain during the first stanza, fold it during the second.*)

The song of the unfolding and folding of the curtain

In pity for man's darkening thought
He walked that room and issued thence
In Galilean turbulence;
The Babylonian starlight brought
A fabulous, formless darkness in;
Odour of blood where Christ was slain
Made Plato's tolerance in vain
And vain the Doric discipline.

Everything that man esteems
Endures a moment or a day,
Love's pleasure drives his love away,
The painter's brush consumes his dreams

The herald's cry, the soldier's tread
Exhaust his glory and his might
A man has nothing but the light
That his resinous heart has fed.
or
Whatever flames upon the night
Man's own resinous heart has fed

A typescript was made from MS. 4; Yeats dated this "March, 1931." The play was printed, apparently from this typescript, in *Stories of Michael Robartes and His Friends,* finished by the Cuala Press in October 1931, and published in March 1932.

vi

Printed Versions of *The Resurrection*

SINCE THE *Adelphi* VERSION OF *The Resurrection* fully represents MS. 2 and the final version MS. 4, my discussion of what Yeats accomplished when he rewrote the play is based on these versions. The beginnings are entirely different: the 1927 version begins with the Hebrew saying he has sent the Syrian to the tomb, the finished play with the Dionysian ceremonies. Then the 1927, or "A" version, continues with the long passage on Judas, first expanded and then cancelled in MS. 3; then the sound of the Dionysian revel is heard, but the Egyptian-Greek does not know what it is. At this point in the final, or "B" version, the Greek says that he has sent the Syrian on an errand, but he does not say what errand. Beginning with the Greek's "What are they doing now?" and continuing for nine speeches the A and B versions run along together; then a long passage in A on the consolations the Hebrew and Greek will find now that they are no longer followers of Christ is telescoped into B's "We can find consolation, but for the Eleven it was always complete light or complete darkness."

After this the versons fall together again for two speeches, then take completely different tacks. What Yeats does is to get all his expository material, including possible views of Christ's nature, into the beginning of his play, while at the same time he cuts away material that he doesn't need. In the A version of this passage there is further discussion of Judas, discussion whether the Jews or Greeks will inherit the Roman world, as well as discussion of Christ's nature. Yeats did his revision partly in MS. 3, partly in MS. 4, and partly after completing MS. 4. The passage describing the Dionysian revelers that follows has been changed completely. In the A version it sounds rather like notes taken from *The Golden Bough*; in the B version the material has been fused into drama. Yeats accomplished the change in MS. 3 and its addenda. Perhaps a comparison of these two passages will reveal more sharply than any other just what Yeats accomplished by his revision.

[From *The Adelphi*, pp. 719–21]

(*A sound of rattles and drums, but nearer now.*)

THE HEBREW: There is that noise again. I can see them now. They are women and some carry on their shoulders a bier with a dead man, while others shake rattles or beat upon drums. Some of the crowd are angry but the Roman soldiers keep them back.

THE EGYPTIAN: Are you certain that they are women and not men in women's clothes with rouged faces?

THE HEBREW: They are passing at the end of the street and the crowd obstructs the view. Now I can see. I think you are right — they walk like men and their cheeks and lips are vermilion — an impossible vermilion.

THE EGYPTIAN: Nor is that a dead man, but a painted wooden image of a dead man. I have seen them in Alexandria — they are new arrivals here. They worship a drunken god called among the Greeks Dionysus, and at the first full moon in March they gather in some field outside the town, one of them with a live kid in his arms. The others stand in a circle and he throws the kid into the midst of them and they fall upon it tumbling over one another and seize it with their teeth and their hands, and tear it asunder, and eat the raw flesh, their heads and garments all spotted with blood. And all the while they keep crying out upon the God Dionysus whose flesh they eat and whose blood they drink.

THE HEBREW: Horrible — only a Greek could have such thoughts.

THE EGYPTIAN: Then they go into the town and march hither and thither, some with a painted image of a dead man upon their shoulders, some dancing and rending their clothes and calling upon their God to rise from the dead.

THE HEBREW: One of the priests has got separated from the rest and is among the crowd under the window. He is drunk and the crowd is making game of him and pushing him about and laughing.

THE EGYPTIAN: Some of the priests are always drunk. It is part of their piety to seem intoxicated by the blood of the God.

THE HEBREW: The drunken man has begun to sing.

Song of the Drunkard.

The drunkard with the painted eyes
Discovered thought is misery,
Now, with drum and rattle, he
Bids a drunken God arise.

THE HEBREW: They eat the flesh and drink the blood of their God. That is what you said.

THE EGYPTIAN: Yes, it is their Sacrament. They say he died for the salvation of men. The Titans, as the story goes, were at war with the Gods and climbed up Olympus, keeping in the woods' shadow. They came where the divine child was playing. They made him run towards them, by shaking rattles which they had brought for the purpose. When the child had come under the shadow of the trees, they tore him in pieces.

THE HEBREW: So that is why the priests have rattles?

THE EGYPTIAN: Certain loose women among the Titans, twelve it is said, twelve Titan women, tried to protect him and in commemoration of that, the priests dress like women, rouge their lips and faces and dance swaying their hips, like women enticing men.

THE HEBREW: Let them cry as loud as they please, even the Greeks cannot raise the dead.

THE EGYPTIAN: Presently they hide their image and parade the streets again, crying out that he has arisen and pretend a great joy and excitement.

[From *Collected Plays*, Eng. ed. pp. 585–88; U.S. ed. pp. 368–69]

THE GREEK (*who is standing facing the audience, and looking out over their heads*). It is the worshippers of Dionysus. They are under the window now. There is a group of women who carry upon their shoulders a bier with an image of the dead god upon it. No, they are not women. They are men dressed as women. I have seen something like it in Alexandria. They are all silent, as if something were going to happen. My God! What a spectacle! In Alexandria a few men paint their lips vermilion. They imitate women that they may attain in worship a woman's self-abandonment. No great harm comes of it — but here! Come and look for yourself.

THE HEBREW: I will not look at such madmen.

THE GREEK: Though the music has stopped, some men are still dancing, and some of the dancers have gashed themselves with knives, imagining themselves, I suppose, at once the god and the Titans that murdered him. A little further off a man and woman are coupling in the middle of the street. She thinks the surrender to some man the dance threw into her arms may bring her god back to life. All are from the foreign quarter, to judge by face and costume, and are the most ignorant and excitable class of Asiatic Greeks, the dregs of the population. Such people suffer terribly and seek forgetfulness in monstrous ceremonies. Ah, that is what they are waiting for. The crowd has parted to make way for a singer. It is a girl. No, not a girl; a boy from the theatre. I know him. He acts girls' parts. He is dressed as a girl, but his fingernails are gilded and his wig is made of gilded cords. He looks like a statue out of some temple. I remember something of the kind in Alexandria. Three days after the full moon, a full moon in March, they sing the death of the god and pray for his resurrection.

(*One of the musicians sings the following song.*)

Astrea's holy child!
A rattle in the wood
Where a Titan strode!
His rattle drew the child
Into that solitude.

Barrum, barrum, barrum (*Drum-taps accompany and follow the words*).

We wandering women,
Wives for all that come,
Tried to draw him home;
And every wandering woman
Beat upon a drum.

Barrum, barrum, barrum (*Drum-taps as before*).

But the murderous Titans
Where the woods grow dim
Stood and waited him.
The great hands of those Titans
Tore limb from limb.
Barrum, barrum, barrum (*Drum-taps as before*).

On virgin Astrea
That can succour all
Wandering women call;
Call out to Astrea
That the moon stood at the full.
Barrum, barrum, barrum (*Drum-taps as before*).

THE GREEK. I cannot think all that self-surrender and self-abasement is Greek, despite the Greek name of its god. When the goddess came to Achilles in the battle she did not interfere with his soul, she took him by his yellow hair. Lucretius thinks that the gods appear in the visions of the day and night but are indifferent to human fate; that, however, is the exaggeration of a Roman rhetorician. They can be discovered by contemplation, in their faces a high keen joy like the cry of a bat, and the man who lives heroically gives them the only earthly body that they covet. He, as it were, copies their gestures and their acts. What seems their indifference is but their eternal possession of themselves. Man, too, remains separate. He does not surrender his soul. He keeps his privacy.

Following the description of the followers of Dionysus, the A version develops further the idea that Christ was a phantom, and contrasts specifically the Greek and Christian mythologies. (This passage was quoted in the description of the *Adelphi* version, above.) It returns, in short, to exposition. The B version moves on directly to the return of the Syrian. Beginning with "There is someone at the door" down through "Though we are so much younger we know more of the world than they do" the A and B versions are much the same. At that point the passages quoted from each of the successive manuscripts begin. The beginnings are similar in A and B, but after the comment on the effect the news of Christ's resurrection will have on the apostles the two versions differ radically. In B the Greek restates his phantom theory and predicts that Christ will shortly appear, thereby preparing us fully for the end of the play. Then in four speeches which replace a long and somewhat didactic discussion in A, Yeats sharply phrases the three contrasting views of Christ's nature — that he is both man and god, that he is only a man, that he is only a god. Then the Syrian develops the theme of the eruption of the irrational into an ordered culture; this is hardly present in A, though at the end the Greek does speak of irrational force. The return of the followers of Dionysus and the appearance of Christ are much the same in both versions, though the Greek's comment on the effect of the rebirth of the new god is much more sharply phrased in B.

Now to summarize briefly what happened between the A and B versions of *The Resurrection*. The content of the play remains much the same. In both Yeats embodies in the Egyptian-Greek, the Syrian, and the Hebrew three concepts of Christ's nature: he is a god whose "body" is a phantom; he is both man and god; he is a man. Yeats places these ideas in conflict and resolves the conflict in favor of the Incarnation, doubling the theme and introducing the concept of recurrence by his description of the Dionysian revelers. But in the B version these essential elements are presented far more dramatically than in A. This is partly a result of paring away irrelevant detail, partly a result of reordering material that is kept, and partly a result of adding new material.

Yeats omits all reference to Judas and the question why he betrayed Christ; what the Greek and Hebrew will do now that Christ is dead; whether the Jew or Greek will inherit the Roman world; the Hebrew's visit to a Greek shrine where he saw an unhatched egg of Leda; the differentiation of man from god in terms of a beating heart and swirling blood; the statement by the Syrian that god has made the ancient world's ceremonial resurrections a reality. Yeats completely reordered his exposition. When the A version opens the Egyptian-Greek says he has sent the Syrian to find out if Christ's body is in the tomb. He withholds this information in B, which opens instead with a needed preparatory account of the Dionysian ceremonies. In the A version the three opposed views of Christ's nature are diffusely developed; in the B version this diffusion has been entirely overcome. The Greek and Hebrew clearly, even sharply present their clashing views that Christ was all god and that Christ was all man. Then the Syrian develops his view that Christ was both man and god, a view which the miracle at the end of the play sustains. Yeats added, near the end of the play, the exchange between the Greek and the Syrian on the irrationality of the resurrection and its devastating effect on the ancient world.

Besides omitting, reordering, and adding Yeats greatly improved his presentation of what he kept, for instance his description of the Dionysian ceremonies. And he greatly improved his language as the quotations above show in detail. The result of all this was a much better play.

In that exciting book *Wheels and Butterflies* this play (a butterfly) is provided with an "Introduction" (a wheel). In the introduction Yeats makes clear that *The Resurrection* is a dramatic statement of part of his personal mythology: Progress is an illusion. In human life as in human history there is no progress, only eternal recurrence. Yeats claims that Ptolemy, Plato, Plotinus all used symbolic systems to express this recurrence, and that a cyclic system is to be found in Indic thought. He had wished, he continues, to give in *The Resurrection* a modern statement of the doctrine of recurrence so that three systems of thought might join battle for the allegiance of modern man: Communism, Catholicism, Cyclism. Yeats picks Lenin and Pope Pius X to represent orthodox Communism and orthodox Catholicism; he himself undertakes to be the orthodox exponent of Cyclism.

However you may take it this is a magnificent irony. Whether Yeats is pulling our leg or whether he is deadly serious — perhaps he is both deadly serious and pulling our leg — we delight to see him with Lenin and Pope Pius X. His after-the-fact statement may help explain why early versions of *The Resurrection* sound like parts of "Dove or Swan" in dialogue, may explain why Yeats had to keep at the play so long to achieve the dramatic tension of the final version. To me it is, however, more than a systemic play. It expresses rational man's terror and shock in the presence of the supernatural; this terror and shock Yeats had experienced again and again during his own esoteric studies. Here, as in *The Words upon the Window-pane,* he conveys some of it to us.

9

A Full Moon in March

THE manuscript record of *A Full Moon in March* is, I think, complete or nearly so, and the play is so short that the successive manuscripts can be reproduced in full. This is one reason for printing them; another is my own great admiration of the play, particularly of its lyrics, for the staging of which Yeats tells us he invented the fable both of this play and that of *The King of the Great Clock Tower* out of which it grew. Yeats was at work on the earlier play in November 1933, when he sent Olivia Shakespear a draft of the song for the opening of the curtain (*Letters*, p. 817). Apparently he was well along with it in January 1934, for on the 27th he wrote to Olivia Shakespear, "I made up the play that I might write lyrics out of dramatic experience, all my personal experience having in some strange way come to an end," a stratagem which worked so well that when he was done there was one song left over — "He had famished in a wilderness" — from which the second play grew. Yeats went to Italy in June 1934, and he took the play with him to show to Ezra Pound. Yeats tells the story of Pound's rejection of the play in his "Preface" to the prose version of *The King of the Great Clock Tower*. A more immediate account is found in a manuscript book inscribed "W. B. Yeats/ Saville Club/ 69 Brook Street/ London": "Rapallo. June. 1934. Gave 'Clock Tower' to Ezra to read. He condemned it — 'nobody's language.' At first I took his condemnation as a confirmation of my fear that I am now too old. I have written little prose for three years. But 'nobody's language' is something I can remedy. I must write in verse, but first in prose to set structure." Yeats continued with a scenario of part of a new version of *The King of the Great Clock Tower,* and with several drafts in verse of the opening of the play.

Undeterred by Pound's criticism, Yeats had the prose play produced at the Abbey on July 30, 1934, along with *The Resurrection.* He was pleased by the success of the play, which he described to Olivia Shakespear in his letter of August 7. He had the play printed in *Life and Letters* in October, and it gave its name to the Cuala Press *The King of the Great Clock Tower,* published in December. Sometime during the winter of 1934/35 Yeats put the prose play into verse. It appeared in this form in Macmillan and Company's *A Full Moon in March,* and this is the form of the play included in *Collected Plays.*

While he was at work on *The King of the Great Clock Tower,* Yeats grew dissatisfied with it. His dissatisfaction is stated in a letter to Edmund Dulac which Allan Wade dated December 10, 1934: "I don't like *The Clock Tower* which is theatrically coherent, spiritually incoherent." Yeats describes in the Preface to *A Full Moon in March* the reason for his dissatisfaction. "In *The King of the Great Clock Tower* there are three characters, King, Queen and Stroller, and that is a character too many; reduced to the essentials, to Queen and Stroller, the fable should have greater intensity. I started afresh and called the new version *A Full Moon in March*" (*Variorum Edition,* p. 857). This was printed in *Poetry* in March 1935, and after careful revision was published in November 1935 in *A Full Moon in March.*

Five manuscripts of *A Full Moon in March* have survived. The final manuscript (MS. 5) is at the National Library of Ireland; the others are in Mrs. Yeats's collection. I have arranged them in what seems to me their progressive order.

MS. 1. A scenario (prose).

MS. 2. A prose draft of the play; drafts of lyrics.

MS. 3. A second prose draft.

MS. 4. Three partial drafts in verse. In the latest of these Yeats is beginning to invent the language of the finished play.

MS. 5. The final draft, complete. The play is nearly finished.

i

Manuscript one

YEATS WROTE THE SCENARIO of the new play in the manuscript book from which Pound's reaction to the earlier play was quoted:

THE GREAT CLOCK TOWER

New version — for private room

Unfolding of curtain discovers Queen and Stroller. Is it true she has announced that she will accept as lover the man who praises her beauty in the best song? She answers it is true, but no man has praised her fitly [two words undeciphered]. Will give herself to a man like him, a man with matted hair, in rags and savage grown, savage from the forests that he has crossed, the wild beasts that have torn him? These terrors have left their mark upon his body. It is for her he has crossed so many forests. Yes, he has come from the end of the world, even in the end of the world they sing songs of her. Then it may be that his song will be the best and that he shall win her. They say that the men whose songs are not good you put to death. They are taken out from her presence, their heads are cut off, and they are put upon stakes, and the stakes are put upon the top of the great tower. But there are none there now; men have grown cowards. Fool, yet nobody has luck with her. Sing. I am ready. Sing. But you have no instrument. I have no instrument because I will not sing. First you must dance for me. When you have danced I will sing. Why should I dance? I declare that you will dance. Then will you sing? No, will not sing your beauty. Did I say that I thought you beautiful? I desire you with an overwhelming passion, because when I first heard your name I knew you were my woman. I did not know whether you were beautiful or ugly, all songs lied. I knew that you were my woman. I am no man's woman. If you will not praise my beauty, what will you sing? My song, and in my joy I shall sing more than one, will command you to my bed, command and you will come. Captain of the Guard, this man has insulted me. Sever his head from his body. When I [have] bathed my hands in his blood, you can take him to the top of the great tower. Put his head upon a stake and leave it. STROLLER, *with folded arms.* When I said that you were my woman, I knew that nothing would come between us, even death. Midnight approaches. Before the first stroke is struck, you will have danced for me. When the last stroke has struck you shall kiss me upon the lips. Hardly shall the last echo of the great bell have died away before you have joined me in my bed. The axe, the axe. I will listen [to] his insults no longer.

Folding and unfolding of the curtain.

(a version of desecration and the lover's night)

In this scenario Yeats seems to regard the play as no more than an alternate version of *The King of the Great Clock Tower.* He drops the King from his title and his cast, he invents the love test, brutalizes the character of the Stroller, and makes the Queen's a speaking part. The germ of the new play is a song beginning "He had famished in a wilderness" left over from the old. Having found no place for this in *The King of the Great Clock Tower,* Yeats had published it twice in December 1934: first by itself in *The Spectator* where it has the title "*The Singing Head and the Lady,*" then without title at the end of his "Commentary on the Great Clock Tower." Yeats's new fable dramatizes the situation suggested by the opening lines of this lyric: "He had famished in a wilderness/ Braved lions for my sake." The words in parentheses at the end of the scenario, "a version of desecration and the lover's night," indicate that Yeats intended to use the song that closed the prose version of *The King of the Great Clock Tower* at the end of his new play (again, Yeats had found no place for this in the revised *Clock Tower*). Yeats's scenario invents a fable that will provide an appropriate setting for these songs.

ii

Manuscript two

IN THIS SAME MANUSCRIPT BOOK Yeats wrote out the first prose version of *A Full Moon in March.* Here he roughs in the dialogue between the Queen and the Stroller, who is becoming a swineherd; at the end he begins to plan the dance that will express the climax of his action.

QUEEN: Captain of the guard, some man is coming. I have felt that disgust I feel always when some lover is coming. It may be that he who [comes] may be that man to whom I shall give myself, for in the last hour I have twice yawned and stretched myself. (*A knock*) Admit the man, Captain of the Guard. (*Enter* STROLLER)

STROLLER: Is [it] true that you have sworn to give your kingdom and yourself to the man who sings you [the] best song of love?

QUEEN: I have sworn it.

STROLLER: The best.

QUEEN: The song that shall most move me; no song yet has moved.

STROLLER: Look well at me. My hair is matted, my clothes in rags, beasts have torn my flesh, I have crossed so many forests I do not remember whether my birth was as foul as my body. Solitude, or so it seems, has driven me mad. Yet my song shall most move you.

QUEEN: Sing your song, but remember.

STROLLER: All those whose songs displease you put to death?

QUEEN: I have sworn it.

STROLLER: What manner of death do they die?

QUEEN: They're taken out from my presence. Their heads are cut off. Then their heads are taken up onto the great tower above us and set upon stakes. But there [are] no heads there now. Men are grown cowardly or can sing no more. [undeciphered sentence of eight words] Maybe you come from the end of the world. What do they say of me — do they sing songs about me? Why do you not answer?

STROLLER: What have I to do with that; I am thinking of our marriage night.

QUEEN: Were it possible that a thing so foul could move me with a song, that thought would make me shudder. Your words make me shudder.

STROLLER: Because I am without fear, I see you as the gods see you.

QUEEN: What do the gods see?

STROLLER: Because I am without [fear] I see your cruelty and desire. What marriage can be like ours, your ice laid against a burning coal, neither melted nor consumed, and yet made one?

QUEEN: What have you come [for], why do you say such things?

STROLLER: You know, there is no need for me to answer.

QUEEN: You mean that I am theme of all song? Your praise of my beauty will most move me?

STROLLER: I shall not praise your beauty — my memory is gone. Yet it seems to me that I was tending [swine] when I first heard your name, and that I covered myself with the excrement of the swine, and laughed.

QUEEN: If I should prefer your song, you would become a king.

STROLLER: What do I care [for] kingdoms — I belong to the swine.

QUEEN: [If] I could not control myself — if I were constrained by an oath or my tears to proclaim the song the best, you would lead me from all this. I shall [call the] Captain of the Guard. He will cut your head from your body.

STROLLER: Yes, yes. I will bring [you] to the swine.

QUEEN: This song shall not be sung. I shall [call the] Captain of the

Guard. He will cut your head from your body. (*The* STROLLER *laughs.*) Stop. Stop laughing.

STROLLER: She would cut my head from my body — she would cut my head from my body.

QUEEN: When your head is [off], I shall be free of you. I shall not be compelled to hear a swineherd sing.

STROLLER: O, I forgot the best of the story. When I sat there heaping the dung of swine upon my body, I foresaw everything. First you shall kneel before me.

QUEEN: I kneel?

STROLLER: Then you shall dance.

QUEEN: Dance for you, dance?

STROLLER: After that I shall [sing] my song. Then, with the last note of the song shall begin our marriage night. You shall conceive of the first coupling, then sink into the bridal sleep.

QUEEN: Captain of the Guard, cut this man's head from his body.

Folding of cloth, etc.

(*Dancer takes place of speaker. Her dress different in that it has red blotches or streaks. Her hands are red. She holds up his head. She holds it so that the blood seems to drip over her body. Then she lays it upon the chair and kneels. Attendants describe her kneeling, and then sing a song that is her song, "I dread you no longer now that you are dead, O beloved, etc." Then dance before the head. Then later, in her hands, again dance. Stands with head in air. Head sings: "What shall be born of us, etc." The marriage night. His blood has poured on her at the first coupling; she conceives of his blood. After that the bridal sleep. The dance, the kiss, the shudder. She sinks down in sleep.*)

In this draft of his play Yeats has fully developed his fable, but he has yet to clothe it in language that will express it. Here he has the Stroller — the inadequate name still lingers from *The King of the Great Clock Tower* — think "of our marriage night" in terms of ice and fire; he begins to develop the beast and excremental symbols that will express "degradation and the lover's night"; he has the Stroller refuse to sing unless the Queen will kneel before him and then dance. In his sketch of the dance that will express the Queen's surrender to love Yeats plans two songs which he never did write, one to begin "I dread you no longer now that you are dead," the other to begin

"What shall be born of us." After finishing this draft of his play Yeats did begin work on two of its songs. In the pages immediately following he wrote several early versions of the "Song of the Head," beginning "I sing a song of Jack and Jill," and of the opening song sung by the Second Attendant, beginning "Every loutish lad in love." I do not print these, for they would add nothing to our knowledge of Yeats at work on a poem.

Yeats continued work on the play in a looseleaf manuscript cover. He first composed another draft in prose (MS. 3), then several drafts in verse which he has cancelled. Finally he composed a verse draft of part of the play which he labelled "B" (MS. 4). Yeats has not cancelled this, and it will be found to be similar to the final manuscript. I give the material in the order in which it occurs in the manuscript cover. I think the first item is later than that which immediately follows it. It is an opening of the play which resembles the opening finally printed. I take it to be a working up of the stage directions at the head of the version which follows it.

iii

Manuscript three

THE SEVERED HEAD

TWO ATTENDANTS

SECOND ATTENDANT: What is to be danced? What shall we find when we pull back?

FIRST [ATTENDANT]: The stage manager told me a full moon in the third month of the year, but what that means I have forgotten, but presently I shall remember. He said some they [word undeciphered] to the stake or [word undeciphered], also Christ upon the cross — and then something strange, something [about] the seed of dead men.

[SECOND] ATTENDANT: But what of the woman we are to see? The moon is not yet full; it comes to the full while they dance. (*He sings* — it comes to the full while they dance.)

[FIRST] ATTENDANT: The woman dances — there is someone else who dances. They know all things who dance.

[This is followed by a full version in prose of the dialogue between the Queen and the Stroller.]

THE SEVERED HEAD

ATTENDANTS *speak as they unfold the curtain.* What is coming before us. Eternal image. What image will this one select? What does the coming dance compel us to say? I remember her. Some [time] I stood among worshippers [?], and I saw her as I see her today. All the cruelty of the past, of winter ice in her face. We must not make it too plain. All see differently. A player queen, with the cruelty of the past upon her face. That will serve.

(QUEEN *discovered*)

QUEEN: Captain of the Guard?

CAPTAIN: I am here.

[QUEEN]: Is there no one at the door?

CAPTAIN: There is no one.

QUEEN: Some man is coming. I have felt all day as I feel when some lover is coming. It may [be] that a man is coming to whom I can give myself. In the last hour I have three times stretched myself and yawned. (*Three knocks*) Admit him, Captain of the Guard.

STROLLER: Is it true that you give yourself and your kingdom for a song?

QUEEN: I have sworn.

STROLLER: For the best song of love.

QUEEN: It must be sung about me and to me.

STROLLER: The man must make love to you in a song, but who shall say whose song is best?

QUEEN: The best song is that shall most move me.

STROLLER: Look at me. My hair is matted and foul, my clothes are ragged, beasts have torn my flesh, I crossed so many forests. I have been in such great solitudes that memory is gone. It may be that my birth is as foul as my body. If my song most move you, will you give yourself to me?

QUEEN: I have sworn. Sing your song, but remember that all those I reject are put to death. No song has moved me yet. A man sings, he is taken out, his head is cut off.

STROLLER: It seems to me that men have grown cowardly or have forgotten how to sing, for it is the full moon [in] March, and I alone have come.

QUEEN: What do they say of me? Do they say that I am beautiful; do they say that I am cruel? Why do you not answer?

STROLLER: I am thinking of our marriage night.

QUEEN: How could a thing so foul move [me] with a song? It is the thought of your approaching death, or the thought of your foulness that makes me shudder.

STROLLER: Because I am without fear, I can see you as the gods can see you.

QUEEN: What do the gods see?

STROLLER: Your cruelty. When I shall touch your body I shall touch that cruelty, and my desire for one is as my desire for the other.

QUEEN: Why did you come, what makes you say such things?

STROLLER: You know there is no need for me to answer.

QUEEN: You mean that your song shall move me more than other men's? Will you praise my beauty as it has [been] praised?

STROLLER: What do I know of beauty? My memory is gone, and yet [it] seems to me that I was attending swine when I first heard your name, and that I rolled in the dung of swine and laughed.

QUEEN: If I should think your song the best, you would become a king.

STROLLER: What do I know of kingdoms? I belong to the swine.

QUEEN: If I should lose control of myself, if I was constrained by my tears, or by the ashen paleness of my face or by the trembling of my limbs to proclaim this song the best, you would lead me away from all this?

STROLLER: Yes, Yes. I will bring you to the swine and there, among the swine, you shall bring forth your farrow.

QUEEN: That song shall never be sung, Stroller. In a moment I shall [call] the Captain of the Guard and he shall cut your head from your body. (*The* STROLLER *laughs.*) Stop. Stop laughing.

STROLLER: There is a story in my country of a woman who stood bathed in a dead man's blood. A drop of his blood entered her body and she conceived.

QUEEN: When you are dead I shall be quit of you. I shall not be compelled to hold your head and sing. When they bring me your head, I shall not touch it even with my hands.

STROLLER: A drop of his blood entered her body, and then she sank down in the bridal sleep.

QUEEN: Captain of the Guard, cut this man's head from his body.

STROLLER: I shall sing, and then with the last notes of the song shall begin the lover's night.

The opening of the play which stands first in MS. 3 was almost certainly written after the draft which follows. While Yeats was working on that draft he for the first time has the Stroller arrive on the eve of a full moon in March. The new opening of the play introduces this configuration, eventually used in the title of the play, which clearly associates the sexual surrender of the virgin Queen with resurrection myths. Does Yeats mean that when the winter of virginity ends in sexual surrender and conception a kind of resurrection takes place? Yeats also alludes in this opening to "the seed of dead men"; again, he introduced this detail during the draft which follows. Yeats must first have composed the draft of the dialogue, then written an overture, so to speak, which hints at themes to be found in the draft.

The initial stage direction in the full draft speaks of a player queen with "winter ice in her face," an indication that the figure of Decima from *The Player Queen* was still active in Yeats's phantasmagoria (Yeats's *Collected Plays*, which includes *The Player Queen*, had just been published).

Yeats has given these drafts a new title, "The Severed Head," an indication that he no longer thought of the play as simply another version of *The King of the Great Clock Tower*, that it was beginning to have for him an identity of its own. In addition to introducing the new themes of the full moon in March and conception from the seed of a dead man, Yeats made some minor changes in his action. The Queen stretches and yawns three times instead of twice, and the comment that men have grown cowardly and no longer seek the hand of the Queen is transferred from the Queen to the Stroller. The style of MS. 3 is so finished that it suggests Yeats may have intended to keep his play in prose. There is not a word too few or too many, all excess has been cut away to achieve a perfect simplicity of statement: MS. 2: "QUEEN: [If] I could not control myself — if I were constrained by an oath or my tears to proclaim the song the best, you would lead me from all this. I shall [call the] Captain of the Guard. He will cut your head from your body." MS. 3: "QUEEN: If I should lose control of myself, if I was constrained by my tears, or by the ashen paleness of my face or by the trembling of my limbs to proclaim this song the best, you would lead me away from all this?"

iv

Manuscript four

YEATS DID NOT PRINT any prose version of this play, however, and in the drafts which follow, found in this same manuscript cover, he began to cast it into verse. Yeats began in the blank verse of the finished play, then momentarily tried using shorter lines, then returned to blank verse.

Q. Captain of the Guard, what man is at the door?
A. There is no man at the door.
Q. No lover has come
But I have felt him in my bones; I think
Because I have yawned and stretched myself three times
In the last hour a man is at [the] door
That I shall take for husband. (*Three knocks*)
Admit the man.

[The draft, which Yeats wrote on the back of one of the sheets of the prose version reproduced above, breaks off here. I think what follows, from a later page, is a continuation of the draft begun above.]

S. Men say that you will take the man to bed
That sings you the best song of love.
Q. So have I sworn
My kingdom and myself for the best song
No man has won me yet.
S. But who decides?
Q. The song that moves me is the best
No song has moved me yet
S. Look steadily
My hair is foul and matted I wear rags
44 I have crossed many forests and the beasts
Have torn me with their claws — my memory is gone
46 Because great solitudes have driven me mad
But when I look into a pool, a face
Looks up that makes me think

[Yeats broke off the draft at this point. The beginning of a draft in short, three stress lines follows immediately.]

Q. What man is at the door
A. There is no man at the door
Q. Some man is at the door
I feel him in my bones
I greatly dread the man
Because for the last hour
I have stretched myself and yawned
(*Three knocks*)
Open — admit the man

[I omit three pages of cancelled versions, and a page on which Yeats wrote drafts of "Every loutish lad in love." I continue with a version marked "B" which has not been cancelled.]

HE. They say that man shall [have] you for a wife
That sings the best.
SHE. That sings his passion best.
HE. And that the kingdom is added to the gift.
SHE. The kingdom and myself thus have I sworn
HE. 37 But what if some blind aged crippled man
Or some base beggar out of his famine sing
Better than full men.
SHE. Some I reject
38a No man abhorrent to these eyes can sing.
39 Some I have punished for their impudence
Of standing there and looking at my face
HE. My hair is foul and matted I wear rags
44 I have crossed many forests and the beasts
45 Have torn me with their claws — My memory's gone
46 Because great solitudes have driven [me mad]
47 But when I look into a stream the face
Trembling upon the stream there makes [me] think
49 My origin is fouler than my rags.
SHE. 50 But you have passed through perils for [my] sake
51 Come a great distance — I permit the song
HE. Therefore I get you if I sing the best
53 But who decides.
SHE. I and my heart decide
I call that song the best that moves me most
But none has moved me yet

HE. You must be won
At a full moon in March the beggars say
57 That moon has come and I am here alone
SHE. You know the cruel journey that you took
Forest and beast and crueller [?] solitude
Some I have killed or maimed because their words
Or else their music put me in a rage
63 And some because they came at all — men hold
That beauty is kind, a melting thing
65 But they that call me cruel speak the truth
A cruel winter of virginity
Go quickly for I have not done you harm
And should not if you go. What keeps you dumb
What pulls your chin upon your breast. Speak out
HE. 70 My mind is running on our marriage night
71 Imagining all from the first touch and kiss
SHE. What makes you think that you can move me most
HE. 74 Because I look upon you without fear
I think as the gods think
SHE. What do they think
HE. Desiring cruelty they made you cruel
I shall embrace that body and embrace
That cruelty desiring both — So great
Is [my] desire you cannot help but yield
SHE. Another question are you like the rest
Trusting [to] some novel simile
Or some ridiculous hyperbole
To praise my beauty and fill out the song
HE. All comes back — I sat among the swine
When I first heard your name and how to win you.
84 I rolled among the dung of swine and laughed
85 What do I know of beauty
SHE. Sing the best
86 And you are not a swineherd but a king
HE. 87 What do I know of kingdoms?

[The draft breaks off at this point; no doubt the continuation was removed from the looseleaf manuscript book we have been following.]

In the three partial versions that come first Yeats achieved some of the language of the printed play, and in the version marked "B" a good deal of it; there some twenty lines are in the form first printed, and others require only slight modification. Although Yeats often uses words and even phrases that occur in the prose drafts, the diction of his verse is much less dependent on the prose than was the diction of *At the Hawk's Well.* This greater originality in word choice makes the verse seem fresher, it indicates a more generous creative economy. Yeats is still inventing new matter, rounding things out, so to speak: the swineherd's question about what would happen if a beggar sang the best song is new, as is the Queen's question about the simile and hyperbole of the swineherd's song. The new speech tags "He" and "She" reduce things to their ultimate essentials. In the "B" draft Yeats is on his way to the finished play.

V

Manuscript five

YEATS COMPLETED *A Full Moon in March* except for incidental revision in a manuscript written on thirteen numbered sheets with the title "The Swine-Herd." If we assume that a continuation of the dialogue in the "B" version has been lost or misplaced, then in MS. 5 Yeats assembled the parts of his play from various drafts. While doing this he continuously refined his diction and versification, and he added some new matter. (The manuscript is very lightly punctuated; I have supplied essential punctuation from the version printed in *Poetry*, but retained all of Yeats's manuscript punctuation.)

THE SWINE-HERD

FIRST ATTENDANT. Did you ask him what the play was about?

SECOND ATTENDANT. He said something about a full moon in March, Christ upon the cross, Caesar dead at the foot of Pompey's statue, but that is nonsense.

FIRST ATTENDANT. Did he say what I must sing?

SECOND ATTENDANT. At first he said sing any love song you could remember, then that you must sing that song with the line "Crown of gold, dung of swine."

Song of the unfolding and folding of the cloth

SECOND ATTENDANT.
11 Every loutish lad in love
12 Thinks his wisdom great enough,
What cares love for this or that?
To get all the town astare,
15 As though Pythagoras wandered there.
16 *Crown of gold or dung of swine.*

17 Should old Pythagoras fall in love
18 Little may he boast thereof.
What cares love for this or that?
20 Days go by in foolishness.
21 O how great their sweetness is.
22 *Crown of gold, or dung of swine.*

23 Open wide those gleaming eyes
24 That can make the loutish wise.
What cares love for this or that?
26 Make a leader of the schools
27 Thank the Lord all men are fools.
28 Crown of gold or dung of swine.

The First Attendant may join in singing the burden at the end of the first or second verse. When the cloth has been folded up by the three attendants, as "The Hawk's Well," they sit at one side or at both sides the stage, where at their entrance they may have placed gong, drum, flute and zither. A Queen is discovered seated. She is veiled.

THE QUEEN. 29 What man is at the door? *She stretches herself, yawns.*

ATTENDANT. Nobody, Queen.

QUEEN. 30 Some man has come, some terrifying man,
Some man that I shall take for husband comes
31 For I have yawned and stretched myself three times.
32 Admit him, Captain of the Guard . . .

ATTENDANT. He comes.

Enter the SWINEHERD

SWINEHERD. 33 The beggars of my country say that he

34 That sings you best shall take you for a wife.
QUEEN. 35 He that best sings his passion.
SWINEHERD. And they say
36 The kingdom is added to the gift.
QUEEN. So have I sworn.
SWINEHERD. 37 But what if some blind aged crippled man
37a Or some base beggar in his famine sing
38 Better than wholesome men?
QUEEN. Some I reject.
38a No man abhorrent to these eyes can sing,
39 Some I have punished for their impudence.
SWINEHERD. 40 So that's the catch. Look well upon me, Queen.
42 My hair is foul and matted — here and there
My flesh seems scarce less ragged than my clothes.
44 I have crossed many forests and the beasts
45 Have torn me with their claws — my memory's gone
46 Because great solitudes have driven me mad,
47 But when I look into a stream the face
48 That trembles upon the surface makes me think
My origin is fouler than my rags.
QUEEN. 50 But you have passed through perils for my sake;
51 Come a great distance: I permit the song.
SWINEHERD. 52 Kingdom and lady if I sing the best,
53 But who decides?
QUEEN. I and my heart decide.
54 We say that song is best that moves us most.
55 No song has moved us yet.
SWINEHERD. You must be won
56 At a full moon in March those beggars say.
That moon has come and I am here alone.
QUEEN. 59 Remember through what perils you [have] come.
60 But I am crueller than solitude,
61 Forest or beast. Some I have killed or maimed
62 Because their singing put me in a rage
63 And some because they came at all. Men hold
That woman's beauty is a melting thing.
65 But they that call me cruel speak the truth,
A cruel winter of virginity.

67 But for a reason that I cannot guess
68 I would not harm you; go before I change.
69 Why do you stand, your chin upon your breast?

SWINEHERD. 70 My mind is running on our marriage night,
71 Imagining all from the first touch and kiss.

QUEEN. 72 What gives you that strange confidence, what makes
73 You think that you can move my heart and me?

SWINEHERD. 74 Because I look upon you without fear
75 I know the thought of God.

QUEEN. What is that thought?

SWINEHERD. 77 Desiring cruelty, he made you cruel.
78 I shall embrace body and cruelty
79 Desiring both, as though I had made both.
You cannot help but yield to great desire.

QUEEN. 80 Another question. You bring like all the rest
81 Some novel simile, some wild hyperbole
82 Praising my beauty?

SWINEHERD. My memory has returned.
83 I tended swine when first I heard your name.
84 I rolled among the dung of swine and laughed.
85 What do I know of beauty?

QUEEN. Sing the best
86 And you are not a swineherd, but a king.

SWINEHERD. 87 What do I know of kingdoms? *Snapping his fingers*
That for kingdoms!

QUEEN. If by my tears or by the trembling of my limbs
89 I should proclaim your song beyond denial
90 More moving than the rest, I leave this throne
91 These corridors, the reverence of servants,
92 What do I gain?

SWINEHERD. A song — the night of love,
93 An ignorant forest and the dung of swine.

QUEEN. 94 All here have heard the man and all have judged.
95 I led him, that I might not seem unjust,
96 From point to point, established in all eyes
That he has brought an insult, not his love.

SWINEHERD. 99 She shall bring forth her farrow in the dung.
100 But first my song — what nonesense shall I sing?

QUEEN. 101 Send for the headsman, Captain of the Guard.

ATTENDANT. I have sent already, Queen.
QUEEN. 103 I owe my thanks to God that this foul wretch,
104 Foul in his rags, his origin, his speech,
105 In spite of all his daring, has not dared
106 Ask me to drop my veil — Insulted ears
107 Have heard and shuddered, but my face is pure.
108 Had it but known the insult of his eyes
109 I had torn it with these nails.
SWINEHERD. *Going up stage* Why should I ask,
110 What do those features matter? When I set out
111 I picked a number on the roulette wheel.
112 I trust the wheel as every lover must.
QUEEN. 113 Pray if your savagery has learnt to pray,
114 For in a moment they will lead you out
115 Then bring your severed head.
SWINEHERD. My severed head! *He laughs.*
116 There is a story in my country of a woman
117 That stood all bathed in blood — a drop of blood
118 Entered her womb and there begat a child.
QUEEN. 119 O foul, foul, foul — I shall be quit of him.
120 I shall not touch his blood.
SWINEHERD. She sank in sleep,
122 Her body in the bridal sleep conceived.
QUEEN. 123 Begone! I shall not see your face again.

She turns towards him, her back to the audience, and slowly drops her veil. The Attendants begin the unfolding of the cloth, or close the stage curtains.

FIRST ATTENDANT. 124 What are you to sing?
SECOND ATTENDANT. 125 The song [of] that ancient Irish Queen, who had put her lover's head upon a stake.
FIRST ATTENDANT. 125a But that has nothing to do with this play,
126 That was quite a different Queen.
SECOND ATTENDANT. I must do what he told me to do.

Second Attendant sings the song of the severed head from the Note in "King of the Great Clock Tower." When the curtain is parted or the cloths folded up again, the QUEEN *is seen standing exactly as before, the dropped veil by her side, but she holds above her severed head of the* SWINEHERD. *Her hands are red, there are red blotches on her. They must not be too realistic — red gloves, red cloth maybe; some kind of harmony or pattern should suggest blood.*

[The song is not included in the MS. It is supplied from "Commentary on the Great Clock Tower."]

127 He had famished in the wilderness,
128 Braved lions for my sake,
129 And all men lie that say that I
130 Bade that swordsman take
131 His head from off his body
132 And set it on a stake.

133 He swore to sing my beauty
134 Though death itself forbade,
135 They lie that say in mockery
136 Of all that lovers said,
137 Or in mere woman's cruelty
138 I bade them fetch his head.

139 O what innkeeper's daughter
140 Shared the Byzantine crown!
141 Girls that have governed cities,
142 Or burned great cities down,
143 Have bedded with their fancy-man
144 Whether a king or clown;

145 Gave their bodies, emptied purses
146 For praise of clown or king,
147 Gave all the love that women know!
148 O they had their fling
149 But never stood before a stake
150 And heard the dead lips sing.

SECOND ATTENDANT. 151 Her lips are moving.

FIRST ATTENDANT. She has begun to sing.

SECOND ATTENDANT. What is she singing? I cannot hear her.

153 Ah, now I can hear.

FIRST ATTENDANT. *Singing as* QUEEN

154 Child and darling hear my song,
155 Never cry I did you wrong,
156 Cry that wrong came not from me
157 But my virgin cruelty.

158 Great my love before you came,
159 Greater when I loved in shame,
160 Greatest when there broke from me
161 Storm of virgin cruelty.

She lays the head upon the throne.

SECOND ATTENDANT. 162 She is waiting.

FIRST ATTENDANT. She is waiting for his song.
The song he came such a long journey to sing,
164 She has forgotten that the dead cannot sing.

SECOND ATTENDANT. Look, look, his lips are moving. *First Attendant laughs as Swineherd.*
165 He has begun to laugh.

FIRST ATTENDANT. He has begun to sing.

SECOND ATTENDANT. *Singing as head.*

166 I sing a song of Jack and Jill.
167 Jill had murdered Jack;
168 *The moon shown brightly;*
169 Ran up the hill and round the hill,
170 Round the hill and back,
171 *A full moon in March.*

Jack had a hollow breast, for Jill
173 Had hung his heart on high;
174 *The moon shown brightly;* . .
175 Had hung his heart beyond the hill,
176 A-twinkle in the sky,
177 *A full moon in March.*

The Queen in her dance moves away from the head. FIRST ATTENDANT *as* QUEEN *laughs.*

SECOND
ATTENDANT. She is laughing. How can we laugh if we love the dead?

FIRST
ATTENDANT. 179 She is crazy. That is why she is laughing.

He laughs again. The dance expresses refusal. She takes up the head and lays it upon the ground. She dances before it. Her dance is a dance of invitation. She takes up the head and dances with the head to drum taps which grow quicker and quicker. Her dance expresses the sexual act. She kisses the head. Her body shivers. She sinks slowly down, holding the head against her breast. Song of the closing of the curtain or the unfolding and folding of the cloth. The song at the end of "Clock Tower" with the line "Their desecration and the lover's night."

[The song is not in the MS. It is supplied from the prose version of *The King of the Great Clock Tower.*]

SECOND
ATTENDANT. 180 Why must those holy, haughty feet descend
181 From emblematic niches and what hand
182 Ran that delicate raddle through their white?
183 My heart is broken, yet must understand.
184 What do they seek for? why must they descend?

FIRST
ATTENDANT. 185 For desecration and the lover's night.

SECOND
ATTENDANT. 186 I cannot face that emblem of the moon,
187 Nor eyelids that the unmixed heavens dart,
188 Nor stand upon my feet, so great a fright
189 Descends upon my savage, sunlit heart.
190 What can she lack whose emblem is the moon?

FIRST
ATTENDANT. 191 But desecration and the lover's night.

SECOND
ATTENDANT. 192 Delight my heart with sound; speak yet again.
193 But look and look with understanding eyes
194 Upon the pitchers that they carry; tight
195 Therein all time's completed treasure is:
196 What do they lack? O cry it out again.

FIRST
ATTENDANT. 197 Their desecration and the lover's night.

A comparison of MS. 5 with the earlier drafts of the play shows that Yeats assembled most of his play from these drafts. The prose the Attendants speak at the opening of the play is adapted from MS. 3; there were multiple earlier drafts of the opening song "Every loutish lad in love." Yeats's decision to have the Queen veiled, and to have her drop her veil as a symbol of sexual surrender just before the Swineherd is taken out is not anticipated in any of the drafts that I have seen, nor is the naming of the Swineherd in the speech tags. The opening dialogue down to the point where version "B" breaks off when the Swineherd says "What do I know of kingdoms" refines the language of B though there are few changes in substance. From here on the play follows the plan of the second prose draft (MS. 3) with some added matter such as the Queen's appeal to the Attendants before she orders the execution of the Swineherd, the Queen's statement that the Swineherd has not seen her face, and the Swineherd's speech "I picked a number on the roulette wheel."

The end of the play shows greater influence from *The King of the Great Clock Tower* than any other part: the dance with the severed head and the song by the head. The Queen's song beginning "Child and darling hear my song" is new. Yeats made many earlier drafts of the song sung by the head, "I sing a song of Jack and Jill." Yeats's plan for the dance suggesting the sexual union of the Queen and Swineherd is more fully worked out than in MS. 3 and more frankly expressed than in the play as printed.

vi

Printed Versions

THE TEXT OF THE FIRST PRINTING of *A Full Moon in March* in *Poetry* for March 1935 is very close to the text of MS. 5. Yeats reworked a few lines and made some changes in the stage directions, but the conformity of manuscript and printed text is, for Yeats's works, unusual. Yeats then carefully revised the play before reprinting it in the book to which it gave its name. The kind of changes made can be traced in the evolution of the speech in which the Swineherd describes his journey — first, MS. 5:

> So that's the catch. Look well upon me, Queen.
> My hair is foul and matted — here and there
> My flesh seems scarce less ragged than my clothes.
> I have crossed many forests and the beasts
> Have torn me with their claws — my memory's gone
> Because great solitudes have driven me mad,
> But when I look into a stream the face
> That trembles upon the surface makes me think
> My origin is fouler than my rags.

In the *Poetry* printing Yeats changed the third line above to "My flesh seems scarce less ragged than my rags." In *A Full Moon in March* the passage reads as follows:

> So that's the catch.
> Queen look at me, look long at these foul rags,
> At hair more foul and ragged than my rags;
> Look on my scratched foul flesh. Have I not come
> Through dust and mire? There in the dust and mire
> Beasts scratched my flesh; my memory too is gone,
> Because great solitudes have driven me mad.
> But when I look into a stream, the face
> That trembles upon the surface makes me think
> My origin more foul than rag or flesh.

The introduction and repetition of "mire" in this passage links it to "Byzantium," written before the play, and to "The Gyres," written after it. "Mire" is a key word in "Byzantium" where Yeats uses it three times and always in conspicuous places: in the final lines of stanzas 1 and 3 and in the initial line of stanza 5.

> The fury and the mire of human veins . . .
> And all complexities of mire and blood . . .
> Astraddle on the dolphin's mire and blood

It is one of Yeats's favorite words when as here with the Swineherd he is creating a symbol of human sensuality. The word is used somewhat differently in "The Gyres" where it forms part of Yeats's description of the violence of the Thirties: "What matter though numb nightmare ride on top/ And blood and mire the sensitive body stain?" The blood aspect of this configuration is reserved for the close of the play where the staining of the Queen's clothes and hands by the blood of the Swineherd represents her sexual surrender and conception.

Eric Bentley in his essay "Yeats's Plays" (*In Search of Theater*, p. 325) calls *A Full Moon in March* "one of the finest examples of [Yeats's] histrionic art." He finds this play a classic example of Yeats's dramatic art because Yeats

> starts from a dramatic situation and resolves it into a single incident; . . . he employs non-verbal arts while subordinating them to the words; . . . he asks for absolutely un-Stanislavskyan actors; . . . his situation is not used to define individual character or as the starting point of a plot, but as a gateway to the "deeps" of the "soul life"; and, finally, . . . we are not left holding a mere Maeterlinckian mood, but are given a theme — namely the idea that if we are to live . . . our wintry and saintly virginity must descend into the dung of passion.

It took Yeats a year to achieve the ultimate dramatic and poetic concentration which Eric Bentley admires. The drafts of *The King of the Great Clock Tower*, out of which *A Full Moon in March* grew, proliferate in many directions. In early drafts the King is the half-legendary Irish chief, O'Rourke of Breffany, whose great-grandfather had married Dervorgilla, and whose "body has inherited a passion/ For women worthy death." As Yeats refined the telling of his fable, this Irishizing almost disappeared, and King, Queen, and Stroller, divested of personality, emerge as emblems of certain eternal aspects of human character. Then the King went, and essential man and essential woman play out an essential human drama.

In *A Full Moon in March* Yeats dramatically presents his ultimate philosophy of love, shows us that love indeed "has pitched his mansion/ In the place of excrement." To accomplish this he uses incidents and situations which echo and re-echo through folklore: the cruel queen, the impossible test, magical impregnation. He associates these with fertility legends more ancient still. We find in the Queen an embodiment of what Denis de Rougemont calls "passion": "To love love more than the object of love, to love passion for its own sake, has been to love to suffer and to court suffering all the way from Augustine's *amabam amare* down to modern romanticism" (*Love in the Western World*, p. 41). And we see in the Swineherd's triumph over this "passion," at the cost of his life, a triumph of what De Rougemont calls "the sturdy Celtic tradition which proclaimed its pride in life" (p. 36). Yeats has created still another fable to express Unity of Being.

In this play, too, Yeats somehow resolves one peculiar form which the love-death amalgam had taken in the Romantic ethos. Romantic literature is full of severed heads to which women make love, to a lover *per force* chaste. Blake's Fair Eleanor took up the severed head of her husband and kissed its pale lips; Stendhal's Mathilde placed Julien's severed head on a marble table and kissed its brow, and so on through Wilde's *Salomé*. There is an echo of these horrors in Yeats's early story, "The Binding of the Hair." If we ignore the uncanny to take this emblematic situation at its simplest it appears to say that part of the Romantic ethos was a desire by some women — and some men — to be loved without responding to the brutal demands of their lover's bodies. I say Yeats has resolved this theme because what is uncanny, deeply troubling in Stendhal grows clear and deeply moving in *A Full Moon in March*.

This comes about, I think, because Yeats has consciously raised his subject to the level of myth, or, in his own word, "fable." Stendhal's protagonists are "personalities," and because they are we look into the psychological depths which Stendhal has imagined for them to discover reasons for what they do. Yeats's protagonists are "characters" from whom personality has been carefully abstracted. In "An Introduction for My Plays," written in 1937 and recently printed in *Essays and Introductions* (p. 530), Yeats wrote: "Browning said that he could not write a successful play because interested not in character in action but in action in character. I had begun to get rid of everything that is not, whether in lyric or dramatic poetry, in some sense character in action; a pause in the midst of action perhaps, but action always its end and theme." In *A Full Moon in March* we find characters in action, and it is because we do that the play moves us so deeply. When protagonists become timeless "characters," as they do here, materials can be used to reveal the depths of the soul life which produce a highly morbid impression when used in connection with "personalities" carefully involved in time.

This play is one of Yeats's finest achievements in his own special dramatic form, the play for dancers. Yeats expressed his hopes for this form in an unpublished dialogue written in 1916, "The Poet and the Actress";

Take anything you will — theatre or speech or a man's body — and develop its emotional expressiveness, and you at once increase its power of suggestion and take away from its power of mimicry or of stating facts. The body begins to take poses or even move in a dance. . . . Speech becomes rhythmical, full of suggestion, and as this change takes place we begin to possess, instead of the real world of the mimics, solitudes and wildernesses peopled by divinities and daimons, vast sentiments, the desires of the heart cast forth into forms, mythological beings, a frenzied parturition.

The phrase "a frenzied parturition" perfectly describes *A Full Moon in March.*

10

Purgatory

THE materials for the study of the composition of *Purgatory*, Yeats's next to last play, are unusually complete: a scenario eight pages long, two manuscripts, four typescripts with corrections in Yeats's hand, and a set of corrected proofs. This material is all in the National Library of Ireland. In TS. 4 the text has nearly reached its final form. Yeats first mentions the play in his letters on March 15, 1938. By June he was planning its production; it was first produced at the Abbey Theatre August 10, 1938. On the first night of the play Yeats made his last public appearance. *Purgatory* was set up for the Cuala Press, along with the rest of *On the Boiler* in the fall of 1938, and Yeats read proof. Yeats died before *On the Boiler* was published, and after Yeats's death, Mrs. Yeats decided that *On the Boiler* had been so carelessly printed that the edition for which Yeats had read proof would have to be destroyed. A new edition was manufactured and published in the fall of 1939.

Yeats conceived *Purgatory*, then, while at work on *On the Boiler*. One of the principal subjects of *On the Boiler* is the need for eugenic reform, a subject about which Yeats had come to feel strongly. This accounts for one of the themes of the play, where the Old Man, product of a misalliance, kills his pubescent son before the boy can carry on the degenerating line. Another theme, the destruction of a house which had at one time been the seat of an established way of life, turns up frequently in Yeats's later poetry. In his statement to the press at the time of the play's first production Yeats said, "In my play a spirit suffers because of its share, when alive, in the destruction of an honoured house. The destruction is taking place all over Ireland today." No doubt Yeats had particularly in mind the destruction of Roxborough House and Moore Park during the Irish Civil War, and the fact that Coole was deserted and, as he had foreseen in "Coole Park, 1929," soon to be destroyed. Happily Yeats died before Coole was torn down. To express these themes Yeats returned to one of his favorite dramatic subjects, the earth bound spirit, already exploited in *The Dreaming of the Bones* and *The Words upon the Window-pane.* As Dr. Trench tells us in *Words,* a spirit becomes earth bound in one of two ways: either death was so traumatic that the spirit of the dead man or woman cannot forget its death and relives it over and over again; or, and this is the doctrine Yeats uses, during life a man or woman commits a crime so monstrous that after death the spirit cannot forget the crime, and recapitulates it again and again. Such a recapitulation becomes for Yeats in this play a kind of purgatory.

Yeats composed the scenario and the two manuscripts in a looseleaf notebook, starting to work always on the right hand page and using the left hand page, the back of the preceding page of his manuscript, for rewriting and revision. The scenario is eight pages long, and the backs of pages one and eight have been used for revision. This manuscript was clearly not all composed at a sitting. Yeats began in ink; near the bottom of page two he shifted to pencil and continued in pencil to the middle of page four. He wrote with a soft pencil in strokes so light they have made no impression on the paper — indeed it seemed to me that every time I returned to this part of the manuscript it was dimmer than it had been the time before. Then Yeats completed the scenario in ink. I tried for days to transcribe it, but was unable to make a transcription full enough to print. I will, however, paraphrase what I could read of it, since it is a record of Yeats at work during the last year of his life, at work on a play which several critics consider his best.

Yeats began by describing the scene of the action more fully than he does in his stage directions. The background is a ruined house, a large window and door of which show. At one side is a garden wall or hedge. A black tree looks white in the moonlight. The characters are to be well lighted by a stream of moonlight falling on the front of the stage. The Old Man and the Boy enter, carrying a pack. The Old Man tells the Boy that they are in a horrible place, that it is because of what happened here that "he and the Boy must live by peddling needles, and pins, and spools of thread." This has happened to a man who has read books, who learned to read them in the ruined house before them. The Old Man announces the doctrine of purgatory: "The dead in purgatory return to the place . . . of their transgression — they return again and again." The house was the house of the boy's grandmother, and here shortly the boy's grandparents will relive a crime committed sixty-three years before. The Old Man's mother had inherited the house from her ancestors. Her father was dead, her mother an old woman, and there was no one to control her. She met his father, the Boy's grandfather, somewhere on the other side of Ireland. He was a groom at an establishment where she had a horse in training. He used to ride with her. They fell in love and married. The Boy says that his grandfather was a lucky man. The Old Man says — and here Yeats breaks into direct discourse, "he was only a drunken devil and spent all she had." The Boy wishes he could marry a rich woman and spend her money.

There is the sound of horse hooves. The Old Man says this is the marriage night of his father and mother. His father has been to the public house for a drink, and his mother is waiting for him at the window. The Old Man sees his mother's ghost at the window; the Boy sees nothing and tells the Old Man he is mad. In the Old Man's vision his father has ridden to the back of the house; his mother goes to let him in. His father takes his mother in his arms and they go to their marriage bed. There the Old Man is begotten, and a dark evil, a curse that has never been broken, begins. The Old Man says that what he has seen is only his mother's thought. She died in giving birth to her son, so never knew the end of the story. But she knows it now. His father spent all her money on drink and horses and women; he never gave his son an education, so on this one night every year she lives through her crime again.

At this point the Boy tries to run away with the Old Man's money. The Old Man threatens to kill the Boy before he can beget a child. They struggle for the knife and the Old Man throws the Boy down. He tells him how he murdered his own father, the Boy's grandfather. The vision returns; this time the Boy sees it too. The scenario ends as follows:

Come, come, come, I say, that I may kill, and my mother find rest now that the evil is finished. (BOY *rises and comes slowly to* OLD [MAN], *who stabs him. The vision fades. As it fades the hoof beats are heard again.*) O my God, she does not understand — her agony, her agonized joy, or her remorse begin all over again. Even when mother sees all [her soul] does not understand that the evil it set in motion is finished. O my God, what is man? Are they never ending, the misery of the living and the remorse of the dead?

By the end of the scenario Yeats has projected himself completely into the character of the Old Man he is imagining. He began with indirect discourse: "the Old Man says that"; "the Boy says that." During the scene where the Old Man envisions his own begetting, Yeats changes to direct discourse and most of the rest of the scenario is a dramatic monologue spoken by the Old Man. A few stage directions interrupt this monologue, and the Boy speaks twice, but even in late typescripts of the play Yeats was still writing speeches for the Boy in order to break up this long monologue. The last line of the scenario stayed pretty much as it was through all the versions of the play. Studying the manuscript of the scenario is curiously exciting, for the impetus of the vision Yeats saw is passed on to the reader by the half-formed words that seem at times literally to have been hurled onto the page.

After he had recorded this dreadful vision in the scenario, Yeats had still to clothe the bare bones of his plot with the flesh of detail, and he had to put the whole into verse. He did this in two manuscripts which are such a tangle of revisions they are nearly indecipherable. Then he made his first typescript from the second manuscript, dictating to his typist and making further revisions as he went along. He continued the process of revision on successive typescripts and then on the proof sheets.

Yeats's struggle for expression has to be seen in the manuscripts to be fully appreciated, but perhaps something of the struggle can be indicated by working through successive versions of the final scene in the play, based on the passage from the scenario which was quoted above. In MS. 1 the Old Man's final speech goes approximately as follows:

195 Hush a bye baby thy/ your father's a knight
196 Thy mother a lady lovely and bright
197 No that is something that I read in a book
× It is my mother I would sing

If I sing it must be to my mother
And I have not the words — Dear Mother,
Because I have finished all that evil
The window's empty sink into your peace
I killed this lad because he had youth
And soon would take some woman's fancy
× And pass the blood pollution on
And he'd pass the pollution on
But I am a wretched foul old man
And thus harmless. ~~When this knife is clean~~ When my knife is clean
And I have picked up all that dropped money
I'll to a distant place and change my [word undeciphered]
× God [word undeciphered] and sing a song or two
× About how the dead tramp [three words undeciphered]
× [Undeciphered cancelled line]
× Dead tramps are soon forgotten
× Until the dead tramp killed in a brawl
Hoof beat
O God release my mother ~~from her dream~~ ~~from her misery~~ from the misery
For I can do no more ~~release~~ appease
223 The misery of the living and the remorse of the dead

[I am very uncertain of the order of the drafts that follow.]

× Horse hoofs
× That sound again horse hoofs again
× That distant sound that horse hoof means
× That she relives her marriage night
× Not because of any outward consequences
× That man can end but because
× Of what has happened to her soul

All dark but for a light that falls
Upon that thunder blasted tree
Cold sweet glistening light

× That distant sound, that horse hoof means
× That sound again horse hoofs again
× That means that she lives her deed

× Horse hoofs, horse hoofs again
× That sound again ~~that horse hoof means~~ that means
× That she relives that past event
× Because of what her marriage did to herself
× To her own soul and what I think
× Not to others but to her own soul
× And what I did is but vain
× O God release my mother's soul
× There's nothing ~~I~~ mankind can do. Appease
223× The misery of the living and the remorse of the dead.

~~That distant sound~~ Hoof beats, hoof beats — that ~~horse~~ hoof beat means
That she must animate that dead night
Again, and again, ~~and yet again~~ on, on, on, on
O God release my mother's soul
There's nothing mankind can do. Appease
223 The misery of the living and the remorse of the dead.

[On an inserted sheet Yeats worked over once again the passage about cleaning the knife and picking up the money.]

× My jack knife
× My knife into the
210 This old jack knife into a sod
211 And pulled it out all bright again
212 And picked up all the money that he dropped
Find out/ I'll hurry to a distant place and there
214 I'll make/ Tell my old jokes among new men

[In MS. 2 the Old Man's speech nearly reached its final form.]

(*He stabs again and again and then sings*)
195 Hush a bye baby, that father's a knight
196 Thy mother a lady lovely and bright
197 No that is something that I read in a book
198 And if I sing it must be to my mother
× And I have not the words. Dear Mother
× Because I have finished all that evil
× The window is dark again. Sink into peace
199 And I lack rhyme.

(*The stage has grown dim, except where the tree stands in white light*)

Study ~~this~~ that tree
That stands there like a purified soul
201 All cold sweet glistening light
202 Dear Mother the window is dark again
203 But you are in the light because
204 I finished all that consequence
I killed that lad because of his youth
He would soon take some woman's fancy
Beget and pass pollution on
208 I am a wretched foul old man
209 And therefore harmless — ~~The knife now I stick~~ ~~that I have stuck~~ When I have stuck
210 This old jack knife into a sod
211 And pulled it out all bright again
212 And picked up all the money that he dropped
213 I'll to a distant place and there
214 Tell my old jokes among new men
× Until the guards have found me or forgot

× All's dark but for a beam of the moon that falls
× Upon that thunder blasted tree
× Bold cold steady light
× That stands there like a purified soul
× In cold sweet glistening light
× That I may study what it's like
× Hoof beat hoof beat that dream returns;
× Her mind cannot prevent ~~that dream returning~~ it and I
× ~~And I am~~ Am twice a murderer ~~and~~ for nothing.
219× And she must animate that dead night
× ~~Again again~~ Again and yet again not once but many times; O God

Hoof beats. O my God hoof beats
216 How quickly it returns: beat; beat
× Her mind cannot prevent that dream retu
217 Her mind cannot hold up that dream
Twice a murderer and for nothing
219 And she must animate that dead night

220 Not once but many times. O God
221 ~~O God~~ Release my mother's soul from its dream;
222 ~~There's nothing~~ Mankind can do no more. Appease
223 The misery of the living and the remorse of the dead.

The first typescript was made from MS. 2. In his correction of this and the other typescripts Yeats expanded the stage directions for the end of the play, and made several verbal changes: "Study that tree/ That stands there" became "Study that tree/ [200] It stands there . . ." The half line "because of his youth" became "for he was growing up"; "Hoof beats, O my God" became "Hoof beats, dear God." Yeats also indicated in the later typescripts how he wanted the verse paragraphed. The version of this speech printed in *On the Boiler* has one other revised passage; Yeats made the revision on the proof sheets of the first setting of that work, the edition which was destroyed: "I killed that lad for he was growing up,/ He would soon take some woman's fancy,/ Beget . . ." became "[205] I killed that lad because he had grown up,/ [206] He would have struck a woman's fancy/ [207] Begot . . ."

Clearly Yeats had a far less difficult time with *Purgatory* than he had with either *The Resurrection* or *A Full Moon in March*. He largely realized his dramatic conception in his scenario and went on rapidly from that to the composition of his play. Mr. F. A. C. Wilson in *W. B. Yeats and Tradition* has shown that many aspects of Yeats's thought— esoteric, historic, political — culminate in *Purgatory*, and that Yeats finds for their expression a fable that is clear, stark, and tragic. This certainly accounts for much of the power of the play as well as for the speed with which it was written. I would like to add this: the play is powerful and was quickly written because in it violent feelings which Yeats usually contained exploded. In his last years Yeats was a deeply troubled man. He could sometimes contemplate the end of a cycle and the advent of a new age of barbarism with the ironic detachment he shows in "The Gyres," but he could not always do so. Yeats felt his message to be urgent, and the world was no more listening to him than it had listened to Blake: the general deafness sometimes drove Yeats to violent expression, here in *Purgatory*, and elsewhere. What Thomas Mann called "human patriotism" drives Yeats powerfully to state that the continuing degradation of the human stock must some how, any how, be stopped, that it is not enough to throw likely couples into bed unless you do indeed knock the others down. Yeats could hardly have stated this more brutally than he does when he plunges us into the dark underside of the human consciousness by the themes of father murder and son murder, and lets us know that even father murder and son murder will not relieve the responsible sinner, the mother, of the burden of her guilt.

In section XVIII of *Estrangement* Yeats draws an analogy between playwriting and the development of a religion:

In Christianity what was philosophy in Eastern Asia became life, biography, and drama. A play passes through the same process in being written. At first, if it has psychological depth, there is a bundle of ideas, something that can be stated in philosophical terms; my *Countess Cathleen*, for instance, was once the moral question, may a soul sacrifice itself for a good end, but gradually philosophy is eliminated until at last the only philosophy audible, if there is even that, is the mere expression of one character or another. When it is complete life it seems to the hasty reader a mere story.

In an essay "An Introduction for My Plays," recently prnted in *Essays and Introductions* (pp. 529–30), Yeats wrote in 1937:

I wanted all my poetry to be spoken on the stage or sung and, because I did not understand my own instincts, gave half a dozen wrong or secondary reasons; but a month ago I understood my reasons. I have spent my life in clearing out of poetry every phrase written for the eye, and bringing all back to syntax that is for the ear alone. Let the eye take delight in the form of the singer and the panorama of the stage and be content with that . . . Write for the ear, I thought, so that you may be instantly understood as when actor or folk singer stands before an audience.

These remarks between them explain why Yeats found playwriting difficult if we add the obvious point that any playwright who rejects all the styles of theatrical production accepted in his day is bound to have a hard time of it. Yeats did usually start with an abstraction, often with some aspect of his personal philosophy: *At the Hawk's Well* began with Yeats's feeling that both the heroic and the passive man will fail to accomplish their ends, that their lives will come to seem a preparation for something that never happens (by a curious irony Yeats was producing this play which so deeply questions the possible ends of heroic action only a few days before the outbreak of the Easter Rebellion in Dublin). *The Words upon the Window-pane* began with speculations as to the true source of Swift's *saeva indignatio; The Resurrection* with a traditional speculation about the nature of Christ. A *Full Moon in March* has its origin in a congerie of ideas that had become central in Yeats's philosophy: Unity of Being, recurrence, "resurrection," and others; in *Purgatory* again many of Yeats's characteristic themes fall together: the state of the dead, especially the kinds of sin that cause a spirit to become earth bound, the degeneration of a people and of a country where all that is "accustomed, ceremonious" is disappearing or has disappeared. These moral and philosophical questions are not intrinsically dramatic; how is a playwright to make them "life, biography, and drama"?

Yeats's answer in all instances save one (*The Words upon the Window-pane*) among the plays we have studied was to invent a fable which usually takes an archetypal pattern involving archetypal persons, and to concentrate his meaning in a cluster of traditional symbols often expressed in lyric poems. Of all those things which life seems to prepare us for which never happen, what is the one which never, never happens? The achievement of immortality by a mortal. So in *At the Hawk's Well* Yeats invents a fable with mythic backgrounds stretching from the Greeks, through the Middle Ages (the search for the elixir), to the present which involves the discovery by an Old Man and a Young Man of a well of immortality. Its waters flow, but both characters miss the moment. Their search is presented against a contrast of domestic repose, stated, ironically, by the well and the tree. Yeats's symbols include the well, the tree, the hawk woman (who is immortal), and others. In *The Resurrection* the *mythos* is the story of God's death and rebirth which ends with what is for Yeats a surprisingly Christian answer, the symbols are the Dionysian rites and the parallel Eucharist which is so central to the meaning that it is merely alluded to in passing (the Eleven are eating a meal consisting of bread and wine). And so on. By these means philosophy in Yeats's successful plays does become "life, biography, drama"; it loses its abstraction.[1]

The second passage quoted expresses Yeats's ideal for the language of his plays. He will write "for the ear alone." It is simple enough to say this, but it expresses a stylistic ambition as exalted as that Yeats expressed for the style of his poems in "The Bounty of Sweden": "to find for them some natural speech, rhythm and syntax, and to set it out in some pattern, so seeming old that it may seem all men's speech." It should be universally accepted that a play must be written for the ear — and Yeats would surely have added written for the speaking voice of the actor, which probably comes to much the same thing. But in our time this has been anything but a common ambition among playwrights. Neither Shaw, O'Neil, nor even Eliot seems to me to write for the ear. Yeats in an unpublished broadcast introducing a radio production of his version of *King Oedipus* (1928) spoke of testing his lines: "Sometimes I went on to the stage and spoke a sentence to be sure it was simple enough and resonant enough to be instantaneously felt and understood in every part of the theatre." His ideal for his translation was to avoid words which were "strange or difficult," and to avoid tiring "the ear by putting those words in some unnatural order." Yeats, as the many manuscripts printed above testify, took the same infinite pains with the language of his plays as he took with the language of his poems. I do not know whether Yeats was a great playwright — how can any of us know when we never get an opportunity to see his plays produced as he intended them to be; even the Abbey Players have lost the trick of doing this — but I do know that the language of his plays is a sheer delight from beginning to end.

PART THREE

Prose

AN INTRODUCTION

DURING EVERY DECADE OF HIS LONG CAREER *Yeats wrote extensively in prose, yet only two of his prose works,* Autobiographies *and* A Vision, *are widely known, and his other prose works have elicited little commentary compared with the massive commentary that is in print concerned with his poems and plays. This situation may be partly explained by the fact that much of Yeats's prose was out of print for a very long time. This is no longer true thanks to that series of extremely handsome books Macmillan and Company has produced in recent years, beginning with* Autobiographies *(1955) and continuing with* Mythologies *(1958),* Essays and Introductions *(1961), and* Explorations *(1962). Yet even now many of Yeats's prose works have never been collected, and must be traced with Wade's indispensable help to their original publication. Yeats also wrote a great deal of prose which he did not print either because it did not please him or was felt to be too private for publication. This is not true of his poems or plays except for juvenilia. The result is that even now the corpus of Yeats's prose cannot be said to be before us, easily accessible and relatively complete, as is the corpus of his poems and plays. Nor have the textual changes Yeats made in his prose been studied with anything like the care that the texts* of his poems and plays have received. Yet Yeats made many changes in the texts of his prose works, so many that any student of his prose has constantly to consult the original editions.

In this account of the development of certain prose works by Yeats I hope to call attention to this textual problem by continuing my discussion beyond the manuscript record to the point at which the text of each work reached final form, and to illustrate the immense labor Yeats expended on his prose. Yeats's statement to Dorothy Wellesley, "The correction of prose, because it has no fixed laws, is endless; a poem comes right with a click like a closing box" (Letters to DW, p. 24), expresses the simple truth concerning his own prose. He put even minor essays through draft after draft, he labored for years on Autobiographies.

I should like to explore for a moment the role the prose works played in Yeats's artistic economy by studying his production during the decade 1910–20. I pick this decade because during these years Yeats became a great writer, his years of hard labor were rewarded by a transubstantiation upward from lower to higher. This will be readily allowed when we recall the poems Yeats wrote between 1910 and 1920. These include all of Responsibilities and The Wild Swans at Coole, and nearly all of Michael Robartes and the Dancer. Yeats never wrote finer poems than "September 1913," "Easter 1916," "In Memory of Major Robert Gregory," and "The Second Coming." During these years Yeats also invented two original dramatic forms, the heroic farce and the play for dancers. After these inventions he wrote some of his finest plays, among them The Dreaming of the Bones.

During this decade Yeats wrote a great deal of prose as may be seen from the table given below, which ignores merely ephemeral prose but includes several prose works (marked with an asterisk) that have never been published.

1910	"The Tragic Theatre" (dated August 1910).
1910–14	* During these years Yeats composed the last forty-five entries of the Journal from which he later extracted "Estrangement," and "The Death of Synge."
1912–17	* Manuscript book and esoteric journal begun Christmas, 1912.
1913	"Art and Ideas."

1914	"Swedenborg, Mediums, and the Desolate Places" (dated October 14), "Reveries over Childhood and Youth" (finished December 25).
1915 (?)	* "Leo Africanus."
1915–16 (?)	* "First Draft" of Autobiographies.
1916 (?)	* "The Poet and the Actress."
1916	"Certain Noble Plays of Japan" (dated April 1916).
1917	Per Amica Silentia Lunae (finished in May).
1918–19	* Two full-length drafts of A Vision, written as a dialogue between Aherne and Robartes.
1919	"If I Were Four-and-Twenty" (published in August).

A word about the unpublished works before we return to the problem of the role of Yeats's prose in his total artistic economy. Between 1910 and 1917 Yeats kept a kind of literary daybook, first in the Journal begun in 1908 and then in the Esoteric Journal. He wrote in them infrequently but regularly. These daybooks are unlike any of his published works, for Yeats, as will be shown below, removed his accidence from the Journal begun in 1908 when he published selections from it in "Estrangement" and "The Death of Synge." These journals contain final and draft versions of many of the poems included in The Green Helmet and The Wild Swans at Coole, informal explorations of lines of thought Yeats later developed in essays such as "J. M. Synge and the Ireland of His Time," reports of séances and esoteric investigations, as well as autobiographical items. "Leo Africanus" and "The Poet and the Actress" point toward Per Amica. In "Leo Africanus" Yeats explores possible interpretations of his own esoteric experiences in an imaginary exchange of letters with Leo Africanus, explorer and writer of the seventeenth century, whose "spirit" had appeared at various séances, claiming to be Yeats's daimon or anti-self. "The Poet and the Actress" is a dialogue wherein a Poet (WBY thinly disguised) and an Actress (Florence Farr even more thinly disguised) discuss the doctrine of the Mask. It is enough to say here that the "First Draft" of Yeats's Autobiographies is described exactly by the title Yeats gave it. It is a rough first draft of the continuation of his memoirs beyond Reveries, which includes much of the material that Yeats was to expand in "The Trembling of the Veil" and

"Dramatis Personae." (I describe it more fully below when I discuss the composition of Autobiographies.)

To return to the problem with which we began, we can now say with some assurance that Yeats used the other harmony of prose to explore his changing critical interests, to express his powerful autobiographical impulse, and to say as much as he wished to say (usually in the form of a personal philosophic speculation) about his esoteric researches. All the works listed above can be assigned to the genres of criticism, autobiography, and philosophic speculation if these genres are broadly conceived, and if we observe that all of Yeats's interests are remarkably combined in the two Journals.

The four essays and the dialogue written during the period being examined are in their different ways critical, and in their different ways remarkably prescient of the development of Yeats's future work: "The Tragic Theatre," short as it is, opens a train of speculation on the nature of tragedy and of our response to tragedy that was to lead Yeats eventually to "Lapis Lazuli" and to the description of the tragic ecstasy in On the Boiler; "Art and Ideas" is an excellent brief illustration of the "identity of Yeats," for the reference (Essays and Introductions, p. 355) to "some Chinese painting of an old man, meditating upon a mountain path" whose meditations, Yeats says, we share, again points to "Lapis Lazuli"; "Certain Noble Plays of Japan" explains the origin of the play for dancers which Yeats invented, the form in which most of his later plays were cast; "The Poet and the Actress" playfully explores the doctrine of the Mask; "If I Were Four-and-Twenty" contains among many delightful things a public announcement of Yeats's intention to spend the next twenty years inculcating the doctrine of Unity of Being.

The impulse toward autobiography was always powerfully present in Yeats, perhaps most powerfully in 1914–17, years during which Yeats at long last decided to give up "returned and yet unrequited love" — decided that is to have done with the Gonnes, both mother and daughter — and get on with his life. The autobiographical element is powerfully present too in Yeats's poems and plays, where indeed it would have to be present given Yeats's belief that a poem should be a personal utterance. Some personal event was so often the origin of poem or play that one has constantly to check the impulse to reduce poem and play, now "intended, complete," to the events out of which they grew.

Finally, it was Yeats's habit, early and late, to use his esoteric investigations — he once estimated that they occupied a third of his time — as a basis for a series of philosophic and religious speculations which began with "Magic" in 1901 (in Ideas of Good and Evil*), continued with "Swedenborg, Mediums, and the Desolate Places" (1914 — Yeats's introduction to volume 2 of Lady Gregory's* Visions and Beliefs*) and* Per Amica *(1918), and culminated in* A Vision *(1925 and 1937). Yeats usually does not say much about the esoteric studies that lie back of these works, perhaps because he entered the arcane world through the back door, so to speak, that is through Madame Blavatsky, MacGregor Mathers, and the séance room; he came out the front door in the company of the neo-Platonists and the writers of the Upanishads. No doubt Yeats was delighted to find himself among these respected persons, though we should always remember that the compelling things here were Yeats's own visions and Yeats's own experience of psychic phenomena. Again, as with the autobiographical impulse, Yeats's esoteric experiences are by no means confined to the prose works which grew out of them directly; these experiences echo and reverberate through his poems and plays from beginning to end.*

This brief analysis of the prose Yeats wrote during the years 1910–19 describes the pattern into which his later prose falls, and suggests its relation to the rest of his work. This pattern was established earlier than 1910; I think it became operative in 1901 when Yeats abandoned a partly finished novel, "The Speckled Bird." After the failure of his novel Yeats seldom attempted narrative writing, gave up, that is, the kind of prose he had most frequently written during the 1890's. From 1901 to the end of his life Yeats's important prose works fall within the genres of criticism, autobiography, and philosophic speculation.

We have seen that Yeats's poems began with a subject or prose sketch, and that his plays began with a scenario. With the prose works we do not find any exact equivalent of subject or scenario, though in prose as in poetry and drama Yeats's process of writing was an accumulative one. On the Boiler*, for example, grew out of an eighteen-page essay on the need for eugenic reform. This event is typical. Yeats usually started a prose work with a rather general statement of his subject, then worked up slowly the detail needed to give this statement life and being. Then he cut and altered and* *rearranged, all the while polishing his phrasing, until he got exactly the expression that he wanted. In writing his prose works, especially the longer ones, Yeats often had great difficulty arranging his material. We will encounter an extreme instance of this difficulty when we examine the manuscripts of "Ireland after Parnell," where a single page will often have at the top a whole series of page numbers indicating the various places it has occupied in the developing manuscript. Finally, with Yeats's prose as with his poems and plays, publication did not mean that Yeats was done with a work. Sometimes Yeats rewrote a published work; he did this with* Stories of Red Hanrahan *and* A Vision. *More often he used a reprinting to make incidental revisions and additions. He made many revisions of this sort in the texts of the prose works included in* Early Poems and Stories *(1925) and in the successive issues of* Autobiographies. *He also dropped a number of his early stories from collected editions, just as he dropped early poems that dissatisfied him.*

In the following chapters I describe the process Yeats went through in writing certain of his prose works. I have picked these works as representative of Yeats's method, early and late: The Celtic Twilight, *written 1888–93,* The Secret Rose, *written 1892–96,* Discoveries, *written 1907,* Autobiographies, *written 1908–36, and* On the Boiler, *written 1938.*

11

The Celtic Twilight, *The Secret Rose*, AND *Discoveries*

UNTIL we get to *Discoveries*, the materials for the study of the composition of Yeats's prose works are incomplete. Such manuscripts as have survived seem to have survived quite by chance, or because Yeats was working at home where his sisters could preserve them. I believe, too, that a census of Yeats manuscripts in libraries and private collections would disclose that much of this early material is scattered throughout the world. One of the maids of the Misses Yeats took to drink; she supported her thirst by selling various items from their collection to book dealers and others. This material still turns up in Dublin from time to time, and no doubt much of it has gone abroad. So for the early works the process of composition can be established in only a very tentative way. There is more material for the study of the stories included in *The Celtic Twilight* than for the other early prose works.

i

The Celtic Twilight

The Celtic Twilght IS A COLLECTION of stories and essays most of which had been printed in magazines and newspapers during the years 1888–93. They are stories that Yeats had heard, or personal experiences thinly disguised. He wrote in Quinn's copy in 1904: "All real stories heard among the people or real incidents with but a little disguise in names and places" (Wade, item 8). Manuscripts of eleven of the stories have survived; there are two different manuscript versions of three of the eleven stories and clippings of magazine or newspaper versions of two other stories. Yeats has corrected one of these. A study of all this material suggests strongly that Yeats worked less hard on his early prose than on his late.

The manuscripts of eight stories are so like the printed texts that they suggest either that these manuscripts are clean copy which Yeats prepared for the press, or, if drafts, that the stories came easily. These eight stories include "A Teller of Tales," "A Knight of the Sheep," "The Sorcerers," "Regina, Regina Pigmeorum, Veni," "The Untiring Ones," "The Eaters of Precious Stones," "Our Lady of the Hills," and "The Golden Age." Two manuscript versions of three of these stories have survived: "Regina, Regina," "The Eaters of Precious Stones," and "Our Lady of the Hills." The later versions of all three, almost identical with what Yeats printed, show revision, but this is not nearly so radical as Yeats's revision eventually became. The principal change in the second manuscript of "Our Lady of the Hills," for example, is a comment added at the end. Yeats let this stand through the *Collected Works* of 1908, but it has been cut out of *Early Poems and Stories*. In the *Collected Works* (V, 142–43) the passage added in the second manuscript went as follows:

And after all, it was not my pretty Protestant, but Mary, Star of the Sea, still walking in sadness and in beauty upon many a mountain and by many a shore, who cast those tassels at the feet of the child. It is indeed fitting that men pray to her who is the mother of peace, the mother of dreams, the mother of purity, to leave them yet a little hour to do good and evil in, and to watch old Time telling the rosary of the stars.

I conclude from this partial evidence that Yeats composed many of the stories collected in *The Celtic Twilight* rapidly, and that he could not or did not in the early 1890's revise with the scrupulous care of his later years. This conclusion is supported by the study of the drafts of "The Host of the Air" in part 1. That poem, written at the same time as these stories, seems to have been rapidly, perhaps too rapidly composed.

Yeats did make a considerable revision of the manuscripts of two stories before he printed them, "Belief and Unbelief" and "The Thick Skull of the Fortunate." He added the story of the little girl taken by the fairies (*Collected Works,* V, 6–7) to "Belief and Unbelief," and cut two rather amusing passages out of "The Thick Skull of the Fortunate." In the manuscript, after telling the story of Egil's thick skull, Yeats adds, "Our critics treat a poet in much the same way"; and the sentence beginning "In some of our mountainous and barren places" reads in the manuscript "In some of our mountainous and barren places and in our seaboard villages we still test each other in this fashion, for lack, perhaps, of poets to hammer."

Two manuscript versions of an eleventh story, "The Religion of a Sailor," have survived, very different from each other. Since these manuscripts more than the others show us how Yeats worked in the 1890's, I have transcribed the first, giving as many of the cancellations as I can read:

We who live far from the simplicity of the elements, in our ~~painted~~ watch houses of intricate thought, must ever find something fascinating in the men of the ~~tide~~ sea and of the wood and of the mountain, and of all these the men of the sea, while apparently most unlike, are really most like ourselves. We isolate ourselves amid our watch houses of ~~speculation~~ thought and look out through ~~the brittle glass windows of our speculations~~ the dim window of our speculations, while they think ~~upon God~~ about God and about the world in ~~the solitude of their~~ their inside house or upon the bridge. ~~To us~~ Before our eyes moves the immensity of ~~the world~~ Hope and Dream ~~thought fantasy~~ and before theirs the immensity ~~of the sea~~ of sky and sea. We and they are alike lonely pilgrims amid storms and darkness and must perforce think much of that unknown city ~~whereto all pilgrims are travelling~~ where every pilgrimage comes to an end. Away in the valley yonder among the corn and the poppies men may well forget all things besides the warmth of the sun upon the face and the kind ~~shelter~~ shade of the hedgerow. One summer a couple of years ago I took my supper with a Captain Moran on board the SS Margaret ~~in Sligo~~ then put into Sligo River from I know not where. We got to talking of the deeper things and of the gulfs which shall devour our dreams or be the fulfillment of our hopes. [On the opposite page Yeats has written a variant of part of this last sentence. He let both versions stand. "of Religion and of the man of the word and I found him a man of many thoughts all flavoured with personality, as is the way with sailors."] He talked quietly in his queer sea manner of heaven and hell ~~and through all he said broke~~ but up through all broke the hard energy ~~of one that had~~ of the man of action buffeted for years against storm and darkness unafraid.

"Sur," said he, "did you ever hear tell of the sea captain's prayer?"

"No," said I, "What is it?"

"It is," he replied, "O Lord, give me a stiff upper lip."

"And what does that mean?"

"It means," he said, "that when they come to me some night and wake me up and say, 'Captain, we're going down,' that I maint make a fool o' mesel. Why, Sur, we war in mid Atlantic and I standin' on the bridge when the third mate comes up to me lookin' mortal bad. Says he, 'Captain, all's up with us.' Says I, 'Didn't you know [when] you joined that a certain percentage go down every year?' 'Yes, Sur,' says [he], and, says I, 'Aren't you paid to go down?' and, says he, 'Yes, Sur,' and says I, 'Then go down like a man and be damned to you.' "

He repeated this sea tale simply and quietly, ~~just like any other matter, and yet do they not contain that heroism born of long~~ just as if he told of the bubbling of the tar between the deck planks in the hot sun, the gathering of barnacles under the keel, or of any other part of the daily circumstances of his ~~profession~~ calling. Yet we whose wills are ever melted into thought and dreams can but look upon him and be full of wonder. Alas that he who does may not dream, and that he who dreams cannot do, and that the world sees no one man who unites them into a double mystery. Yet it [is] as well perhaps, for when that lover's knot of Time and Eternity is tied, voices are heard in the air and the hearts of men take fire and the old things are torn up by the roots and planted in new places. But Captain Moran [word undeciphered] upon his way in peace and I pen upon him but words. [undeciphered sentence]

In MS. 2 Yeats revised this story drastically. He cut out of the first paragraph the long comparison between the artist and the man of action, and reduced local detail when he changed "Sligo River" to "a western river." The first paragraph in MS. 2 ends rather differently from the printed story (*Collected Works,* V, 134–35; *Early Poems and Stories,* 259–60). In MS. 2 the paragraph ends as follows: "We got to talking of religion and the meaning of the world, and I found him a man of many notions all flavoured with personality as is the way with sailors. He talked in his queer sea manner of heaven and hell, and up through all his words broke the hard energy of the man of action." Yeats kept the passages of dialogue pretty much as they were written in MS. 1, and then cut out the entire final paragraph of commentary. In MS. 2, then, Yeats got his story into the form in which it was printed, except for the end of his first paragraph. There can be no doubt that the little anecdote stands out more sharply once it is relieved of its commentary; it is at once more simply and more circumstantially told. The long comparison between the man of action and the man of thought and the vaguely phrased prophesy of the coming of a new and changed world, both cut away, are so characteristic of Yeats in the 1890's — indeed of his generation — that one is glad this record of it has not disappeared. Yeats was literally haunted by his vision of a new dispensation.

Yeats's sisters used to clip his early stories and paste them into scrapbooks, several of which have survived. Sometimes, when he was preparing copy for a book, Yeats would cut out these clippings and write his corrections onto them. There is an example of this practice among the manuscripts of *The Celtic Twilight.* Copy for "Drumcliff and Rosses" was prepared from the version printed in *The Scots Observer.* Yeats had originally called the piece "Columkille and Rosses," and had started it by quoting the third stanza of Allingham's poem, "The Fairies":

High upon the hill-top
The old king sits;
He's now so old and grey,
He's nigh lost his wits
With a bridge of white mist
Columkille he crosses,
On his stately journeys
From Sleive-league to Rosses.

On the margin of the clipping Yeats has written and initialed this note: "A mistake. Allingham's Columkille and Rosses are in Donegal." He then revised the essay, taking out all references to the poem. There is also a clipping, apparently from a newspaper, of "Concerning the Nearness Together of Heaven, Earth and Purgatory." This was not used as copy for *The Celtic Twilight,* where the text was slightly revised, for there are no markings on this clipping. The clipping proves, however, that the piece had appeared in some serial before it was collected. Wade has not noted this.

In two of the many reprintings of *The Celtic Twilight,* Yeats carefully revised his text. Allan Wade notes these changes in his descriptions of *The Celtic Twilight,* 1902 (item 35), and *Early Poems and Stories,* 1925 (item 147). In the 1902 edition Yeats added seventeen new stories and wrote notes on or made additions to several of the old ones. He omitted "The Four Winds of Desire." In *Early Poems and Stories* Wade notes changes in the texts of seventeen stores. A collation of the texts of these stories as they were printed in *Collected Works* and in *Early Poems and Stories* shows that nearly all the revisions are omissions of passages of commentary. They carry on, as it were, in the successive printings of these stories the kind of revision Yeats made of the manuscript of "The Religion of a Sailor," leaving them more simply, more circumstantially told. Yeats cut concluding sentences or paragraphs of commentary from thirteen stories, as well as incidental sentences of commentary found in the body of certain stories. He also changed the tone of the book somewhat by cutting out elaborate personifications, and sentences befogged by the mists of the celtic twilight. In short, he treats these stories just as he treated certain of his early poems when he revised them for this collection. The following are typical of the kinds of passages Yeats cut:

> Perhaps he may have found and gathered . . . the Lily of High Truth, the Rose of Far-sought Beauty, for whose lack so many of the writers of Ireland, whether famous or forgotten, have been futile as the blown froth upon the shore. ["*The Last Gleeman,*" Collected Works, V, 72.]

> This old man always rises before me when I think of X——. Both seek — one in wandering sentences, the other in symbolic pictures and subtle allegoric poetry — to express a something that lies beyond the range of expression; and both, if X—— will forgive me, have within them the vast and vague extravagance that lies at the bottom of the Celtic heart. The peasant visionaries that are, the landlord duellists that were, and the whole hurly-burly of legends — Cuchulain fighting the sea for two days until the waves pass over him and he dies, Caolte storming the palace of the gods, Oisin seeking in vain for three hundred years to appease his insatiable heart with all the pleasures of faeryland, these two mystics walking up and down upon the mountains uttering the central dreams of their souls in no less dream-laden sentences, and this mind that

finds them so interesting — all are a portion of that great Celtic phantasmagoria whose meaning no man has discovered, nor any angel revealed.

[*Final paragraph of "A Visionary,"* Collected Works, V, 15–16.]

ii

The Secret Rose

MATERIALS FOR STUDY of the composition of *The Secret Rose* are fragmentary, but extremely interesting. Among the Yeats papers is a full manuscript of "Costello the Proud," and a scrap of manuscript of the final paragraph of "The Rose of Shadow." All the stories collected in *The Secret Rose* had appeared in magazines, and these versions can be compared with those found in a nearly complete set of page proofs of *The Secret Rose,* also in Mrs. Yeats's collection. These proofs not only establish the nature of the copy Yeats provided his publisher; they also, if we compare them with the text of the first edition, make it possible to determine the changes Yeats made in the text while the book was going through the press. A study of these materials shows that such manuscripts as remain are very similar to the texts published in the magazines; that Yeats did not greatly alter the magazine versions of most of the stories in preparing copy for his publisher, though he did revise five of them substantially; finally, that he literally rewrote the book while it was going through the press.

The complete manuscript of "Costello the Proud," with two drafts of the opening, is signed, and dated on the back, though not, I think, in Yeats's hand, "Aug. 1895." As is usual in Yeats manuscripts, there are no paragraph breaks (Yeats always adjusted the paragraphing of his prose very late in the process of revision), but apart from this the manuscript is very close to the version of the story first printed in a yearbook called *The Pageant,* published for the holiday book trade in the winter of 1895–96. Part of the final paragraph of a manuscript version of "The Rose of Shadow" has survived. Here, too, no changes of importance were made in the magazine version. The manuscript fragment reads:

. . . hidden by a huge mass of white flame that roared but gave no heat and in the midst of the flame was the form of a man crouching on the storm. His heavy and brutal face and his vast naked limbs were scarred with many wounds and his eyes full of white fire were fixed upon the girl under their knitted brows. The rest of the roof rolled up and then fell with a crash and the storm rushed through the house.

The text of this passage both in *The Speaker* (July 21, 1894) and in the proof sheets of *The Secret Rose* was the same, except that "part naked" in *The Speaker* became "partly naked" in the proof:

. . . lost in a shapeless mass of flame which roared but gave no heat, and in the midst of the flame was the form of a man crouching on the storm. His heavy and brutal face and his part(ly) naked limbs were scarred with many wounds, and his eyes were full of white fire under his knitted brows. The rest of the roof rolled up and then fell inward with a crash, and the storm rushed through the house.

To keep things together and at the same time to indicate what is coming, this passage read as follows in the first edition of *The Secret Rose*. Yeats made the changes in proof:

. . . lost in a formless mass of flame which roared but gave no heat, and had in the midst of it the shape of a man crouching on the storm. His heavy and brutal face and his partly naked limbs were scarred with many wounds, and his eyes were full of white fire under his knitted brows.

No doubt it seemed to Yeats when he began that it would be an easy task to collect the short stories he had written since the appearance of *The Celtic Twilight*. In a letter to his sister Lily, dated January 1, 1896, he wrote "my new book *The Secret Rose* is nearly finished and will be out about June I imagine or perhaps earlier." By this he meant, presumably, that he had the copy about ready for the printer. It was fifteen months later, on March 31, 1897, that he wrote to O'Leary "I send a copy of *The Secret Rose*." The various items finally included had all appeared, or were appearing, in magazines, beginning with the one called "The Book of the Great Dhoul and Hanrahan the Red," printed in *The National Observer* on November 26, 1892, and ending with "The Death of Hanrahan the Red" which appeared in *The New Review* in December 1896. Five of the stories appeared in 1896 while Yeats was at work on the collection, but there is no reason to suppose they were not all written when he began that work.

If we compare the magazine versions of these stories with the proof versions, we can determine exactly what Yeats did to them when he prepared his copy for the printer. Copy for one item included in *The*

Celtic Twilight, prepared on a clipping of the periodical version has, as was noted above, survived. It seems probable that Yeats prepared copy in this way for a majority of the stories included in *The Secret Rose,* for the magazine and proof texts are often very similar, and Yeats seldom produced two manuscript versions of any work without introducing changes. The texts of the following stories are close enough to the magazine versions to make it probable that copy was prepared in this way: [1] "The Crucifixion of the Outcast," "Out of the Rose," "The Curse of the Fires," "The Heart of the Spring," "Costello the Proud," "The Twisting of the Rope," "Kathleen the Daughter of Hoolihan," "The Curse of Hanrahan," "The Rose of Shadow," and "The Old Men of the Twilight." The proofs of *The Secret Rose* provide one piece of definite evidence that Yeats sent in printed copy. Hanrahan was originally "O'Sullivan," and then, throughout the proofs, "O'Hanrahan" or "O'Haurahan"; but on page 162 of the proofs the name "O'Sullivan" appears in place of the changed name. It seems more likely that Yeats missed a correction here than that his pen slipped in producing a new manuscript version.

Yeats radically revised the text of six items: the introductory poem, "To the Secret Rose," "The Binding of the Hair," "The Wisdom of the King," "The Book of the Great Dhoul," "The Vision of Hanrahan," and 'Rosa Alchemica." For all of these he must have provided new copy. Another story, "The Death of Hanrahan," appeared in a magazine in December 1896, so Yeats must have provided copy for it too.[2] Two examples of magazine versions will illustrate the kind of changes made. The first is from the story originally called "Wisdom." The magazine version of a paragraph which begins on page 27 of the first edition of *The Secret Rose* went as follows:

There was a broad-shouldered boy in the dun, who had long yellow hair, and was skilled in boxing and the training of horses; and one day when the king walked in the orchard, which was between the foss and the forest, he heard his voice among the salley bushes which hid the waters of the foss. "My blossom," it said, "I hate them for making you weave these dingy feathers into your beautiful hair, and all that the bird of prey who sits upon the throne may sleep easy o' nights"; and then the low musical voice he loved answered: "My hair is not beautiful like yours, that is heavy as a shower of gold thread woven by the merchants of Cathair."

In the proof "boy" becomes "young man" and the comparison of the boy's hair to a shower of gold thread is omitted; many new changes were introduced between the proof and the final versions.

The second illustration comes from the earliest of the Red Hanrahan stories, called "The Devil's Book" when it appeared in *The National Observer* on November 26, 1892. Yeats remained dissatisfied with the language of the Hanrahan stories until he rewrote them with Lady Gregory's help in 1904. In the magazine version he has Hanrahan, then O'Sullivan, speak in this absurd fashion.

'Whist now, and I'll tell you. Father Gillen says I am a limb o' Satan, but I am goin' to hold out until he has ruz the neighbourhood, as Father Clancey has ruz Conroy on me. Ye heard tell how the Finians were sent down into Hell because they were powerful strong haythens in their day . . .'

The proof version of this is much better:

'Be quiet now and I will tell you what I want the Book for, and I will tell you no lies about it, but the truth. Father Gillen says I am a limb of the great Dhoul, but I am going to hold out until he has raised the neighbourhood as Father Clancey raised on me. You have heard tell how the Fianna was sent down into Hell because they were great heathens . . .'[3]

But the most interesting thing about the production of *The Secret Rose* is what Yeats did to the book while it was going through the press. Mrs. Yeats has in her collection 256 pages of partly corrected page proof printed for Lawrence and Bullen by Richard Clay & Sons, Bungay. These are no doubt the author's duplicate set. A comparison of these page proofs with the first edition will show that Yeats has not left one stone upon another: he rewrote the book while it was being printed.

The page proofs bear the printer's stamp and the dates 2, 4, 6, and 8 November, 1896. The printer no doubt thought the book nearly done; the page numbers were in place and the running titles — in the side margins — were all set up. Yeats made so many changes that the earliest page in the completed book to agree with the proofs is that numbered 221, the beginning of "Rosa Alchemica," and that was only achieved by introducing ahead of it a new page with a half title on one side and an epigraph on the other. The changes are so radical as to raise immediately the question whether these are the first proofs Yeats saw. Certainly the setting of a book directly in pages was and is a most unusual practice. Yet there is some evidence that this may have happened. As has been noticed, there are several places in the proofs where the compositor has left blanks, presumably because he could not read copy; throughout he set "Haurahan" for "Hanrahan" more often than he got it right. One would suppose that Yeats would have filled in the blanks and corrected the name while reading the galleys had galley proof been provided. Since there is a strong probability that much of the book was set up from printed copy — the magazine versions of the stories — Bullen may have thought that the process of production could be shortened by setting the book directly in pages.

While revising the proof Yeats made several kinds of general revision throughout. The magazine versions of the stories had used many West Ireland place names. These Yeats replaced with made-up names: "Bulben" becomes "the mountain of Gulben," "Aghamore" becomes "the Great Field," "Balladrihid" becomes "Townland of the Bridge," "Lough Naminbrach" becomes "Waters of the Speckled Bag," "Bally Gawley" becomes "Hill of Awley," "Markree Wood" becomes "Steep Place of the Strangers," "Rosses" becomes "the Three Headlands." Yeats replaced many words of Gaelic origin with English equivalents: "ollaves" becomes "men of law," "meering" becomes "mear of a territory," "eric" becomes "the penalty of blood." He got rid of all "Mac's" and "O's," and "Ni's," replacing them by "son of" and "daughter of." "Poteen" becomes throughout "the brew of the Little Pot." He made innumerable changes in diction and phrasing, usually replacing the rejected term by a simpler one. Here are some examples from "The Binding of the Hair": "recited a battle-tale" becomes "spoke them a story," "lyrics" becomes "songs," "preternatural bravery" becomes "extreme courage," "stray lines and phrases" becomes "vague words." The result of hundreds of such verbal changes is a more direct style.

Yeats changed many titles and character names. "Wisdom" became "The Wisdom of the King," "Costello the Proud, Oona Mac Dermott and the Bitter Tongue" became "Of Costello the Proud, of Oona Daughter of Dermott and of the Bitter Tongue," "The Devil's Book and O'Hanrahan the Red" became "The Book of the Great Dhoul and Hanrahan the Red." Indeed the change from "O'Hanrahan" to "Hanrahan" changed the titles of all the Hanrahan stories.

Since all the running titles had been set, these title changes alone caused over a hundred resets. There were dozens of changes in character names, most of them caused by the dropping of "O," "Mac," and "Ni," but others as well. In the story "Where there is nothing, there is God" "Brother Moal Calumb" becomes "Brother Dove," "Brother Moal Melruan" becomes "Brother Bold Fox," "Brother Fintain" becomes "Brother Fair-brows," and "Aodh" becomes 'Olioll" (except once on page 33 where Yeats forgot to make the change; this is still wrong in the *Collected Works* of 1908 – see VII, 75).

The effect of these changes can be seen clearly if we compare the proof version with the final version of several passages. Here are the first three sentences of "The Crucifixion of the Outcast":

Proof version:

A man, with thin brown hair and a pale face, half ran, half walked, along the road that wound from the south out the town of Sligech. Lua Ech Ella was his name, and he was a gleeman, as was denoted by his short particoloured doublet, his pointed shoes, his bulging wallet. Also he was of the blood of Ernaans, and his birth-place was Gort-an-oir: but his eating and sleep-places were the four provinces of Eri, and his abiding place was not upon the ridge of the earth.

First edition:

A man, with thin brown hair and a pale face, half ran, half walked along the road that wound from the south to the Town of the Shelly River. Many called him Cumhal, the son of Cormac, and many called him the Swift, Wild Horse; and he was a gleeman, and he wore a short particoloured doublet, and had pointed shoes, and a bulging wallet. Also he was of the blood of the Ernaans, and his birth-place was the Field of Gold; but his eating and sleeping places were the four provinces of Eri, and his abiding place was not upon the ridge of the earth.

As we would expect from Yeats, the poems used were nearly all revised. It is characteristic that three versions of "To the Secret Rose," that published in *The Savoy* in September 1896, that found in the proofs, and the final version are all different. The poem was entirely reset in a smaller type-face between the proof and the final versions. Hanrahan's song on pages 161–62 has not one line the same in the proof and final versions. The proof version ran:

Veering, fleeting, fickle, the winds of Knocknarea,
When in ragged vapour they mutter night and day,
Veering, fleeting, fickle, our loves and angers meet:
But we bend together and kiss the quiet feet
Of Kathleen-Ny-Hoolihan.

Weak and worn and weary the waves of Cummen Strand,
When the wind comes blowing across the hilly land;
Weak and worn and weary our courage droops and dies,
But our hearts are lighted from flame out of the eyes
Of Kathleen-Ny-Hoolihan.

Dark and dull and earthly the stream of Drumahair
When the rain is pelting out of the wintry air;
Dark and dull and earthly our souls and bodies be:
But pure as a tall candle before the Trinity
Our Kathleen-Ny-Hoolihan.

The version printed in *The Secret Rose* read:

O tufted reeds, bend low and low in pools on the Green Land,
Under the bitter Black Winds blowing out of the left hand!
Like tufted reeds our courage droops in a Black Wind and dies:
But we have hidden in our hearts the flame out of the eyes
Of Kathleen the Daughter of Hoolihan

O tattered clouds of the world, call from the high Cairn of Maive,
And shake down thunder on the stones because the Red Winds rave!
Like tattered clouds of the world, passions call and our hearts beat:
But we have all bent low and low, and kissed the quiet feet
Of Kathleen the Daughter of Hoolihan.

O heavy swollen waters, brim the Fall of the Oak trees,
For the Grey Winds are blowing up, out of the clinging seas!
Like heavy swollen waters are our bodies and our blood:
But purer than a tall candle before the Blessed Rood
Is Kathleen the Daughter of Hoolihan

In spite of the fact that every change here is for the better, from weak to strong, from personal to mythic, Yeats again rewrote this poem entirely when he revised *Stories of Red Hanrahan* in 1903–4.

The changes so far studied do not alter the meaning of the stories; rather they are matters of style and phrasing. The changes in "Rosa Alchemica" were substantive. The version in *The Savoy* opened with a paragraph which summarized the story. Yeats cut this introduction, no doubt thinking it something of a "come on" for magazine readers. There were also many changes in parts II and III. The most interesting change, however, was in the description of the iconography of the Rose, to which Mr. Ellmann has drawn attention in *The Identity of Yeats* (pp. 64–76). In the proof version Yeats included this description of the symbolic rose tree on his front cover. The passage does not occur in *The Savoy* version, and was cut out of the final version. It reads: "In the box was a book bound in velum, and having a rose-tree growing from an armed anatomy, and inclosing the faces of two lovers painted upon the one side, to symbolize certainly the coming of beauty out of corruption, and probably much else." (Page proof of *The Secret Rose*, p. 249.) The passage which follows this, describing the smaller rose icon which Yeats used on his back cover, did appear in *The Savoy* and was allowed to stand in the final version.

There was one other substantial cut, this time of a passage that had appeared in *The Savoy*. Again, it is made particularly interesting to us by Mr. Ellmann's study of Yeats's use of the word "mood" (*Identity*, pp. 56–61). In the cut passage, Yeats used the term "mood" in a somewhat different sense from those Mr. Ellmann describes — the term has almost the sense of *Zeitgeist*. Yeats introduced the cut passage with the following general statement, which Mr. Ellmann quotes (p. 59):

In this way all great events were accomplished; a mood, a divinity, or a demon, first descending like a faint sigh into men's minds and then changing their thoughts and their actions until hair that was yellow had grown black, or hair that was black had grown yellow, or cities crumbled away and new cities arisen in their places, and empires moved their border, as though they were but drifts of leaves.

Yeats then continued with the passage which he cut, now only to be found in the rare *Savoy* text:

I remembered, as I read, that mood which Edgar Poe found in a wine-cup, and how it passed into France and took possession of Baudelaire, and from Baudelaire passed to England and the Pre-Raphaelites, and then again returned to France, and still wanders the world, enlarging its power as it goes, awaiting the time when it shall be, perhaps, alone, or with other moods, master over a great new religion, and an awakener of the fanatical wars that hovered in the grey surges, and forgot the wine-cup where it was born. [*Page proofs of* The Secret Rose, *pp.* 253–54.]

Yeats seemed to feel the production of his book was rather slow. On August 12, 1896, he wrote "I shall publish this autumn a book of phantastic stories called *The Secret Rose.*" [4] Early the following year he wrote that the book "was to have been out in December but has been postponed till February" (*Letters,* p. 280). Actually, it was postponed till April. One can well understand why.

This revision of the stories in *The Secret Rose* was by no means Yeats's last. He detached the Hanrahan stories from the others and published them separately in 1905 (Wade, item 59). In this revision he dropped his first story, "The Book of the Great Dhoul and Hanrahan the Red," and replaced it by a new introductory story, "Red Hanrahan," which he had published separately in December 1903. He completely rewrote "The Twisting of the Rope," and radically revised all of the other stories without greatly changing their content. A short passage from "Hanrahan and Cathleen the daughter of Hoolihan" will illustrate the kind of changes Yeats made with Lady Gregory's help:

Mary Gillis, who was pouring the Brew of the Little Pot into a noggin which stood upon a creepy-stool at his feet, ceased to pour, and said: 'Are you thinking of leaving us?' [The Secret Rose, *p.* 160.]

Mary Gillis was pouring whiskey into a mug that stood on a table beside him, and she left off pouring and said, 'Is it of leaving us you are thinking?' [Collected Works, V, 228.]

The tone of the story has been changed completely in the new version, where the natural has replaced the highly artificial, the colloquial the affectedly folk-lorish. What a relief when a "noggin" becomes a "mug," a "creepy-stool" a "table."

Yeats twice revised the texts of the other stories included in *The Secret Rose,* once when he was preparing his *Collected Works* and again when he was preparing *Early Poems and Stories.* In the section of *Collected Works* called *The Secret Rose,* Yeats dropped two stories entirely, "The Binding of the Hair" and "The Rose of Shadow." He revised the texts of the stories he kept and arranged them in a different order. The most interesting thing about these revisions is that Yeats put back into his stories many of the Sligo place names he had carefully cut out while revising the proofs of *The Secret Rose.* Of the revised stories the text of "Of Costello the Proud" shows the most change, especially in the opening pages of the story. The text of "Rosa Alchemica" shows the greatest stability; there was some incidental revision, but the changes are not substantive.

When preparing "The Secret Rose" for *Early Poems and Stories,* Yeats dropped still another story, "Where there is Nothing, there is God," and again revised all the others. Again, "Of Costello the Proud" was revised most heavily. Yeats put back into it many of the "Mac's" he had cut out in revising his original page proof. But most of Yeats's revisions of this story and the others are cuts. He cut out many descriptive passages, and passages of commentary. A result of these cuts is that the stories are told far more simply and directly than in the first edition. Again, "Rosa Alchemica" was very little changed, though two of the changes are worth noting. Yeats introduced a Byzantine reference (*EPS,* p. 467) not in the first edition when he changed "glittering in the light of the fire as though they were wrought of jewels" (*SR,* p. 224) to read "glittering in the light of the fire as though of Bizantine mosaic." The other change was the omission of a long passage on the old Irish gods (*EPS,* p. 483) which Yeats had allowed to stand in *Collected Works* (VII, 123–24).

iii

Discoveries

THE MANUSCRIPTS of the first seventeen sections of *Discoveries* have survived. They were composed in two manuscript books used in 1906; these also contain two versions of the important essay, "Poetry and the Tradition," two essays which Yeats suppressed from the printed *Discoveries,* and part of a long essay without a title which Yeats left unfinished. No manuscripts of the last four sections of *Discoveries,* written in 1907 after Yeats returned from his Italian tour, have come to light. Yeats appears to have grown fond of these brief, informal meditations on literary and philosophic subjects, for in 1908 he started another series of essays done in the same manner. These he never printed though the manuscripts have survived. The texts of the essays included in *Discoveries* were very little revised after their first publication in Bullen's short-lived *Gentleman's Magazine;* the text found there is substantially that found in the Dun Emer edition of 1907 and in volume VIII of *Collected Works.* There was further incidental revision made when Yeats was preparing *The Cutting of an Agate* (1912), especially in "The Tree of Life," but I scarcely know of a prose work by Yeats so little changed in successive editions. I should like to examine the whole of this characteristic manuscript, section by section, comparing it with printed versions.

Yeats nearly achieved in his first draft the version of "Prophet, Priest and King" that he ultimately printed, though the end of the essay gave him trouble. There are three conclusions in the manuscript, and before he printed it Yeats softened the criticism of the Irish Catholic Church made in the third draft. In the first draft the essay ended: "As I put away the book I thought, 'the soldier is half and the priest is half, and there can be [no] sound life where the two halves do not come together!" Yeats cancelled this, perhaps because its meditative tone seemed unurgent, and wrote this direct statement on the opposite page: "The English have driven away king and prophet, and one cannot have a sound community if one has not prophet, priest and king." He drafted a third version in the other manuscript book used in writing *Discoveries;* here he explores a vatic mode:

"A people cannot prosper without prophet, priest and king, and from Ireland England has driven away the king and the prophet has turned demagogue and this is our priest!" Outside religious emotions [there is in] Ireland nothing that has reality, though there is the representation, the image, the phantom of everything that man can desire, and this is because the prophet who should reveal realities, Heaven and Hell open, is but culling from this or that.

The printed text combines parts of drafts 2 and 3, and omits the final sentence of draft 3, which would undoubtedly have offended Irish readers:

The English have driven away the kings, and turned the prophets into demagogues, and you cannot have health among a people if you have not prophet, priest and king.

The first draft of "Personality and Intellectual Essences" I quote entire to allow comparison with the printed version.

INDIVIDUALITY AND PERSONALITY

My work in Ireland has continually set this thought, "How am I to make my work mean something to vigorous and simple men, the bulk of whose life is not with art but with cattle or a shop, or teaching in a national school, [or] dispensing medicine." [I] have not wanted "to elevate them" or "educate them" as these words are understood, but to make them understand my vision, and I have not wanted a large audience, certainly not what is called a national audience, but enough people for accidental and temporary man to lose himself in the lump. In England, where there has been so much systematized education, one only escapes the accidental and temporary among students, but here there is the right audience could one get their ears. Always I have come back to this certainty: "What moves men is what they live by, and [word undeciphered] they live by, and that is might of personality." The gestures, the intonations that show them in a book or a play the strength, the essential moment of a man who would be exciting in the market or at the dispensary door. They must go out of the theatre with the strength they live by excited within them. They must really [?] see before them on the stage the passions that could, whatever its chosen way has been, strike down an enemy, or fill a long stocking with money, or move a girl's heart. They have not much to do with the speculations of science, though they have a little, or of metaphysics, though they have a little. Their legs will soon tire on the road if there is nothing in their hearts but vague sentiment, and an affectionate feeling about flowers, though that is good at moments, will not lift the cart out of the ditch. An exciting person, whether hero of a play or himself the writer of poems, will display or imply the greatest volume of personal energy, and this energy must be of the body as of the mind. One must say to oneself continually, have I given him the root, as it were, of all faculties necessary for life, and only when one is sure of that may one give the one faculty that for the moment fills the imagination with joy. Villon, the robber, could have written them plays or songs — if they and he had the one language, the one tradition — but Shelley could not, and since men came to live in towns and to read printed books and become specialized, it has become more and more possible [to] produce Shelleys, less and less possible to produce Villons. The last Villon dwindled to Robert Burns because the higher faculties had faded upward into some sort of vague heaven and left the lower to lumber where they best could. In literature, partly from the lack of the spoken word that knits us to normal men, we have lost the personality but we have gained individuality, if I may use individuality to describe the identity of the soul as distinguished from the identity of the whole man, impressing itself through the image, the personality, upon the common senses. There are two ways before literature, upward into ever growing subtlety, with Verhaeren, with Mallarmé, with Maeterlinck, until at last there has arisen a new agreement among studious and refined men and until passion turns this agreement into a new religion; or downward, taking the soul with it, until all is simplified, tempered, solidified again, and a Don Quixote, an Ulysses, a Gil Blas is once again a possible imagination, and poetical drama, the mirror of personality, a living form again. We should choose our way. Upward with the bird till common eyes have lost us, or downward among the market carts, but if it is downward we must see to it that the soul goes with us. The bird song is always beautiful; the tradition of modern imagination, growing always more musical, more lyrical and more melancholy, casting up now a Shelley, now a Swinburne, now a Wagner, is, it may be, leading us [to] God, for it is known that his kingdom is not of this world. If we turn from all that, we must have the soul tight within our bodies or it will slip away, for it has grown so fond of a beauty accumulated by subtle generations that it will for a long time be impatient with our search for power. If it begins to slip away, [we] will go back, for Shelley's Chapel is better than Burns's Beer House, except when one is tired at the day's end, and always better than that very uncomfortable place where there is no beer, the machine shop of the realists.

Though Yeats did not change the substance of this essay when he revised it, he did alter the wording of every sentence to achieve in the finished essay a style that is at once tighter and more euphonious; he also cut and expanded to make the line of his thought clearer. A comparison of these two passages shows Yeats tightening his syntax and increasing euphony:

Always I have come back to this certainty: "What moves men is what they live by, and [word undeciphered] they live by, and that is might of personality." The gestures, the intonations that show them in a book or a play the strength, the essential moment of a man who would be exciting in the market or at the dispensary door.

I have always come to this certainty: what moves natural men in the arts is what moves them in life, and that is, intensity of personal life, intonations that show them in a book or a play, the strength, the essential moment of a man who would be exciting in the market or at the dispensary door. [Essays and Introductions, *p. 265.*[5]]

The longest cut was one of three lines made following the words "solidified again" in the manuscript reproduced above. Yeats twice expanded his thought: he added a new sentence before the reference to Villon, and he expanded his final sentences. Here is the new sentence:

I even doubt that any play had ever a great popularity that did not use, or seem to use, the bodily energies of its principal actor to the full. [Essays and Introductions, *p. 266.*]

Near the end of his essay Yeats changed ". . . tradition . . . is . . . leading us to God, for it is known that his kingdom is not of this world" to read ". . . traditions . . . are . . . the frenzy of those that are about to see what the magic hymn printed by the Abbé de Villars has called the Crown of Living and Melodious Diamonds"; he also revised ". . . be impatient with our search for power" to read ". . . be impatient with our thirst for mere force, mere personality, for the tumult of the blood" (*Essays and Introductions*, p. 267). Yeats had his thought firmly in mind when he wrote his first draft. During revision he sharpened contrasts, tightened his syntax, made his rhythms more subtle.

The next essay, "The Musician and the Orator," was in the MS. this brief but telling scrap. I quote the second draft:

Music is the most impersonal of the arts, and that is why musicians dislike words, which are the principal expression of personality. They are afraid they will not be able to digest them. They masticate them for a long time, until they are broken and softened and mixed up with spittle. Then they swallow them.

Some time before Yeats printed *Discoveries* he added the sentences now used to introduce the passage quoted above. He also rephrased and softened the sentences quoted from the manuscript.

"A Guitar Player" – called "The Banjo Player" in the *Gentleman's Magazine* and Dun Emer Press texts – and "The Looking-glass" show verbal alteration between first draft and printed texts, but no alteration in substance. Yeats composed "The Tree of Life" in another manuscript book, though already it is numbered "6," the place it still has in *Discoveries*. This seems to have come easily, and Yeats did not much revise it. "In Praise of Old Wives' Tales" followed "The Looking-glass" in the original manuscript; there Yeats began the anecdote immediately. He inserted the first sentence, which serves as a transition from "The Tree of Life," at some later time. The manuscript versions of "The Play of Modern Manners" and "Has the Drama of Contemporary Life a Root of Its Own" are essentially what Yeats printed. A misprint in "Why the Blind Man in Ancient Times Was Made a Poet" persisted through the *Collected Works* of 1908. Yeats wrote, "In the art of the greatest periods there is something careless." This was printed "In the *heart* of the greatest periods." Yeats finally set the passage right in *The Cutting of an Agate*. Misreadings of this sort are fairly common in Yeats's texts; they probably came about because it was his habitual practice to dictate from his prose manuscripts to a secretary, who in this instance heard "heart" when Yeats said "art." When Yeats was revising typescripts, he rather frequently made revisions to accommodate a word which his typist had misheard if he had himself forgotten his first intention. The manuscript of this essay is a very rough first draft which had to be considerably revised.

Yeats did two versions of "Concerning Saints and Artists." In the second version he expanded a mere scrap to the essay that we know. This is what he originally wrote in the manuscript of *Discoveries:*

Some years ago I took hashish with a number of the followers of St. Martin, who were strangers to me. It had little effect upon me, because [two words undeciphered] but the third or fourth time that it affects one decisively, but the followers of St. Martin all began to dance at about midnight, and to talk together. We could not understand each other, for I had little French nor they [word undeciphered] English, but after the dance had gone on for a while a young man ran over to me in great excitement, pointing to a piece of paper on which he [had] made a circle with a dot in it. He cried out "God, God."

The original manuscript of *Discoveries* continued with the essay now called "In the Serpent's Mouth," which grew directly from the passage quote above. The manuscript of "In the Serpent's Mouth" begins "There is an old saying that God is a circle whose centre is everywhere." The manuscript of "In the Serpent's Mouth" is, again, a rough first draft.

The manuscript of "The Subject Matter of Drama" is so typical of this period that I quote a long passage from it, transcribing it exactly, even to the original punctuation. In the manuscript Yeats wrote opposite his quotation from Blake "verify quotation"; and indeed Yeats had got it quite wrong. He first wrote, "The newest water is the best and the oldest wine." Yeats seldom remembered quotations exactly. Not only is the manuscript characteristic, the revisions Yeats made before printing it are also characteristic. These may be studied by comparing parallel parts of the manuscript and published versions.

Water is experience, immediate sensation, & wine is emotion, & is with the intellect as distinguished from imagination, this enlarges the bounds of experience, separating from all but itself, from illusion, from memory, creating among other things science and good journalism. Emotion upon the other [hand] grows intoxication, & delightful after it has been enriched, from memory & old experience, & it is precisely this antiquity of emotion that has been deepened by the emotion and experience of many men of genius in many ages, that distinguishes the cultivated man. The subject matter of his meditation, & invention is old, and he will disdain a too conscious originality in these things as in those matters of daily life, where is it not Balzac who says we are all conservatives. He is above all things well bred, & whether he write or paint, will not desire a technique that denies or obtrudes, his long & noble descent. Dante did not deny his master Virgil, nor Corneille & Racine their masters, for till our own day imitation was conscious or all but conscious, originality unconscious & therefore deeper, far more a part of the man himself than ours is. It was not capable of quick analysis & needed sometimes many generations to reveal, but it is our imitation that is unconscious & awaits the revelation of time. The more religious, the more stationary is the subject matter of an art, the more ancient will be the emotion it arouses in the circumstances it calls up before the eyes. When in the Middle Ages the pilgrim to St. Patrick's Purgatory found himself on the lake side, he found a boat made out of a hollow tree to ferry him to the cave of vision. In religious painting & poetry, crowns and swords of an ancient pattern take upon themselves new meaning, & it is impossible to separate our idea of what is lofty, from a mystic stair, upon which not men and women, but robes, jewels, incidents, ancient utilities float upward slowly, over an almost sleeping humanity putting on emotional and spiritual life as they ascend until they are swallowed by some far glory, that they even were too modern & momentary to endure. All art is dream & what the day has done with is dreaming ripe, & what art has moulded religion accepts, and at last as it were all is in the wine cup, all is in the drunken phantasy & the grapes stammer.

Below I quote the parallel passage from the published version of *Discoveries* (*Essays and Introductions,* pp. 284–85) to allow direct comparison:

Water is experience, immediate sensation, and wine is emotion, and it is with the intellect, as distinguished from imaginaton, that we enlarge the bounds of experence and separate it from all but itself, from illusion, from memory, and create among other things science and good journalism. Emotion, on the other hand, grows intoxicating and delightful after it has been enriched with the memory of old emotions, with all the uncounted flavours of old experience; and it is necessarily some antiquity of thought, emotions that have been deepened by the experiences of many men of genius, that distinguishes the cultivated man. The subject matter of his meditation and invention is old, and he will disdain a too conscious originality in the arts as in those matters of daily life where, is it not Balzac who says, 'we are all conservatives'? He is above all things well-bred, and whether he write or paint will not desire a technique that denies or obtrudes his long and noble descent. Corneille and Racine did not deny their masters, and when Dante spoke of his master Virgil there was no crowing of the cock. In their day imitation was conscious or all but conscious, and because originality was but so much the more a part of the man himself, so much the deeper because unconscious, no quick analysis could unravel their miracle, that needed generations, it may be, for its understanding; but it is our imitation that is unconscious and that waits the certainties of time. The more religious the subject matter of an art, the more will it be as it were stationary, and the more ancient will be the emotion that it arouses and the circumstance that it calls up before our eyes. When in the Middle Ages the pilgrim to St. Patrick's Purgatory found himself on the lake side, he found a boat made out of a hollow tree to ferry him to the cave of vision. In religious painting and poetry, crowns and swords of an ancient pattern take upon themselves new meanings, and it is impossible to separate our idea of what is noble from a mystic stair, where not men and women, but robes, jewels, incidents, ancient utilities float upward slowly over the all but sleeping mind, putting on emotional and spiritual life as they ascend until they are swallowed up by some far glory that they even were too modern and momentary to endure. All art is dream, and what the day is done with is dreaming ripe, and what art has moulded religion accepts, and in the end all is in the wine cup, all is in the drunken fantasy, and the grapes begin to stammer.

Comparison of these two versions can show us exactly what Yeats accomplished during revision. To begin, his own punctuation of his prose manuscripts, here and elsewhere, nearly always disfigures his sense. Whereas his verse manuscripts are in their early stages almost without punctuation, prose manuscripts are far too heavily punctuated. Clearly Yeats had a habit of putting in a comma or dash whenever he paused or hesitated in developing his thought; perhaps these commas and dashes also reveal a poet's longing for line ending and caesura. So, while revising, Yeats had to adjust his punctuation. He had also to straighten out his syntax and grammar; had to clear up the reference of pronouns, for example, and adjust the agreement of nouns and verbs. So far Yeats's revising parallels the revising that every writer does. But study of Yeats's prose manuscripts shows not only that his first drafts were better than most of us can manage, but also that he could improve them more during revision than most of us can. This is partly a matter of improved diction and phrasing, partly a matter of delicate adjustment of repetitions, partly, as we would expect from a poet, a matter of the careful handling of sound and rhythm. With Yeats's prose as with his verse he often makes something fine or even great out of an unpromising first draft.

I do not claim that Yeats accomplished such an absolute result in the present instance. "The Subject Matter of Drama," though typical of Yeats's thought in 1906, is not one of the great moments in his prose. Yet even here Yeats greatly improved his first draft by revision. Compare, for example, the passages in which Yeats contrasts the imitation practiced by older writers with the imitation practiced by writers of his own time:

Dante did not deny his master Virgil, nor Corneille & Racine their masters, for till our own day imitation was conscious or all but conscious, originality unconscious & therefore deeper, far more a part of the man himself than ours is. It was not capable of quick analysis & needed sometimes many generations to reveal, but it is our imitation that is unconscious & awaits the revelation of time.

Corneille and Racine did not deny their masters, and when Dante spoke of his master Virgil there was no crowing of the cock. In their day imitation was conscious or all but conscious, and because originality was but so much the more a part of the man himself, so much the deeper because unconscious, no quick analysis could unravel their miracle, that needed generations, it may be, for its understanding; but it is our imitation that is unconscious and that waits the certainties of time.

Here Yeats's revision shows all the improvements claimed for it above.

Yeats made some revisions of the manuscript of "Two Kinds of Asceticism," but none are of particular interest. The telling image "how heavy a quiver of the crow-feathered ebony rods" is not found in the manuscript of "The Black and the White Arrows." Very often Yeats's happiest phrases were added in revision. "His Mistress's Eyebrows" follows "The Tresses of the Hair" in the original manuscript; it was not very much revised. Yeats did two versions of "The Tresses of the Hair" and then made further revisions before publishing it.

We poets and painters are the pursuers of all that winds and changes and runs [into] itself again. Mistress Nature covers her eyes away from us. She keeps them for a better lover, but she lets us play with the long serpent-like tresses of her hair. Maybe we have lived many times, and if we cry with Hafiz "I have made a bargain with that brown hair before the beginning of time and it shall not be broken through unending time," she may listen [to] us and let us gaze at moments even in her eyes.

Hafiz cried to his beloved, "I made a bargain with that brown hair before the beginning of time and it shall not be broken through unending times," and it may be that Mistress Nature knows that we have lived many times, that all that winds and changes and runs into itself belongs [to] us. She covers her eyes away from us; she keeps her eyes for a better lover, but she lets us play with the long serpent-like tresses of her hair.

Hafiz cried to his beloved, 'I made a bargain with that brown hair before the beginning of time, and it shall not be broken through unending time,' and it may be that Mistress Nature knows that we have lived many times, and that whatsoever changes and winds into itself belongs to us. She covers her eyes away from us, but she lets us play with the tresses of her hair. [Essays and Introductions, *p.* 290.]

Discoveries and "Poetry and Tradition" when taken together constitute a new beginning in Yeats's prose which exactly parallels a change that was slowly taking place in his poetry. In a word, the conception of a poem and essay as a "personal utterance" is becoming operative. *Discoveries* is full of Yeats's personal experiences, from it you could surmise what Yeats was doing when he wrote (running a theater, travelling in Italy). "Poetry and Tradition" grows directly out of Yeats's recollections of John O'Leary and Lionel Johnson. In both, Yeats's style is changing, losing the opal hush quality of his prose of the 90's. In subject, method, and style these essays are very unlike characteristic works written then, such as "Rosa Alchemica" and "The Adoration of the Magi." Though probably Yeats did not know it, he was about to begin his *Autobiographies*.

12

Autobiographies AND *On the Boiler*

YEATS'S *Autobiographies,* which are generally regarded as his greatest prose work, were written and published over a period of years. The earliest writing was done in 1908, the latest in 1934; the first parts to be published appeared in 1915, the latest in 1935. To study the successive drafts of *Autobiographies,* then, is to study Yeats's method of composing prose over a period of twenty-six years. For our special purpose we will rearrange the work in the order of its composition, beginning with "Estrangement," written 1908–9, then continuing with "The Death of Synge" 1909–14, "Reveries over Childhood and Youth" 1914, "The Trembling of the Veil" 1920–21, but based on the "First Draft" written, I think, in 1915–16, "The Bounty of Sweden" 1924, and "Dramatis Personae" 1934.

The early drafts of the various parts of *Autobiographies* available in Mrs. Yeats's collection and elsewhere are much fuller for some of its sections than for others. The Journal from which Yeats extracted "Estrangement" and "The Death of Synge," is in Mrs. Yeats's collection. I have compared the manuscript with the published texts and so am able to say exactly what Yeats did when he prepared parts of it for publication. The manuscript and successive typescripts of "Reveries over Childhood and Youth" are widely scattered. One corrected partial typescript is still in Dublin. The manuscript and two corrected typescripts were sent to John Quinn in 1915, and were sold with other items from his library in 1924.[1] I have not been able to locate this material. Yeats's continuation of his memoirs in the manuscript he labelled "First Draft" is in Dublin, along with successive drafts of "The Trembling of the Veil" and "The Bounty of Sweden." The final manuscript of "Dramatis Personae" is in the Houghton Library, and a corrected partial typescript dictated from it, is in Dublin. If Yeats wrote earlier manuscript versions of "Dramatis Personae," and I am inclined to think he did because in the manuscript at Harvard the text of the work is highly finished, these seem not to have survived. The materials available for study of Yeats at work on *Autobiographies* have, then, forced me to concentrate on "Estrangement" and "The Death of Synge," on "First Draft" and "The Trembling of the Veil." There is very little to say about "The Bounty of Sweden" save that in his first manuscript Yeats achieved approximately what he printed.

i

"Estrangement" and "The Death of Synge"

YEATS BEGAN A JOURNAL in December 1908. For a while he wrote in it regularly, sometimes making several entries in a single day. There are 244 entries in the entire Journal: entries 1–3 were made in 1908, entries 4–203 in 1909, entries 204–28 in 1910, entries 229–31 in 1911, entries 232–38 in 1912, entries 239–42 in 1913, and entries 243–44 in 1914.[2] The entries included in "Estrangement" were all written between December 1908, and March 14, 1909; those included in "The Death of Synge" between March 14, 1909, and October 1914. The Journal is a record of Yeats's thought and feeling during a period of great strain in his personal and professional life. Synge was dying, his relations with Maud Gonne after a happy interlude had again taken up their old pattern of strain and frustration, he was directly involved in the productions of the Abbey, he was writing very little poetry and much of what he did write disappointed him, he was literally obsessed by *The Player Queen*.

There is some evidence that Yeats intended his Journal to be a record of his thoughts when he was separated from Maud Gonne, and that he planned to show it to her when they were together. It is written in a bound manuscript book which was, I think, a gift from her; at any rate it is identical in design with a larger manuscript book which she gave him in June 1908, and he began it during a visit to her in Paris made in December of the same year. Yeats writes in entry 44, "I am writing this that a friend for whom and for myself I write may know me for good and evil." There is one piece of evidence that the friend may have been Florence Farr. In a letter to her which Wade has on strong evidence dated March 1909, Yeats writes of his Journal as follows: "I have a large MS book in which I write stray notes on all kinds of things. These will make up into essays. They will amuse you very much. They are quite frank and the part that cannot be printed while I am alive is the amusing part."

Yeats published four extracts from this Journal under the title "The Folly of Argument" in *The Manchester Playgoer* in June 1911, but he made no extended use of it until much later. In 1926 the Cuala Press published "Estrangement," in 1928 "The Death of Synge." I have been unable to determine exactly when Yeats prepared the texts of these books. Yeats used 61 of the first 95 entries of his Journal for "Estrangement," 50 of the remaining 149 entries for "The Death of Synge." With very few exceptions he kept to the original order of his material. "Estrangement" begins with what was entry 5 in the Journal, the next section was entry 4. Clearly Yeats chose to begin with entry 5 because it states his intentions for his Journal, hence could serve well as a preface. There was one important change in the order of material. Sections XXVIII and XXIX of "Estrangement" refer to Lady Gregory; Yeats there calls her A—— C——. The 51st entry in the Journal served as a basis for part of "Estrangement" XXIX, and for all of XXXIV, where Lady Gregory is named. Apparently Yeats wished to obscure the fact that "Estrangement" XXVIII and XXIX also referred to Lady Gregory. He accomplished this by introducing later entries between the published parts of entry 51. Sections XXXV and LIV have also been placed in an order different from that in the Journal, why I do not know. With these few exceptions, Yeats kept to the original order of his material in both "Estrangement" and "The Death of Synge." In several places he combined journal entries to make up sections.

Yeats did omit a great deal of the Journal, some 133 of its 244 entries are entirely omitted, and long sections are sometimes cut from entries used. In commenting on his omissions in an unpublished "Preface" intended for "Estrangement," Yeats wrote that the omitted matter was either too private or too trivial for publication. Some of the omitted entries are trivial, though not many. The compelling reason behind Yeats's omissions was his respect for his own privacy and for that of his associates. Then, too, he had come to use this Journal as a manuscript book — Yeats eventually used all his Journals as manuscript books, though often he began them intending to restrict their use, say, to a record of esoteric experiences. He wrote out in this Journal either draft or final versions of twenty-six poems, most of them printed in *The Green Helmet and Other Poems*, though some appeared in later collections and others have never been published. There are besides prose versions of poems, ideas which Yeats was working up into speeches, comments on various works finished or in progress, corrections to poems already printed, and so on. The original Journal was, in short, among other things a record of Yeats's literary life. Yeats omitted nearly all these entries from "Estrangement" and "The Death of Synge." These omitted sections are among the most interesting of all to the student of Yeats's work. It is the omission of this material that more than anything else changes the tone of the Journal as published from the tone of the manuscript.

An even larger group of omitted entries concerned persons still living in the 1920's. There were many unfavorable comments on the circle that surrounded George Russell (AE), on persons who had failed to help during the *Playboy* crisis, on Henry Stephens, Synge's executor, on George Moore, on various members of the Abbey company. Yeats's comments were often bitter, though never, I think, without cause. He was very occasionally scandalous, though far less often than reports of his conversation would lead one to expect. Most of these omissions reflect, I think, Yeats's wish to respect the privacy of persons who had become involved in one way or another with his far from private career. This went so far that in a section which he did publish he suppressed the name of Miss Beatrice Elvery, now Lady Glenavy, from a report of a conversation about the literary element in painting.

By far the largest part of the omitted material was personal, often highly personal. While he was keeping this Journal, Yeats suffered some sort of nervous breakdown. He omits all reference to this, and to the trouble he had in getting his work done. He omits all entries which tell of the difficulties at the Abbey Theatre, and a few which show a rather childish snobbism. In many highly interesting omitted entries he comments on weaknesses of his personality: his desire to convince always, his failure to listen, his indecisiveness. He also omitted nearly all references to his esoteric interests. In the original Journal there are many entries concerning his horoscope, accounts of dreams and visions, reports on séances attended, and so on. He omitted, too, comments on certain events in his personal life, such as a quarrel with John Quinn and a serious misunderstanding with Lady Gregory brought about by an insulting letter Edmund Gosse wrote to her.

All of these omissions, taken together, largely explain why the tone of the Journal is quite different from the tone of "Estrangement" and "The Death of Synge." What was an intimate, autobiographical account of some years important in Yeats's life becomes a series of meditations on men and events, sometimes rather vatic in tone. The Journal is warm, immediate, trivial, often funny, irritated and irritating, sometimes scandalous or vituperous. One would, I think, never guess from reading "Estrangement" and "The Death of Synge" that the Journal had these qualities. In both, life has lost most of its accident.

It remains to say how and to what extent Yeats revised the entries which he did print. First of all, he did not put anything new in beyond adding a clarifying sentence here and there; this is rather contrary to his usual practice. The Journal text was far less revised for "Estrangement" than for "The Death of Synge"; indeed, Yeats's method of dealing with his original is different enough in the two books to suggest that he made his redactions from the Journal at different times. The tone of "Estrangement" is more informal and colloquial than the tone of "The Death of Synge." It reads more like the actual Journal, and because the whole was originally written within four months, the entries printed have greater continuity.

Yeats made his printed Journal less personal throughout both "Estrangement" and "The Death of Synge." He accomplished this by omitting nearly all names; in two places he did add names, those of Florence Farr and Hugh Lane, both of whom had died after the entries were made. In an effort to avoid giving offense, presumably, he deleted most others. His practice is illustrated by Section XXII of "The Death of Synge"; in the Journal this read:

April 5. Walked home from Gurteen Dhas with Magee and spoke of Dunsany. Was fool enough to tell how I had taken two of Dunsany's ideas and made a scenario for his play. Thought I had cured myself of this kind of boasting. Why should I want Magee's good opinion? Do I doubt myself, or was it only a desire to prove Russell, of whom we had been talking, sterile? A not very amiable result. Came home cross — had been in Egypt's brick kilns. Magee states everything in slightly argumentative form. This means that the soul is starved by the absence of self-evident truth. Good conversation unrolls itself like the spring or like the dawn, while all effective argument, all merely logical statement, must found itself on the set of facts and experiences common to two or more people. Each hides what is new and rich.

All of the persons mentioned here were alive when Yeats printed "The Death of Synge"; if it were to be used at all, the passage would have to be revised. Indeed Yeats revised so drastically that his meaning in the printed version is not quite clear. Throughout his revisions Yeats seems consciously to have tried to conceal the extent of his estrangement from the group of people who made up the circle of George Russell.

Yeats also, and this was his constant practice, toned down passages which might seem to reflect on the Catholic Church, even when that reflection was not his own. Section x of "The Death of Synge" reports a conversation with the martyr-patriot MacDonagh. Originally this went as follows:

March 23. MacDonagh in today. Very sad about Ireland. Says that he finds a barrier between himself and the Irish-speaking peasants, who are "cold, dark and reticent" and "too polite." He watches the Irish-speaking boys at his school. When nobody is looking at them and they are alone or with the Irish-speaking gardner, they are merry, clever and talkative; when they meet an English speaker or one who has learned Gaelic, they are "stupid." They are a different world. Read him my note on Taylor. [Five entries before the one being quoted, Yeats wrote a comment on J. F. Taylor's *Owen Roe O'Neill.* Yeats did not include this in *The Death of Synge.*] and he said, "I wonder, was he a Catholic? I do not know any Catholics except a few priests. All nearly [Nearly all?] conform, but they are unbelievers. It cannot last long. Even some priests do not believe. They 'form their conscience,' that is the phrase. I was nine years in a monastery, but I had to give it up." I asked about monastic life and he said, "Everybody is very simple and happy enough. There is a little jealousy sometimes. If one brother goes into town with the Superior, another brother will be jealous, and they drink sometimes more than is good for them."

The entry ended much like the printed version. This seems mild enough, but the cult surrounding MacDonaugh was such that it would undoubtedly have given offense.

Yeats appears to have tried systematically to soften the statement of his growing conservatism and generally antidemocratic bias. The passage on which section XXI of "The Death of Synge" is based illustrates this, as well as Yeats's unwillingness to state in print his dislike of many of Shaw's plays:

I see that between *Time*, suggestion, and *Cross-roads*, logic, lies a difference in civilization as well as of art. The literature of suggestion, richest to the richest, does not belong to a social order founded upon argument, but to an age when life conquered by being itself and the most living was the most powerful. What was leisure, wealth, privilege but a soil for the most living? The literature of logic, most powerful in the emptiest, subduing life, conquering all in the service of one metallic premise, is the art of democracy, of generations that have only just begun to read. They fill their minds with deductions, just as they fill their empty houses, where there is nothing of the past, with machine-made furniture. I used to think that the French and Irish democracies follow, as John O'Leary used to say, a logical deduction to its end, no matter what suffering it caused, because they were Celtic. I now believe that they do this because they have lost by some break with the past the self-evident truths, "naked beauty displayed." The English logicians are as ignorant perhaps, but more timid, yet they have Shaw and those arid translations of Ibsen, both barricades.

The purpose of most Yeats's other revisions seems to have been the improvement of his style. Some sections, usually very short ones, have been printed just as they were originally written. Most sections were revised only a little, made a little neater than in the original. The manuscript of section VI of "The Death of Synge" is an example of this:

I think all happiness depends on having the energy to assume the mask of some other self, that all joyous, or creative life, is a rebirth as something not oneself, something created in a moment and perpetually renewed; in playing a game like that of a child where one loses the infinite pain of self-realization, a grotesque or solemn painted face put on that one may hide from the terrors of judgment, an imaginative Saturnalia that makes one forget reality. Perhaps all the sins and energies of the world are but the world's flight from an infinite blinding beam.

Before printing this passage, Yeats achieved a clearer expression of the thought in the second part of the first sentence above by introducing the verbs "we put on," "we invent," by changing the order of his material, and by revising his punctuation. "We put on a grotesque or solemn painted face to hide us from the terror of judgment, invent an imaginative Saturnalia where one forgets reality, a game like that of a child, where one loses the infinite pain of self-realization" (*Autobiographies*, pp. 503–4).

A few sections have been extensively re-written. Section LIII, the most revised in "Estrangement," is an example; the manuscript reads:

March 12. There is a sinking away of national feeling which is very simple in its origin. You cannot keep the idea of a nation alive where there are no national institutions to reverence, no national success to admire, without a model of it in the mind of the people. You can call it "Kathleen-ny-Houlihan" or the "Shan van Voght" in a mood of simple feeling, and love that image, but for the general purposes of life you must have a complex mass of images, making up a model like an architect's model. The Young Ireland poets created this with certain images rather simple in their conception that filled the mind of the young—Wolfe Tone, King Brian, Emmet, Owen Roe, Sarsfield, the Fisherman of Kinsale. It answered the traditional slanders on Irish character too, and started an apologetic habit, but its most powerful work was this creation of sensible images for the affections vivid enough to follow men onto the scaffold. As was necessary, the ethical ideals involved were very simple, needing neither study nor unusual gifts for the understanding of them. Our own movement began by trying to do the same thing in a more profound and enduring way. When I was twenty-five or twenty-six I dreamed of writing a sort of *Légende des Siècles* of Ireland, setting out with my *Wanderings of Oisin* and having something of every age. Johnson's work and, later, Lady Gregory's work carried on the dream in a different form; and it was only when Synge began to write that I saw that our movement would have to give up the deliberate creation of a kind of Holy City in the imagination, a Holy Sepulcher, as it were, or Holy Grail for the Irish mind, and saw that we must be content to express the individual. The Irish people were not educated enough to accept as an image of Ireland anything more profound, more true of human nature as a whole, than the schoolboy thought of Young Ireland. When the attack began on Lady Gregory's style, because of the peasant elements, I was confirmed in this. You can only create a model of a race which will inspire the action of the race as a whole, as apart from exceptional individuals, if you share with it some simple moral understanding of life. Milton and Shakespeare inspire the active life of England, but they do it through exceptional individuals whose influence on the rest is indirect. We must not try to create a school. We have no understanding of life we can teach to others. If we could create a conception of the race as noble as Aeschylus and Sophocles had of Greece, it would be attacked on some trivial ground and the crowd would follow either some mind which copied the rhetoric of Young Ireland, or the obvious sentiments of popular English literature with a few Irish thoughts and feelings added for conscience' sake.

Meanwhile, the need of a model of the nation, of some moral diagram, is as great as in the early nineteenth century, when national feeling was losing itself in a religious feud over tithes and emancipation. Neither the grammars of the Gaelic League nor the industrialism of the *Leader*, nor the attacks on the Irish party in *Sinn Fein* give any sensible image for the affections. Yet from Lady Gregory almost always, from parts of Synge, from Katharine Tynan and Lionel Johnson, from O'Grady, from my work could be taken material that would enable a school of journalists with very simple moral ideas to build up an historical and literary nationalism as powerful as the old and nobler. They could then bid the people love and not hate.

Two examples will show how Yeats revised this entry:

It answered the traditional slanders on Irish character too, and started an apologetic habit, but its most powerful work was this creation of sensible images for the affections vivid enough to follow men onto the scaffold. [MS.]

. . . answered the traditional slanders on Irish character and entered so into the affections that it followed men onto the scaffold. ["Estrangement"]

Yet from Lady Gregory almost always, from parts of Synge, from Katharine Tynan and Lionel Johnson, from O'Grady, from my work could be taken material that would enable a school of journalists with very simple moral ideas to build up an historical and literary nationalism as powerful as the old and nobler. [MS.]

Yet in the work of Lady Gregory, of Synge, of O'Grady, of Lionel Johnson, in my own work, a school of journalists with simple moral ideas could find right building material to create a historical and literary nationalism as powerful as the old and nobler. ["Estrangement"]

Yeats's Journal, 1908–14, is far the finest he ever wrote; indeed I think it a masterpiece of its genre. "Estrangement" and "The Death of Synge" do not, because of the many changes and omissions made, more than suggest its real quality. In its entirety it is a very fine and moving book, and furthermore a book that reflects all of Yeats's interests from the most lofty to the most trivial. And in it are to be found the seeds of much of the work that Yeats was to do during the next decade. Like the 1930 *Diary*, more adequately represented in the published version, though here too many sections of the manuscript are omitted, it is a seminal book. This Journal needs to be known entire.

ii

"Reveries over Childhood and Youth"

THOUGH MY STUDY of the composition of "Reveries over Childhood and Youth" is necessarily incomplete, I will describe the results of an examination of the corrected partial typescript found in Dublin, and of a collation of the first edition with the text printed in *Autobiographies*, 1926. The typescript is extensive, breaking off just before what is now the last paragraph of section XXVIII. Study of it shows that at the time it was produced Yeats was still adding to and taking things out of his text in quite his usual way. The cuts are far more interesting than the additions. They show that Yeats was trying hard to remove passages that might give offense to his family. In section II the paragraph beginning "It was through the Middletons perhaps" ends as follows in the typescript: "I have never heard that they have peasant blood, but they are like some that I have known whose avenues change to grassy ruts while the damp comes through their walls and the plaster cracks in the generation after a peasant marriage." The memory pictures recorded in VII were once three instead of two. The second of these read "Another picture is at Bedford Park where we now lived. My sister had opened the door one morning before breakfast, and found upon the doorstep a relation who had escaped after being shut up for some temporary fit of madness. When we looked at her we were ashamed. We knew that we must telegraph to her keeper and send her away. She had put her trust in us, and we were going to betray her." In section x the passage on the Miss Furys read "that they might look at their ancestral stones and forget that they had come to the counter and the cording up of parcels."

A cut made in xiv is more interesting. In the typescript Yeats wrote after the words "take pleasure in his own nakedness" the following: "Then one day, perhaps, he will lie down in the sun where he has bathed and heap the sand upon his body until, astonished, he discovers, through the pressure of the sand, the change in his body." The deleted passage is almost identical with Yeats's description of his own first experience of orgasm, found in "First Draft." In xxviii Yeats cut this sentence about J. F. Taylor: "Rumour made him out to be the illegitimate son of a great Dublin lawyer."

Sometime after this typescript was prepared Yeats made the following additions: Section vi, the last sentence of paragraph 2; section xxv, the last sentence of paragraph 2; the whole of section xxvii; the beginning of section xxviii, down through the words "loss of sixpence." Only the last two additions are substantive; they show that Yeats did not make these changes in order to spare himself. Section xxvii describes Yeats's youthful timidity and his efforts to overcome it; the added portion of section xxviii tells how poor he was.

When Yeats first issued *Autobiographies* in 1926, he considerably altered the text of "Reveries over Childhood and Youth" in order to cut out of it material he had dealt with more fully in "The Trembling of the Veil." In xxiv he cut several sentences from the paragraph on Dowden beginning "I was vexed when my father called Dowden's irony timidity" because they anticipated the paragraph on Dowden in xii of "Ireland after Parnell." He made severe cuts in the descriptions of O'Leary and Taylor in xxviii, again because they anticipated v of "Ireland after Parnell." He made the longest cut of all in xxix, which had ended with a passage describing Yeats's literary and national hopes for Ireland, all dealt with much more fully in "Ireland after Parnell" and "The Stirring of the Bones." Besides cutting the passages listed, Yeats made a good many minor changes in his phrasing and paragraphing, and added substantially to the passage in III beginning "other ancestors or great-uncles bore a part in Irish history." These changes show that Yeats had learned more about the history of his family since completing "Reveries."

iii "First Draft"

YEATS FIRST WROTE about his young manhood in a manuscript known as "First Draft," which, though its method is different, describes most of the events covered in "The Trembling of the Veil." I shall first attempt to date this important manuscript, and then go on to consider its relation to "The Trembling of the Veil." This comparison will show that Yeats omitted much intimate detail, and that while the general order of the two works is similar the handling of specific material is not.

Yeats himself wrote the following on the outside of the envelope containing this manuscript: "Private. A first rough draft of Memoirs made in 1916–17 and containing much that is not for publication now, if ever. Memoirs come down to 1896 or thereabouts. W.B.Y. March 1921." Yeats's manuscript actually covers events down to 1898, and there is a good deal of evidence to indicate that he wrote it in 1915 and 1916. The only reference to the "First Draft" in Yeats's *Letters* is in a letter to JBY which Wade dates "circa November-December 1915." Yeats wrote "I am going on with the book but the rest shall be for my eye alone" (p. 603). On the back of the last sheet of the manuscript is a draft of "Lines Written in Dejection," which Ellmann has dated October 1915. We can conclude from this evidence that Yeats was at work on "First Draft" in 1915. There is also evidence that Yeats was working on "First Draft" in 1916, after the Easter Rebellion. In section XXVI of the manuscript Yeats recalls his earliest visit to Lissadell and his impressions of Constance Gore-Booth; he then writes of "the life sentence she is now serving." In section XXXIII Yeats either recalls or forecasts the central image used in "Easter 1916," the image of the stone in the midst of the stream of life. Yeats himself dated this poem September 25, 1916. Finally, there is internal evidence which indicates strongly that Yeats had completed "First Draft" before he wrote *Per Amica* in the early months of 1917. In section XL of "First Draft" Yeats describes many of the visions described in *Per Amica*. I feel reasonably certain that the account in

Per Amica is the later of the two. In *Per Amica* Yeats has generalized his experiences, made them less personal. On the whole I think it unlikely that Yeats was still writing "First Draft" in 1917.

The manuscript of "First Draft" is written on four different kinds of paper, and may represent several autobiographical essays on different subjects roughly put together. Yeats repeats himself in a good many places, he assumes antecedent information which he does not give, and the only thread holding the various parts together is the thread of chronology. Since the manuscript is written on loose leaves, I separated these according to the different types of paper used, trying to discover whether Yeats had in fact put together several shorter essays composed at different times. I think this probable, but I was not able to arrive at a certain conclusion. If Yeats did do this, he destroyed so many parts of the separate manuscripts and wrote so many revisions while putting them together that it is not now possible to determine even the exact order in which the various parts were composed. My own conclusion is that Yeats first wrote an account of his relations with Maud Gonne on punched, unlined paper, and later assembled around this the other material included in "First Draft."

The content of "First Draft" roughly parallels the content of "The Trembling of the Veil," and even part of the content of "Dramatis Personae." A comparison of the material in "First Draft" used in expanded form in those books can be deferred until we get to the story of their composition. The things which Yeats included in "First Draft" but omitted from the published account of his life are these: He omitted all but the public aspects of his relations with Maud Gonne, he omitted the charming story of Diana Vernon, he omitted a frank account of his own sexual development and of the results of the years of sexual frustration which the affair with Maud Gonne entailed. He omitted several analyses of his own character and personality. He omitted many details from the account of his attempt to revive the Young Ireland movement in 1892–93, of the Jubilee Riots of 1897, and of the dedication of the foundation stone for the Wolfe Tone Memorial in 1898 — this especially when he had harsh things to say. He did not altogether omit accounts of his own esoteric experiences, but they are much more to the fore in "First Draft" than in *Autobiographies* where they have been generalized and to an extent depersonalized. He omitted some very amusing scandalous stories about his associates in the Rhymers' Club. Yet in spite of these many omissions, we will find that when Yeats continued his *Autobiographies* he added far more than he left out.

As for the tone and method of the manuscript, it resembles "Reveries over Childhood and Youth" much more than "The Trembling of the Veil." "Reveries" is largely a narrative, held together by chronology and association; so is "First Draft." In neither the published nor the unpublished work does Yeats stop very often to speculate or even to comment on the men and events he describes. "The Trembling of the Veil," to the contrary, is one of Yeats's most carefully and elaborately patterned books. By the time Yeats came to write it he had established all his principal doctrines: the Mask, Unity of Being and Unity of Culture, his analysis of personality types in terms of the phases of the moon. He had developed, in short, what he called "the System." In "The Trembling of the Veil" men and events are described systemically, and Yeats's speculations often grow complex. The style, too, of the later work is elaborately rhetorical; it resembles the style of poems such as "Nineteen Hundred and Nineteen" and "Meditations in Time of Civil War," written at about the same time.

There is not even a hint of these intellectual or stylistic complexities in "First Draft." That seems to have been hastily written in a very direct style — there are remarkably few figures of speech — and never revised. Yeats does not attempt to form his material into any pattern, rather he shifts from topic to topic following a time sequence or an association. And yet "First Draft" is an extremely moving work; this partly because the direct simplicity of the style is attractive, but largely because of Yeats's complete honesty and candor. We have seen that Yeats removed most of his accidence from the Journal begun in 1908 when he edited parts of it for publication. He did the same thing when he entirely rewrote his account of his life from 1887 to 1898 in "The Trembling of the Veil." The fascination of "First Draft" is no doubt impure, nonliterary — an interest in a man rather than an aesthetic interest — but the fascination is great.

iv

"Four Years"

YEATS'S LETTERS do not establish exactly when he began to write "Four Years," the continuation of his memoirs. A letter to George Russell, written March 14, 1921, makes it clear that the work was by then well along. Probably Yeats began it during the winter of 1920/21. It was finished before June 1921, when the first parts of it were published. Besides the relevant sections of "First Draft," two complete manuscripts of "Four Years" have survived, the earlier unsigned, the later signed and so carefully, even beautifully written as to suggest that Yeats may have prepared it for sale to John Quinn. Perhaps it has remained among the Yeats papers because the death of J. B. Yeats in 1922 relieved Yeats of the necessity of sending manuscripts to Quinn. In this signed manuscript the text of "Four Years" has very nearly reached the form in which it was first printed by the Cuala Press. I will compare "Four Years" to the corresponding parts of "First Draft," then describe its composition and the revision Yeats made of it before he included it in "The Trembling of the Veil."

Though the date March 1921 on the envelope containing "First Draft" makes it certain that Yeats consulted it while writing "Four Years," a comparison of the two strongly suggests that Yeats did not work with the earlier manuscript open before him. With one exception, "Four Years" is in no sense a rewriting of the corresponding parts of "First Draft." The order of incidents is entirely different, much new material has been added, and there are few verbal echoes of the earlier work. The exception is a very frank passage on Maud Gonne found only in MS. 1 of "Four Years," which I will discuss while describing that manuscript. Here I think Yeats did write with "First Draft" open before him.

The following sections of "First Draft" contain material that corresponds to that used in the indicated sections of "Four Years":

"First Draft"	"Four Years"
1	12, 13
2	8, 9, 10, 11
3	19
4	20
5	16
6	14, 15
8	17
9	6, 7, 9
10	5

As this table of correspondences indicates, the order of material is quite different. "First Draft" begins with Kelmscott House and William Morris, goes on to Wilde, the theosophists, Mathers, Ellis, Johnson and Symons, the Rhymers, Henley, R. A. M. Stevenson, Maud Gonne; "Four Years" after four introductory sections which are new begins with Maud Gonne, goes on to Henley, Wilde, Stevenson, Kelmscott House and Morris, Nettleship, Ellis, the Rhymers, the theosophists, Mathers. In every instance except the passages on Maud Gonne and Ellis, the material in "Four Years" is much fuller than the corresponding material in "First Draft." This can be seen by comparing the account of Henley found in the two works. Section IX of "First Draft" goes as follows:

W. E. Henley was my chief employer. I had become one of that little group of friends who gathered at his house near Bedford Park—did he open his doors once a week or every fortnight?—and who were afterwards the staff of his *Scots Observer* and *National Observer*. He alarmed me and impressed me exactly as he did those others who were called Henley's young men, and even today [when I meet] some one amongst them, showing perhaps the first signs of age, we recognize at once the bond. We have as it were a secret in common: that we have known a man whose power no others can know because it has not found expression in words. I never cared for anything in Henley's poetry except the early gay verses in the measure of Villon, and I know that their charm was the image of that other man's face, and I thought his prose violent and laboured; but I was ready, as were all those others, to test myself and all I did by the man's sincere vision. I scarcely shared an opinion of his and yet, afterwards, when I heard that he had said to somebody, "I do not know if Yeats is going up or going down," I doubted myself. His hold was, perhaps, that he was never deceived about his taste, that he wished one well, and could not flatter. I made no difference that I differed from his judgment of other men. He despised all of Rossetti but "The Blessed Damosel," never spoke of Pater and probably disliked him, praised impressionist painting that still meant nothing to me, was a romantic, but not of my school, and founded [the] declamatory school of imperialist journalism. Lame from syphilis, always ailing, and with no natural mastery of written words, he perhaps tried to find his expression in us, and therefore all but loved us as himself.

He re-wrote my poems as he re-wrote the early verse of Kipling, and though I do not think I ever permanently accepted his actual words, I always knew that he had found a fault. He brought into his violent politics his natural generosity, and I always felt that I suffered no loss of dignity from his opposition to all I hoped for Ireland. I remember his saying, "It is not that I do not think Ireland fit for self-government, it is as fit as any other country" — Ireland's unfitness was the stock argument made [in] his time — "but we have to think of the Empire. Do persuade those young men that this great thing has to go on." There was comfort in such an attitude of mind, and he could admire as I could the folklore and folksong that Hyde had begun to discover, and he was to write of Parnell, "He has been eighteen years before the country and we knew nothing of his character but that he was haughty," and describe, if my memory does not deceive me, Parnell's hatred of the British Empire as "noble." He wanted to found a paper in Ireland and try his chances there. I was drawn to him also, I doubt not, by his aristocratic attitudes, his hatred of the crowd and of that logical realism which is but popular oratory, as it were, frozen and solidified. I did not help him in the reviews and leaders, which we believed to have created and perhaps had created such a terror among innocent sentimental writers and all flatterers of public taste, for in the puritanism of my early twenties I objected to anonymity, but I wrote for him many poems and essays about Ireland, and came to feel that the necessity of excluding all opinion was my first discipline in creative prose. I forget to whom it was he said after publishing "The Man who dreamed of Faeryland," "Do you see what a fine thing one of my boys has written?"

Though I claim for this all the virtues I have ascribed to "First Draft," when it is compared to VI and VII of "Four Years" it will at once be seen how greatly Yeats expanded and modified his account of Henley. By including new material and changing his order, Yeats puts Henley before us more substantially. In VI of "Four Years" Henley is involved in Yeats's systemic analysis of personality; here too Yeats worked in the thematic refrain that helps to hold his book together, that is his rejection of everything Tyndall, Huxley, and Bastien-Lepage stood for. (Yeats developed this refrain in section II: he opposed the realistic painting of Bastien-Lepage to the work of Blake and Rossetti, which he admired; he detested Huxley and Tyndall because they represented the new science which had deprived him of the religion of his childhood.) The extension and enhancing seen here is typical. Finally, parts of sections XVI and XVII and all of section I–IV, XIV, XV, XVIII, XXI, and XXII of "Four Years" are in no way anticipated in "First Draft."

Now for an account of the differences between the two manuscripts of "Four Years." To begin, MS. 1 contains several passages which Yeats omitted from MS. 2 and from the Cuala Press edition. Two omitted passages concern Maud Gonne, one Edwin Ellis, one Madame Blavatsky. The first passage on Maud Gonne to be omitted was a frank account of Yeats's impressions of her when they met for the first time in 1889. When this is compared with section v of the final text of "Four Years," added when Yeats revised "Four Years" for inclusion in "The Trembling of the Veil," it is found to be more intimate and fuller than the passage by which Yeats eventually replaced it. It contains, for example, a criticism of Maud Gonne's political attitudes, which Yeats describes as "derived from Boulangist adventure." Yeats must have written this account of meeting Maud Gonne with "First Draft" open before him, for the later account is full of verbal reminiscences of the first. I think this was the only time Yeats used "First Draft" in this way. The second passage to be omitted followed what is now section XIV, where Yeats tells of editing a selection from the Irish novelists. In the omitted passage Yeats says that while reading these Irish novelists he found himself continually putting Maud Gonne into the desperate situations of their various heroines, especially when the heroine was a woman "who confides and is betrayed." "The impression," Yeats says, "was so painful that for years I would not open a novel with the betrayed woman for its theme." In MS. 1 the passage on Ellis ends with a long description of his incredible domestic life and of his obsession with sex. Here also Yeats wrote of Madame Blavatsky's followers "set down to their vegetarian meal," and adds, "at times she would mock through the folding door, 'My children, have you had any vegetarian babies?' " In MS. 2 and all subsequent versions Yeats records Madame Blavatsky's mockery but does not illustrate it. Surely the explanation of these omissions is that Yeats came to feel he had written too frankly, too much in the spirit of "First Draft."

Yeats also added a number of passages in MS. 2 and in the Cuala Press edition of "Four Years." The passage in the analysis of "Innisfree" in section XV beginning "I had begun to loosen rhythm" is an addition. Yeats did not write of Mathers at all in MS. 1; in MS. 2 he wrote a short passage which parallels the first paragraph of present section XX. Yeats printed this in his first edition. The sentences on the Mask at the end of XXI beginning "Among subjective men" were also added in MS. 2. Both manuscripts ended with a paragraph on Rolleston which was omitted from the Cuala Press edition, and neither contains the paragraph on Rolleston Yeats introduced into the Cuala Press version near the end of what is now section XVII.

Besides these omissions and additions, Yeats of course made hundreds of verbal changes. The suppressed passage on Rolleston from the end of both manuscripts will illustrate their general relation and provide a gloss on "Under Ben Bulben":

He was ten years older than I, and I thought him a possible leader, and many another thought as I did, but all wholesome things — Wordsworthianism and the Spectator newspaper — allured him to his end. He combined an interest in morals with an incapacity for moral discovery, but who could take his mind from watching a mind and body that had the beauty of some Roman copy of a Greek masterpiece of the best period. He was my first public disappointment, and because of it I have tried to choose my moralists from the unwholesome edge of the Mareotic Sea where men fight their own shadows.

[*Transcribed from the unsigned* MS. *of "Four Years."*]

He was ten years older than I, and I thought of him as a perfect leader, but all wholesome things, Wordsworthianism and the Spectator newspaper allured him to his end. He combined an interest for morals with an incapacity for moral discovery, yet who could take his eyes from watching a body that had the beauty of some Roman copy of a Greek masterpiece of the best period. He was my first public disappointment, and because of it I have tried to choose my moralists from the unwholesome edge of the Mareotic Sea where a man whips his own shadow.

[*Transcribed from the signed* MS. *of "Four Years."*]

The revised passage is both smoother and more sharply phrased than the original.

There is an example in the present section XVI of a kind of textual error frequently found in Yeats's prose; this particular one was never put right. Yeats's account of Nettleship in both manuscripts has him defend his "lion pictures" as follows: " 'Everybody should have a *raison d'etre*' was one of his phrases. 'Mrs. E——'s articles are not good but they are her *raison d'etre,*' and, another day, 'My lion pictures are my *raison d'etre.*' " Without the last clause, which has already dropped out of the Cuala Press edition, the anecdote has lost its point.

When Yeats revised "Four Years" for inclusion in "The Trembling of the Veil," he made several extensive additions and rewrote the conclusion so that it pointed forward to "Ireland after Parnell." Manuscripts and typescripts of most of these additions have survived. The new material included section IV, about Florence Farr, and section V, about Maud Gonne. Section V replaces the much longer account of Maud Gonne, described above, which Yeats included in MS. 1 and suppressed from MS. 2. He completely revised the end of section XIX, dealing with Madame Blavatsky, and more than doubled the length of section XX, on Mathers. Here everything following the first paragraph is new. Section XXIII was also rewritten.

Yeats both conceived and wrote the rest of "The Trembling of the Veil" as a unit. The work was divided into books very late in the process of composition. The early manuscripts are headed "Memories" or "Memoirs," and the sections are numbered consecutively throughout. I have been unable to determine exactly when Yeats started to work on the continuation of his memoirs. On June 10, 1921, after the first section of "Four Years" had appeared in *The London Mercury*, Yeats wrote to Lady Gregory of Warner Laurie's offer of 500 pounds for the right to issue his memoirs in a limited edition. The surviving manuscripts testify to such difficult and protracted labor on the composition of "The Trembling of the Veil" that it is hard to believe that Yeats wrote the work between June 1921, and May 1922, when he dated the "Preface." Perhaps Yeats had started writing before he received Laurie's offer.

V
"Ireland after Parnell"

"IRELAND AFTER PARNELL" apparently gave Yeats far more difficulty than any other section of *Autobiographies*. In addition to the principal manuscript, I was able to assemble an earlier version nearly complete from an envelope labelled "Stray Pages." This also contained many other drafts of passages which caused Yeats particular trouble. Yeats's difficulties had, I think, two sources: he was trying to write about controversial events, most of the actors in which were still alive, in a way that would not offend; he had great trouble deciding how to arrange his material. He at first arranged it chronologically, putting the Ely Place material first — Yeats apparently stayed there in

September and October 1891 — and then proceeding to the O'Leary-Taylor section where he writes as though he were living with O'Leary. Actually, the first of Yeats's letters written from Lonsdale House, Clontarf, O'Leary's home, was dated November 1892. Perhaps Yeats rearranged his material because he wanted to put his account of the Dublin theosophists at the end where it provides a logical bridge passage to his next book, "Hodos Chameliontos." The manuscripts make it certain that Yeats remembered the order of events; he remembered quite well that he had stayed with the theosophists on Ely Place before he lived with O'Leary.

Yeats's account of the attempt to revive the Young Ireland Movement in 1891–92, which occupies sections I through XII of "Ireland after Parnell," runs parallel to an account of the same events in sections XIII–XV, XVIII, and XX of "First Draft"; there is no account in "First Draft" of the strange society at Ely Place. As would be expected, Yeats speaks of men especially, though to some extent of events, much more frankly in "First Draft" than in "Ireland after Parnell." He discusses more of the people involved — Sigerson, Richard Ashe King, Oldham — and is often rather sharply critical. The main change, however, is the complete omission of the relation of all this political activity to his wooing of Maud Gonne. The "First Draft" makes it clear that Yeats entered active politics with two purposes: he wanted to make himself a successful man of action because he thought such a man would appeal to Maud Gonne, and he wanted to keep her busy in Ireland on relatively safe projects. At one point in "First Draft" Yeats writes that behind his efforts "was much patriotism and more desire for a fair woman."

Since the composition of "Ireland after Parnell" is at once complicated and characteristic, it seems worthwhile to go through it section by section, using the section numbers assigned to it in *The Trembling of the Veil*, and unchanged in *Autobiographies*, as a guide.

i. I have found only one draft of this section, which indicates that Yeats had little trouble with it. It is a direct continuation of "Four Years." The Cuala Press "Four Years" has its last section numbered XXIII; in the principal manuscript of "The Trembling of the Veil" this section is numbered XXIV.

ii. Yeats made full first and second drafts of this, besides partial drafts of the passages on the Mansion House butler and on the poetry of the Young Ireland Movement. The merits of this verse were a matter of sharp dispute between Yeats and his opponents, and Yeats, as he always did when this subject came up, wrote a lengthy analysis. He cut this sharply, no doubt because it was hardly germane to his purpose. The section was greatly improved by this revision.

iii. Yeats did a much revised first draft of this section; later he rewrote it completely in the principal manuscript.

iv. Yeats got so nearly what he wanted in his first draft that he was able to incorporate this into the principal manuscript.

At this point the early versions took quite a different turn. Yeats, following the order of actual events, went on to his memories of Ely Place. It was not, I think, until rather late in the process of composing "Ireland after Parnell" that Yeats decided to change the order of his material. The evidence for the changed order is conclusive, though too complicated to be easily presented. Perhaps it is enough to note that the first draft of what is now section v began, "I left Ely Place to share a lodging with old John O'Leary."

v. The first draft of this passage follows the present order of the material rather closely down to the point where the passage on Taylor begins. The account of O'Leary was much longer, and it included material that Yeats had already printed in his essay "Poetry and the Tradition." This was followed by the account of Parnell's passionate nature which Yeats eventually put at the end of section XI. Then came the passage on Taylor. The kind of changes Yeats made during the process of composition can be seen by comparing the first paragraph on Taylor as Yeats eventually printed it with this version from an early draft:

John Taylor while he was speaking seemed more than any man's equal because he did not seem a man, being pure rage, and rage within our minds was raught to passion equal with his own, not by hatred as with lesser men, but by self-recognition. No maxim, no principle clung to the memory, all was passion and that noble. But he had no personality; speech over one saw again ill-fitting clothes, a wrinkled umbrella, a stiff ungainly body, and heard his rancorous voice speaking its scorn of this man or that. No great career was possible to him; no party would accept him, no government lift him to great position; he was too notorious for a temper that carried him to the edge of insanity.

vi. Yeats did a draft of the passage on Douglas Hyde, without the introductory sentence. He added this and the anecdotes leading up to the quotation "The periwinkle and the tough dog-fish/ Towards evening time have got into my dish" in the principal manuscript.

vii. The passages on O'Grady and Johnson were very considerably revised after the first draft, but the material used was much the same.

viii. Here there was so little revision that two pages from the first draft, originally numbered 37 and 38, were incorporated into the principal manuscript.

ix. In this section, Yeats comments on the failure of his schemes. As would be expected, he worked through many drafts before he achieved the philosophical attitude he eventually displayed. There is a jungle of manuscript versions, all of which reflect deep disappointment at the failure of his schemes, and some remaining bitterness. Yeats felt that had his plan to combine the nationalist movement with a revival of Irish culture succeeded, Hyde might have been saved from politics and that O'Grady would have had real influence on "Irish education and nationality."

x. It is possible to follow the growth of this section in detail; it illustrates how Yeats went about building up a characteristic passage. The earliest draft that I have found is on three unnumbered sheets filed in the envelope labelled "Stray Pages":

I went to stay with my uncle George Pollexfen in Sligo whenever exasperation hurt [?] endurance, or my purse emptied, and it emptied very often now, for the split in the Irish party had doubled the newspapers and halved their readers. I began to put my watch back. They could no longer afford literary criticism. On one of these visits I got a letter from John O'Leary to announce that the young men had turned against me, and I could do no more. He had warned me, he pointed out, not to talk and walk with them as an equal, but to keep myself apart and to hide my thoughts, but I had refused to listen. I went to Dublin, found that some projects both he and I had thought important must be given up, and that I could do no more, and I think I returned to Sligo.

Yeats wrote a second version of this, which became so very messy that he copied it fair into the principal manuscript, introducing a few improvements as he copied. He did get the passage about as he wanted it in this second draft, save for a long addition which he drafted separately, along with other additions which he added to the principal manuscript before the book was printed. I transcribe the passage from the principal manuscript.

I was at Sligo when I received a letter from John O'Leary, saying that I could do no more in Dublin, for even the younger men had turned against me, were "jealous," his letter said, though what they had to be jealous of God knows. He said further that it was all my own fault, that he had warned me what would happen if [I] lived on terms of equality with those I tried to influence. I should have kept myself apart and alone. It was all true: through some influence from an earlier generation, from Walt Whitman, perhaps, I had set in public bars, talking but drinking nothing; I had talked late into the night at many men's houses; shown all my convictions to men that were but ready for one; and used conversation to explore and discover among men who looked for authority. I did not yet know that intellectual freedom and social equality are incompatible; and yet, if I had, could hardly have lived otherwise, being too young for silence. In Nationalist Dublin there was not—indeed there still is not—a society where a man is heard but never overheard, and where he speaks his whole mind gaily, and is not the cautious husband of a part; where fantasy can play before matured into conviction; where life can shine and ring and lack utility. Mere life lacking the protection of wealth cannot choose its company, taking up and dropping men merely because it likes or dislikes their manners and their looks, and in its stead opinion crushes and rends, and all is hatred and bitterness: wheel biting on wheel, clatter and roar, a mill of argument grinding all things down to mediocrity. If, as I think, minds and metals correspond, the goldsmiths of Paris foretold the French Revolution when they substituted steel for gold in the manufacture of the most expensive jewel work, and made those large, flat steel buttons for men of fashion whereby the card players were enabled to cheat by studying the reflections of the cards.

The manuscript of the long passage inserted into this section at some later time, beginning "The trouble came from half a dozen obscure young men" and ending "without intellectual freedom there can be no agreement" is so nearly what Yeats printed that it hardly seems worth transcribing, though the fact he added it is characteristic of his method of composition.

Yeats's first draft of "Ireland after Parnell" ended at this point and "Hodos Chameliontos" began. Then, apparently when he decided to transpose the Ely Place section to the end, Yeats assembled two sections of commentary.

xi. Yeats lifted the passage on Parnell from his account of O'Leary, where it had been cancelled. The rest of the section was, so far as I can determine, added in the principal manuscript.

xii. Most of this was added in the principal manuscript, and what was old was given a new organization there. In the original draft of the section on O'Leary there were passages that corresponded to the description of Unionist society, and the passages on Fitzgibbon and Dowden. The original version of the Dowden passage was franker:

Dowden, another old friend of my father's, was our principal enemy, for academic youth admired him and all Dublin looked upon him as our one great man of letters. He did not attack us openly, and was in private friendly, but he managed by silences and evasions and indirect allusion to suggest that we were of no account. All his youth had been spent over books, scarcely perhaps even reading the newspapers, and, as is the way with [the] sedentary, he lost his head with political excitement. The rise of Irish nationality meant to him, as all nationality means to the revolutionary socialist, an affront to his international ideal of progress. He could be complimentary, even enthusiastic in conversation or private letters; he would have thought himself false to Shakespeare and Goethe and above all to Wordsworth did he not discourage us when in the public eye.

xiii, xiv, xv. Yeats's account of the community of theosophists at Ely Place and of George Russell was perhaps more revised than any other part of this much revised book. In the early drafts Yeats, as we have noticed, put his account in its proper chronological place; then, when he prepared his principal manuscript, he transposed it to the end. He did achieve in this final manuscript pretty much what he kept, but the way to this was hard and long.

The early drafts are disorderly, held together by a thin chain of association. There are at least three drafts of the introductory paragraph. The intermediate draft includes this amusing account of the attitude towards love taken by the Dublin Theosophists:

If we spoke of love poetry, we preferred the love poetry where one sang at the same moment not only the sweetheart, but some spiritual principle — "All must be 'Vita Nuova.' " We were full of Platonism, not of Plato but of current conversation, and it was perhaps now that I began to write love poems which my fellow countrymen, discerning the presence of some abstraction which [was] plainly not "the finest peasantry upon earth," found very obscure.

Yeats went on directly from this introductory paragraph to his account of the rivalry between the black-bearded engineer and George Russell, and of Russell himself, which he eventually transferred to the next section. He included in this account of Russell the story Russell told of the old religious beggar met on Two Rock Mountain; this became the first paragraph of what is now section xv. Then Yeats returned to the community at Ely Place and wrote first of the red-haired girl and then of the young Scotsman and the American hypnotist. He reversed the order of this material in the final draft, and put part of it into the third paragraph of section xv. It was the red-haired girl who saw the vision of the young man in the coffin.

In two early drafts Yeats devoted a whole section to an account of his attendance at a séance where black magic was practiced. He had already used this material as the basis of a story in *The Celtic Twilight* called "The Sorcerers," where the style employed makes it seem remote and therefore unexciting. Perhaps because he had so used it Yeats cut it sharply in his principal manuscript, and made it paragraph two of section xv. Here is the second and fuller account of the incident:

Dublin was in a strange, fantastic mood, the old religious outline broken or bent out of recognition, and much of that mood argued itself out at our meetings. The priests were blamed for the defeat of Parnell and for many months the people in the streets had ceased to salute a priest. A little later, when I shared a lodging with Mr. John O'Leary, the head of the Fenians, an old Dublin dentist called to recommend a change of religion. He had long been a Mohammedan, he said, and if only Mr. John O'Leary would recommend that religion to the Irish people, they would find it very satisfactory, for Mohammedans had no priests; and, when a year or two later a member of the community at Ely Place took to preaching the ancient Irish gods upon Kingstown pier, he found an interested, half friendly audience.

The most remarkable visitor at our debates while I was there was a magician of an exceedingly medieval sort. Twenty years afterwards I was told that he was a shape-changer and never came twice in the same body. Somebody had said, perhaps, that he was never twice the same, which was true, and rumour had taken it literally. He always took the side of religious orthodoxy, but his point of view seemed to change, either as we thought at the time from some whimsical idea of disguise, or, as I now think possible, because his personality was itself without fixity. He filled us with alarm because he was looking for a clairvoyant, and some of the women were convinced that while he was speaking he was trying to bring them under some hypnotic power, and that he only spoke that he might look full into their faces.

I got into talk with him and was invited to his lodging, and told that he had learned magic from his father, but where his father had learned it he would [not] tell me, and he had a number of friends who shared in its practice. He told me that I had seen nothing of it but effects upon the mind and the mind's eye; he claimed that he could call up forms as solid as my own, and that the furniture would wheel itself about the room. While he talked I felt or fancied a nervous strain, and when my head began to ache was convinced that he had tried to hypnotize me, and was angry, for I had at that time — why I do not know — a dread of all loss of consciousness.

He promised me a demonstration of his powers, and I arrived, still angry because of my headache, and as we must give to all such experiments at least that measure of sympathy we give to a player upon the stage, I may have spoiled the demonstration. He told me that they sat as a rule in a room hung with black curtains, but as they could not admit a stranger there he had arranged his apparatus in the dining room. He had a brass dish for burning herbs, a large bowl, a skull with symbols painted upon it, two crossed daggers, and certain wooden implements shaped like quern stones, or small wheels holed in the middle as for an axle, but with the rim thicker at one side than the other. A third man joined us and all three of us had to put on black dresses which covered us completely except for the eye holes, the kind of dress worn by Roman societies for burying the dead and by inquisitors in old engravings, and these black dresses were, he told me, to blot out our individual characters. He then killed a black cock, which he took out of a basket, and let the blood drip into the bowl, and began an invocation in what I supposed was Arabic, and when I asked what a word was that came many times he said it was an Arabic word but would not translate it.

In a short time I got the same feeling of strain and the same headache, and was angry again. Presently the third man cried out in what seemed a voice of agony, "O God: O God," and when I asked him why he had said that, he said he had not spoken. He cried out "O God" again a little later, but still would not admit that he had spoken. Presently he and the invoker saw various things, a serpent, pillars of black and white

I have record of, and could not understand why I saw nothing. I believed myself surrounded by evil spirits, and that I might lose consciousness, and after about an hour insisted upon the gas being lit and the séance brought to an end. I said to the evoker, "What would have happened if his spirit had overcome me," and he answered, "His character would have been added to your own." The problem for me was who called out "O God," and I still told myself that I had no evidence for more than dramatization, but was convinced that the dramatist was a spiritual being.

When Yeats composed the principal manuscript of "Ireland after Parnell" he transposed the Ely Place material to the end and arranged it in its present order. He first introduced his readers to Ely Place and to certain minor members of the community there. He then put all his Russell material together to form the first part of what is now section XIV. This he concluded with a long new passage which begins with a sentence that now reads, "He had, and has, the capacity, beyond that of any man I have known," and so on, and ends with the section. Yeats drafted this new passage at least twice, changing his first draft radically, but achieving in the principal manuscript approximately the expression he has kept. The radical nature of his revision can be seen by comparing the earlier draft of the final paragraph with the published version, since this is very close to the version found in the principal manuscript. Yeats first wrote:

As I watch Russell and as I watch myself, I understand that he and I are life praisers more and more true to species; I putting the legs of the compass before I draw my circle always nearer and nearer to one another, and he always enlarging his interests; and that his propaganda, his benevolence, all those things that have of late years filled me with impatience, are right. I think he would not have disappointed even my hopes had he, instead of meeting with our modern subjective romanticism, met with some form of traditional belief which would have described all that it [i.e. romanticism] admires and praises as evil when present in his own mind, and so have turned his intellect upon his mind. That, though it might have embittered his life, would have turned him into a great religious teacher, and given style and thought a never relaxed intensity.

In the published version of this passage, nearly achieved in the principal manuscript, Yeats expresses his difficult thought more clearly, and in "systemic" terms:

I think that Russell would not have disappointed even my hopes had he, instead of meeting as an impressionable youth with our modern subjective romanticism, met with some form of traditional belief, which condemned all that romanticism admires and praises, indeed, all images of desire; for such condemnation would have turned his intellect towards the images of his vision. It might, doubtless, have embittered his life, for his strong intellect would have been driven out into the impersonal deeps where the man shudders; but it would have kept him a religious teacher, and set him, it may be, among the greatest of that species; politics, for a vision-seeking man, can be but half achievement, a choice of an almost easy kind of skill instead of that kind which is, of all those not impossible, the most difficult. Is it not certain that the Creator yawns in earthquake and thunder and other popular displays, but toils in rounding the delicate spiral of a shell?

Finally, Yeats took a few bits and pieces left over from his account of Ely Place after he had revised it, and put them into section xv, adding to them the paragraph with which he now ends.

In spite of the protracted struggle in the principal manuscript to achieve the expression he wanted, Yeats made a good many more changes before publishing "Ireland after Parnell." Nearly all of these changes were made to accomplish a further toning down. Here is a detailed account of the changes Yeats made:

i. The principal manuscript is nearly the same as the printed version.

ii. Yeats cancelled the first part of this section, and wrote a new draft of his material down through the words "to practise deception." The manuscript of this new draft is filed separately along with drafts of other changes and additions.

iii. This was a good deal revised. In particular Yeats cancelled an introductory passage: "Looking backward after all these years I think I was doing work of great importance, though it was not such a waste of vitality as I have sometimes thought it. Young men in Paris or in London had for a generation or so been fighting the same fight. What else did Verlaine mean when he wrote, 'Take rhetoric and wring its neck'? But I had greater stupidity and greater passion against me."

iv. Little changed from the principal manuscript.

v. What Yeats kept of this is little changed, but he did cancel a long passage which repeated part of the substance of section XII. The picture of Dublin in the 1890's which emerges is so much franker than the published version that it is worth quoting:

[Taylor] was the tyrant of a society that turned everything to argument, and where we interrupted one another without apology and were quick to hate and to despise; and I, who had known society in London where argument was old fashioned and heated voices in the worst taste, was like a man who has forgotten the use of weapons and yet finds himself in some half-civilized country. On discovering that one of the most ill-mannered of the conversationalists was himself exceedingly sensitive [to] every slight, [I] got into the habit of repeating a sentence I had read in some seventeenth century book upon magic: "The toad is so timid that if you frown upon it for a quarter of an hour it will die. I have killed many toads in this way." It was a society without leaders or social discipline, and all the more in need of both because full of character and talent. The land war, just dying out after twenty years of bitterness, had impoverished the landed gentry, had separated them from a Nationalist Ireland which had in their eyes robbed them and robbed their children, and Trinity College was their university and shared their passions, while the great lawyers owed honour and emolument to government alone, and seeing that public spirit as young men understood it could but impoverish them, lived as if under the receiver of an airpump. I knew little about them except from my father's reports or from one or two chance meetings in his studio, but they had probably better manners than Nationalist Ireland — wealth is a great civilizer — but even less culture. A certain Lord Justice Fitzgibbon, an old acquaintance of my father's, had a newspaper reputation for learning and taste, and I was presently to see a letter of his denouncing some project of mine because I had tried to substitute "giants and fairies" for "Shakespeare and Kingsley." But no matter what his list had been, he had been without influence. We thought him a corrupt politician, hinting that he had changed his politics twice for the sake of office, and mocking at that oratory full of Victorian moral fervour, which had a great local reputation.

All these persons sincerely felt that contempt for Nationalist Ireland of which they made so great a parade, and believed the claims made in speech after speech that they were "the wealth, the culture, and the intellect of Ireland," and Nationalist Ireland secretly thought the claim but true. The old Nationalist leaders, who had once been followed by the most romantic devotion, were displaying in every newspaper and at every public meeting their incredible ill breeding. The principal Parnellite newspaper, the organ of a party which believed that its leader had been murdered, had just in the incoherence of its rage described an opponent as having two left legs and a bad smell. They were sincere men, some would have given their lives to avenge their leader, but they had no language befitting passion, nor the social restraint that can hide its lack, and what had seemed the noble tragedy of Ireland became for nine years a ghastly jeering grotesque puppet show. I longed for some man or woman, preferably some woman of rank or beauty, who would gather us together without too predominate, too exclusive an attention to opinion and intellect, and bring us into measure and sweetness, and I wearied out with my importunity the most beautiful of my friends.

vi, vii, and *viii* are very like the published version.

ix. This is also close to the published version, though Yeats toned down the final paragraph. The passage which now reads "this man's venery, that man's drink" once read "This man's sodomy, that man's drink."

x. As was noted above in the account of the composition of the principal manuscript, Yeats drafted and inserted a long addition to this section after his manuscript was completed. It is the passage beginning "The trouble came from half a dozen obscure young men" and ending "Without intellectual freedom there can be no agreement."

xi. Much the same.

xii. There were a good many revisions here. The most interesting shows Yeats playing with the idea of using one of his key words, "perning," in an unusual context. There can be no doubt of his intention, for he has repeated the word in the margin of his page, clearly forming every letter. He did not fully work out the phrasing that the change to "perning" would have required. The passage occurs towards the end of the first paragraph: ". . . and Unionist Ireland had reacted from that seething, and perning to a cynical indifference, and from those fixed ideas to whatever might bring the most easy and obvious success." It is rather surprising to find Yeats using "perning" to refer to social change; was he perhaps trying to relate various realms of his experience in a new way? Yeats cancelled a repetitive passage at the end of the second paragraph, and deleted, perhaps in proof, a

happy phrase from the sentence on Wordsworth. This once ended, "was cut and sawn into planks to wall the village pond."
xiii, xiv, and *xv* were, after the immense pains Yeats had taken with them, in nearly the form published.

vi
"Hodos Chameliontos"

AN EXAMINATION of the manuscript of the section of "Memoirs" which Yeats eventually called "Hodos Chameliontos" indicates that Yeats had far less trouble with this part of *Autobiographies* than he had with "Ireland after Parnell." I believe that many of the pages of the principal manuscript are Yeats's first drafts; evidence for this statement includes the fact that there are only two pages in the "Stray Pages" envelope which are earlier drafts of revised passages inserted into this part of the principal manuscript, and the section and page numbers used.

These are the principal differences between the manuscript and the first edition: The manuscript of section II gives a more detailed account of the colors used in Yeats's experiments with symbols. As published, the passage says only that the colors were classified as "actives" and "passives." The manuscript reads: "In the symbolism which I used, yellow and red are classified as 'actives' while purple, green and white are 'passives,' and I soon discovered that if I used yellow and red he could see nothing." The last sentence in the published version of section V, that about Strindberg's friend, is not in the manuscript. There are two manuscripts of section IX; both show that there is a misprint near the end of the first paragraph which has never been corrected. This misprint, like those noticed earlier, probably grew out of the failure of the typist to whom Yeats dictated to hear accurately what he said. The manuscripts show that Yeats wrote ". . . had [Dante and Villon] cherished any sort of specious optimism"; this became "had they cherished any species of optimism."

When Yeats revised "The Trembling of the Veil" for inclusion in *Autobiographies,* 1926, he added section VI.

Yeats assembled the esoteric experiences described in "Hodos" from events that occurred at widely separated intervals. Many of them occurred during the 1890's and are recorded in "First Draft," but the incident described in section V wherein Yeats drove away an accidentally invoked Diana by a symbol of dismissal was first recorded in July 1913, in the Journal begun in 1908.

July 1913. I told the control that I had evoked in a girl's mind a Diana in a cave by imagining geometric symbols and a moon, which she did not see, for her eyes were shut. I had not foreseen the Diana. Her trance grew too deep, and I tried to lighten it by making an exorcism very faintly, a stupid action, with the result that the girl started and said, "Diana is angry; you are driving her away too quickly." She had not seen my gesture and would not have understood it if she had.

[*Transcribed from the* MS.]

As usual, the parallel passages in "First Draft" and "Hodos" show no verbal reminiscences of "First Draft," and the order in which Yeats arranges events in the two works is not the same. Nor is Yeats's material fully anticipated in "First Draft"; there is, for instance, no account there of Mary Battle's visions. Sometimes experiences which Yeats refers to in "Hodos" are more fully described in "First Draft." The sentences in the final paragraph of "Hodos," section II, describing differences between the accounts of a vision told by one of Yeats's friends when entranced and when waking summarize a full description of the incident told in section XXI of "First Draft." Once again I conclude that Yeats was not working with "First Draft" open before him.

vii "The Tragic Generation" and "The Stirring of the Bones"

THE MANUSCRIPT OF THAT SECTION of "Memoirs" which Yeats later called "The Tragic Generation" appears to have been written without undue trouble. Yeats was thoroughly familiar with his material, for one of his most popular lectures, called "Friends of My Youth," was about the Rhymers, and he had written a rather full account of their tragic fate in "First Draft." The relation of "The Tragic Generation" to "First Draft" is exactly the same as the relation of "Four Years": Much of the material used is common to both, though it is expanded and added to in "The Tragic Generation"; Yeats's explanation in systemic terms of the tragedy that engulfed so many of his friends is entirely new; the style of the two works is quite unlike. Since the results of my detailed comparison are so nearly the same as those arrived at in the discussion of "Four Years," I will not repeat the comparison, but rather support my conclusion by quoting from "First Draft" Yeats's description of his first meeting with Synge so that it may be compared with the passage on Synge in section XIX of "The Tragic Generation."

I went to Paris . . . and stayed for a time at the Hotel Corneille near the Luxembourg, and there met John Synge for the first time. I liked him, his sincerity and his knowledge, but did not divine his genius. Some chance caller introduced us. "There is an Irishman," he said, "living on the top floor." He was reading French literature, Racine mainly, and hoped to live by writing articles upon it in English papers. I persuaded him that Symons would always be a better critic, and that he should go to Ireland ([he] knew Irish; I told him of Aran where I had just been) and find expression for a life that lacked it. "Style comes from the shock of new material" was his own phrase later on.

In "The Tragic Generation" Yeats's account of the first meeting with Synge is fuller: it includes, for example, recollections of Yeats's trip to Inishmaan in place of the bald "I told him of Aran where I had just been"; it assigns Synge to a phase of the moon; it ends with an analysis of his character.

The idea of putting together his accounts of the tragedies that overtook so many of his contemporaries apparently occurred to Yeats while he was writing "Four Years." He took out of the unsigned manuscript of "Four Years" a long account of Lionel Johnson and put the material into the principal manuscript of "The Tragic Generation."

In the principal manuscript Yeats achieved nearly the version of "The Tragic Generation" which he published, and there are not among his discarded drafts anything like the number of versions that exist for parts of "Ireland after Parnell." There are several partial draft versions of the account of Wilde's catastrophe, and early drafts of what are now the openings of sections III and IV. Below is an account of the principal changes Yeats made in his manuscript before publication; when no reference is made to a particular section, this means that the versions in the manuscripts are essentially what Yeats published.

iii. This section was thoroughly revised and expanded. The revised version expresses Yeats's difficult meaning more clearly.

iv and *v.* Between these two sections Yeats wrote out the material which he put into section XXIII of "Four Years" when he revised it for inclusion in *The Trembling of the Veil.*

vi. Yeats's comment at the very end was added after the completion of the principal manuscript. This section was at one time part of the manuscript of "Four Years."

ix. Yeats greatly improved the expression of this section by extensive revision done after the completion of the principal manuscript.

x. The final sentence is not in the manuscript.

xi. The reference to Herodiade, and the quotation, are not in the principal manuscript.

xiii. Yeats wrote more specifically of the various insults he suffered at the time of the *Savoy* crisis, and he named the "well-known house" to which he refers. It was Stopford Brooke's.

xiv and *xv.* These were apparently written out separately on smaller paper, and incorporated into the principal manuscript. Yeats somewhat changed the order of his material. The anecdote about Beardsley drunk once immediately followed the Wilde anecdote.

xviii. This was considerably revised before *The Trembling of the Veil* was printed, and the end of paragraph one and the whole of paragraph two largely rewritten before being reprinted in *Autobiographies* in 1926. The passage on William Sharp, and with it the sentence at the end of the preceding paragraph beginning "When the nature turns to its spiritual opposite" as well as the first sentence of the paragraph which follows, that on Paul Verlaine, were added after the manuscript was completed. The manuscript preceded directly from the account of Mathers to that of Verlaine.

xix. Yeats improved this section by extensive verbal revision.

xx. The fourth short paragraph was badly misprinted in *The Trembling of the Veil.* Yeats subsequently put this right, so it now conforms to his intention in the manuscript. A short paragraph later transferred to section v of "The Stirring of the Bones" once concluded this section. It is the paragraph beginning "I am at Maud Gonne's hotel."

Included with the manuscript is a typescript of section XI through XX of "The Tragic Generation" and of "The Stirring of the Bones" in the form printed in *The Trembling of the Veil.* This was evidently transcribed from the manuscript, not dictated. Many blanks were left in the typescript, and Yeats filled in the words that his typist could not read. By the time Yeats had finished with this typescript he had essentially the text he printed.

Yeats made an extensive addition to "The Stirring of the Bones" after this had appeared in *The Trembling of the Veil*. He printed this addition under the title "A Biographical Fragment, with Some Notes" in *The Criterion* and *The Dial* in July 1923, and used it to begin section VI of "The Stirring of the Bones" in *Autobiographies*, 1926. Yeats returned to his original version with the words "I was in poor health." No manuscript of this addition, called by Yeats "The Vision of an Archer," has come to light; however, I have seen a manuscript and a typescript of Yeats's first Note on his vision.

The material of both the original version of "The Stirring of the Bones" and of the addition is most of it included in "First Draft"; indeed this section of *Autobiographies* is more fully anticipated in "First Draft" than any other. When Yeats was writing his "Vision of the Archer," now section VI, he may even have worked with "First Draft" open before him, since there are many verbal similarities between the two.

Except for the addition to section VI, the manuscript of "The Stirring of the Bones" runs along pretty much like the version Yeats printed. Certain difficulties occur in the text because Yeats did not carefully compare the typescript made of the manuscript with the original. In section I, for instance, Yeats wrote that the money Maud Gonne "collected would go to the monument, not to her friends," and, a few sentences later, "and no gain at all perhaps to the monument." The typist misread "monument" and put "movement" instead; Yeats did not correct the error. The typist missed a passage near the beginning of section II. Yeats had drafted it on the back of the preceding page of his manuscript, and the typist missed the cue-in. Yeats has not cancelled the passage, and in its original form his second sentence was a better introduction to the anecdote about the Frenchman and to his father's phrase "unity of being." In the manuscript this second sentence ended "just in so far as it was not my business, and in all probability because of an anecdote and certain words about Unity of Being overheard in childhood." Yeats added the poem that closes section II after he had finished his manuscript; he rearranged the items in section V.

viii
"The Bounty of Sweden" and "Dramatis Personae"

THE NEXT PART of *Autobiographies* to be written was "The Bounty of Sweden." Yeats finished this late in January 1924. The manuscript of "The Bounty of Sweden" has survived; I have not seen a manuscript of the lecture "The Irish Dramatic Movement." Writing "The Bounty of Sweden" seems to have given Yeats little trouble, for the manuscript is closer to the version printed than any other Yeats manuscript that I have examined. Yeats seems to have gotten almost exactly what he wanted in his first draft, an event almost unique.

The section of *Autobiographies* called "Dramatis Personae" was the last to be composed. Yeats wrote it in 1934. The manuscript is in the Houghton Library at Harvard; among the Yeats papers in Dublin is a heavily revised typescript dictated from the manuscript, beginning with section XII and continuing to the end. The manuscript in the Houghton Library is unusually clean for Yeats; there is little or no evidence of the kind of travail that often occurred when he composed. A comparison of the manuscript with the revised typescript makes it evident that Yeats dictated the typescript from his manuscript, introducing some changes. He then revised the typescript radically. His revised typescript is so like the version printed by the Cuala Press that it seems fairly certain Yeats accomplished "Dramatis Personae" as we know it in one manuscript and one heavily revised typescript.

Yeats in his later years became marvelously adept at revising, one might almost say rewriting, a typescript. I give below the original typescript version of section XV of "Dramatis Personae"; following it I give the revised typescript:

I saw Moore daily, for we were writing *Diarmid and Grania*. Lady Gregory thought that collaboration would injure my own art. Coleridge calls "the sense of beauty" a "simultaneous interaction or relation of parts, each to each, and of all to the whole," and Moore's mind was diagrammatic, argumentative, or to adopt the language of our own time, spatial. At first we argued constantly about words which contained nothing for him that reason had not put there. In later years, through a knowledge of the stage, and through the exfoliation of my own style,

I learnt the necessity for prosaic words whenever it was necessary to give the impression of an active man speaking. In dream poetry, in "Kubla Khan", in "The Stream's Secret", every line, every word, can carry its unanalysable, rich associations; experience can follow experience; but if we dramatize some possible singer or speaker we remember that he can only feel intensely some one thing. Here and there in correcting my early poems I have made certain stanzas more prosaic; turned, for instance, "the curd, pale moon" into "brilliant moon", [that] it all might seem, as it were, coldly remembered, except some one vivid image. When I began to rehearse a play I had the defects of my early poetry; I insisted on obvious all-pervading rhythm. Later on I found myself constantly saying that only the line or two in which the beauty of the passage came to its climax must rhythm be obvious. Moore thought all effective drama objective, he said after a performance of Russell's *Deirdre:* "Who are his people — clerks, ours were cattle merchants". He wanted always words as they are spoken by active men and women; he was wrong, not because his words were prosaic, but because their associations were exclusively modern, as when he insisted for days upon calling the Fianna "soldiers". He had no historical instinct; in *The Story Teller's Holiday* he makes a young man in the thirteenth century go to the "salons" of "the fashionable ladies" in Paris, and in his last story men and women of the Homeric age read books. Our worst quarrels, however, were over his attempts to be poetical. I have an early draft of a play where the dying Diarmid threatens Fion: "I will kick you down the stairway of the stars". At last my letters to Lady Gregory show that we made peace, Moore accepting my judgment upon words, I his upon construction. To that he would sacrifice what he thought the day before "the best scene in any modern play" and without apparent regret, all must receive its light and warmth from the central idea; nothing being in itself anything. He would have been a master of construction, but that his training as a novelist made him long for descriptions and reminiscences. If *Diarmid and Grania* failed in performance, and I am not sure that it did, it was because the second act, which should have moved swiftly from incident to incident, was reminiscent; almost a new, first act. My training in the poetical drama had made me aware of this, that Moore over-bore me with his vehemence.

Now the revised version, where Yeats very nearly achieves what he printed:

I saw Moore daily, we were at work on *Diarmid and Grania*. Lady Gregory thought such collaboration would injure my own art & was perhaps right. Because his mind was argumentative, abstract, diagrammatic, mine sensuous, concrete, rhythmical, we argued about words. In later years through a knowledge of the stage, and through the exfoliation of my own style, I learnt that occasional prosaic words gave the impression of an active man speaking. In dream poetry, in "Kubla Khan", in "The Stream's Secret", every line, every word, can carry its unanalysable, rich associations; but if we dramatise some possible singer or speaker we remember that he is moved by one thing at a time, certain words must be numb and dry. Here and there in correcting my early poems I have introduced such numbness and dryness, turned, for instance, "the curd, pale moon" into "brilliant moon", that all might seem, as it were, remembered with indifference except some one vivid image. When I began to rehearse a play I had the defects of my early poetry; I insisted upon obvious all-pervading rhythm. Later on I found myself saying that only in those lines or words, where the beauty of the passage came to its climax must rhythm be obvious. [Because Moore thought all drama should be about possible people set in their appropriate surroundings, because he was fundamentally a realist — "who are his people" he said after a performance of George Russell's *Deirdre* "ours were cattle merchants" — he required many dry, numb words. But he put them in more often than not because he had no feeling for words in themselves, none for their historical association.] [3] He insisted for days upon calling the Fianna "soldiers". In *The Story Teller's Holiday* he makes a young man in the thirteenth century go to the "salons" of "the fashionable ladies" in Paris, in his last story men and women of the Homeric age read books. Our worst quarrels, however, were when he tried to be poetical, to write in what he considered my style. He made the dying Diarmid say to Fion: "I will kick you down the stairway of the stars". My letters to Lady Gregory show that we made peace at last, Moore accepting my judgment upon words, I his upon construction. To that he would sacrifice what he had thought the day before not only his best scene, [but] "the best scene in any modern play" and without regret: all must receive its being from the central idea; nothing be in itself anything. He would have been a master of construction, but that his practice as a novelist made him long for descriptions and reminiscences. If *Diarmid and Grania* failed in performance, and I am not sure that it did, it failed because the second act, instead of moving swiftly from incident to incident, was reminiscent and descriptive; almost a new first act. I had written enough poetical drama to know this and point it out to Moore. After the performance & just before our final quarrel the letters speak of an agreement to rewrite this act, I had sent Moore a scenario.

What Yeats accomplished in revising his typescript can be seen most effectively if we set several passages side by side:

Original	*Revision*
Coleridge calls "the sense of beauty" a "simultaneous interaction or relation of parts, each to each, and all to the whole," and Moore's mind was diagrammatic, argumentative, or to adopt the language of our own time, spatial. At first we argued constantly about words which contained nothing for him that reason had not put there.	Because his mind was argumentative, abstract, diagrammatic, mine sensuous, concrete, rhythmical, we argued about words.
I learnt the necessity for prosaic words whenever it was necessary to give the impression of an active man speaking.	I learnt that occasional prosaic words gave the impression of an active man speaking.
. . . we remember that he can only feel intensely some one thing.	. . . we remember that he is moved by one thing at a time, certain words must be numb and dry.
I have made certain stanzas more prosaic	I have introduced such numbness and dryness
. . . coldly remembered	. . . remembered with indifference
Moore thought all effective drama objective, he said after a performance of Russell's *Deirdre:* "Who are his people — clerks, ours were cattle merchants". He wanted al-	Because Moore thought that all drama should be about possible people set in their appropriate surroundings, because he was fundamentally a realist— "who are his

ways words as they are spoken by active men and women; he was wrong, not because his words were prosaic, but because their associations were exclusively modern, as when he insisted for days upon calling the Fianna "soldiers".

people" he said after a performance of George Russell's *Deirdre* "ours were cattle merchants"—he required many dry, numb words. But he put them in more often than not because he had no feeling for words in themselves, none for their historical association. He insisted

. . . sacrifice what he thought the day before "the best scene in any modern play" and without apparent regret, all must receive its light and warmth from the central idea; nothing being in itself anything.

. . . sacrifice what he had thought the day before not only his best scene, [but] "the best scene in any modern play" and without regret: all must receive its being from the central idea; nothing be in itself anything.

The improvement, the enhancement of the second versions is in each instance apparent. Perhaps the finest strokes were the excision of the reference to Coleridge and the quotation, which sadly breaks Yeats's tone; the invention of the phrase "words must be numb and dry," which, slightly varied, is twice repeated: "Numbness and dryness" "dry, numb words"; and the subtle touches which changed "all must receive its light and warmth from the central idea; nothing being in itself anything." Yeats's ability to revise so effectively while working on typescripts made the production of his later prose much less physically laborious than the production of his earlier. He generally used this method of rewriting in later years.

IX

On the Boiler

THE COMPOSITION OF *On the Boiler*, Yeats's last prose work, can be studied in detail from the following materials: 1] A manuscript of twenty-one pages headed "Beltaine," cancelled, and then "Poet's Corner." This is Yeats's manuscript version of the part of *On the Boiler* called "To-morrow's Revolution" and sections I and II of the part called "Private Thoughts." Yeats removed this manuscript from his looseleaf binder and filed it on January 4, 1938. 2] The carbon copy of the typescript Yeats dictated from this manuscript; the title is now "First Principles," and the typescript is headed "First Dictation." With this carbon are twelve sheets, some typed and some manuscript, which are additions to or revised versions of parts of "First Principles." 3] A manuscript of thirty-seven pages, containing drafts of the material now found on pp. 9–14 and 25–38 of *On the Boiler*. 4] The first complete typescript, heavily revised throughout by Yeats. 5] Two additional typescripts, a first copy and a carbon, with further manuscript revisions. These are not always identical on the two copies. In these typescripts Yeats achieved pretty much the text he published. 6] Thirteen proofsheets of the original setting of *On the Boiler*, with manuscript corrections by Yeats and by Mrs. Yeats.[4]

The list of drafts given above shows that *On the Boiler* cost Yeats a great deal of effort, so much, indeed, that on June 22, 1938, he wrote to Dorothy Wellesley, "Yesterday I reminded myself that an Eastern sage had promised me a quiet death, and hoped that it would come before I had to face *On the Boiler No. 2*." What Yeats says in *On the Boiler* he largely said again in "Under Ben Bulben," his poetic last will and testament; this fact, taken together with the immense effort he spent composing *On the Boiler*, shows that he took the work very seriously. Its informal, easy tone is, as one would at this point expect, a result of much hard work; these are not mere jottings, mere table talk, even though Yeats's content is miscellaneous.

Yeats thought of *On the Boiler* as the first issue of a biannual miscellany whose publication might help to solve the financial problems of the Cuala Press; it was to be "*a Fors Clavigera* of sorts – my advice to the youthful mind on all manner of things, and poems" (to DW, Nov. 11, 1937). On November 20, 1937, he again spoke of the work he was planning. "In my bi-annual (my *Fors Clavigera*) I shall do what I thought never to do – sketch out the fundamental principles, as I see them, on which politics and literature should be based." He was writing in December, and took the partially finished work with him when he left Ireland for Monte Carlo late in that month. He reported working on it in January and February. By March 8–9, 1938, the work had reached nearly its present form, for on those days Yeats corrected the first complete typescript. When Yeats left Monte Carlo late in March, *On the Boiler* seemed ready for the press. Yeats was in

England from March 23 to the middle of May; sometime after he returned to Dublin, Yeats made his final revisions and wrote a "Preface" which he dated July 1938. On July 13 he wrote, "Before I left Dublin I gave 'On the Boiler' to Higgins, who is to send it to the printer." Yeats was not yet done with revision and addition, however, for in the same letter he adds, "I am writing a new 'Crazy Jane' poem — a wild affair." This poem, "I am tired of cursing the Bishop," eventually became part IV of the section "Ireland after the Revolution," and a new part III had to be added to introduce the poem. Eventually, *On the Boiler* was set up, and Yeats read proof, though progress through the press was so slow Yeats changed the date of the "Preface" from "July" to "October" in the proof corrections. This version of *On the Boiler* was never published; the version finally published in September 1939, was a new edition. (See Wade, items 201 and 202.)

Yeats, as usual, accumulated *On the Boiler;* as with most of his prose works, he did not compose it in its present order. The part completed first was an essay which in typescript runs to eighteen pages. This Yeats called successively "Beltaine" — a title which expressed his hope for publication in the spring of 1938, "Poet's Corner," and "First Principles." In the finished work this essay forms the section called "To-morrow's Revolution" and parts I and II of that called "Private Thoughts." It stated in Yeats's emphatic way his belief in the need for eugenic reform. It was directly inspired, as Yeats indicates, by his reading R. B. Cattell's impressive book *The Fight for Our National Intelligence.* Eventually Yeats put in front of this essay the matter now found in "The Name" and "Preliminaries," and that which follows it beginning with part III of "Private Thoughts." That he did this later is proved by a note Yeats included in the manuscript of these parts of *On the Boiler;* there, at the beginning of what became part III of "Private Thoughts," Yeats wrote "After First Principles now in typescript." Yeats dictated from the manuscript of "First Principles" to Mrs. Yeats, no doubt watching over her shoulder as was his usual practice. Mrs. Yeats made a first copy and a carbon, heading them "First dictation." Yeats in several places revised his dictation while the sheets were still in the typewriter; the carbon copy shows that certain cancellations were made by drawing a line through the offending passage while it was still on the roller. The revised dictation follows immediately. Fourteen corrections were made in this way. In another place Yeats apparently told Mrs. Yeats to leave a blank to be filled in.

The passage read, "Ricketts made pictures that suggest ——— by their colour." Mrs. Yeats later wrote in the correct name, "Delacroix." The carbon copy of the "First dictation" was kept intact.

Yeats began his correction of "First Principles" on the first copy of this dictation. Twelve of these sheets, much overwritten, were incorporated into the first complete typescript of *On the Boiler* (pages 1–3 and 10–18); the middle portion of the essay was so drastically revised that Yeats made an intermediate version. This revised portion is partly typescript, partly manuscript. Probably not all of Yeats's revisions have survived. When the process of composition grew complex, and here it was very complex, Yeats often destroyed abandoned intermediate versions to avoid confusion.

As nearly as I can reconstruct it, the revision of the typescript of "First Principles" went as follows: Yeats cancelled the first paragraph, though later he used much of the material in it in his "Preface." He changed the title twice, first to "The Coming Revolution," then to "To-morrow's Revolution." Parts I and II of this section (*On the Boiler*, pp. 14–15) he twice revised, once in pencil and once in ink. During the pencil revision Yeats gave the parts subtitles which he later cancelled. The cancelled subtitle of part I is, I believe, "Patter"; that of part II is certainly "A Text." Except for the cancellation of the first paragraph these revisions were not radical; they improved the phrasing and added illustration.

The part now numbered III (pp. 16–18) was completely reworked, probably reworked more than once. During this reworking Yeats composed most of the notes now attached to part III, and altered his text radically. In the dictation of "First Principles" there was only one note in place of the five now found; this Yeats did not retain, though he incorporated its substance into note 2, page 17. Yeats composed his notes in manuscript on the margins and backs of the typed sheets intermediate between the "first dictation" and the first complete typescript, and on separate sheets which he inserted; indeed he did two drafts of one of them, note 2, page 17. Clearly Yeats wishes to bolster his argument by citing authorities on the mental and physical degeneration of the various West-European peoples. The text itself is, as a result of many revisions, a shorter (by about 200 words), clearer, and more specific statement of the thesis stated in "First Principles." The process of revision can be followed in these successive versions of a sentence found on page 17.

First dictation: "Mother-wit is not everything, without acquired habits and skill, Gray's Milton is not much of a man, ~~but no training, no environment can give it~~ but no habits, no skill can give it."

Revision of first dictation: "Mother-wit is not everything, without acquired habits and skill, Gray's Milton would remain decidedly 'inglorious,' but no habits, no skill can give it."

Intermediate typescript sheet: "This mother-wit is not everything, Gray's Milton remained for lack of acquired skill "mute, inglorious," but it outweighs everything else by, let us say, six to one, and is almost always hereditary like the speed of a dog or horse."

This intermediate sheet as corrected in Yeats's hand: "This mother-wit is not everything; Gray's Milton remained for lack of acquired knowledge 'mute, inglorious'; but it outweighs everything else by, let us say, six to one, and is hereditary like the speed of a dog or horse." Yeats used the fourth form of this sentence in his first complete typescript. When Yeats revised this typescript, he dropped down into the sentence we are studying an allusion to Bluebeard and St. Augustine which had been part of the preceding sentence.

As corrected on the first typescript: "This mother-wit is not everything; it may have been the same in Blue Beard and St. Augustine; Gray's Milton remained for lack of acquired knowledge 'mute, inglorious'; but it outweighs everything else by, let us say, six to one, and is hereditary like the speed of a dog or horse." Yeats was not yet done with this sentence. In typescripts 2 and 3 "everything; it may" became "everything and may"; "Milton" was put into quotation marks only in the printed text. This run of successive drafts of a single sentence shows the lengths Yeats went to in order to achieve the lively allusiveness of "To-morrow's Revolution."

Part IV was also carefully revised. Yeats did his first revisions of the beginning of this passage down through a sentence now found in the middle of page 19 ("That increase, too, can be calculated mathematically") on pages 7 and 8 of his dictated "First Principles." At that point his revision became so complex that he did a manuscript version of the passage which now begins "But even if all Europe" and ends with a quotation from *A Vision*. Yeats dictated from these corrected sheets and from this manuscript when he put the first complete typescript together, and introduced many further changes during his dictation.

Part v of "To-morrow's Revolution" and parts i and ii of the section now called "Private Thoughts" correlate with pages 9 through 18 of the dictated "First Principles." Their revision was less radical. There are no intermediate versions, the corrections were made directly on the typed sheets of "First Principles," and from page 10 on the actual sheets of "First Principles" were re-numbered and incorporated into the first complete typescript of *On the Boiler*. Yeats introduced the new section heading "Private Thoughts" in this first typescript at the point marked vii in "First Principles." There another subheading has been cancelled; I believe it read "The Philosophical Method."

Yeats surrounded this core of material with a variety of other matter. He wrote a manuscript version of this material which on the whole correlates closely with the version printed in *On the Boiler*. He added two passages after completing his first draft; the manuscript of these additions has been placed at the end of the first draft. These added passages are parts iii and iv of "Ireland after the Revolution," (the story about George V and the last Crazy Jane poem) and the paragraph about Diana Murphy and the importance Yeats attached to having artists avoid distortion in representing the human body, now included in part vii of "Other Matters." The last Crazy Jane poem was composed in July 1938; I have found no indication of the date when the passage on Diana Murphy was added.

Yeats dictated to his typist from these manuscripts, introducing changes as he dictated. All of this material except that which became part iii of "Private Thoughts" was both composed and revised with relatively little trouble. The manuscript of the sections now called "The Name" and "Preliminaries" was composed on twelve numbered sheets. It is unusually clean for first drafts by Yeats, and relatively few changes were introduced into the subsequent typescripts. Yeats continued his manuscript after what is now part ii of "Private Thoughts." He picked up the pagination of "first dictation," numbering the first page of the continuation "19," and writing "After First Principles now in typescript." Yeats composed the first draft of what is now part iii in blue ink; his corrections of the manuscript were made in black ink. Hence it is possible here to separate what Yeats originally wrote from his corrections. In most Yeats manuscripts this cannot be done with any certainty.

Part III of "Private Thoughts" gave Yeats a great deal of trouble. There are many versions, and the order of versions is hard to establish. I believe that Yeats wove two manuscripts together when he dictated this passage for the first complete typescript. In addition to the two manuscript versions, there is an intermediate typescript version of part of the passage. After dictating the first complete typescript, Yeats practically rewrote the passage on the sheets of that typescript.[5] This radical revision was necessary. The manuscript version first composed, which can be largely reconstructed because of the different color of the ink, is nearly incoherent. Yeats in the passage as printed in *On the Boiler* states his meaning as clearly as the esoteric nature of his doctrine permits.

Part IV of "Private Thoughts" came more easily; the printed version does not differ greatly from the manuscript. The quotation with which it ends is from *Sigurd the Volsung,* in the translation of William Morris. In the manuscript at the point where the quotation is introduced, Yeats wrote, "Quote passage from Sigurd already given in Wheels and Butterflies" (see *Wheels and Butterflies,* London, 1934, pp. 74–75). Yeats copied the quotation out in longhand on the first complete typescript. While revising this typescript Yeats had an idea for an addition at this point, though he abandoned it almost at once. He wrote on the typescript, "When I return next from the Button-Moulder, and I hope not too much altered, I shall play my part as doubtless I played in the past in the driving of the Blatant Beast. (Quote poem about Hound Voice)" Yeats cancelled this blatant but charming egotism. The manuscript of part V was little revised.

The following section is now called "Ireland after the Revolution"; this section of the manuscript was called "Their Application," meaning, presumably, the application of the "first principles." The heading became "Applications" in the first complete typescript, where Yeats supplied the present title in revising. Parts I and II of this section still follow the manuscript very closely, indeed were probably less revised than any other part of *On the Boiler.* Both the manuscript and the first typescript continue with what is now part V. We have already noted that parts III and IV, the last Crazy Jane poem and its introduction, were late additions. The manuscript of part III, now found at the end of the principal manuscript, was typed and inserted into the second and third typescripts, where it was thoroughly revised. The last Crazy Jane poem was inserted into TS. 2. What is now part V is a slightly revised version of the passage which concluded this section in the manuscript and first typescript.

The original manuscript continues with a short passage about the Cuala Press, which Yeats has cancelled. He continued, under the heading "Other Matters," to compose a first draft of what is now part I of that section. Opposite it, on the back of the preceding page of the manuscript, is another cancelled version of the same material headed, simply, "Other." The manuscript continues through part VI pretty much as printed, though there was, of course, much revision of the manuscript itself. In composing his description of the tragic ecstasy on page 35, Yeats filled the margins of the sheet on which he was writing and most of the verso of the preceding sheet.

Only the first paragraph of part VII of "Other Matters" was composed in the principal manuscript. Paragraph two is not found there, nor does it appear in the first complete typescript. A manuscript of a portion of this second paragraph (down through the words "Greek proportions") is included among the loose sheets filed at the end of the principal manuscript along with the first drafts of other additions. In the first complete typescript at the end of the paragraph, which then constituted all of part VII, Yeats wrote and then cancelled the instruction, "Insert here the first section of 'News for the Delphic Oracle.' "

Part VIII, the final paragraph of *On the Boiler*, was composed in the original manuscript. The text makes it clear that Yeats intended to end with "The Statesman's Holiday," then called "Avalon," although his instruction "quote the whole of Avalon" is not in the manuscript; it was inserted in the first typescript.

On the Boiler was accumulated around an essay called "First Principles," on the physical and intellectual decadence of the West-European nations. This essay, much revised, was supplied with an introduction. Other matter was added to it, which both comments on this main theme and to an extent softens its impact by suggesting that civilization will somehow continue after tomorrow's revolution — continue at least in Ireland. Yeats wished especially to state the artist's role during the crisis which he foresaw; as he put it in "Under Ben Bulben," the artist is to "Bring the soul of man to God,/ Make him fill the cradles right." *On the Boiler* is a kind of Yeats miscellany, yet it has the unity of theme Yeats sought to achieve. He wrote in his Preface, "In the new publication I shall write whatever interests me at the moment, trying, however, to keep some kind of unity, and only including poem or play that has something to do with my main theme." Yeats followed this principle of selection, including "Why Should Not Old Men Be Mad," "I am Tired of Cursing the Bishop," "The Statesman's Holiday," and "Purgatory," all of which have as their theme some aspect of the degeneration which is Yeats's subject. During the long process of composition Yeats considered at one time or another including "Hound Voice," part of "News for the Delphic Oracle," "The Statues," and "Three Marching Songs." All of these appear either in his text or in an early typed Table of Contents; indeed the "Three Marching Songs" were even set in type. No doubt Yeats omitted all of them because they less obviously concern his theme.

An examination of the many drafts of *On the Boiler*, though clearly it is not one of Yeats's major works, shows that late as well as early Yeats's process of composition was an accumulative one, and that expression which satisfied him came only after a bitter struggle. Yeats often complained of the sheer drudgery of his profession; after examining so many of his manuscripts one can see why. Even at the end of his life, at a time when some commentators have felt an overmastery of the resources of language led to a certain glibness of tone, Yeats achieved precise diction, easy phrasing, and an effective order both within the sentence and the total work only after expending great effort.

BIBLIOGRAPHY / NOTES / INDEX

BIBLIOGRAPHY

The usual bibliography found at the end of a work on Yeats seems addressed to specialists who have no need of its help. I shall try, while keeping the needs of readers of this book in mind, to cast a somewhat wider net.

Yeats's Manuscripts.

Most of the Yeats manuscripts are in Dublin. The family collection of Yeats's papers is nearly intact, and it is overwhelmingly abundant. Mrs. Yeats did give the manuscripts of Yeats's plays to the National Library of Ireland in 1958. The National Library has accessioned these manuscripts and placed them in folders, but they had not been recorded in the public catalogue in 1960. They are difficult to use because the various drafts of individual plays have not been arranged successively, and because Yeats often worked on plays in his manuscript books which remain in the family collection. (For only two of the plays which I discuss are all the manuscripts at the National Library — *At the Hawk's Well* and *Purgatory*.) The family collection is uncatalogued, which explains why in my notes of ascription I have tried to identify for future scholars the manuscripts quoted by referring to some physical characteristic of the manuscript such as an inscription in the front of it. In the United States the Houghton Library has a number of important manuscripts and many manuscript letters. In addition it has five reels of microfilm reproductions of manuscripts in Mrs. Yeats's collection, which contain copies of all Yeats's manuscript books save two (a manuscript book given Yeats by Maud Gonne in the summer of 1908 and the manuscript of the 1930 Diary), and much other material. Houghton also has a photostatic copy of the "First Draft" of Yeats's *Autobiographies.* There are restrictions on the use of all of this material.

John Quinn collected a considerable number of Yeats manuscripts and other items which were dispersed during the sale of his library (Anderson Galleries, Sale No. 1820, Thursday, March 20, 1924). The Yeats items were numbered in the sale catalogue from 11338 through 11610. There is a copy of the sale catalogue, partly priced and giving the names of the original purchasers, in the library of the American Antiquarian Society, Worcester, Massachusetts. These items from Quinn's library are very hard to locate. Inspection of such manuscripts from Quinn's library as I have run into strongly suggests that they had been, so to speak, "concocted" — written out for Quinn by WBY after a work was complete or nearly so. Letters by Yeats are being acquired by libraries in the United States in ever increasing numbers. In short, a census of Yeats manuscripts in American libraries would be very useful.

Yeats's Printed Books.

With Yeats not only the first edition but all successive reprintings of his works must, because of Yeats's habit of constant revising, be examined by a scholar who wishes to study the evolution of one of his texts. This is no longer so necessary with the poems because of the Allt-Alspach *Variorum Edition,* and the forthcoming variorum edition of Yeats's plays will be invaluable since the early plays were more than revised; they were rewritten, often several times. The prose works will continue to raise problems because they too were frequently revised. Again, Mrs. Yeats has a complete or nearly complete run of Yeats's printed books. The library of Trinity College, Dublin, since it is a deposit library for Great Britain, has a very rich collection. In the United States both the Harvard and Yale libraries have fine collections. In recent years two important collections, neither of which I have seen, have come to American libraries: the P. S. O'Hegarty collection to the library of the University of Kansas, the Allan Wade collection to the library of Indiana University.

There is as yet no standard edition of Yeats's works, with the result that writers on Yeats bewilder their readers by the variety of their citations, often to books that are rare or have been long out of print. The "definitive edition" of *The Poems of W. B. Yeats* published by Macmillan and Company in two volumes in 1949 was limited to 350 copies and hence cannot be found in most libraries. (It is hardly definitive, but it is the best we have.) Both the English and American editions of *Collected Poems* are less satisfactory, for both ignore the reordering of Yeats's narrative and dramatic poems made for the definitive edition, and they have other defects. Given this situation, probably the best solution is to cite the *Variorum Edition* (described below), since it is generally available. This is based on the text of the definitive edition.

The *Collected Plays* issued by Macmillan and Company (London) in 1952 is generally regarded as the standard edition of Yeats's plays; Colonel Alspach's variorum will use this text. It is not altogether satisfactory as G. B. Saul's *Prolegomena* (see below) makes clear, but again it is the best we have. *A Vision,* issued by The Macmillan Company (New York) in 1956 states on its title page that it incorporates the "author's final revisions," and is generally regarded as standard. The edition published in 1961 in Macmillan Paperbacks appears to have been printed from the same plates. The four volumes of Yeats's prose printed by Macmillan and Company (London) beginning in 1955 with *Autobiographies,* and continuing with *Mythologies* (1958), *Essays and Introductions* (1961), and *Explorations* (1962) have filled a long felt need by getting Yeats's prose back into print. Their textual authority has yet to be determined.

Basic Scholarly Books on Yeats.

Allan Wade's *A Bibliography of the Writings of W. B. Yeats,* London, 1951, was reissued with important additions and an index in 1958. This index enables the book's users to find quickly the first and subsequent appearances of works which have become sections of collected editions. Allan Wade's revision was completed by Mr. Rupert Hart-Davis. This is one of the finest bibliographies I have ever used. G. B. Saul's *Prolegomena to the Study of Yeats's Poems*, Philadelphia, 1957, and *Prolegomena to the Study of Yeats's Plays*, Philadelphia, 1958, are more than bibliographies, though they are that among other things. Each contains a vast amount of information, and any student of Yeats's poems and plays would be well advised to begin here.

Three volumes of Yeats's letters have been published since his death if we omit the separate publication of his letters to Katharine Tynan, all found in Wade: *Letters on Poetry from W. B. Yeats to Dorothy Wellesley* (London, New York, Toronto, 1940); *W. B. Yeats and T. Sturge Moore: Their Correspondence*, ed. Ursula Bridge (London, 1953); and *The Letters of W. B. Yeats*, ed. Allan Wade (London, 1956). Wade's collection is the most comprehensive and has an excellent index. Wade does not, however, index his own biographical essays on Yeats, though these constitute by far the best short account of Yeats's career that we have had. I suspect that unpublished letters of Yeats will continue to turn up for a very long time, but that his best letters are in print.

The Variorum Edition of the Poems of W. B. Yeats, eds. Peter Allt and Russell K. Alspach (New York, 1957), is indispensable, a great work of modern scholarship. Colonel Alspach's variorum edition of the plays should follow shortly, perhaps before this book is in print.

A Concordance to the Poems of W. B. Yeats, ed. Stephen M. Parrish (Ithaca, 1963), seems to me the finest concordance to a poet's work ever to appear. We are just at the beginning of understanding its usefulness. It is based on the text of the Allt-Alspach *Variorum*, and lists the variant as well as the final readings.

There is as yet no standard biography. Hone in *W. B. Yeats, 1865–1939* missed a great opportunity, for Mrs. Yeats made all Yeats's papers available to him and told him he could print anything he wanted to. He found it easier on page after page to quote Yeats's "First Draft of *Autobiographies*" almost verbatim without indicating that he was doing this.

Other Books and Articles on Yeats.

Of these there are no end, nor is there likely soon to be one. Perhaps the best way into this maze is to start with G. B. Saul's two *Prolegomena* (see above), then to move on to the present by means of the annual bibliographies printed in *PMLA*. (There are very few articles and, I think, no books devoted exclusively to Yeats's prose.) I list below the works on Yeats which I have cited:

Eric Bentley, *In Search of Theater*, New York, 1953.
Richard Ellmann, *The Identity of Yeats*, New York, 1954.
Lady Gregory's Journals, 1916–1930, ed. Lennox Robinson, London, 1946.
Joseph Hone, *W. B. Yeats, 1865–1939*, London, 1942.

Thomas Parkinson, *W. B. Yeats: the Later Poetry*, Berkeley and Los Angeles, 1964.
———. *W. B. Yeats: Self-Critic*, Berkeley and Los Angeles, 1951.
Jon Stallworthy, *Between the Lines: Yeats's Poetry in the Making*, Oxford, 1963.
John Unterecker, *A Reader's Guide to William Butler Yeats*, New York, 1959.
F. A. C. Wilson, *W. B. Yeats and Tradition*, New York, 1958.
———. *Yeats's Iconography, London*, 1960.
Yeats: a Collection of Critical Essays, ed. John Unterecker, Englewood Cliffs, N. J., 1963.

Other Works Cited.

Aspects of Poetry, ed. Mark Linenthal, Boston and Toronto, 1963.
David Hayman, *A First-Draft Version of Finnegans Wake*, Austin, 1963.
Pope, *The Twickenham Edition of the Poems of Alexander Pope*, General Editor John Butt, London and New Haven, 1939–61.
Pope and His Contemporaries: Essays Presented to George Sherburn, eds. James L. Clifford and Lewis A. Landa, Oxford, 1949.
Denis de Rougemont, *Love in the Western World*, trans. Montgomery Belgion, New York, 1956.
Arnold Toynbee, *The Study of History*, Oxford, 1934.
W. B. Yeats, *Collected Works* [in eight volumes], Stratford-on-Avon, 1908.
———. *Early Poems and Stories*, New York, 1925 (the poems are now to be found in *Collected Poems*, the stories in *Mythologies*).
———. *On the Boiler*, Dublin, 1939 (parts of *On the Boiler* are included in *Explorations*).
———. *Wheels and Butterflies*, London, 1934 (Yeats's introductions, and the text of *Fighting the Waves* — omitted from *Collected Plays* — are reprinted in *Explorations*).
———. "First Draft of *Autobiographies*," unpublished ms. (the ms. is in Mrs. Yeats's collection; there is a photostatic copy at the Houghton Library).
———. "A Journal begun in December 1908," unpublished ms. (Yeats made "Estrangement" and "The Death of Synge" from this Journal. The ms. is in Mrs. Yeats's collection; there is a microfilm copy at the Houghton Library).
———. "The Speckled Bird," MS. and TS. of an unfinished and unpublished novel, which are in Mrs. Yeats's collection. There are microfilm copies at the Houghton Library.

NOTES

Notes to Part 1, an Introduction

[1] See Jon Stallworthy, *Between the Lines* (Oxford, 1963), pp. 177–200. My "Yeats's Byzantium Poems" was first published in PMLA, March 1960, pp. 110–25, and in a revised form has been twice reprinted. For the details of these reprintings see note 2.

[2] Twice in the revised version of my "Yeats's Byzantium Poems," and in Jon Stallworthy's *Between the Lines,* pp. 91–92. Mr. Stallworthy is right (*Between the Lines,* pp. 89–91) when he concludes that I did not know of the existence of these MSS. when I wrote "Yeats's Byzantium Poems"; I first saw them in Dublin in the summer of 1960. The revised version of "Yeats's Byzantium Poems" first appeared in *Yeats: a Collection of Critical Essays,* ed. John Unterecker (Englewood Cliffs, N. J.: Prentice-Hall, 1963) and was reprinted in *Aspects of Poetry,* ed. Mark Linenthal (Boston and Toronto: Little, Brown, 1963), pp. 64–103.

[3] Thomas Parkinson studies this ms. on pp. 96–97 of *The Later Poetry,* but does not reproduce it. His observation "The initial notes for the poem . . . are also the notes for stanza 5" led me to develop the argument presented below that the composition of "Among School Children" began in the middle of the finished poem.

[4] Mr. Parkinson reproduces part of this ms. in a somewhat different arrangement on pp. 97–98 of *The Later Poetry.*

[5] I have stated elsewhere (*Sewanee Review,* Autumn, 1958, pp. 673–74) my conviction that the long line of editors and copy readers who added punctuation to Yeats's own versions of his poems have done us no favor. I now state my conviction again because Jon Stallworthy has recently supported the other view: that Yeats's punctuation needed correction and improvement (*Between the Lines,* pp. 12–13), quoting a letter by Yeats to this effect. I cite as further evidence for my case Yeats's punctuation of "News." With punctuation as with syntax (see *Letters on Poetry,* pp. 192–93) and even meter Yeats was perhaps too diffident about the authority of his own views.

Notes to Chapter 1

[1] Yeats writes in Section XIX and XX of the "First Draft" of his *Autobiographies* that "Into the Twilight" grew out of an estrangement from Maud Gonne, caused in part by a scandalous story about them which was making the rounds in Dublin. Yeats comments: "I went to Sligo seeking to call to myself my courage once again with the lines 'Into the Twilight': Did not the dew shine through love decayed 'Burning in fires of a slanderous tongue'?"

2 Yeats's discussion of "personal utterance" in section xxx of "Reveries over Childhood and Youth" was probably written in 1914.

Notes to Chapter 2

1 Marion Witt's "The Making of an Elegy," *Modern Philology*, November 1950, indicates that there are MSS. of this poem in the New York Public Library. See p. 117 of her essay.

Notes to Chapter 4

1 The Slieve Aughty or Echtge Mountains lie directly east of Thoor Ballylee in Co. Galway.
2 I use the word "rhyme" here and elsewhere to stand for assonance or consonance as well as rhyme.
3 The word "Irishry" is an example of how the alchemy of poetry can transmute base metal into gold. Yeats found the word in Toynbee (*The Study of History* — Oxford, 1934 — II, 425). He quotes a passage where Toynbee uses the word in the "Introduction" written for the proposed Dublin Edition and recently printed in *Essays and Introductions:* "He then insists that if 'Jewish Zionism and Irish Nationalism succeed in achieving their aims, then Jewry and Irishry will each fit into its own tiny niche.' " Later in his "Introduction" Yeats himself uses the word "Irishry" several times, always in quotation marks: "[Irish literature] may do something to keep 'the Irishry' living." "It may be indeed that certain characteristics of 'the Irishry' must grow in importance." "I am joined to 'the Irishry.' "

Notes to Chapter 5

1 Jon Stallworthy prints a transcription of part of the first draft of "Ribh considers Christian Love insufficient" on pp. 10–11 of *Between the Lines.*
2 The notebook may be seen in its original state in a microfilm copy at the Houghton Library, but the contents have since been removed and placed with other MSS. of the works represented.
3 The first named of the three shows this interesting evolution: "craftsman" (item 6), "artist," "workman." Yeats is here moving towards the more inclusive word and at the same time echoing "work" in line 17 of this draft.
4 Yeats's intention here is made more certain still when we observe that in revising "Cuchulain's Fight with the Sea" for *Early Poems and Stories* (1925) Yeats closed the poem with the line "And fought with the invulnerable tide." That "invulnerable" was still echoing in Yeats's mind in this context is proved by these lines from *The Death of Cuchulain* (1939), shortly to be written:

> *Cuchulain*. . . . Then I went mad, I fought against the sea.
> *Aoife*. I seemed invulnerable.

Notes to Chapter 6

1 This song has a curious history. It is not found in TS. 1. Yeats gave it the title "The Well and the Tree" and included it in Macmillan's *Responsibilities*, published October 10, 1916. The *Harper's Bazaar* version of the play, printed in March 1917, does end with this song, though it is not quite in its final form. Wade says in his description of the Cuala Press *Wild Swans at Coole* (item 118) that the song does not appear in the magazine version of the play. He was mistaken about the *Harper's Bazaar* text.

2 Though all of this is true, and indicates that Yeats is using archetypal characters and situations, I wish mildly to challenge the critical usefulness of F. A. C. Wilson's discussion of this play in terms of its archetypes (*Yeats's Iconography*, pp. 27–72). His is one of many recent studies that has led me to doubt whether archetypal criticism is the way in and through. If *At the Hawk's Well* is a grail legend, so too is *Heart of Darkness*, and once a reader has observed this of both works he is still left with nearly everything to do. Archetypal materials are materials and nothing or at least not much more than that; we become almost painfully aware of this when we note that archetypes cluster most heavily in Tom Mix movies and the Horatio Alger books — indeed there you find almost nothing else. The critical problem remains what it always was: what has the artist done with his materials? Archetypes — like biographical fact, historical fact, ideas, or what have you — are at the outset inert, dead even until they have been fully transformed by what Yeats called the artist's "phantasmagoria." This I take to be his version of Coleridge's esemplastic or fusing-all-to-one imagination, at least it had come to mean something very like that by the time Yeats wrote "A General Introduction for my Work" in 1937. One hasn't gotten very far in his reading of *Romeo and Juliet* when he perceives in it a rite of spring. There are many rites of spring, and not all of them are works of art; indeed some of them, to paraphrase Uncle Toby on "Lispius . . . who composed a work the day he was born," should be wiped up.

Notes to Chapter 7

1 Mr. Murray Krieger has been making the point in recent addresses — I heard him make it in an address given in April 1964 — that many critics construe an artist's relation to his time far too simply. If I understood him correctly, he granted that to a degree an artist is produced by his age, but noted also that the artist helps produce his age and often shows a surprising prescience regarding times to come. The following example is mine, not Mr. Krieger's (and I hope I have understood him): the kind of evidence adduced in Louis Bredvold's "The Gloom of the Tory Satirists" (from *Pope and His Contemporaries*, eds., Clifford and Landa) seems inadequately to explain their gloom. Pope did not write "Dunciad IV" because, or only because he was depressed by the tone of public life near the end of Walpole's administration and unaware that the glories of Pitt's administration were just around the corner. Neither

the low tone nor the glories would have affected Pope on any deep level; a better explanation may be one like that which Yeats educes to explain Swift's *saeva indignatio*. Certainly Pope, like Swift, would have regarded everything that was to come for a very long time as "ruin."

Notes to Chapter 10

1 The method of *The Words upon the Window-pane* is different. By the time Yeats wrote it he had invented an Anglo-Ireland which had at least something of the Unity of Culture exemplified by Justinian's Byzantium (See *A Vision*, "Dove or Swan," section IV where Unity of Being was possible). Clearly Swift, because of his *saeva indignatio*, hardly exemplified Unity of Being. Was the cause of his *saeva indignatio* biographical? Yeats explores the question while demonstrating the *saeva indignatio* in the dreadful dialogue between Swift and Vanessa, but has Corbet suggest at the beginning and end of the play that the true source of the *saeva indignatio* was the fact that Swift foresaw "the ruin to come." Yeats does not choose between these explanations. The point seems to be that as a cycle nears its end Unity of Being is impossible to achieve, for whatever reason.

Notes to Chapter 11

1 I exclude the items which appeared in 1896 because of the time difficulty. Even with some of these, printed copy might possibly have been used. Yeats always demanded proofs from magazines and newspapers, and sometimes corrected proofs were pasted into his volumes of cuttings. For example "Where There is nothing, there is God" appeared in *The Sketch*, October 21, 1896. The version there given is so nearly the same as that found in the proofs of *The Secret Rose* as to make it almost certain one was set from the other.

2 On page 197 of the proofs, the compositor has left a blank in the text of "The Death of Hanrahan" where, presumably, he could not read ms. copy.

3 Page proofs, pp. 132–33. The compositor has left a blank for the place name after "raised"; Yeats supplies "Great Spring." Five blanks were left in the proof of this story, an indication that the compositor was working from ms. copy.

4 *Letters*, p. 266. At the time of writing, Yeats still expected that "The Tables of the Law" and "The Adoration of the Magi" would be included.

5 I quote the text of *Essays and Introductions* because *Essays* (1924) has been out of print for so long it has become difficult to locate a copy. In comparing the two texts I note changes in *Essays and Introductions*, usually in punctuation, though there are some verbal changes. The publishers say nothing about the provenance of the texts printed in *Essays and Introductions*. I do know that before his death Yeats had carefully revised the text of *Essays*, and that his revisions had been written into a copy of that book still in Mrs. Yeats's library; therefore the text of *Essays and Introductions* may well represent Yeats's final wishes. Only a complete collation would settle this question.

Notes to Chapter 12

1 Anderson Galleries, Sale No. 1820, Thursday, March 20, 1924. The MS., lot 11546, was sold to Dr. Rosenbach; the TSS., lots 11547 and 11548, were sold to the Brick Row Book Shop. Information from the annotated sale catalogue at the American Antiquarian Society, Worcester, Massachusetts.

2 My numbering. Yeats numbered his entries in the earlier sections of this Journal, but he repeated some numbers and skipped others.

3 The passage in brackets was inserted into the original typescript.

4 Parts of *On the Boiler* have recently been reprinted in *Explorations*. I continue to refer to the first publication of *Boiler* because of omissions from the text in *Explorations*.

5 Some notion of the complexity of this revision can be given by working back from a passage in its final form to the sources of its sentences in the several versions. The sentences of the first paragraph of part III of "Private Thoughts" have the following sources: "But if I would escape . . . intellect and knowledge" in the first sentence is a radical revision of the original MS. The last half of the first sentence — "and besides . . . ivory balls" was written into the first complete typescript, as were the next two sentences, beginning "The mathematician" and ending "place it occupies." The next sentence — "During the seventeenth century . . . would live after" — is a revised version of a sentence that occurs both in the original MS. and on an odd MS. sheet which Yeats used when his revision became so complicated he needed more space. These are also the source of the final sentence — "Nature or reality . . . is measureable."

INDEX